AF571762

there is no eye

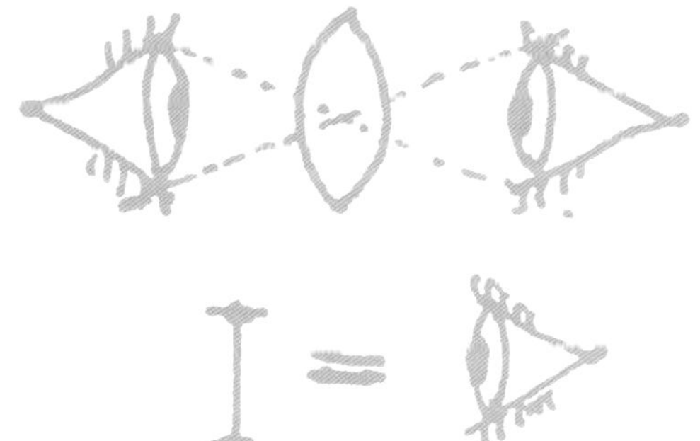

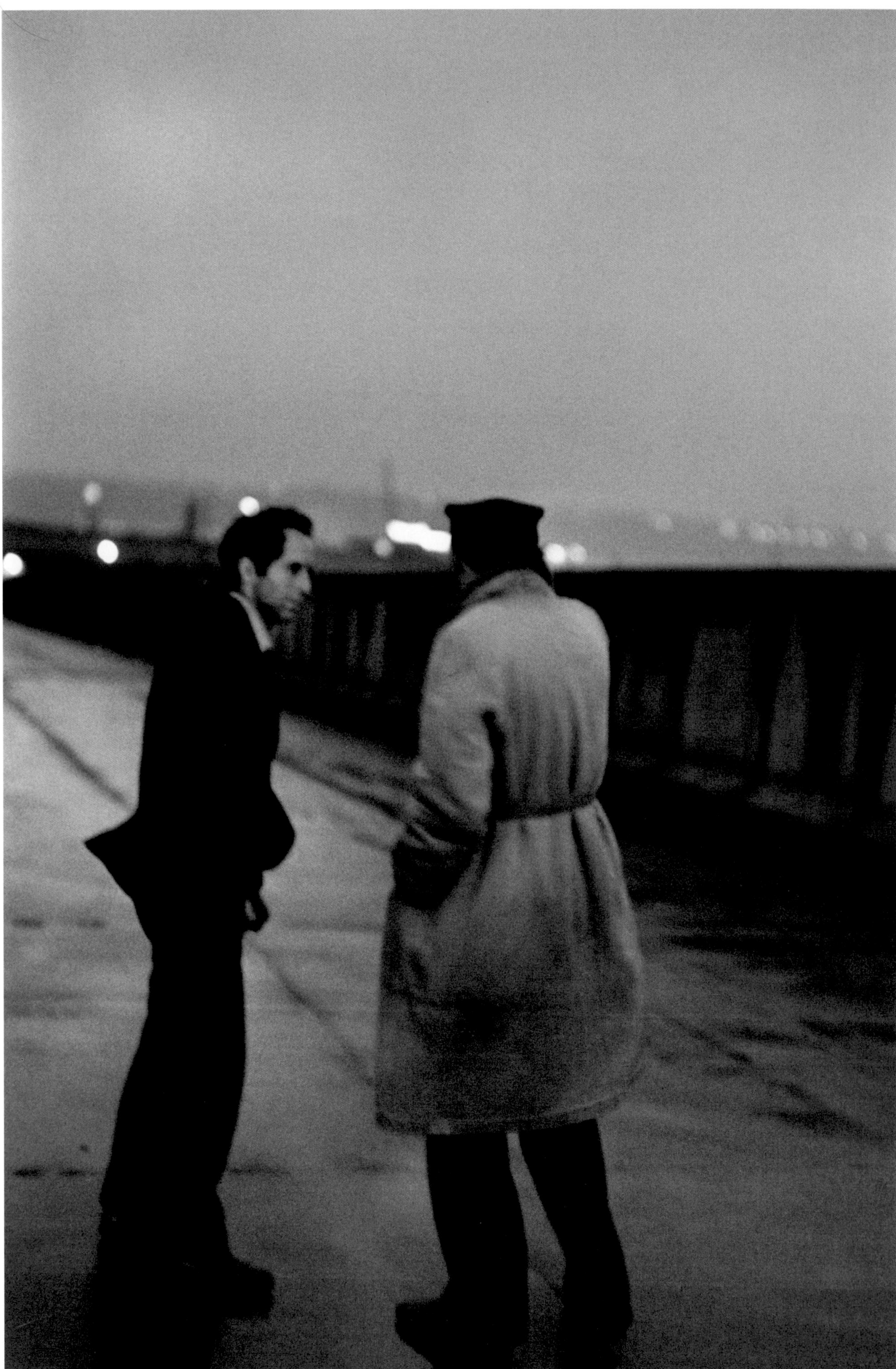

there is no eye

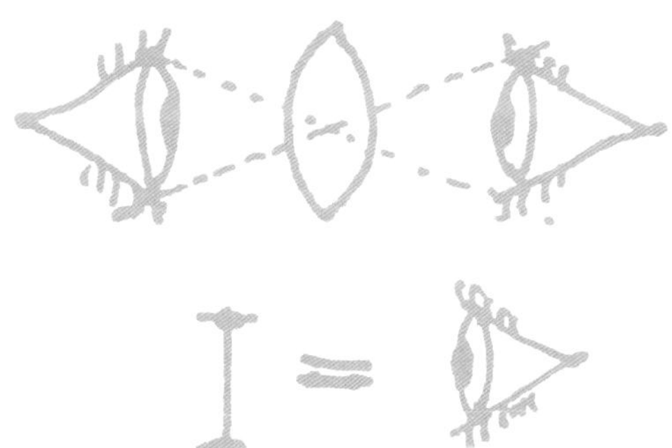

JOHN COHEN PHOTOGRAPHS

INTRODUCTION BY GREIL MARCUS

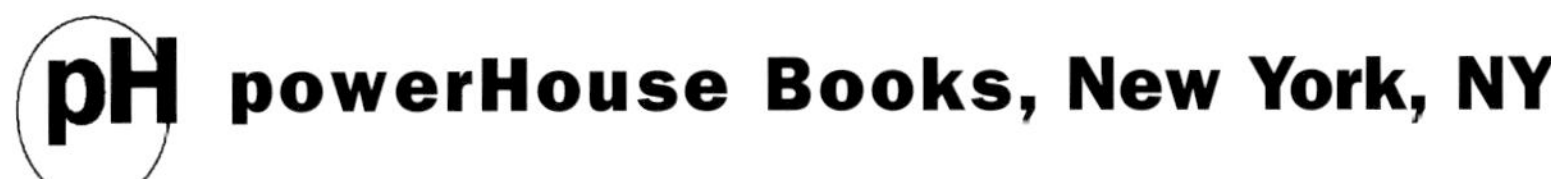
pH powerHouse Books, New York, NY

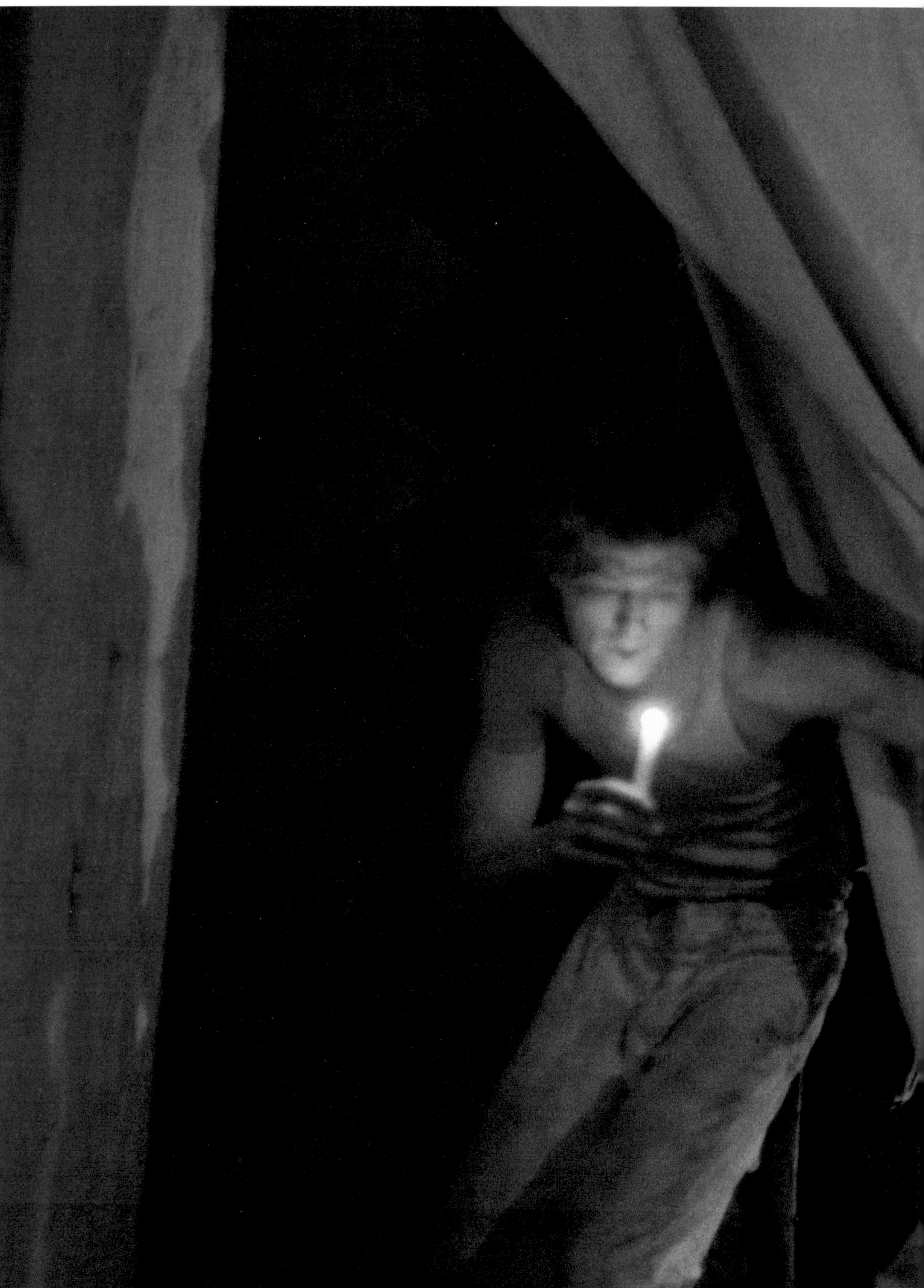

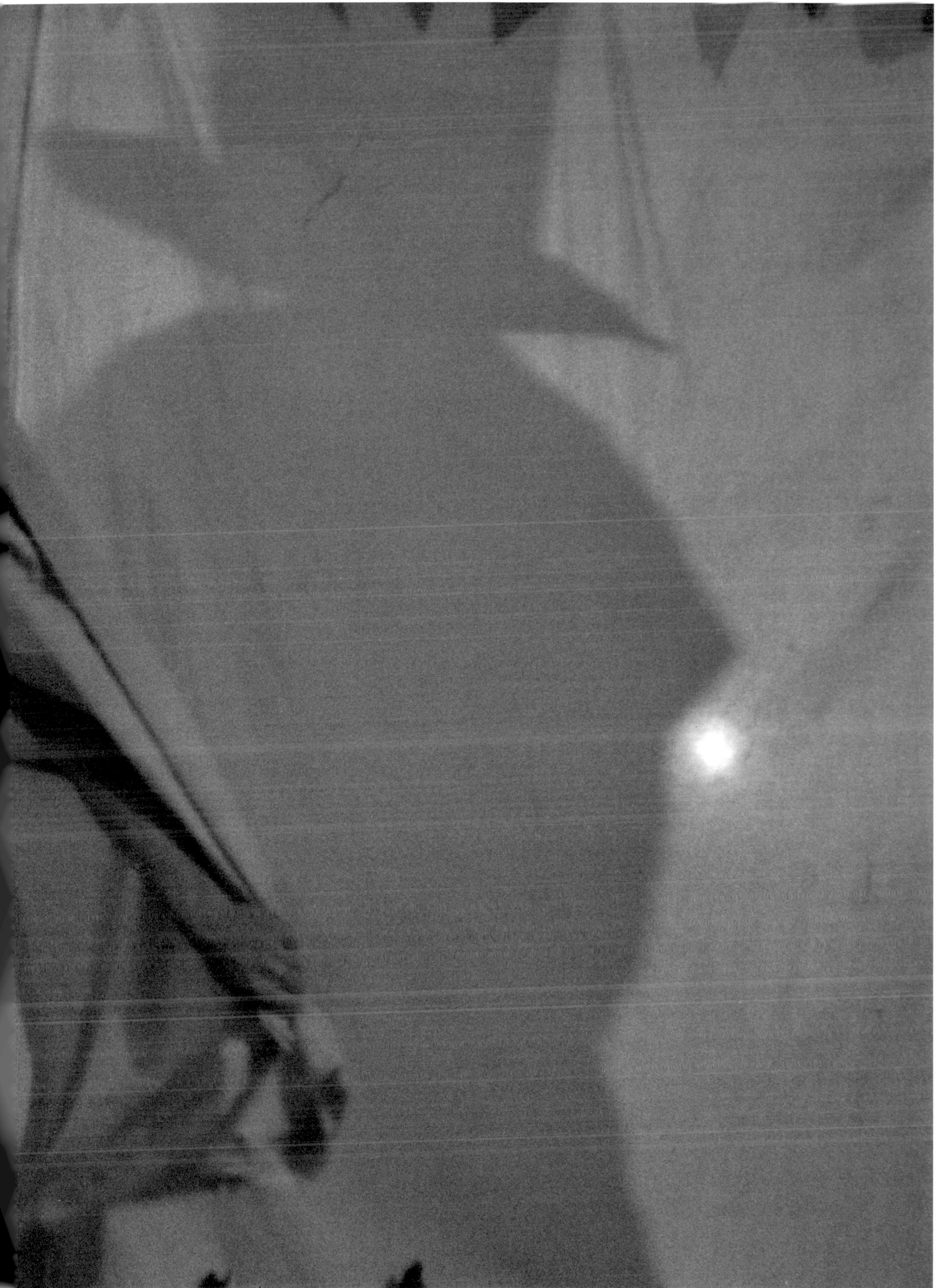

INTRODUCTION You can look at John Cohen's THERE IS NO EYE and see through very familiar eyes: the New York City eyes of Helen Levitt and Walker Evans, Evans' country eyes, the highway eyes of Robert Frank, even Margaret Bourke-White's doubting eyes in Holiness churches. These were photographers who, whatever their claims of artlessness, knew what they were looking for. Emptiness for Evans and Frank, a matter of a place that in some essential way fended off its inhabitants. Pathos for Levitt: the pathos of knowing how to wait for the unlikely event, scene, artifact, or happenstance that could give a glimmer of individuality to streets that seemed to make everyone the same. For Bourke-White, the revelation of foreignness, of people not like us, right here in our own country, making the viewer wonder, at best, what the country really is.

John Cohen's argument is that the picture exists outside of the photographer's intentions, or even his or her desire. The picture—not the event, scene, artifact, or happenstance, but the image—may exist, in and of itself, in some realm of natural composition to which we have no access, but whether this is true or not the photographer will only ever capture part of the picture that he or she thinks they have found. This doesn't make photography mystical; it makes it frustrating. The photographer's best, most fully realized pictures are also his or her most inscrutable, or rather the inscrutability is a quality the photographer helplessly records but cannot translate. The pictures mock the one who took them.

There is a formal version of this little drama here in "Frank, Leslie, Corso," a picture taken during the filming of the 1959 Robert Frank-Alfred Leslie "life among the beatniks" movie, *Pull My Daisy*. The two filmmakers and poet Gregory Corso make a circle of male camaraderie so complete the frisson of the picture is less in its vision of a happy brotherhood than of "we few, we happy few"—that is, the exclusion of the photographer from this brotherhood, his exclusion and, as you look, yours. You are not wanted here. You have noticed the men in the picture, but they are elsewhere, and will never notice you.

The formality of this picture's escape from its photographer, though, merely hints at the displacement in two pictures that, one might think, only John Cohen would have made. They exclude the photographer and the viewer even more forcefully than the portrait of the beat boys, but they are also

⇇ Robert Frank and Larry Rivers, New York City, 1959

← Red Grooms "The Burning Building," 1959

irresistible: looking glasses you want to travel through. The pictures do not quite hold still on the page; for an instant you might think you can go right into them, put your hand through the paper.

"Roscoe Holcomb, Daisy, Kentucky" is a picture of a man standing in front of an outbuilding. He holds a banjo; with a hat on his head, he squints through his glasses. The man's posture is so straight that for all you know he could have been standing here for a century, waiting for someone to recognize that he knows something no one else knows. Cohen took Holcomb's picture in 1959, but there's no sense of time in the photo: not historical time, not passing time. In this picture, time does not pass. It doesn't stand still; past, present, and future move in and out of frame. Holcomb is dead now, but there is something in the picture, or something in Holcomb's way of standing of which the picture only captures a figment, that does not allow even the prospect of death to enter the world the picture shows. I look at this picture with absolute confidence that Roscoe Holcomb is now standing right where he stood for Cohen.

A Peruvian child strides across a rocky field high in the Andes. She is wearing a short shift that does not cover her legs; behind her are thatched huts, llamas resting on the ground or on their feet, and most of all, distance. She seems to be on top of the world, or in another world. The year is 1957. The only proof that the picture is not pre-Columbian is one's knowledge that there was no photography before the nineteenth century—but no one has told the girl in the picture. Now you know something she doesn't—but she isn't interested. That you encountered her is an accident; she hasn't encountered you at all.

You want to know more, though. As with the picture of the man descending a dark Harlem staircase, you want to know where he came from, where he's going, if his visit to the apartment he has left was a success or a failure, and if it was a failure, what he's going to do about it. But with the Peruvian girl you can't even be this specific; you can't frame the questions, only feel the wish.

Up against these eyeless pictures, those of Evans, Frank, Levitt, and Bourke-White can seem almost propagandistic. That is, they make arguments; you are aware that the photographer wants to tell you something, to convince you of something, to accept a certain point of view. Here there is no point of view. There is something else; I don't know what to call it, so I won't try.

—Greil Marcus, October 2000

→ Q'eros, Peru, 1956

⇉ Naushon Island, Massachusetts, 1971

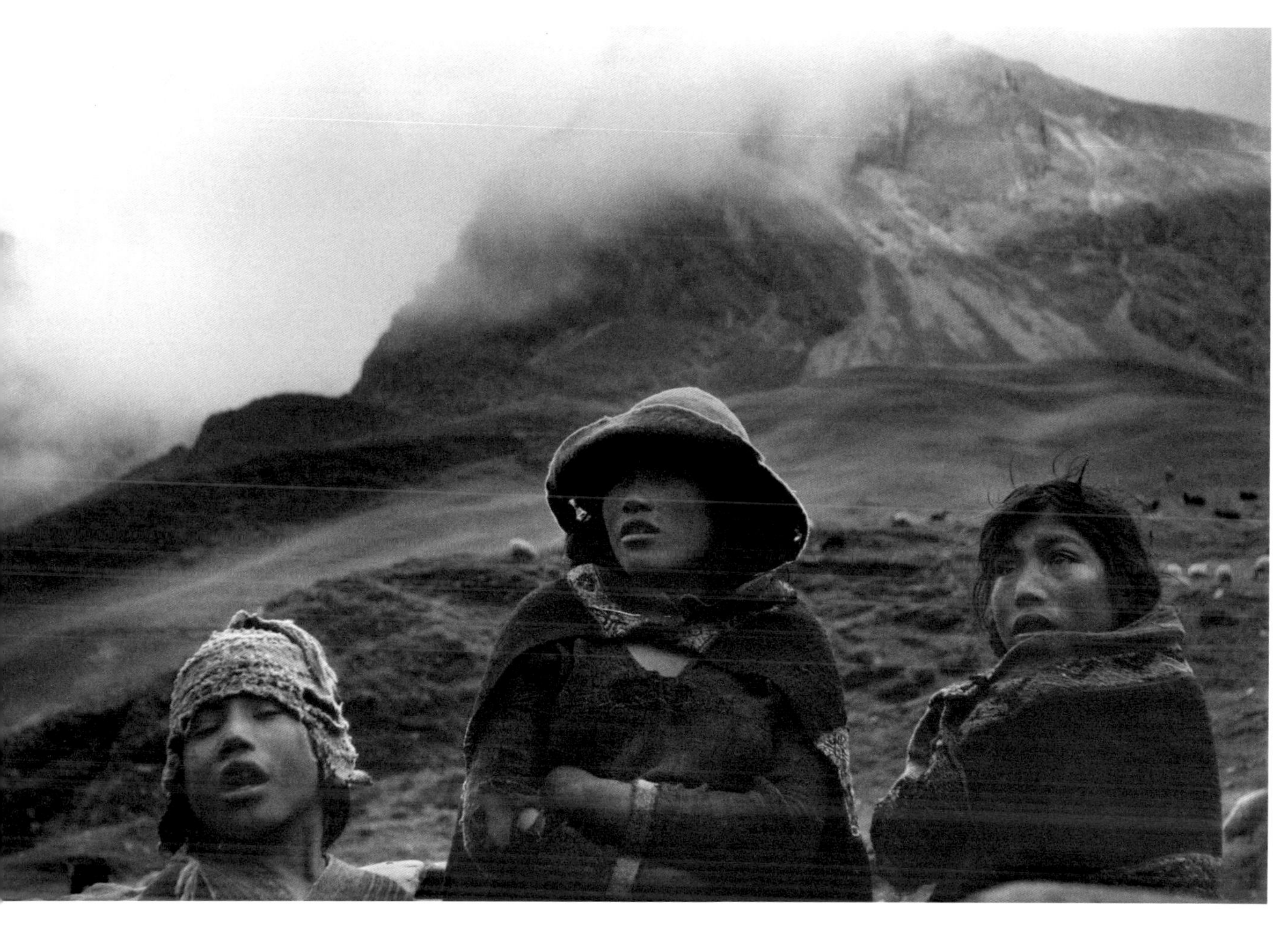

On the Voyager space craft is a recording
of a young girl singing an Andean huayno.
She's singing in Quechua, and her song is
included as a sample of the sounds
of our planet. Twenty years after its departure
from Earth, the spacecraft is traveling out
beyond the solar system. My recording of that
Peruvian girl will theoretically outlast all of us.

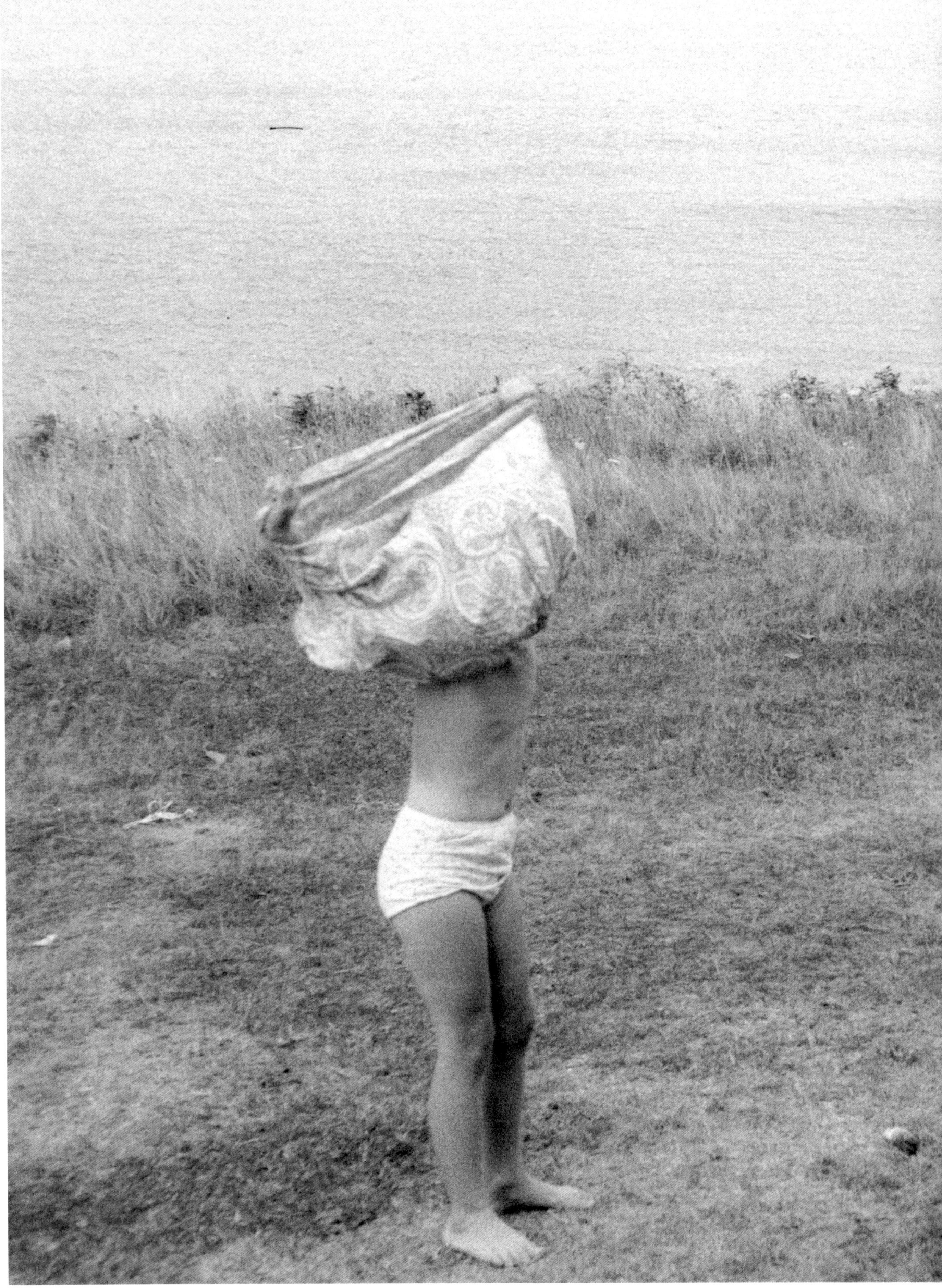

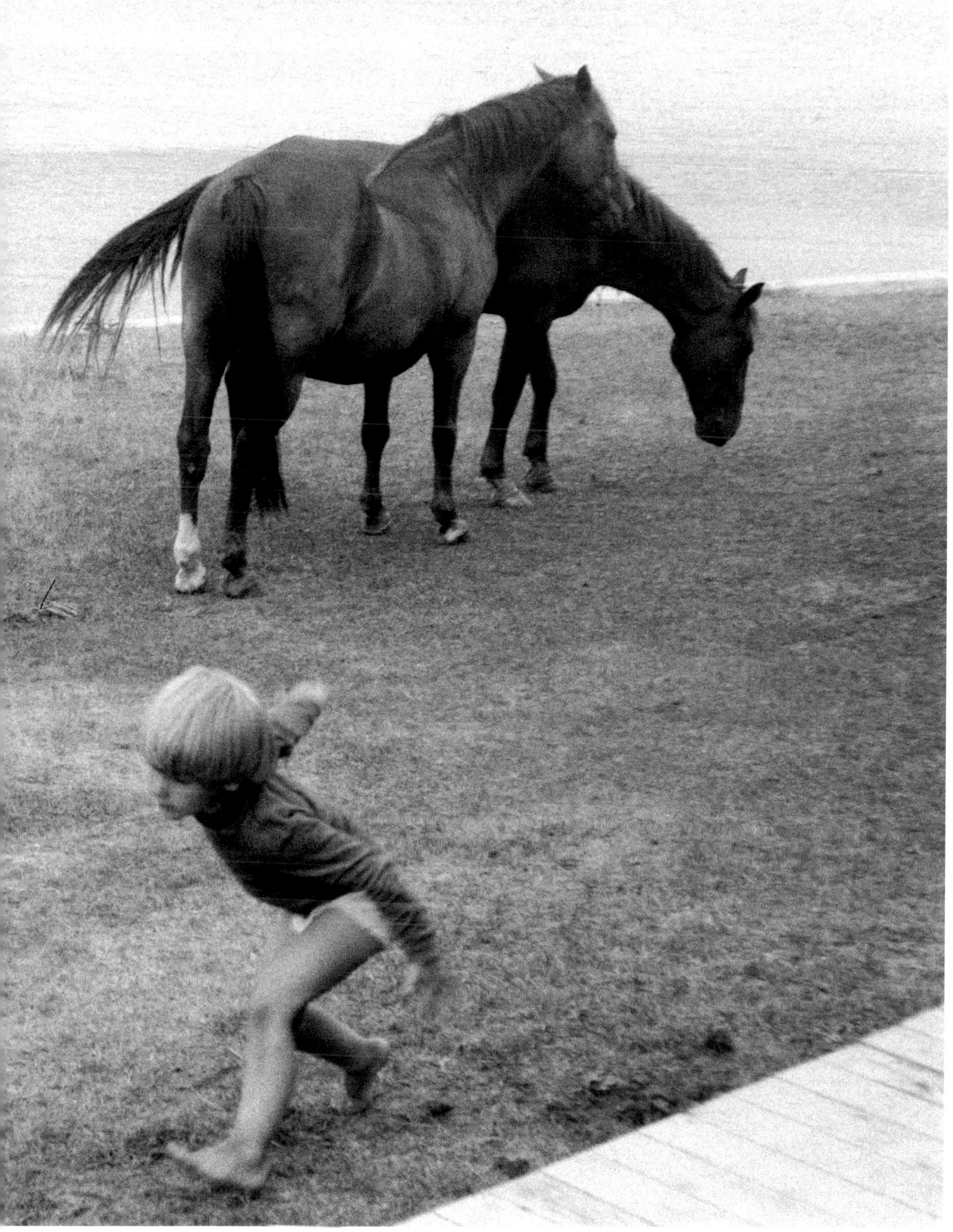

An immense willow tree has collapsed into
the stream. Up on the hill above it, the
sound of parkway traffic gets louder
each year. I've walked away from twenty-five
years of university teaching, completed
fifteen films, performed music through
several generations, and done nine field-
recording projects of traditional musicians,
all of which are very dear to me.

Like the birds that fly in enormous circles
at the start of their long migrations, I set out
to get a vision of a wider world. Intangible
forces have driven my path. Along the way I
confronted myself. If I could explain why
I've done all this work I probably wouldn't
have had to do it. Now the kids have grown up
and moved out. Penny is gone—
I look at what I've done. It's all there in the
barn: a storage cabinet filled with old photographs,
another with reels of 16mm films,
studio drawers are packed with drawings.
All this is a record of my search.

I'm getting ready to start again...
hoping for an empty head
so I can see clearly as before.
Will I ever get there?

→ Putnam Valley, New York, 1999

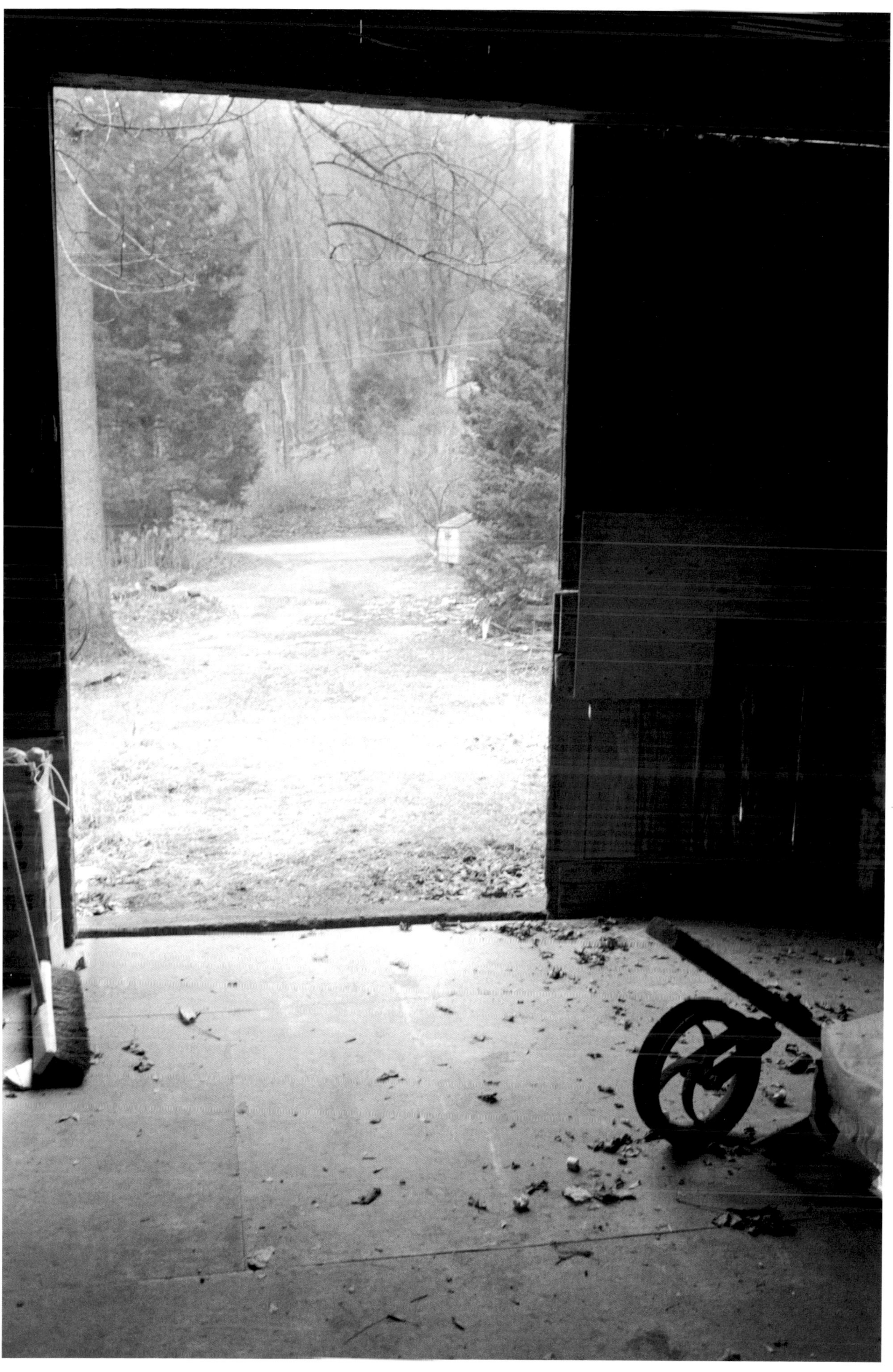

KEEPING TIME As a kid, bubble gum cards shaped parts of my world-view. One showed a soldier during World War Two who was blown into the sea during a naval battle. From his vantage point, clinging to a scrap of wreckage, he witnessed the entire Battle of Midway, with airplane duels, submarine attacks, and battleships destroying and being destroyed. I was attracted to this possibility of having an inside view without being part of the action. I always wondered whether the water was cold and if the wreckage he clung to was slimy or full of splinters.

As a child raised with a diverse mix of music around our house, I got the idea that music could have special spiritual qualities. I heard this in the Negro spirituals that were sung at home. In the excitement of childhood, this spiritual focus soon got lost; there was too much other music to enjoy. Years later when I was recording music in Kentucky, I heard Roscoe Holcomb say, "music…it's spiritual. You can take a small kid that can't even sit alone, and pull the strings on some sort of instrument, banjo or fiddle, and it draws the attention of that kid. It draws the attention of the whole human race. That is why I say it is a gift."

For years I've made many photographs of people playing music that brings a community together, calls up old spirits, and evokes family memories. Music making transcends everyday life. Music that involves dances or religious rituals can get very intense. After a festival, people often comment, "it filled my deepest needs." Sound, dance, motion, artistic and spiritual matters, even economics and politics contribute to this feeling. But language is an inadequate tool for expressing it. Try to describe these deepest needs and you wind up with a list of cliches. My travels have been in pursuit of music and art which filled such deep needs. I got to experience and inhabit these things personally—not just as a listener—along with a wish to be consumed by them.

I started photographing in the streets of New Haven and then in Black Gospel churches in Brooklyn. Then I went to Europe, Morocco, and Peru. New York's art world during the Beat Generation was the home base from which I traveled to photograph and record music in East Kentucky. My involvement was always with outsiders: artists, poets, mountain musicians, fiddlers, Peruvian Indians, Scottish and Greek Gypsies. They all broadened my vision of the world.

I sat with Andean Indians as they implored the gods for the health of their animals and for their own survival. I photographed Gospel singers going into trances. Mountain musicians sang with a sharp edge to their voices. I met Roscoe Holcomb in Kentucky and his singing cut into me. Around the same time I was hanging out with Beat poets and Abstract Expressionist painters in New York. They and Roscoe had the same effect on me. They didn't seem so different from each other, out there wailing and putting their worlds together in unexpected ways. I wanted to make a visual statement encompassing both documentary and subjective ideas, to find a way to integrate feeling with seeing. I was often torn between a need to document (describe) what was in front of me and the desire to follow intuitive visual impulses. This set up an internal dialog, a debate between conceptual and creative thinking. I walked the line between these ideas all my life.

My photographic ideas were formed before there were galleries in which to show. I rarely thought of photographs as something to hang on a wall. At that time the only way to have your work seen was in magazines, and the only way to make a living with photography was in fashion, advertising, or photojournalism. That was not what I wanted to do. Some photographs in books were like poetry to me, triggering ideas, stimulating images in the mind. There were images that were too active to sit still on a wall. They could find an expressive life inside a book, generating feelings that remained after it was closed. One early idea I had was to be a painter but that was overtaken by photography. Photography won out between the prospect of a life in front of an easel or photographing out in the world. It could be personal, subjective, and documentary. The lens became like the balance point in an equation that had the visible world on one side and the interior world on the other.

I'm also a musician and for forty years have performed with the New Lost City Ramblers (NLCR), a string band which plays old time Appalachian music. We've pointed to down-home sounds and authentic performance styles. Although we never had a hit record, we've influenced the shape of folk music and affected the work of musicians such as Bob Dylan and Jerry Garcia. We introduced the notion that it was okay for city singers to play roots music in traditional styles. Other musicians have taken up our ideas. Now there are many old time fiddle bands playing better than we do. Some are as good as the old-timers we learned from.

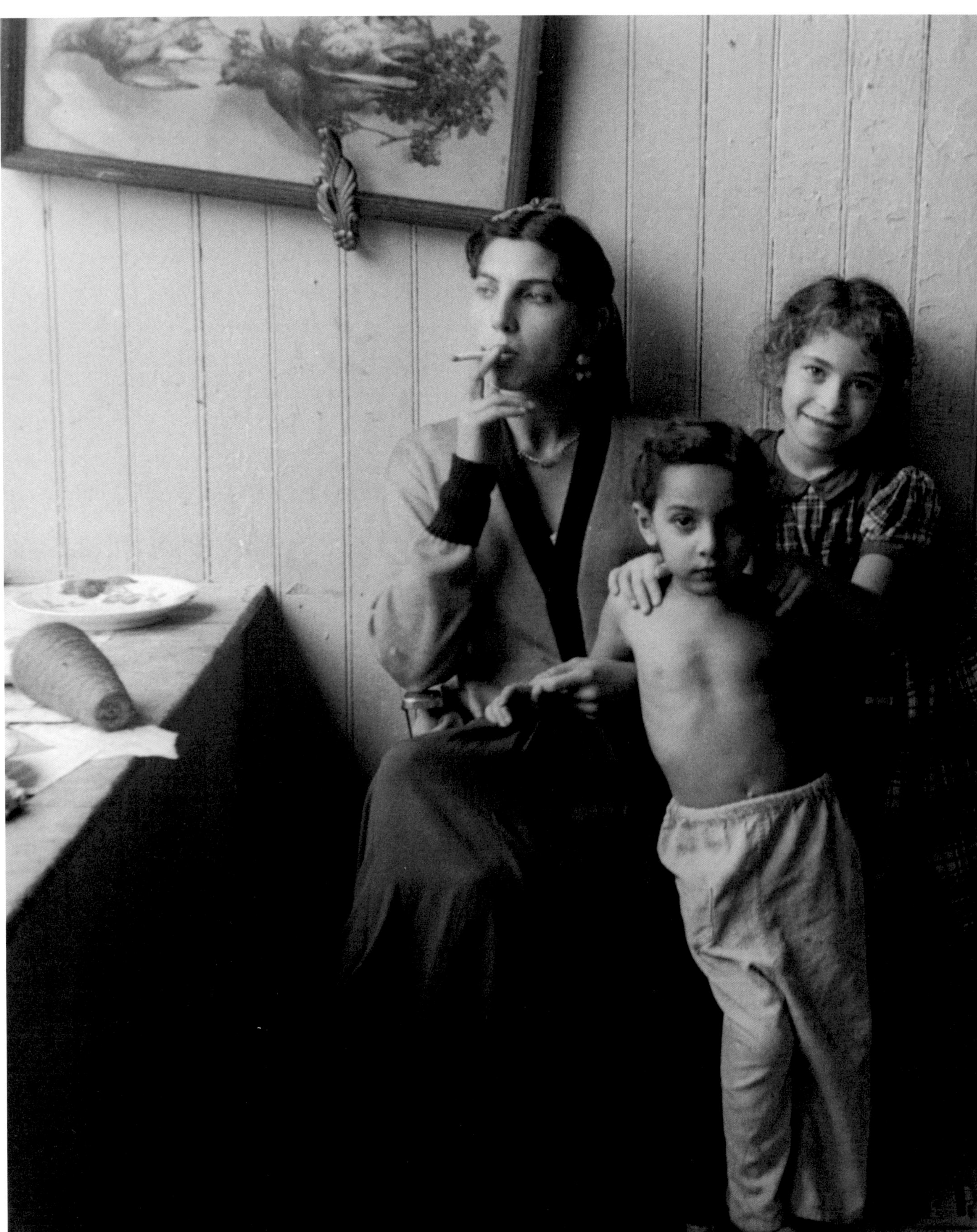

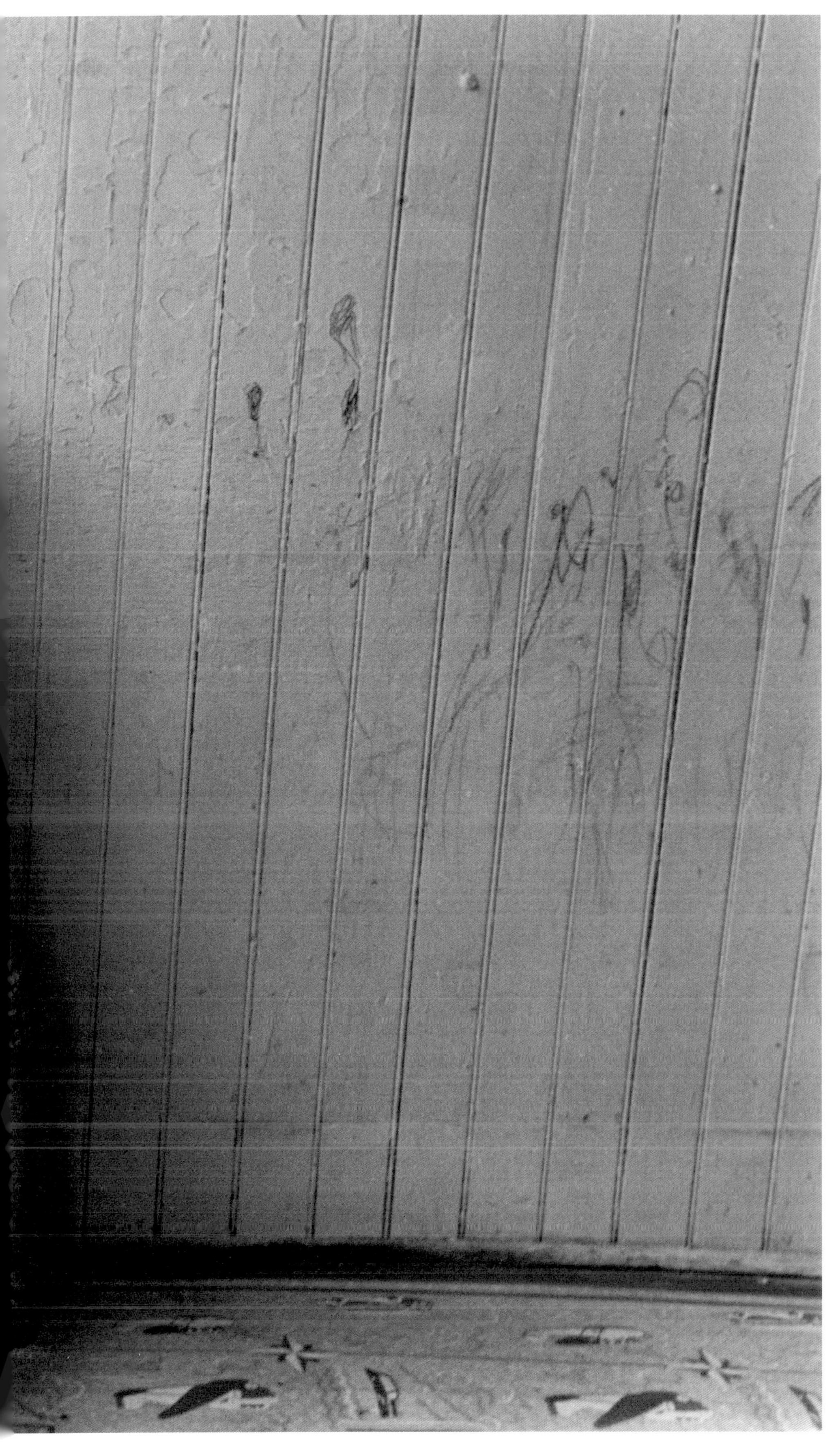

Gypsies, Oak Street, New Haven, 1955

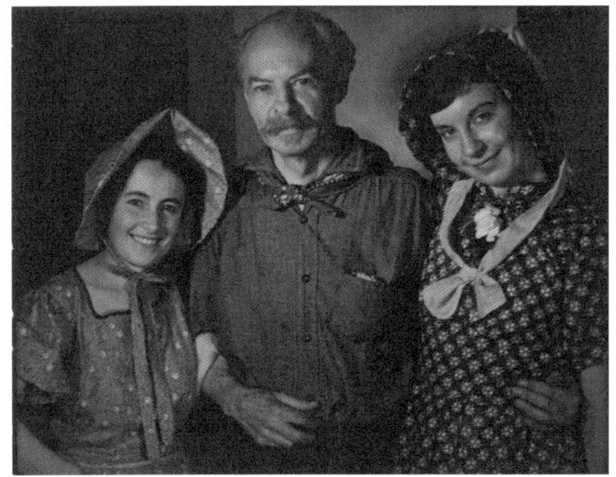

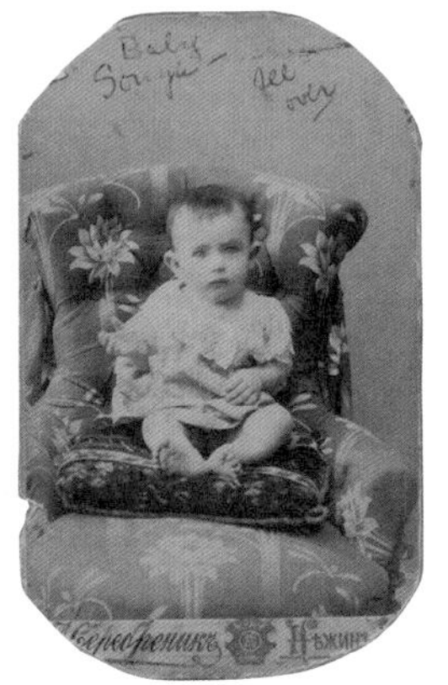

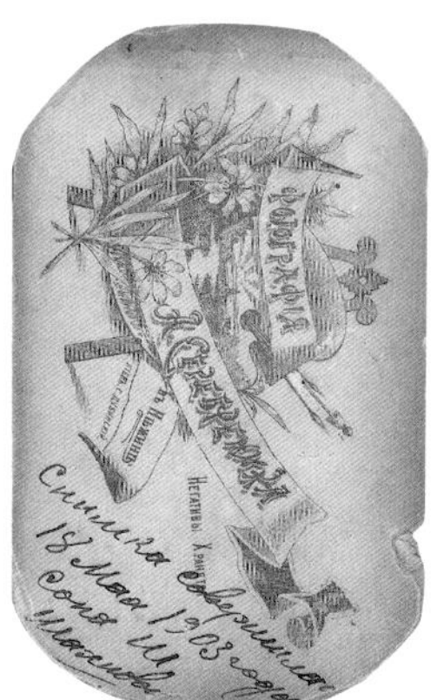

Although my grandparents were immigrants, I do not sing or play their music. My adventure, journey, involvement and evolution in music has been with America. When the NLCR started, I could only hear country music on distant radio stations broadcasting late at night, and the advertisements were directed at listeners whose values seemed very different from mine. Listening to commercial advertisements for the Lord's Last Supper on a plastic tablecloth became the discovery of America for me. Ever since, whether playing or recording music, making films, or photographing, I always seem to end up in the home of someone with an image of the Lord's Last Supper on a plastic tablecloth.

FAMILY As a child I had heard my parents sing sentimental songs and folk songs. Out in the world, I eventually heard the tougher, hard biting music of traditional singers who made my childhood seem like a sheltered illusion. Yet throughout it all, the music conveyed the message that there was another kind of a life out there.

In traditional societies, when you get close to the musician you are close to the heart of the people. Approaching a community through its music gives immediate and intimate access to their deep-rooted feelings. It could be in a bluegrass bar or at a ritual ceremony in the Andes. For the photographer or filmmaker, there is a great responsibility attached to such access. In the presence of music, people open up. Performers offer their music to their audience, and music fills their needs. People reach out to touch the music, and in turn, it lifts them. Things that were shut off are now exposed, especially the spirit. I heard a Peruvian Indian woman in Q'eros sing to her female alpacas:

↑ (left) My mother, Sonya as a Folk Dancer, New York City, photo by Gjion Mili, 1930s
↑ (center and right) Sonya in Russia, 1903 (front and back)

"Mother, mother,
Open me up
And speak inside me."

Before I was born my parents did folk dancing which they continued until we moved to the suburbs. Probably they learned these dances at a Lower East Side settlement house in New York City. Both were children of recent immigrants from Russia. My mother would dress in peasant outfits. When I was little, I came to believe that she had been a Russian peasant. "Smells like Rasha," she would say when we were out in the countryside. She sang folk songs in a way that was different from the cultivated voice she produced from her singing lessons. She was working on a "trained" voice, with vibrato and coloratura. It made me uneasy to hear it. There was something there that smothered her joy. She sang European folk songs in her natural voice, with an open pleasure that I connected with the beauty of nature. Where did she learn these songs? Was it as a little girl, before they all came to America? She sang pastoral songs about a "little birch tree growing in the meadow," and some others that had a disturbing aspect I worried over.

"Paul on the hillside, he seemed so dejected
Reynard, the fox, must be somewhere around.
Cluck cluck cluck cried a hen on the hillside
Now to my mother I can never go home."

Without the awareness of intellect, I found comfort in these old songs of my parents. How did my mother know about this stuff? Why was she singing about it? I was certain this was something she knew first-hand, perhaps from her family in Russia. But they weren't the only songs my parents sang, and I never could deal with the grief and overwhelming emotional load that was conveyed in some of the Jewish songs. That music was too close to weeping and shrieking from the heart, and it didn't soothe me, either, when my father invented piano settings to accompany them (he played a type of stride piano that later made him seem like a genius to me). I liked least hearing my mother sing folk songs while vacuuming the house with the radio playing classical music.

I have a faint memory of my father carrying me as a baby while singing, "Swing low, sweet chariot, coming for to carry me home." As I grew, the idea that there was "spiritual music" came to me. I heard Negro spirituals sung at home with a depth and seriousness that was not in the Yiddish show tunes or the Gilbert and Sullivan light operas which my parents sang with mindless pleasure. I hadn't yet learned to differentiate between singing spirituals and being a Negro gospel singer. Recently I found a book of Negro spirituals that my father had bought in 1925. How did he, a child of immigrants, grow to have this longing? Towards the end of his life he had a dreadful accident that put him into an intensive burn care hospital with 24-hour private nurses. He was barely conscious and nearly delirious. One of the nurses, an old black woman from Jamaica, told me he found out she knew some old spirituals and they spent their time singing together. My old Jewish father and this nurse found healing through music from the past, in that chariot "coming for to carry me home."

Spirituals and folk songs were different from the popular music I heard on the radio. They were connected to home, yet distinct from Old English Christmas carols or the children's records of "Songs of Safety" which were also in the house.

Ice skating is nice skating
But here's some advice about ice skating
Never skate where the ice is thin,
Thin ice will break and you'll fall right in
And come out with icicles under your chin
If you skate where the ice is thin.

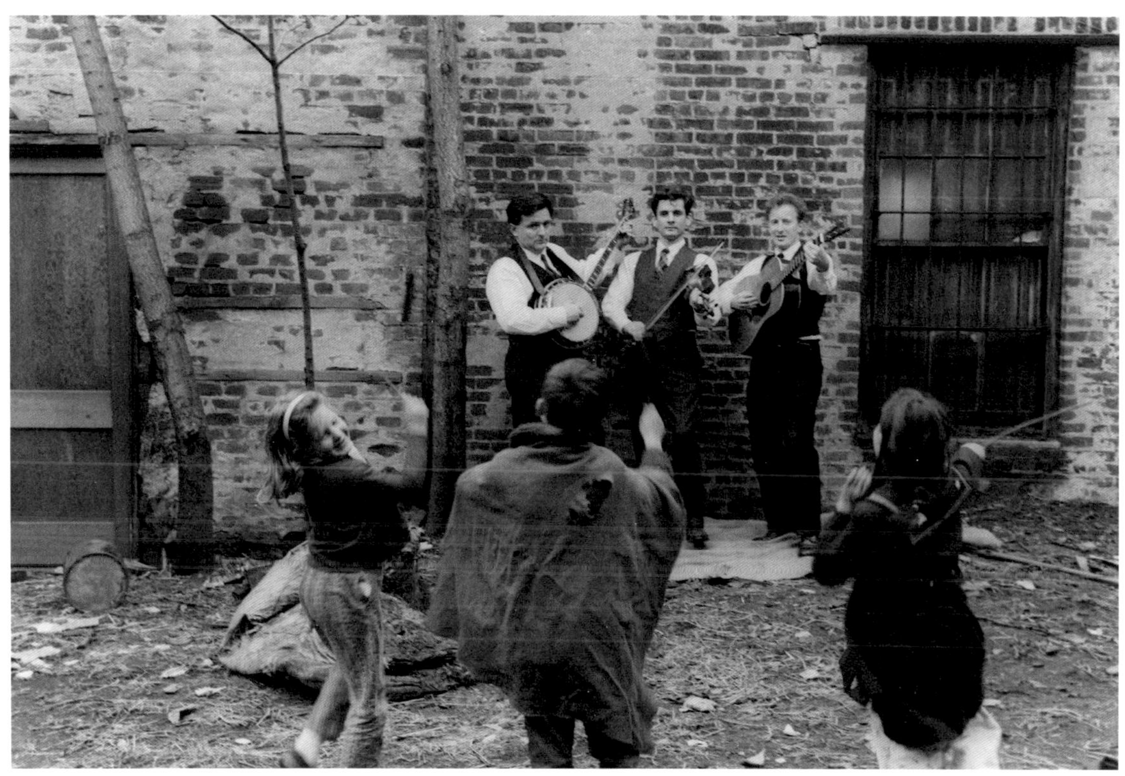

MUSIC AND ART

When I was nine we moved to Long Island. It took me a long time to develop a full resentment of the suburbs. The first inkling came when I visited friends whose families had expensive living rooms that we were forbidden to enter. We weren't permitted to sit on the sofa or walk on the carpet, but instead were sent down to the "finished basement."

My family didn't have a finished basement. Our cellar had an oil burner, concrete walls, and a washing machine with a crank driven clothes wringer. Down there I made collections of photos from magazines. Eventually this became the place where my paintings and drawings were stacked floor to ceiling, alongside storm windows and summer screens. In my bedroom I made paintings of moonlight entering my body. I also did accurate drawings of birds nesting outside the window. I drew a country farm market and painted imagined fiddlers. I have no memory of how I got the idea to be an artist. No one in my family, neither in my parents' families or grandparents' families, were artists. It was from my own private need, something awfully close to myself. With little exposure to "art," I got my early inspiration from comics and advertising. I resisted any attempts to provide me with "art lessons," rebelled

↑ The New Lost City Ramblers (Tom Paley, Mike Seeger, John Cohen) photo by Robert Frank, 1961

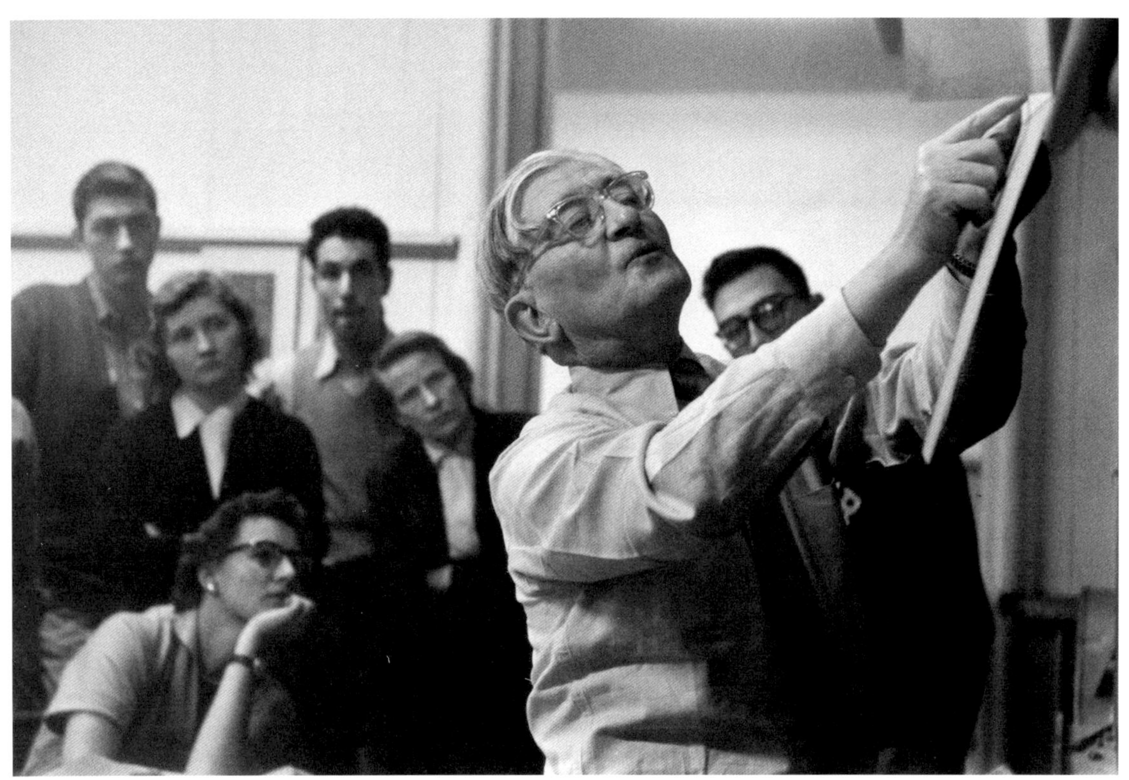

against the teacher who was hired, and mercilessly drew funny ears on top of his serious charcoal chiaroscuro rendering of a vase. Whatever my idea of art was, I insisted that it would come from me.

During the summer I turned sixteen I first heard the "Dust Bowl Ballads" of Woody Guthrie, along with several albums of early hillbilly songs and fiddle tunes assembled from commercial recordings. Within a short time this music became part of my private rebellion against middle class life. It reawakened memories of my imagined peasant mother and sent me looking for a larger world outside the suburbs.

In high school I learned the guitar instead of the typewriter and my afternoons were spent listening to Woody Guthrie sing about migrant workers in California.

↑ Josef Albers at Yale, 1955

"Ramblin' around your city, ramblin' around your town
I never see a friend I know, as I go ramblin' around.

The peach trees they are loaded, the limbs are bending down.
I pick 'em all day for a dollar boys, as I go ramblin' around.

Sometimes the fruit gets rotten, falls down on the ground.
There's a hungry mouth for every peach, as I go ramblin' around."
—Woody Guthrie

Woody's experiences didn't resemble my life in Long Island at all and I started to pursue a path that didn't require feeling good or bad about a finished basement. I was the only one in high school who played guitar. It didn't make me popular, it marked me as strange. I listened to records of old-time fiddlers, Leadbelly, Pete Seeger, the Almanac Singers, Hobart Smith, and Texas Gladden. Library of Congress recordings introduced the sound of chain gang songs with their wild energy and sense of beauty in the midst of horrible prison farms. This blew a hole in the walls of my sheltered life. Rosalee Allen's country music show was on the radio, broadcasting from New Jersey. I didn't like the twang of the steel guitar or the style of the Nashville singers and couldn't imagine singing that way. I didn't respond to Hank Williams either, probably because it spoke of some Honky Tonk life to which I had no connection. But on hearing the ballad of Barbara Allen on this radio show I felt some kind of a special light shining through. The story was so old and mysterious.

From William's grave grew a red, red rose
And from Barbara's grew a green briar.

Why was this song on a country music radio show? It suggested that somewhere in America, in the midst of the commercial environment, something ancient was still alive and being sung.

At Williams College I couldn't stomach the fraternity atmosphere and spent my time drawing, hiking the mountain trails of northwestern Massachusetts, and teaching myself the five-string banjo. My advisor told me I should be out playing sports, not practicing the banjo in my room. The college library had an entire set of the Library of Congress field recording collections, which I listened to a lot. I got good grades, made the Dean's List, and transferred to the art school at Yale University in 1951.

As one "last fling" preceding art school, I hitchhiked south to experience Appalachian music first hand. At a Virginia gas station I heard Earl Scruggs' bluegrass music blaring across the country-side. In Asheville, North Carolina, I asked the police if I could sleep in the jail (they wouldn't allow it). I telephoned Bascom Lunsford, the "Minstrel of the Appalachians," but he wouldn't see me when he learned I was from New York and I knew of Alan Lomax and Pete Seeger and my last name was Cohen.

At Yale I studied painting with Josef Albers and the collection of artists he assembled to teach with him. He had been at the Bauhaus in Germany and later was a central figure at Black Mountain College. He would say things such as "I believe in search, not research" and new worlds started opening to me.

Then I saw some photographs that disturbed me in a way I can still remember. They appeared in *Life Magazine*, announcing the winners of a young photographers' contest. In the midst of photo-journalism and picture stories the three images by Robert Frank were unlike anything I had experienced. Frank's work made me realize that art could be personal, biographical, even sentimental at the same time it was surreal. He used the strongest formal devices to convey these feelings in visual terms. I don't understand why Frank's work meant so much to me but it offered an alternative to the "classical" notions of painting and art history that I had picked up at college. It suggested a sense of action where an artist might move through the world and make images from his own experience. Two years later I took up photography.

I met Robert Frank through Herbert Matter. Both were artist-photographers in retreat from the Swiss bourgeois life, and both were generous and encouraging to me. Matter was an inspiring teacher at Yale. Since he rarely dispensed technical advice, some students didn't consider him a good teacher.

Yet, I probably learned more from him than from anyone. He was most respectful and encouraging of his students' beliefs, spoke very little, and would sometimes sit and share long silences. His photography critiques were sparse but full of insights. He would look over a stack of photographs. "That's nice," he would say, or "that's very nice," or "that's always nice." He had studied painting in Paris with both Ozenfant and Léger. He told how he brought them a portrait he had done. Léger said the head was good, but the body was not. Ozenfant said the body was good, but the face was not. "After that," said Herbert, "I only answered to my own heart." He was making films in black churches, looking for the roots of jazz dancing. Matter and his wife Mercedes were involved in the New York art world. They spoke of first hand experiences and conversations with Jackson Pollock, de Kooning, Calder, Guston, Franz Kline, as well as Giacometti, and even Mondrian. There were works by all these artists on the walls of the Matters' house. I would sit there and take it in like an intimate experience with wonderful art in the room. Robert Frank was not involved in the art world. He was mistrustful of movements and organizations and was more drawn to individuals with quirky human qualities. People I met around him happened to be artists and photographers but were totally unique.

In art school, along with studio painting, I'd go out and have "adventures" with my camera. I photographed in the streets of New Haven, especially the ghetto of Oak Street. It was a mixture of Blacks, old Russian Jews, and Gypsies. Photography led to a street education. In my senior year, I made black-and-white portraits of Gypsies. When I took them prints they would color them in with lipstick and hang them in their storefront windows (the first public exhibition of my work). Perhaps the photographs were better than my paintings at that time. The visiting painter Marca Relli from New York noticed this and told me, "Things are tough, but stick with it and they'll get better." Later that day I visited the Gypsy fortune-teller down the street and after she took all the money I had on me (forty-five cents) she told me, "Things are tough, but stick with it and they'll get better."

↱ Jack Kerouac, Chinatown, New York City, 1959

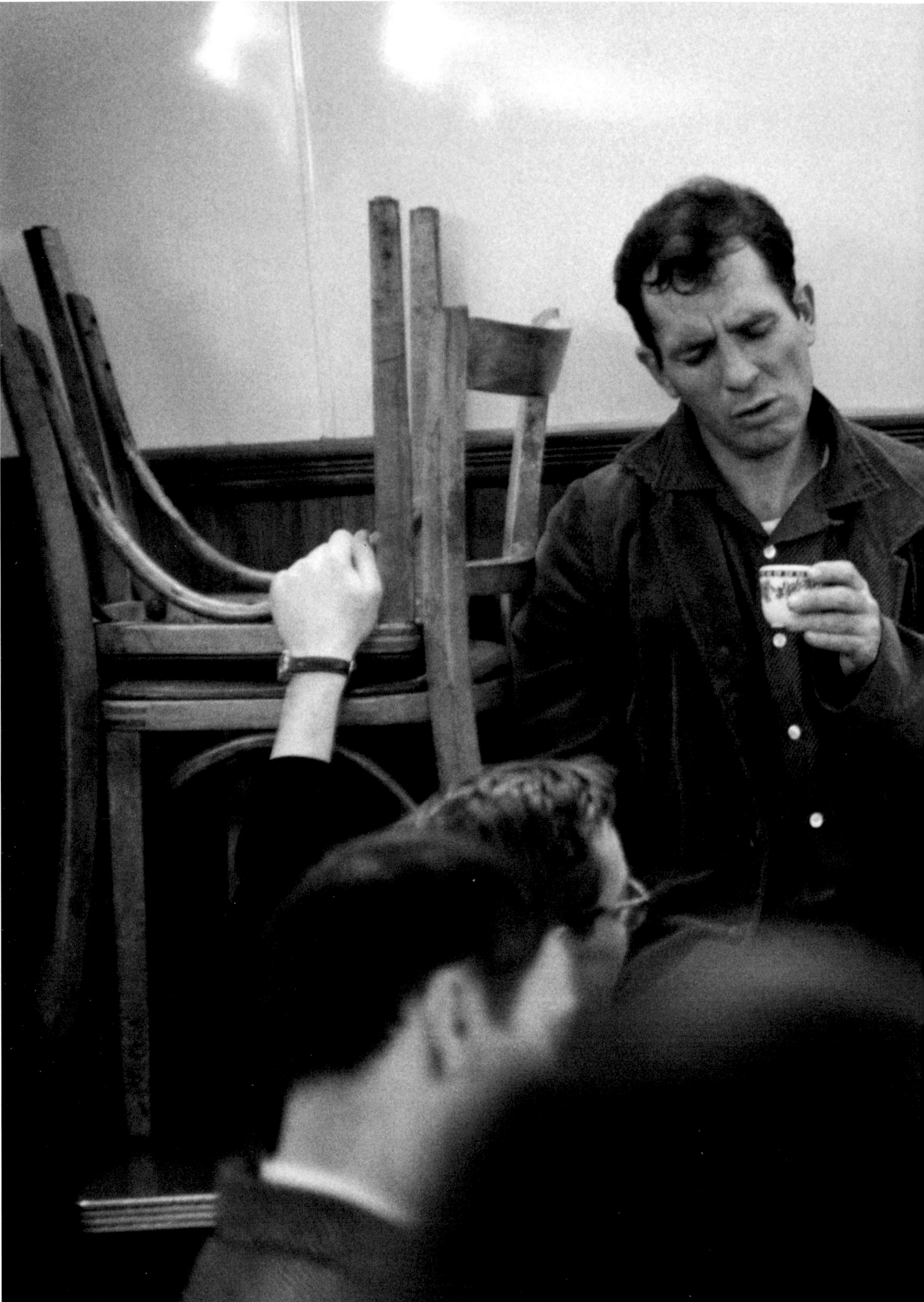

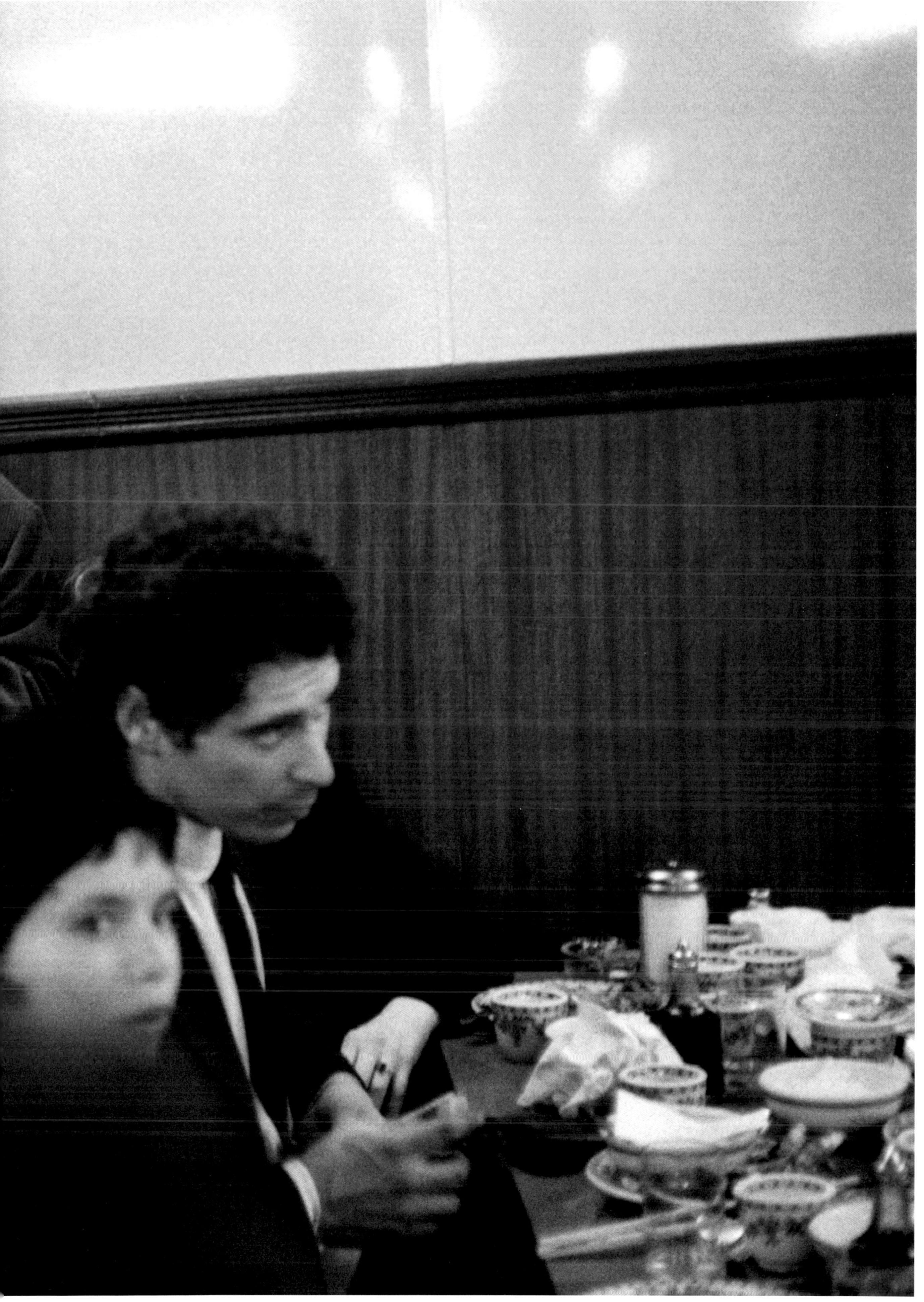

→ Third Avenue, New York City, 1962

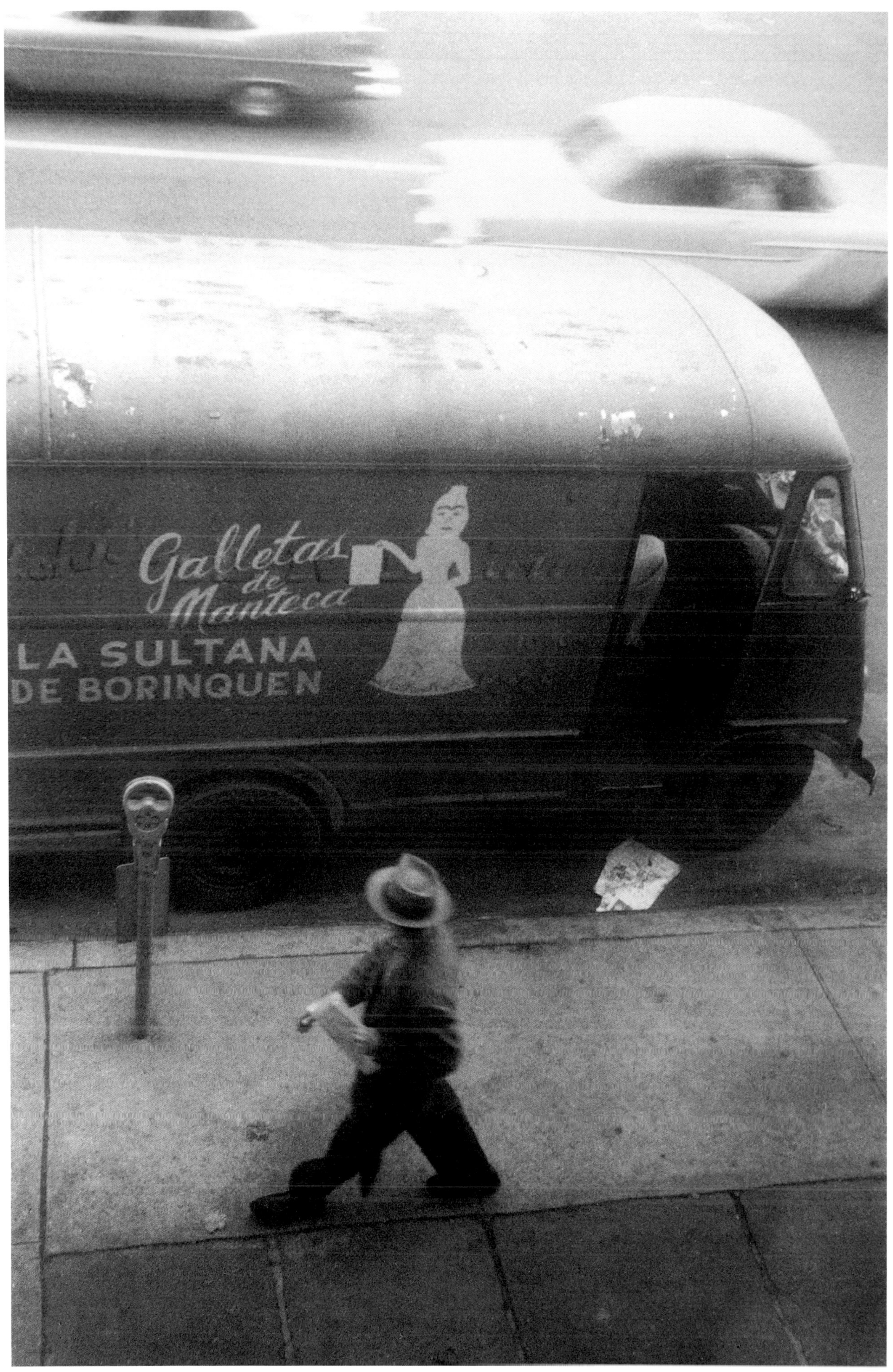
Galletas de Manteca
LA SULTANA
DE BORINQUEN

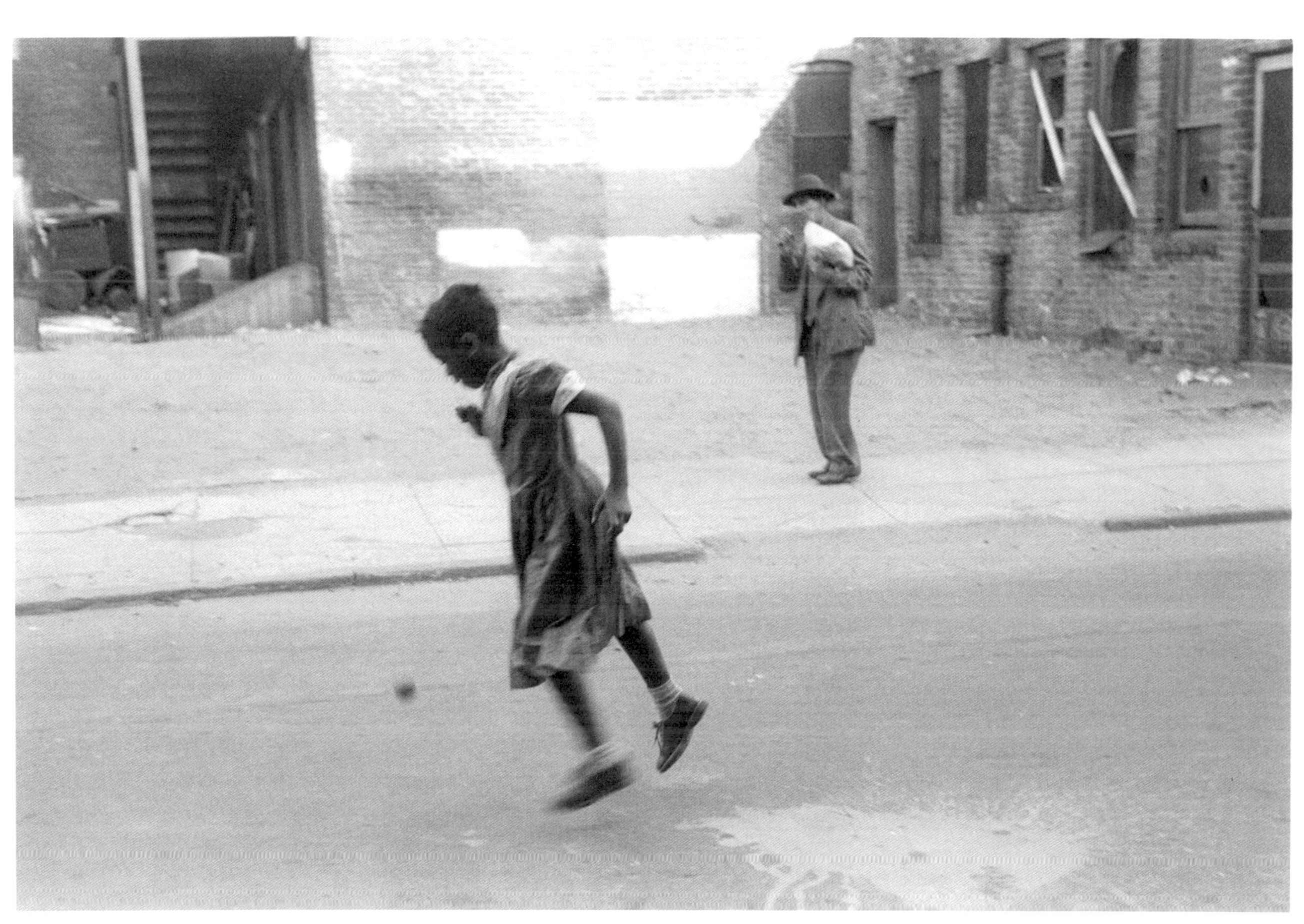

↑ Oak Street, New Haven, 1955

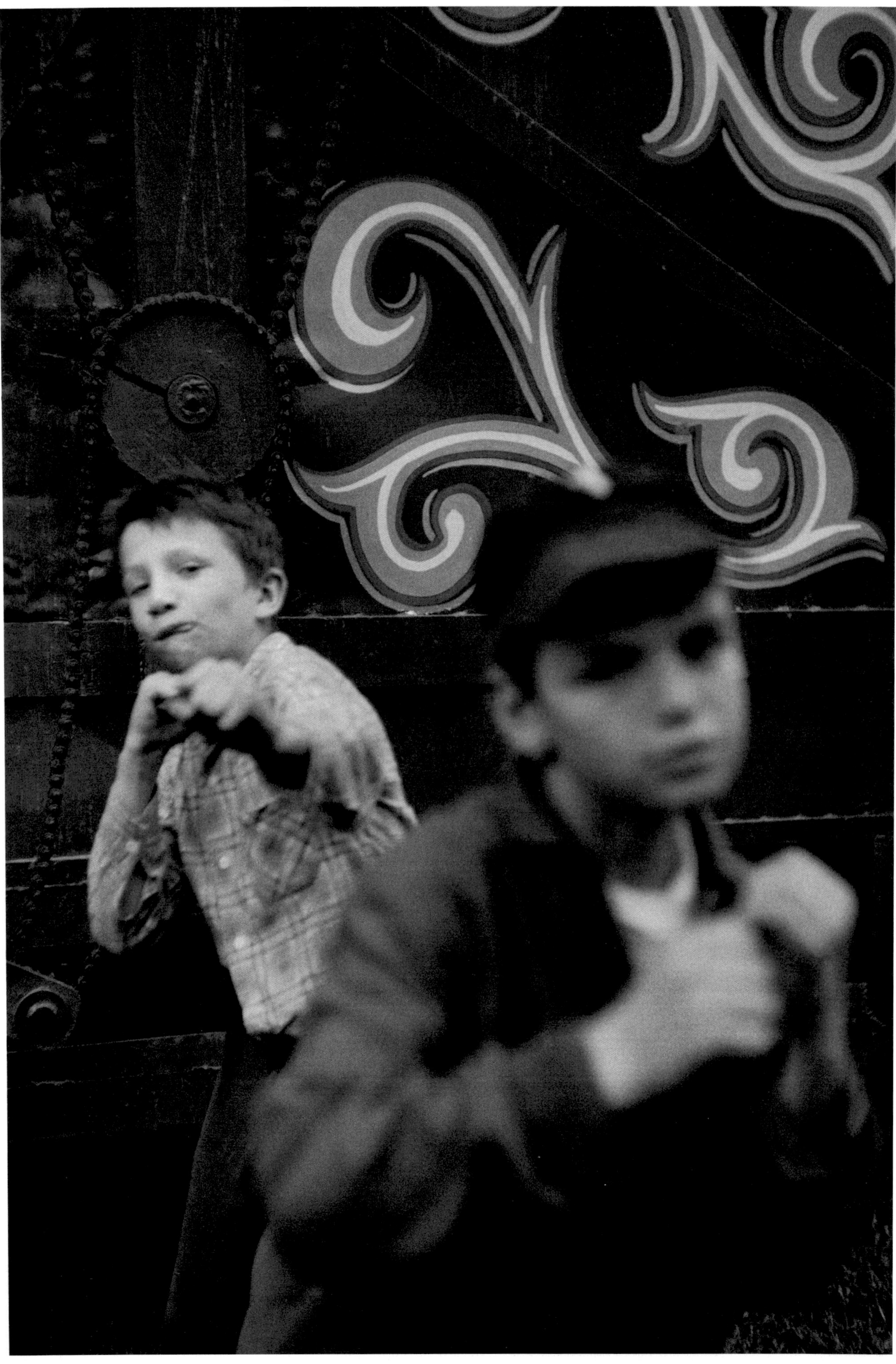

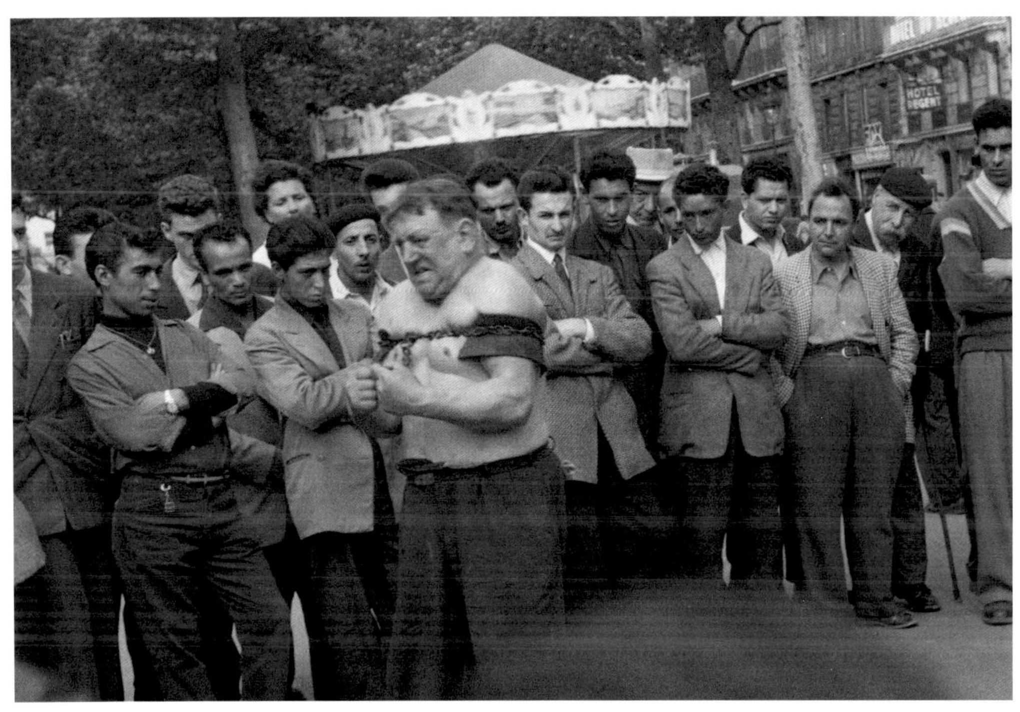

← Philadelphia, 1961

↑ Paris, 1955

→ Penn Station, New York City, 1955

⇉ Oak Street, New Haven, 1955

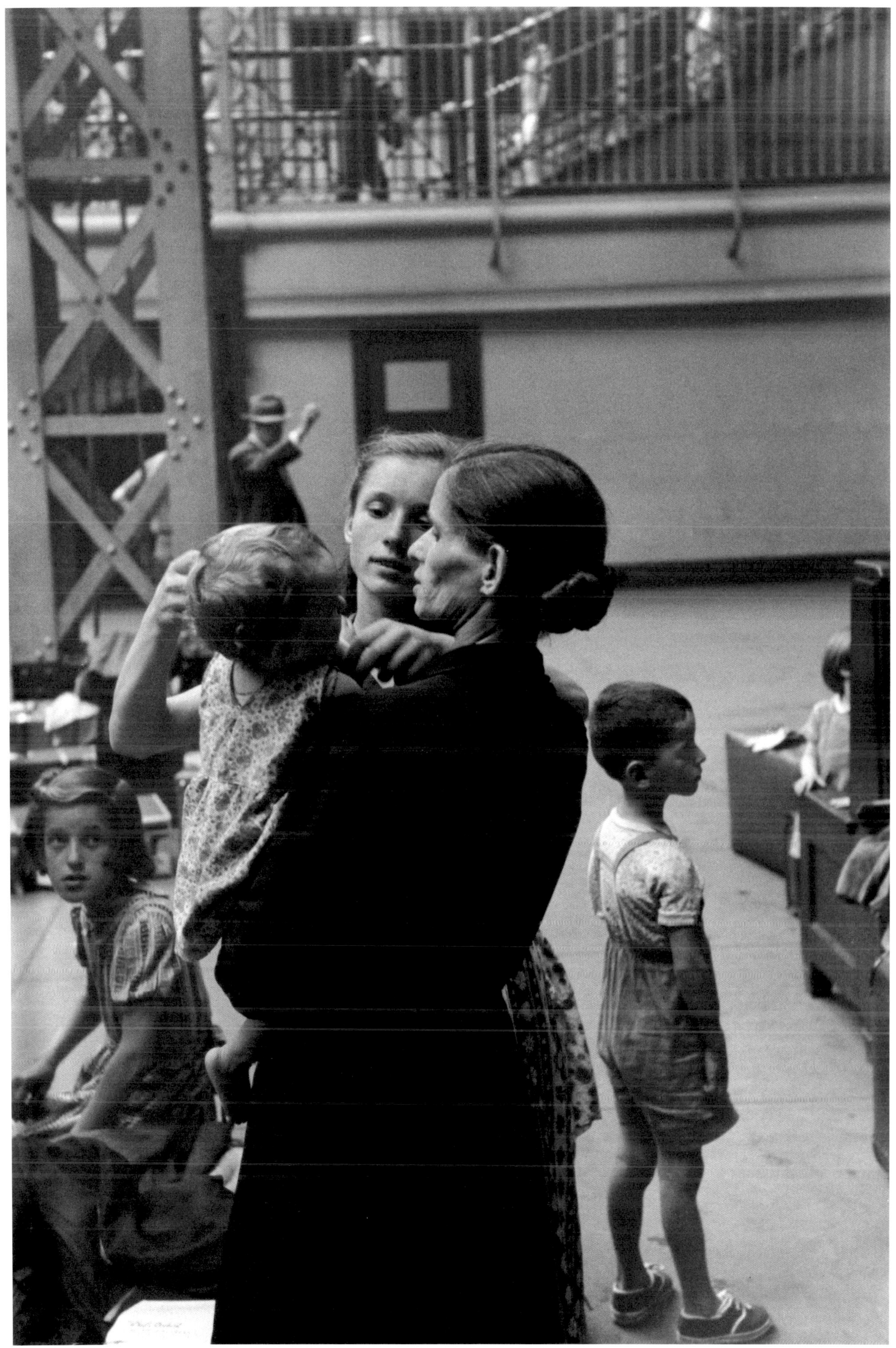

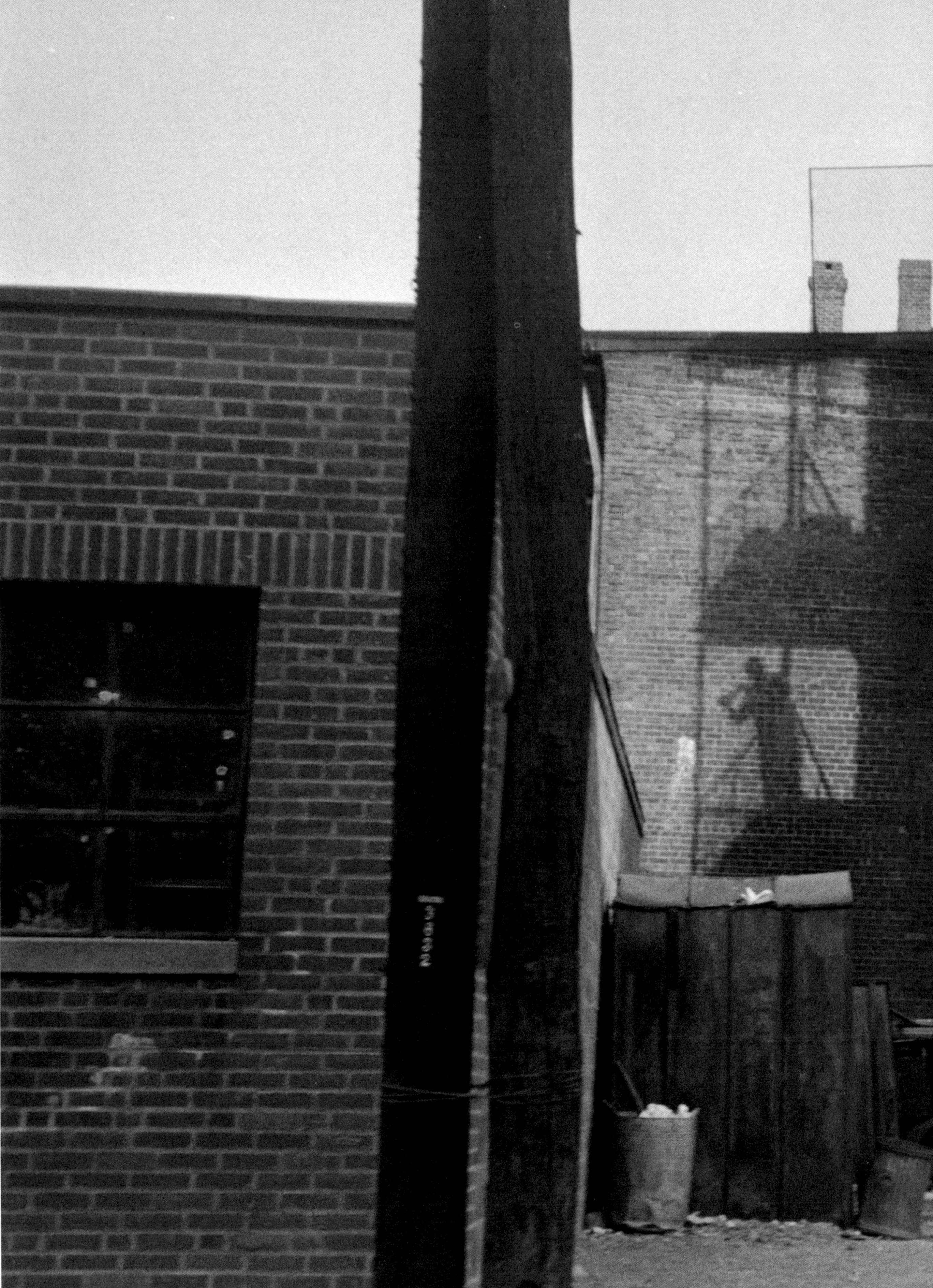

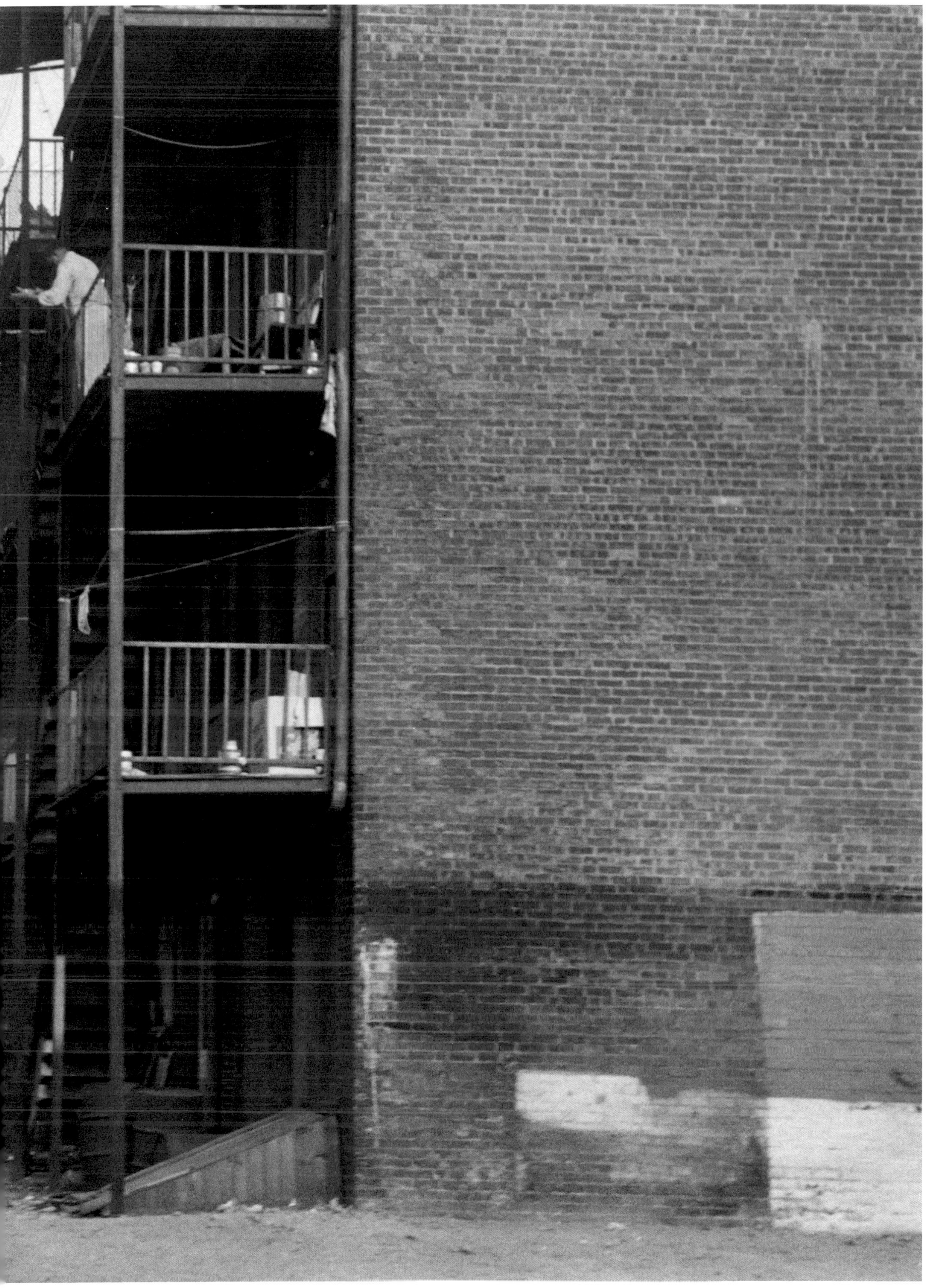

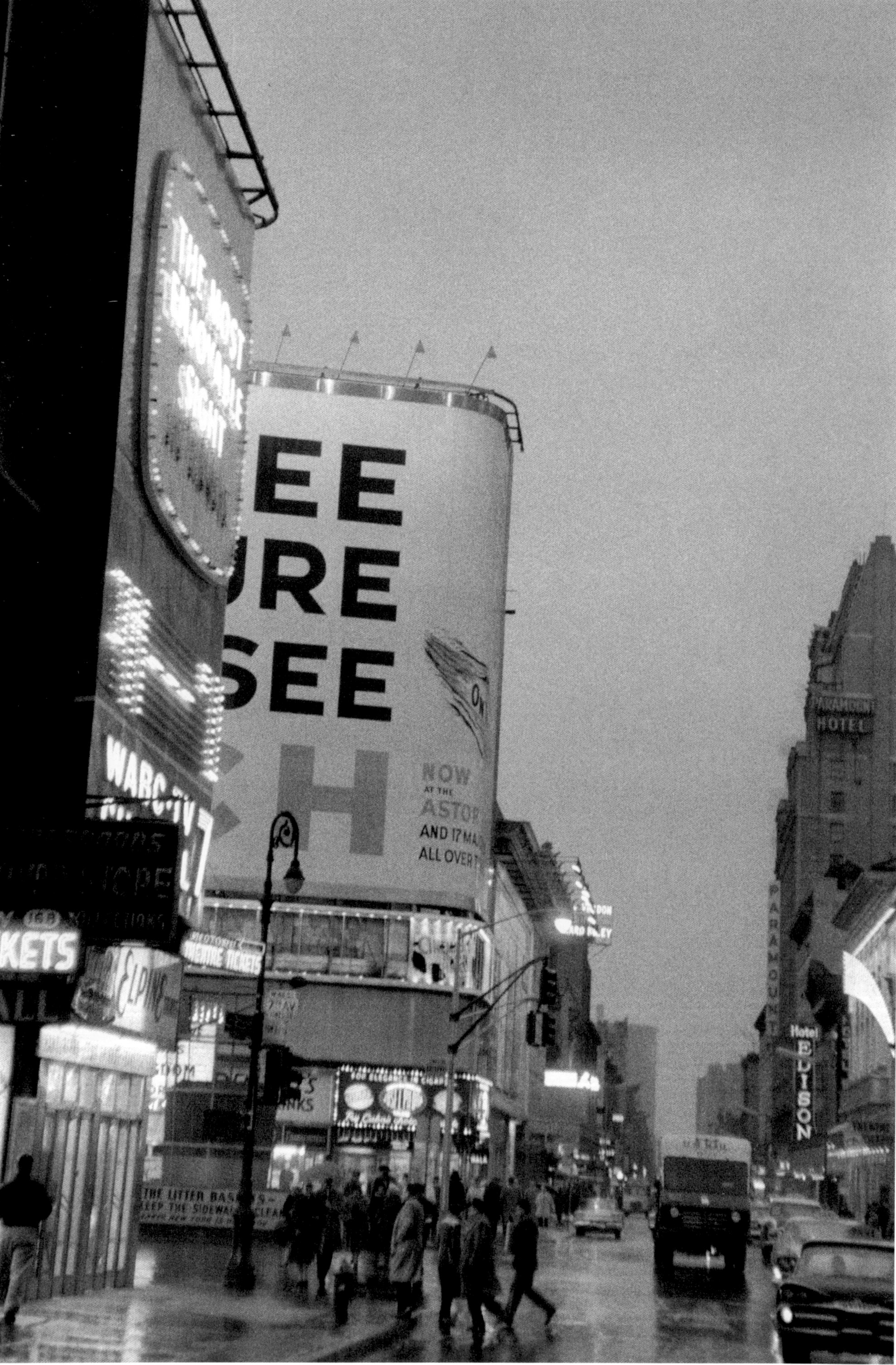
EE
URE
SEE
NOW
AT THE
ASTOR
PARAMOUNT
HOTEL
Hotel
EDISON
THEATRE TICKETS
KETS

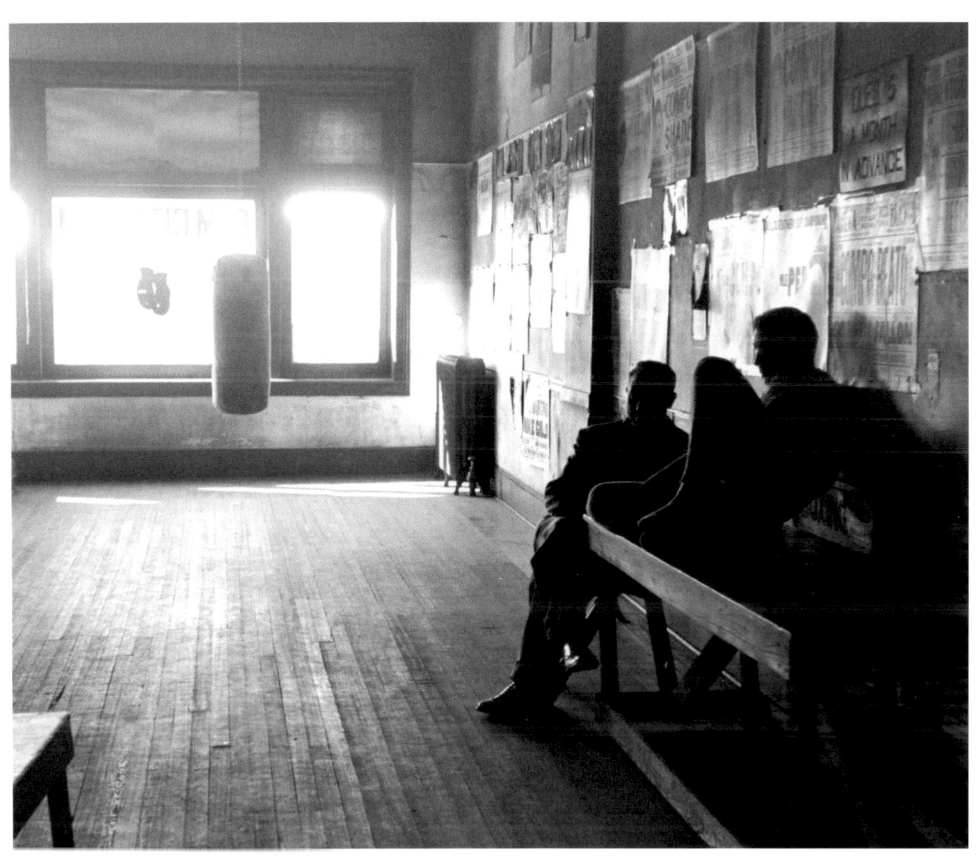

← Times Square, New York City, 1962

↑ New Haven, 1955

⇉ London, 1981

13
2
30
113
159
74

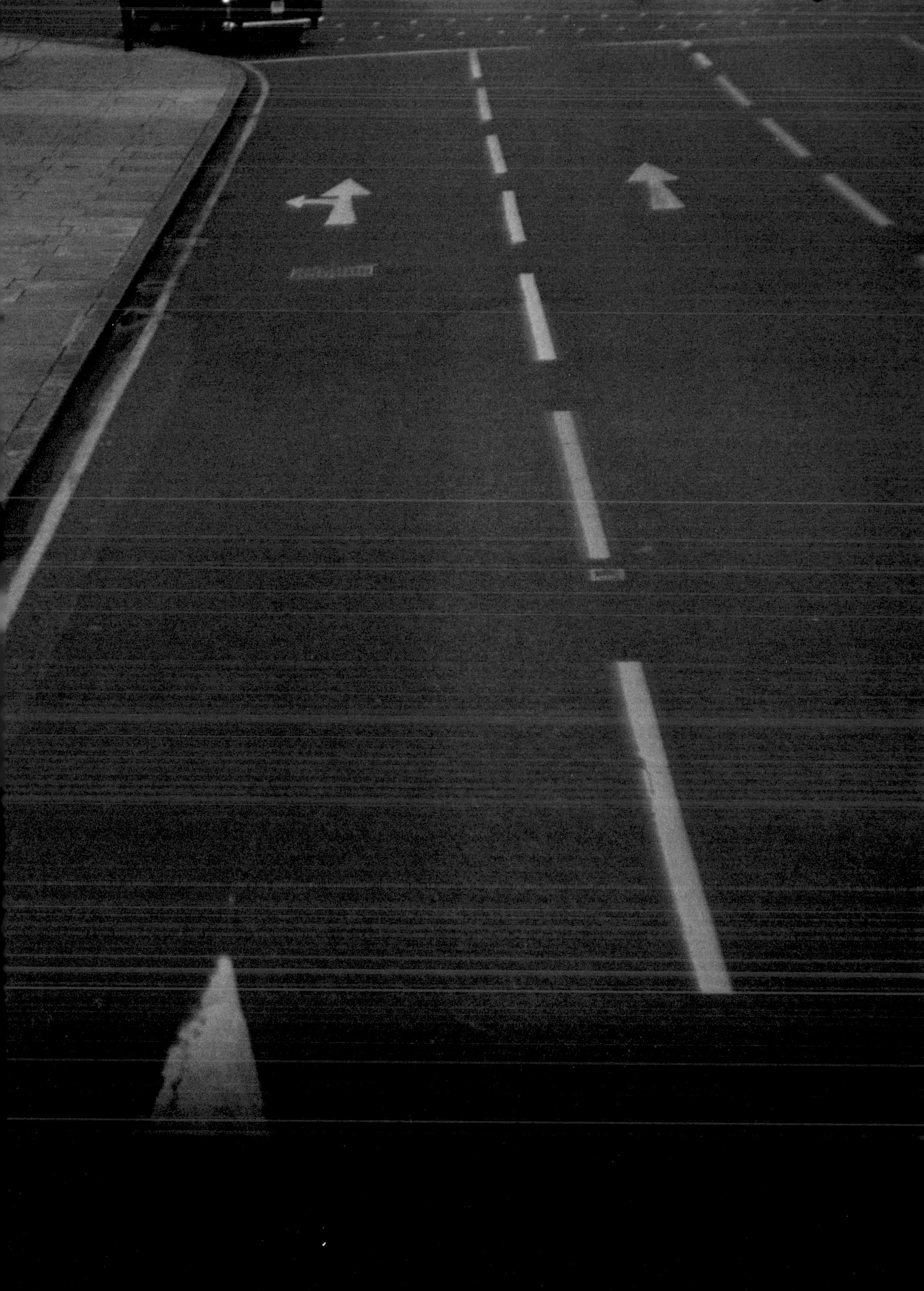

GOSPEL TRUTHS Harlem on a Sunday morning listening for the sound of Gospel music. I heard it coming from high in a building and climbed five dark flights of stairs to a room where seven people were dancing, singing and shouting. Six of them were in trances. The congregation went through this transformation every week. The weight of their New York existence was carried away in a rush of energy, taken in the name of religion.

Reverend Gary Davis was a powerful singer and incredible guitar player. I started visiting him in 1952, hung out at his house, documented his music, and took him to concerts. At that time I was unaware of the great records he had made in the 1930s as Blind Gary. In New York he often performed and begged in the streets. He invited me to a testimonial show in Harlem which honored him. I brought my parents. I vividly remember how upset my mother got when a women in the congregation started screaming and going into fits.

In the store front services and testimonial gatherings the music was built on rock-solid beats and driving rhythms, coupled with hand clapping, passionate singing and an incredible building of tensions followed by ecstatic release. That's when the yelling and spirit possessions took over, where the dancing and stomping began.

I first encountered Gospel music when I was fourteen at a summer camp. The entire kitchen staff came from a town in rural South Carolina and would gather in the barn after work and sing songs like "Walk Around My Bedside, Lord." The piano pounded out the rhythm and the women walked around as they sang. I was very impressed.

I recognized that feeling again when I accompanied Herbert Matter on his filming forays to Black churches in New York City. Later I attended such services on my own. In every sense they filled my needs with a great mix of spirit, music, dance, trance, and raw energy. There wasn't room for anything else.

→ Harlem, New York City, 1954

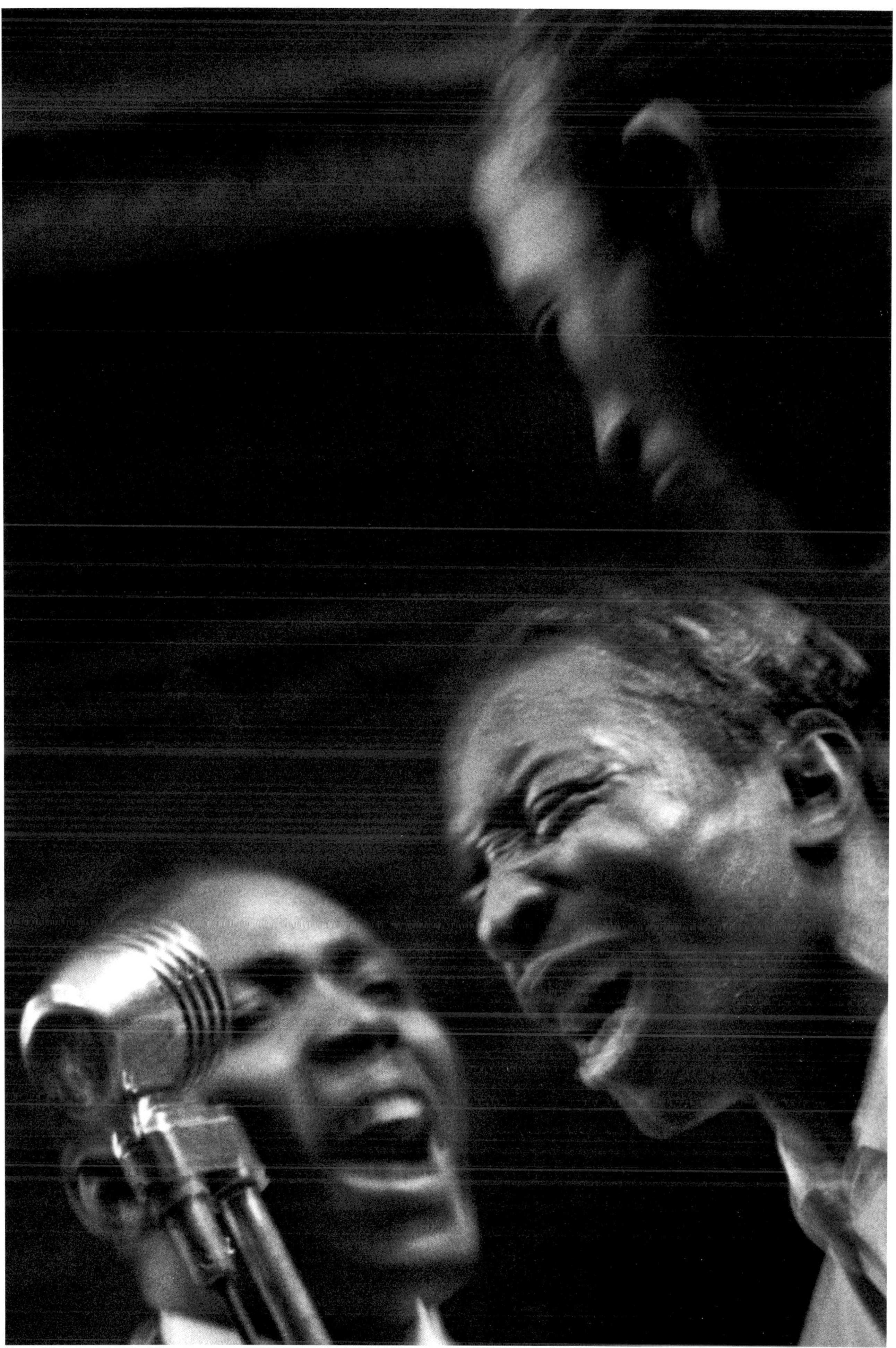

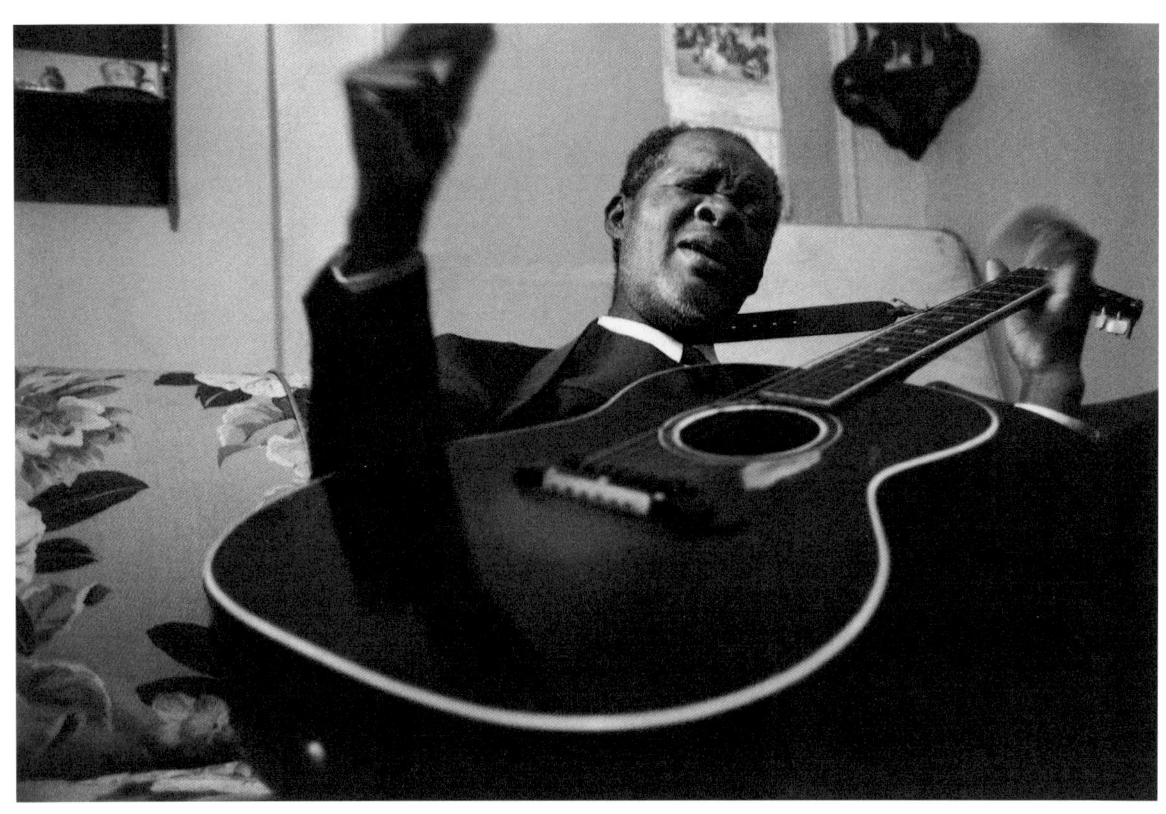

↑ Reverend Gary Davis, New York City, 1954

→ Harlem, New York City, 1957

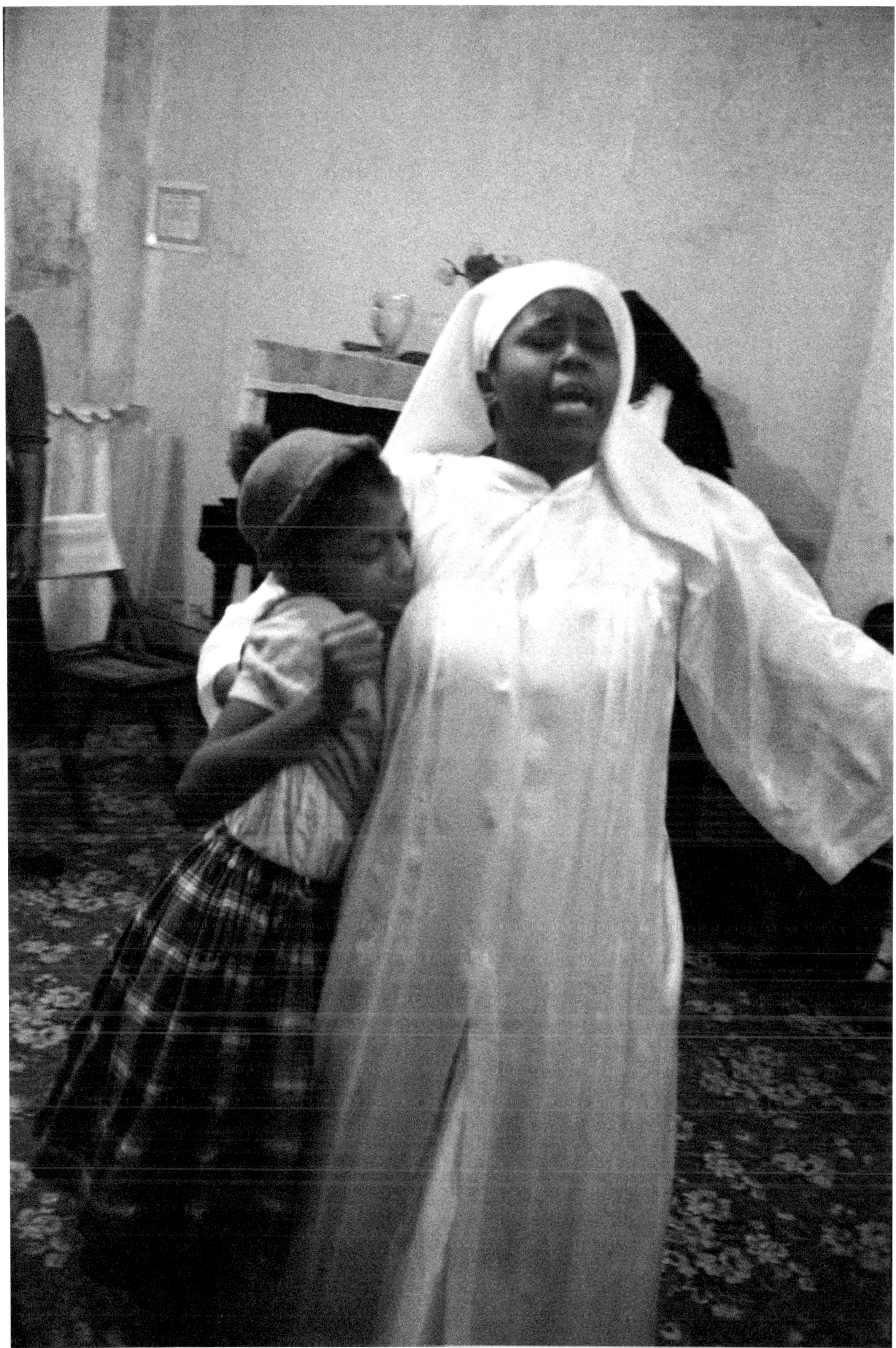

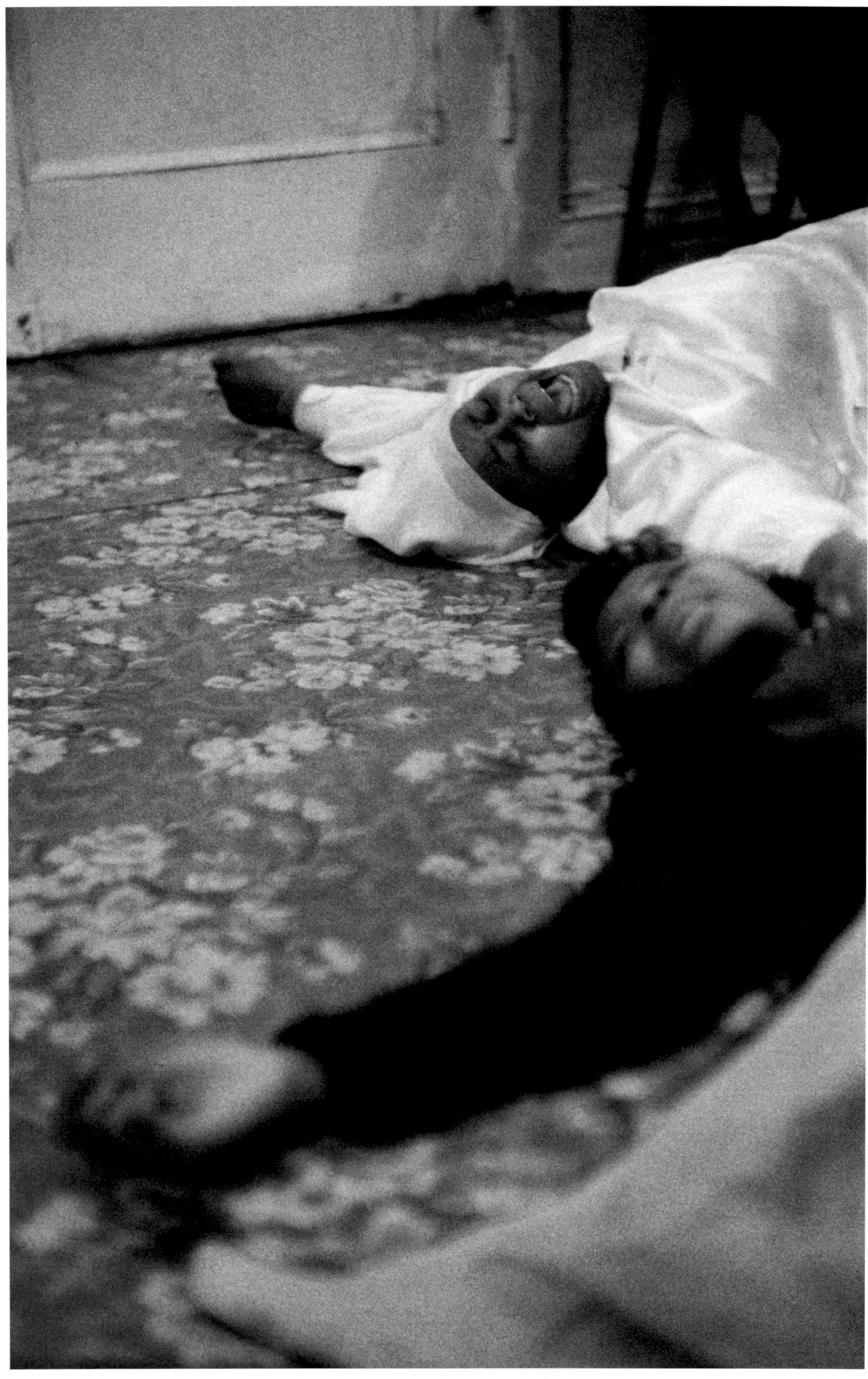

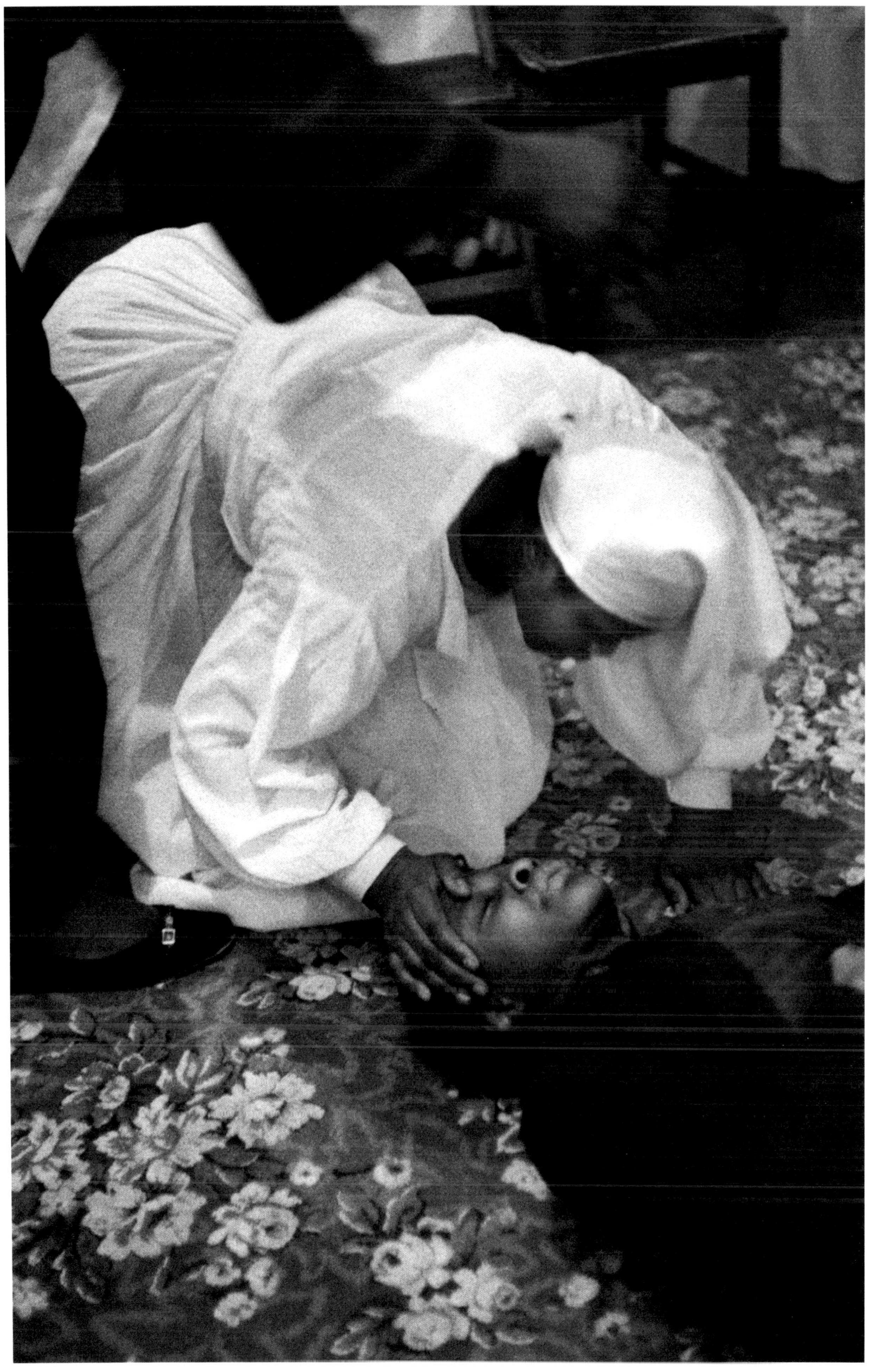

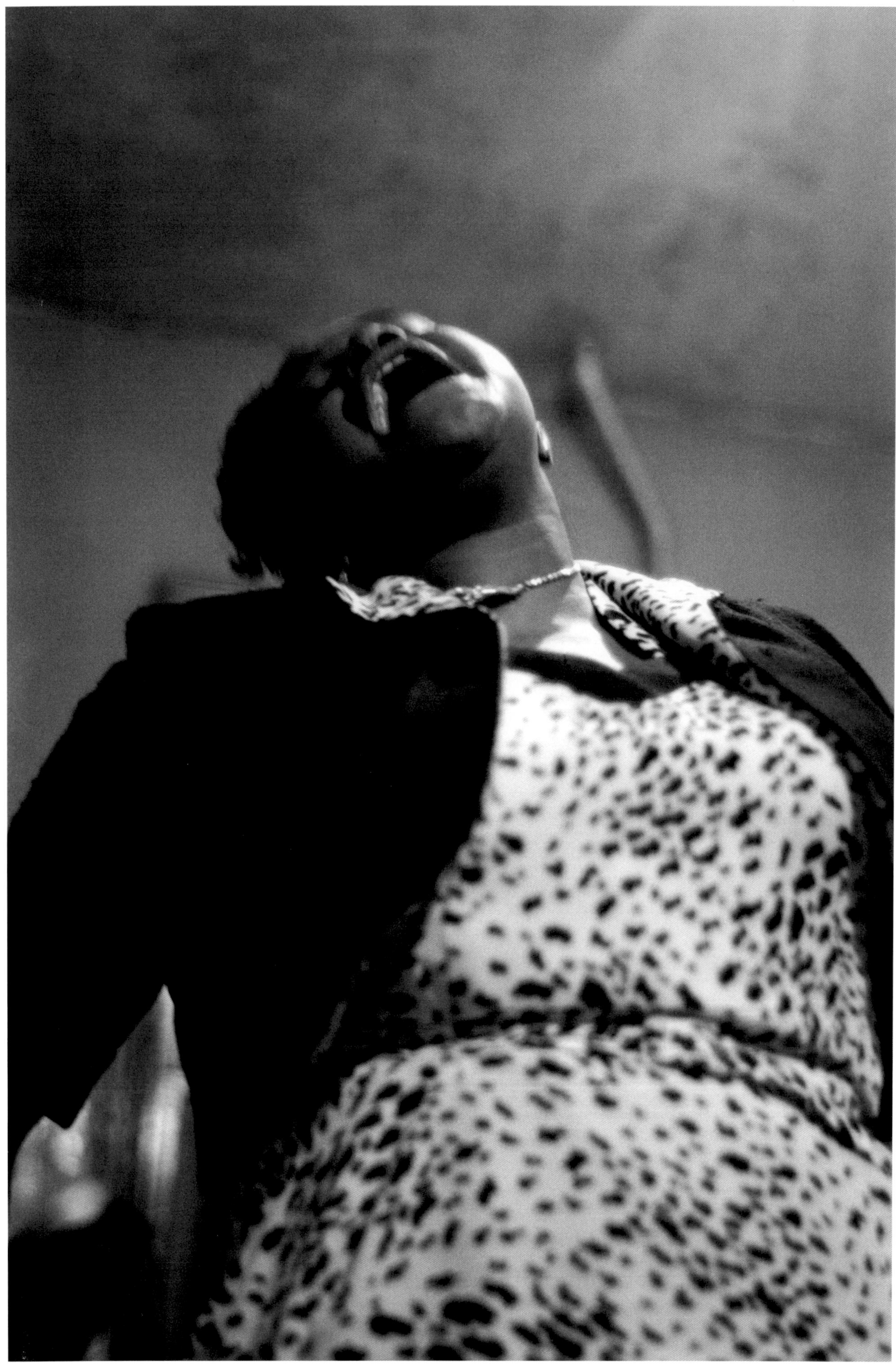

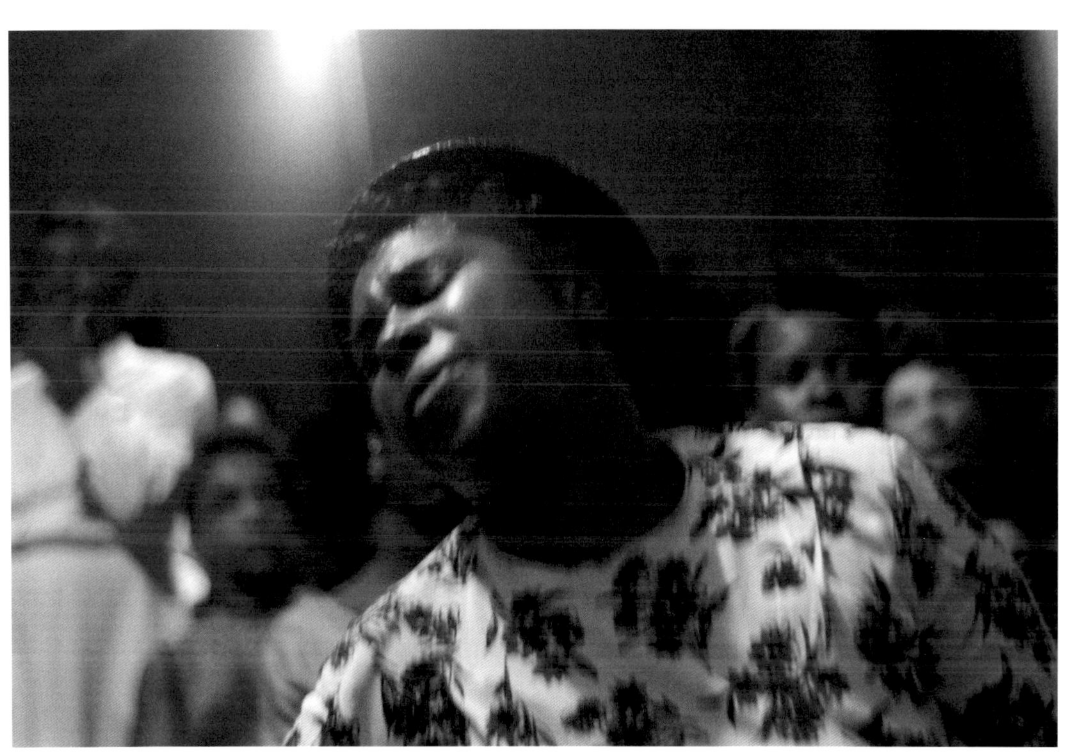

⇇ Harlem, New York City, 1957

← East New York, Brooklyn, 1956

↑ East New York, Brooklyn, 1956

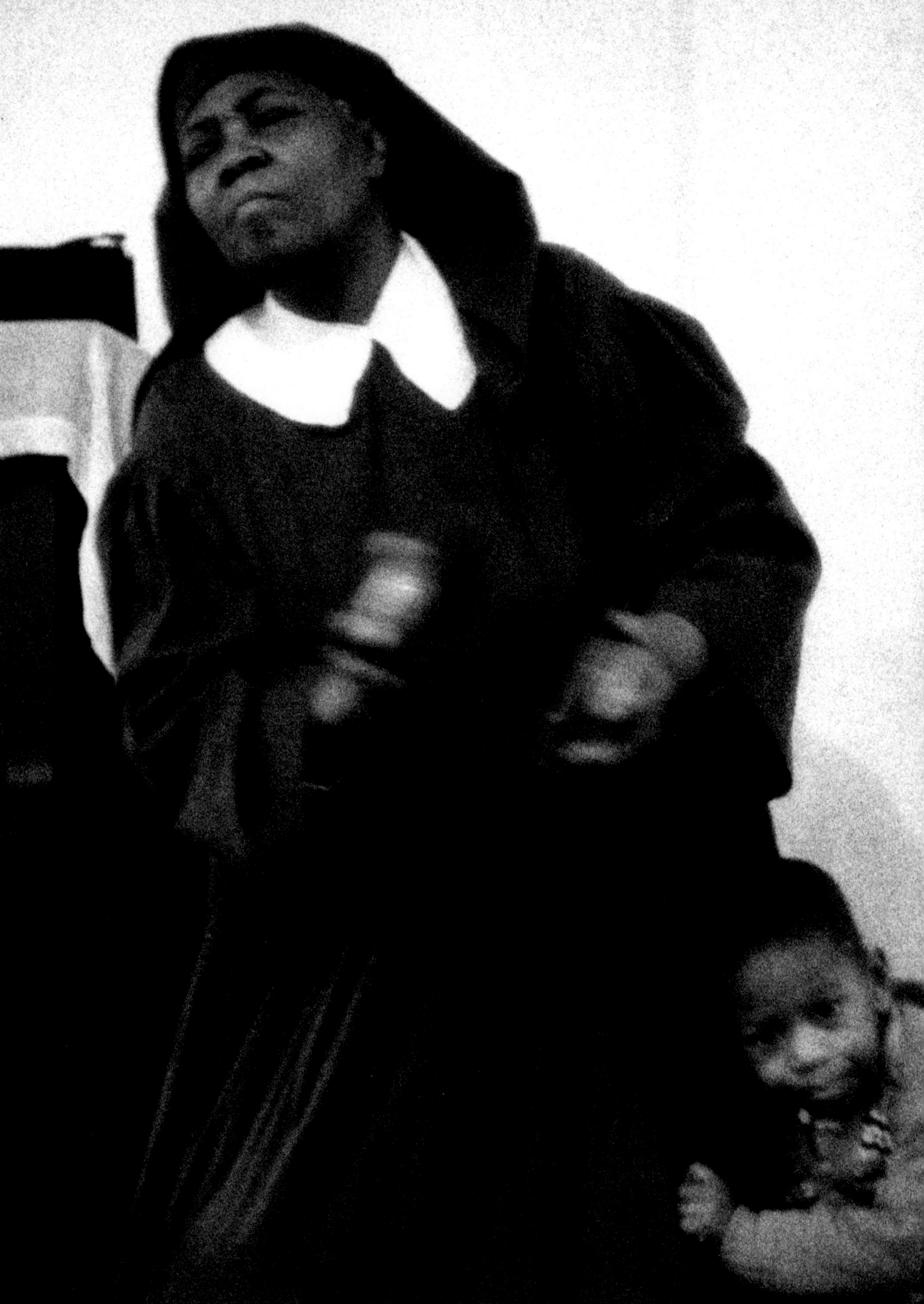

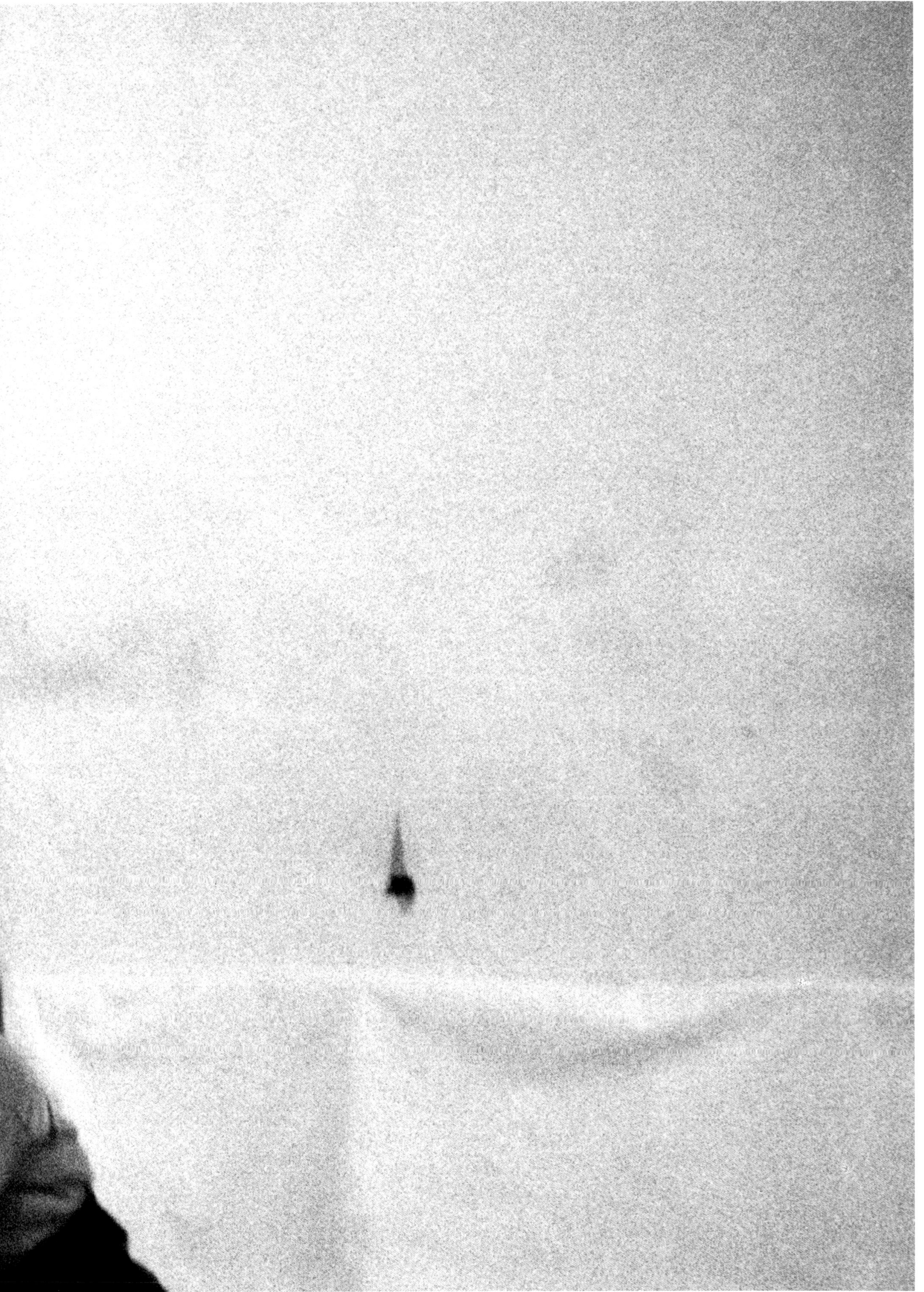

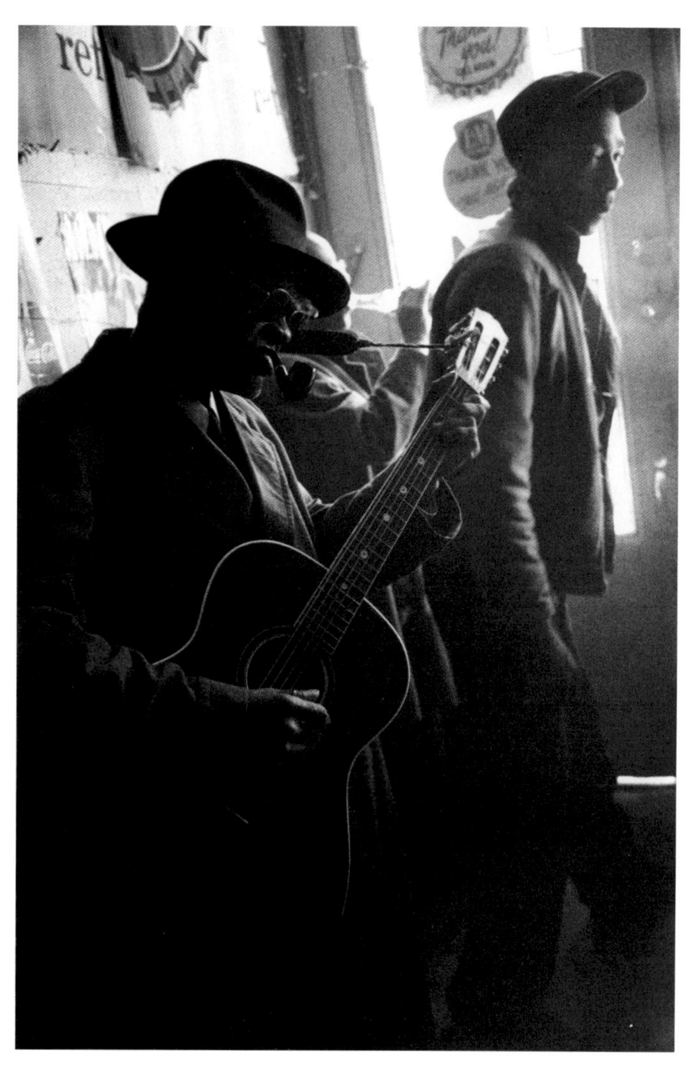

← Harlem, New York City, 1957

↑ Reverend Gary Davis, New York City, 1954

→ Reverend Gary Davis, New York City, 1954

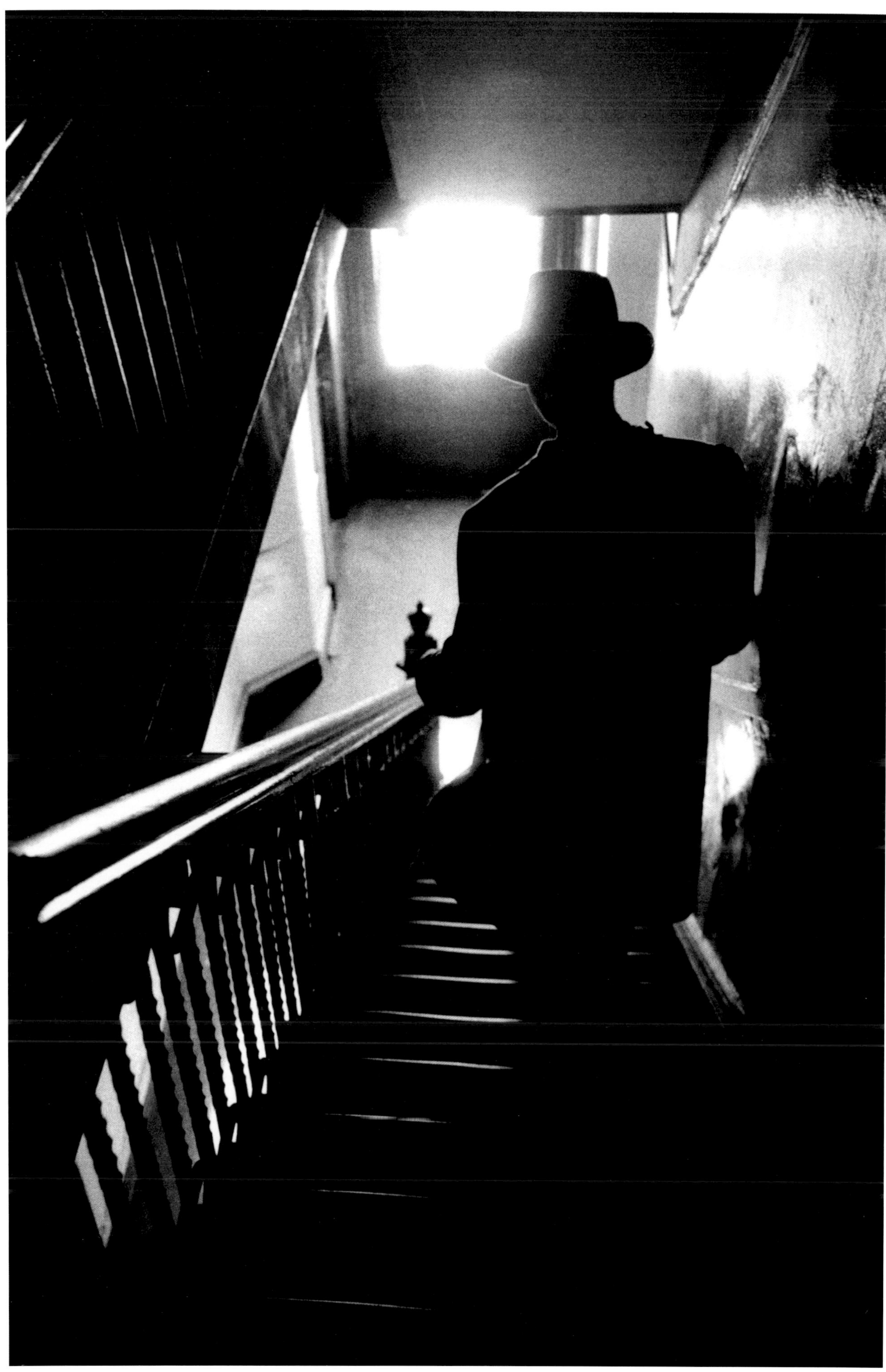

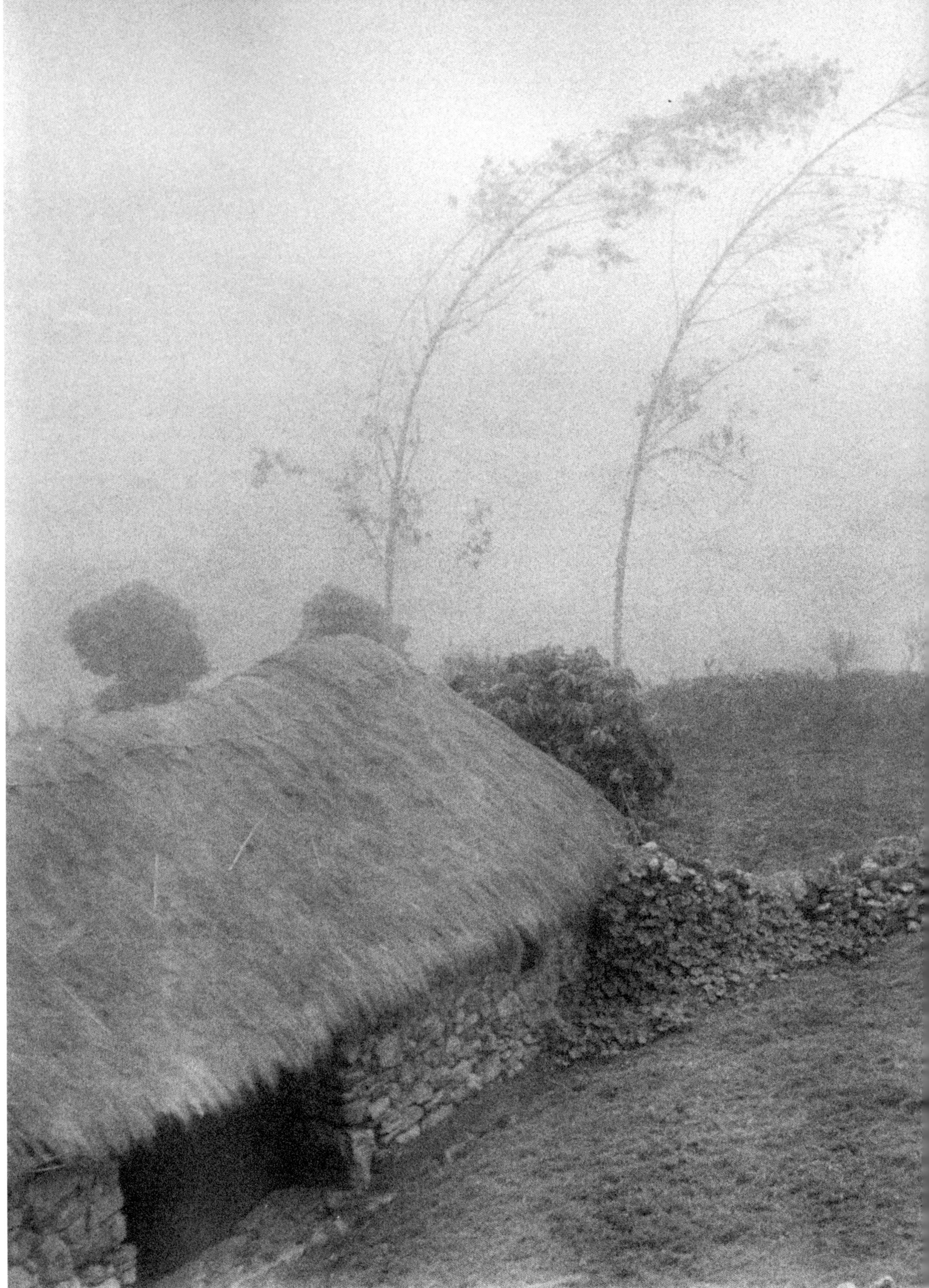

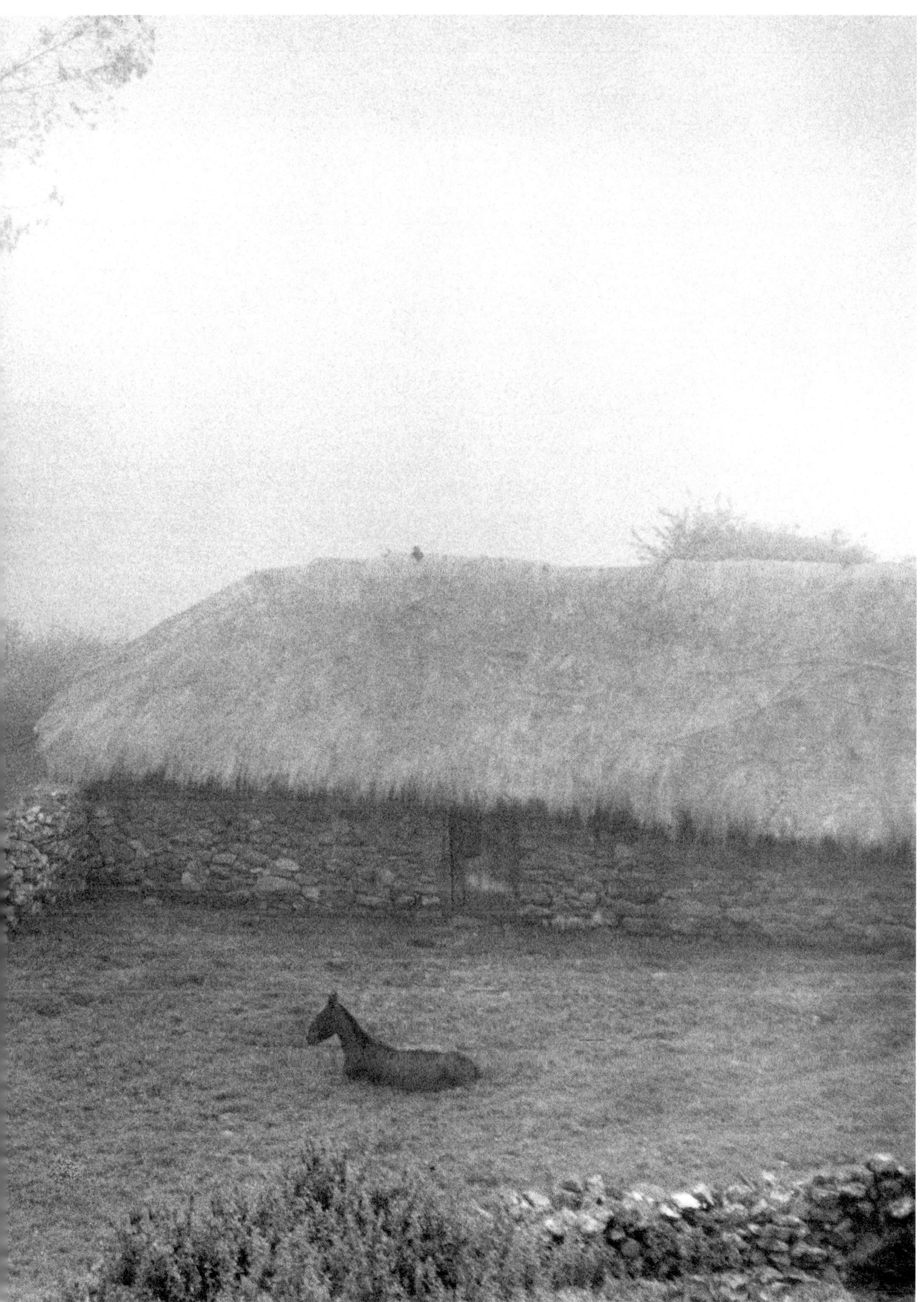

THE SHAPE OF SURVIVAL Over the tears of time, the Andean people of Peru have put the world together in their own way. There is an unbroken thread that runs from before the Incas to the Indians today, as well as a continuing struggle with Western ideas. I've traveled to the Andes more than eight times to photograph, record music, document weaving, and make films. It has been very hard on my body, and exhausting to view the social disparities that exist there. Yet, after every trip I returned to America with new realizations and ways to look at my life.

I showed a Q'eros woman my photograph of her husband who had recently died. Tears flowed down from her eyes and she refused to look at more photos "if there were any of him."

In a New World archaeology class I wondered whether the conclusions drawn by archaeologists held any resemblance to the lives of the Indians today. I did a paper about pre-Columbian textiles, and I searched out everything that had been written about Paracas fabrics. At the Brooklyn Museum, standing before a beautiful Paracas textile, I wondered why the weaver had used a specific sequence of colors and why there were random interruptions to these patterns. The color series resembled music to me. I found myself in a dialog with a weaver who had lived 2000 years ago about choices she had made in this design. It led me to my own questions and I could not find answers in the books. Standing there, my sense of time evaporated, and I don't know whether five seconds or five hours went by. The only place I could conceive of finding answers was among the descendants of the weaver. Ask the people who make the weaving. Three months later I was on my way to Peru.

Before I left, my father had asked what I'd be doing the following year. I told him my idea. He asked again the next week, and I told him again. He said, "That's an idea. Now what are you going to do?" I told Herbert Matter of this conversation. His response was, "well, at least you have an idea."

On my first trip to the Andes in 1956, I was in the house of a Protestant missionary. He had come to Peru to convert the Indians from their Catholic practices. On his bookshelf was a guidebook for missionaries and under music and dance it said, "Dancing among the Indians is mostly sexual. Couldn't this be replaced by competitive games?" I could imagine the Indians abandoning their religious rituals, done with music and dance, to take up soccer. I found myself comparing the competitive basis of capitalism to the spiritual needs of the Indians. The comparison was ugly and I naively hoped

← Hautun, Q'eros, Peru, 1957

→ Kiku, Q'eros, Peru, 1957

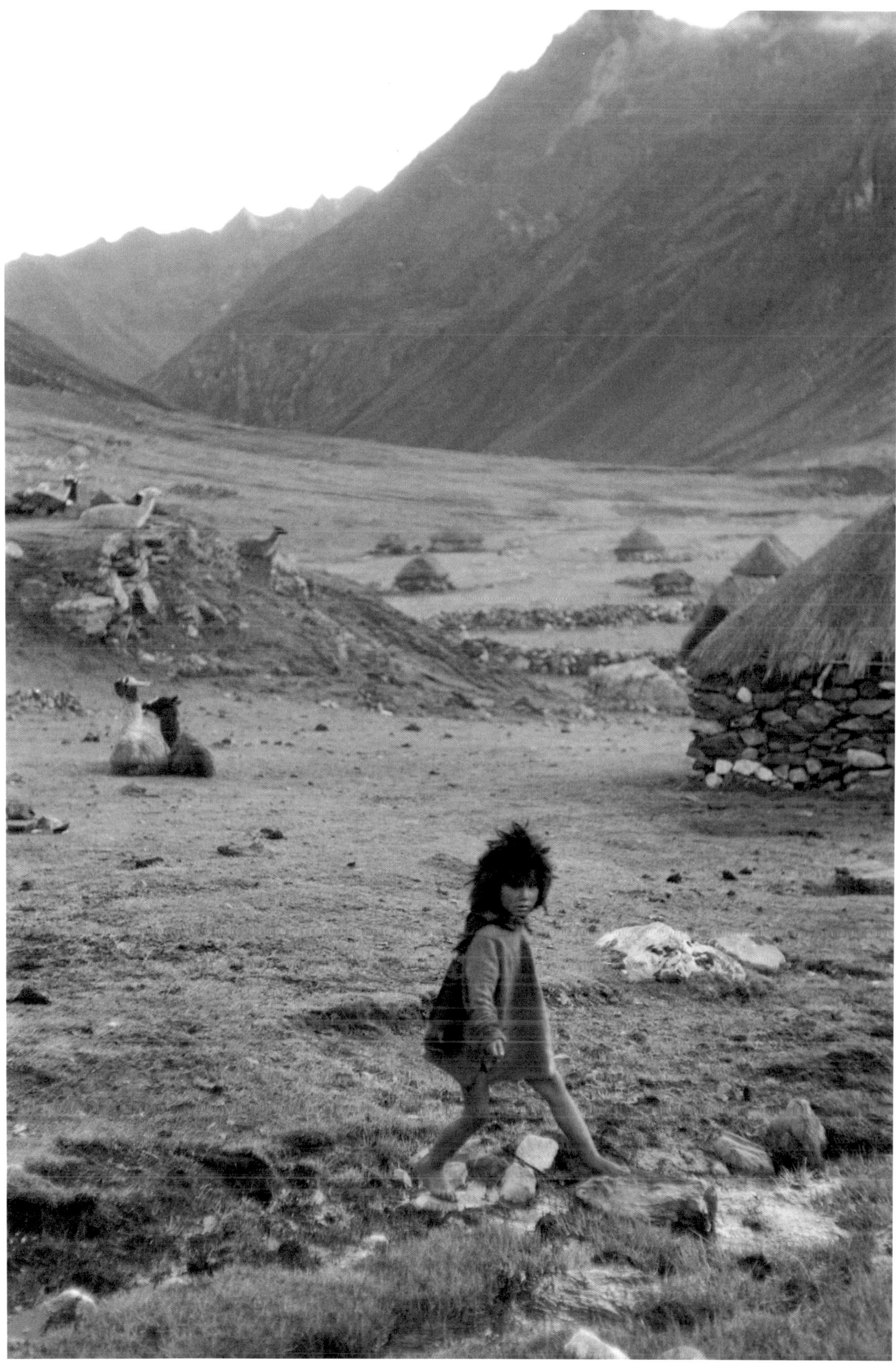

that by showing the beauty of Indian life, my photographs would challenge the missionary's program. All bets were off, however, when someone pointed out that sex is a competitive game.

When meeting a weaver at her work, it was often an uneasy situation. She would be sitting on the ground by her adobe house setting up her loom. I would approach as an unknown force, a foreigner. I'd observe the weaving for a while but couldn't speak her language. But I knew two words of Quechua; they were "Ima Sumac" (the name of a popular Peruvian singer who had been promoted in the U.S.). So I'd say those words which mean "how beautiful" and the weaver would smile at my compliment. Then I'd point to part of the weaving and ask, "Ima ima su tiki?" (How do you do that, what is it called?) By writing down her words I could build a vocabulary of weaving terminology and learn the process in her terms.

I observed and photographed things which I didn't understand until much later. The acts which were done around the weaving—sprinkling some corn beer on the corners of the loom before starting the weaving, pouring some corn beer on the ground in honor of mother earth, flicking beer to the cardinal directions—looked like rituals. For the purpose of my study this didn't add weaving information, but over time the strength of the Indians' dedication to the powers of nature became primary to me. What began as exotic and extraneous became my central concern.

In 1956 on my first trip to the isolated region of Q'eros, we had to cross a snowy pass at 15,000 feet above sea level to get to the far side of the Andes. In this dizzying altitude I photographed three children in a high valley and asked for directions. They were alone with no adults around and I had no reason to stay. It was only a moment. That photograph of them hung in my studio for years. I stared at it a lot. Twenty years later, when I made my first film of Q'eros, I found myself gazing into the face of a man whom I didn't know. I couldn't stop looking at him and realized that this was the little boy in my photograph, now grown up. His name is Raymundo Quispe Chura and I've seen him a lot on later trips. I've watched him age more rapidly than I have. Once Raymundo picked up a rock and held it to his face exactly as I held my camera. He was showing me what a photographer looked like to him. He's told me many things. While filming the rituals around Carnival season when the Q'eros make offerings to the gods for the health and fertility of the alpacas, Raymundo told me about the song he sang for the ceremony. He said, "Without the song we can't have the festival, and without the festival there is no song."

This left me wondering. If their songs and flute tunes are an integral part of their ceremonies, is it possible the Q'eros have no separate category called "music"? When they play a particular melody or sing at my request, perhaps they have only been accommodating my conception of music all these years. Raymundo gave me the words to the song "Kius" which was used in the ritual.

"Kius, Kius, they are recording my voice.
The tall hill I am to climb, I hope the festival there
will be strong."

His text was a description of what his plans were at that moment. It was truly documentary. Although the song was given as part of the ritual, his text was of the moment and would change from hour to hour, a passing state of mind.

The "Palcha" and "Kius" are parts of a cycle of rituals, imploring the gods for the health of their animals. They sing and throw palcha flowers at the animals. The gods are known by the name Huamani, which also means hawk or eagle. The wild animals belong to the gods while the domesticated animals belong to the Q'eros. These rituals are repeated each year. As each season comes into focus, so do its songs.

Among the animals in a corral, a woman sang her Palcha song. It wasn't directed at anyone who was there, nor at the tape recorder. It revealed a spiritual world that intermingled with the daily one.

Suffering takes away the happiness of my valley
People leave and die
Scatter the palcha flower, Huamani
One or two of you alpacas have gone away (died)
Why do we have to die?
Scatter the palcha flower, Huamani
Alpaca who leads the way forward,
With your little sister
Wouldn't you nurture me?
Together you are sleeping
Scatter the palcha flower, Huamani
Hurry, move on
Don't look at me, mother, for you are sacred
Scatter the palcha flower, Huamani

3 Andrea Quispe Chura, Wayuna Pampa, 1977

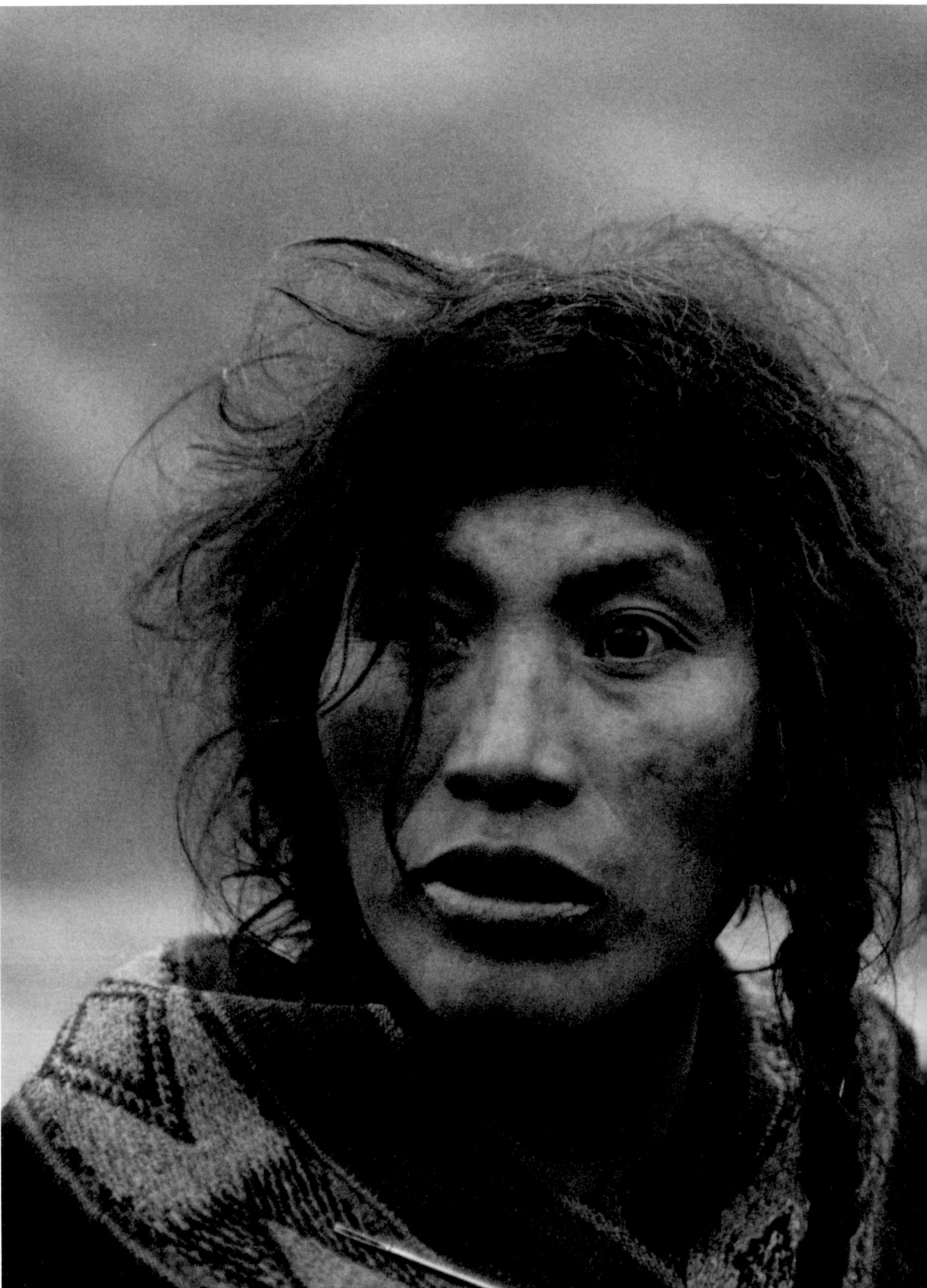

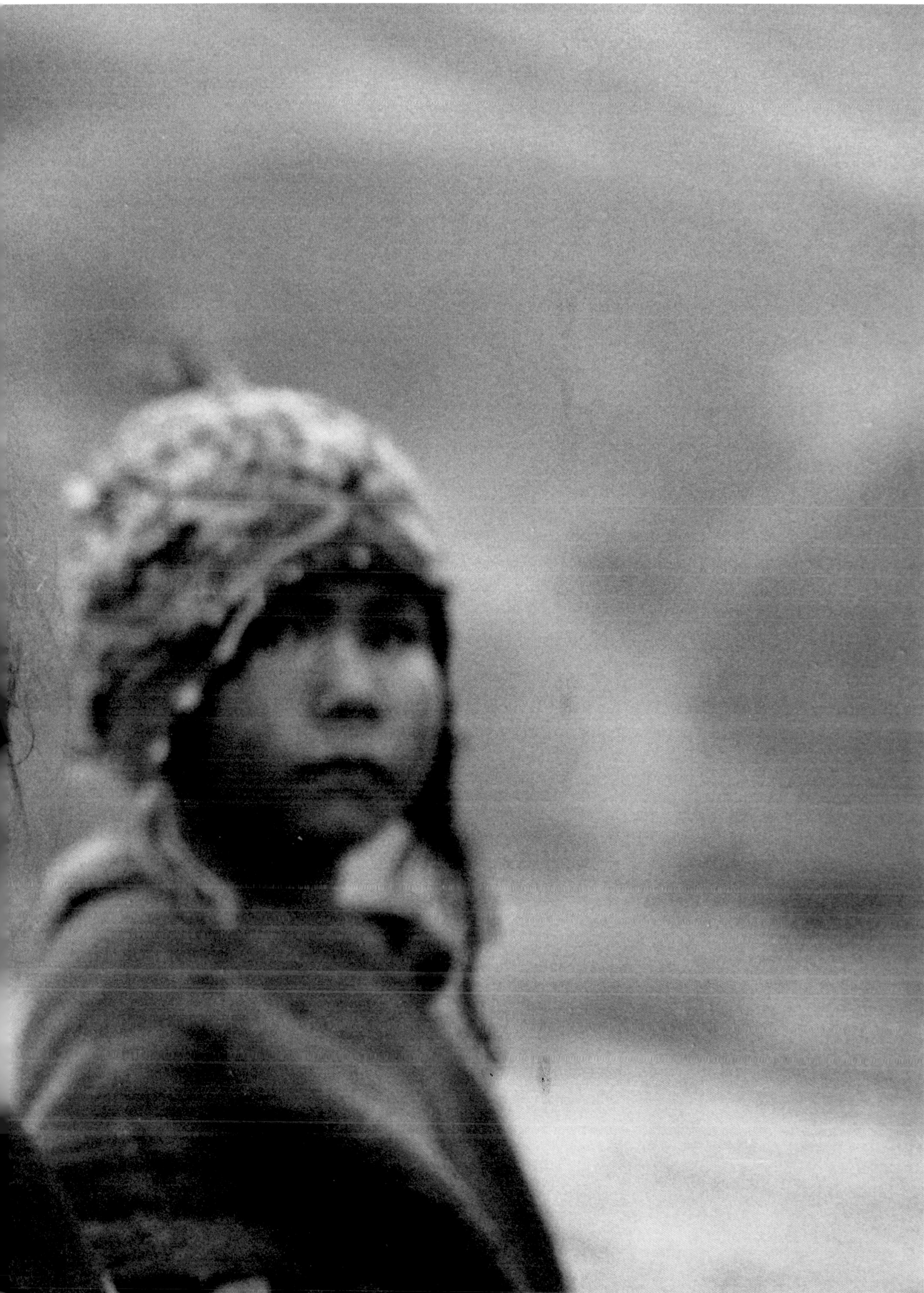

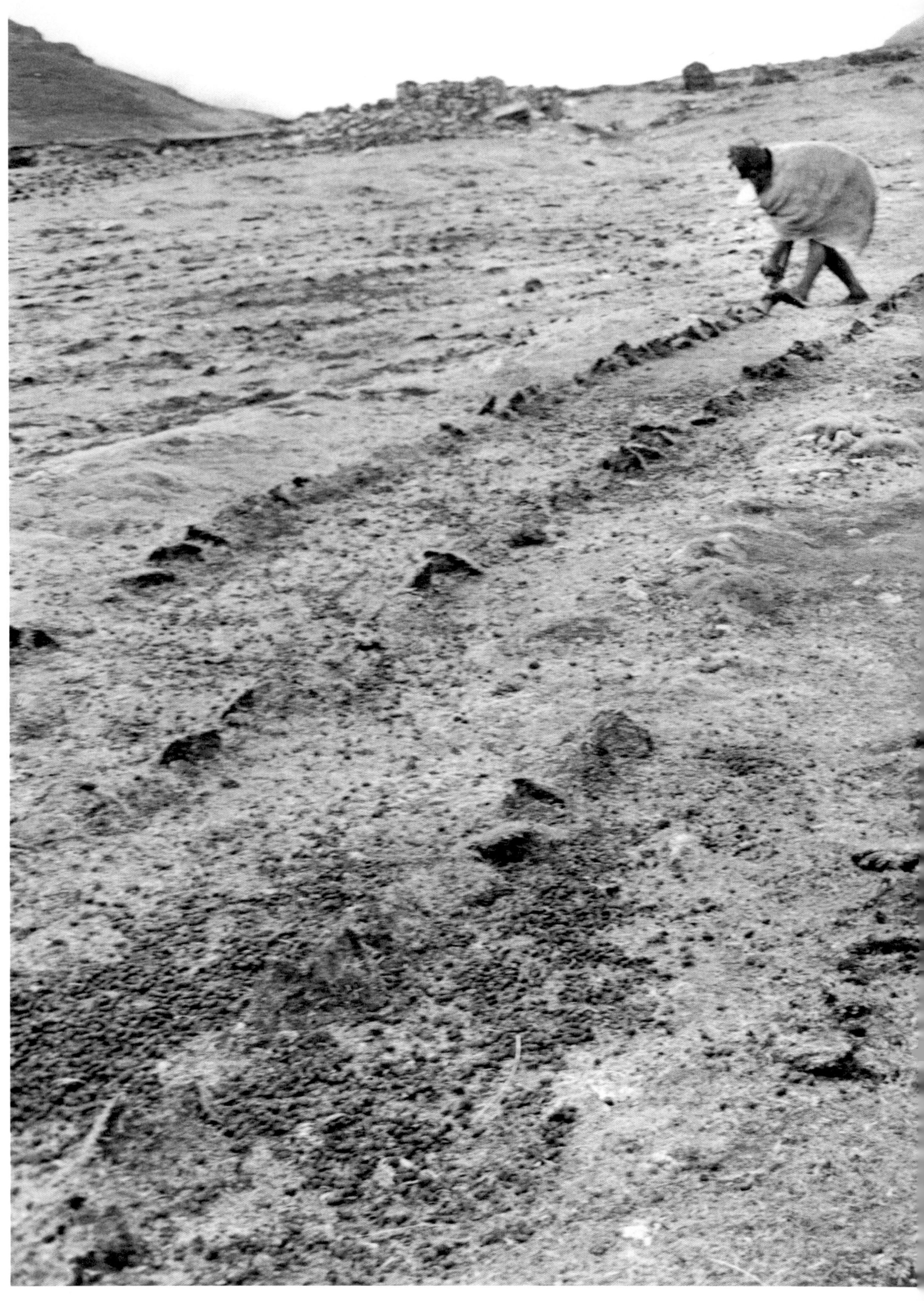

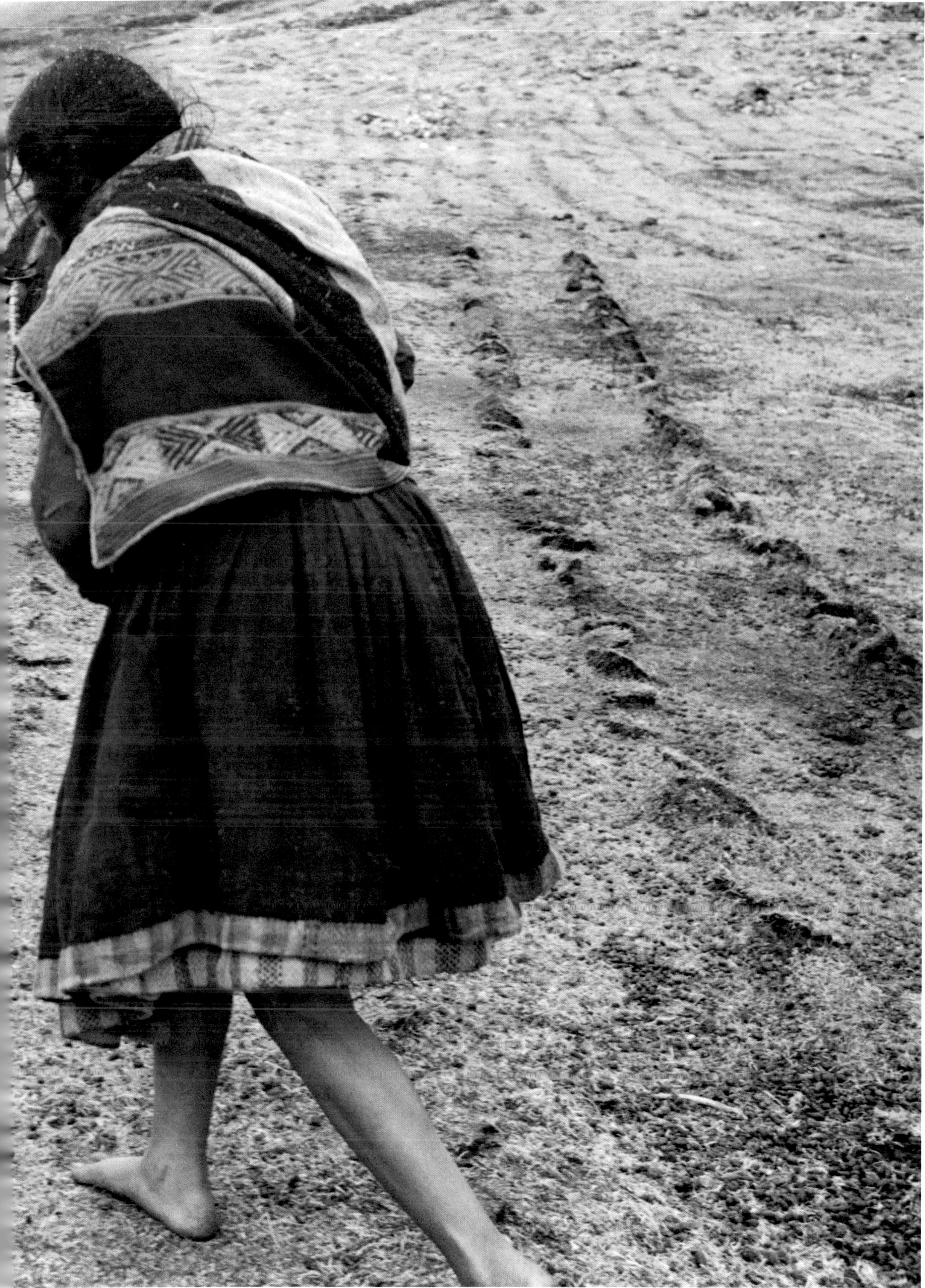

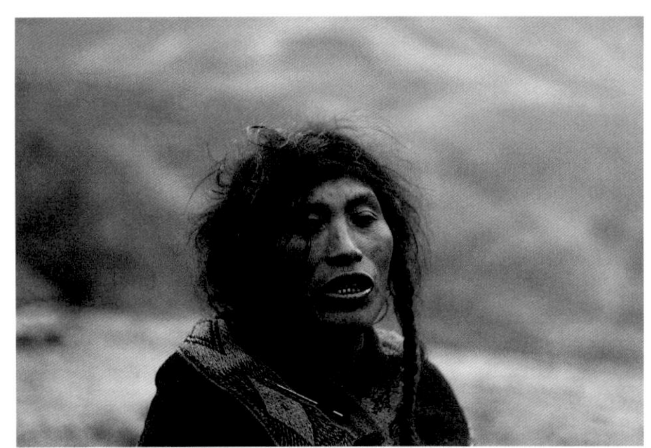

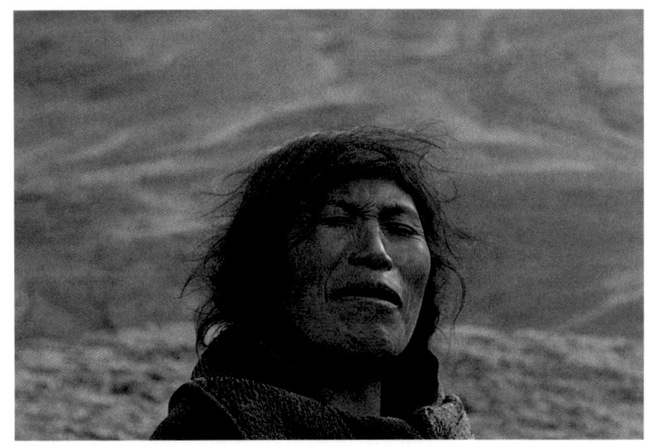

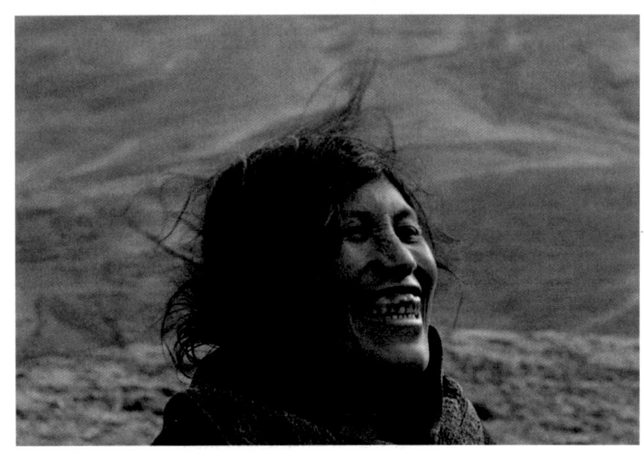

← Kiku, Q'eros, Peru, 1964

↑ (all) Andrea Quispe Chura, Q'eros, Peru, 1977

→ Wayuna Pampa, Q'eros, Peru, 1956

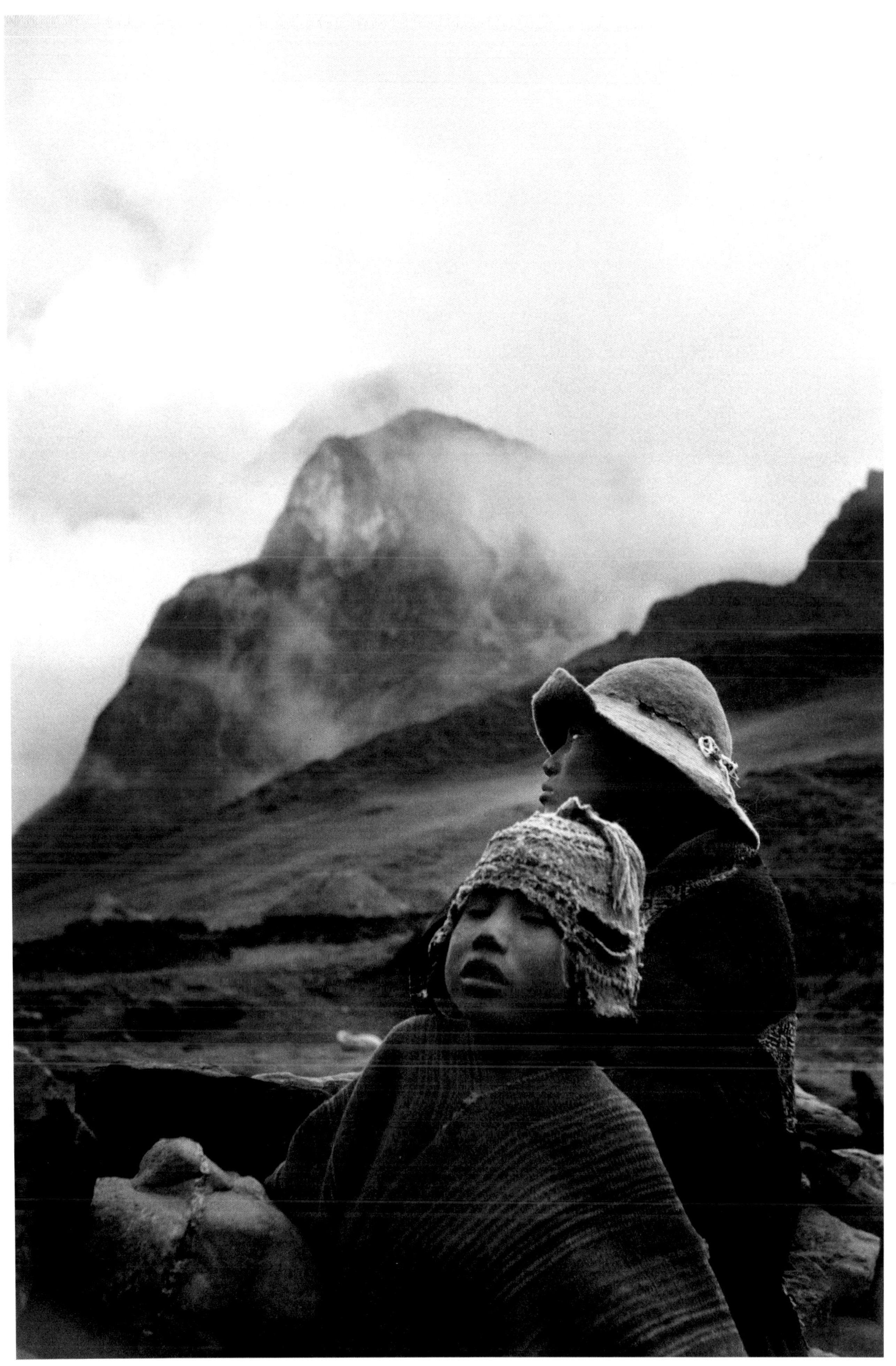

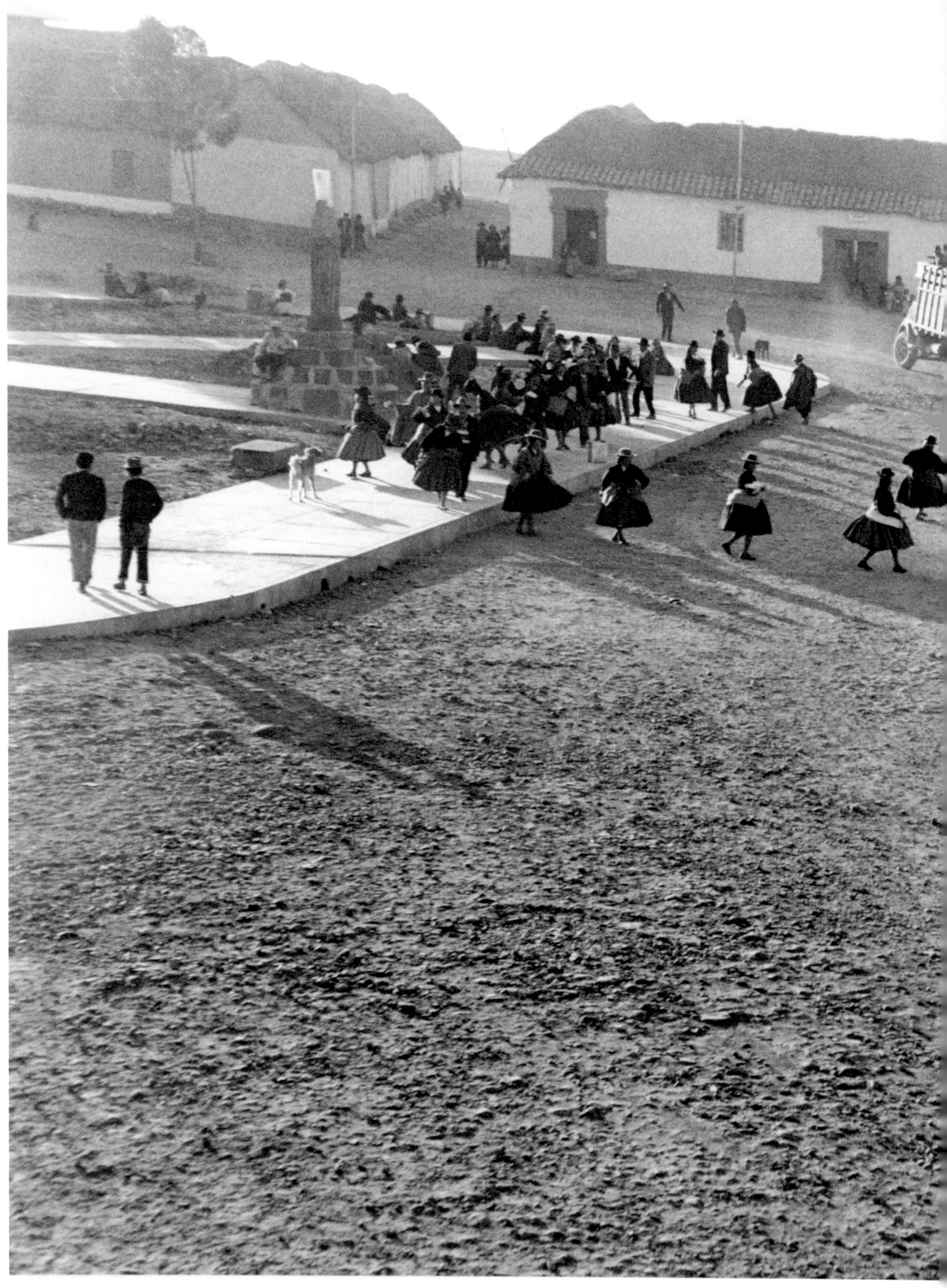

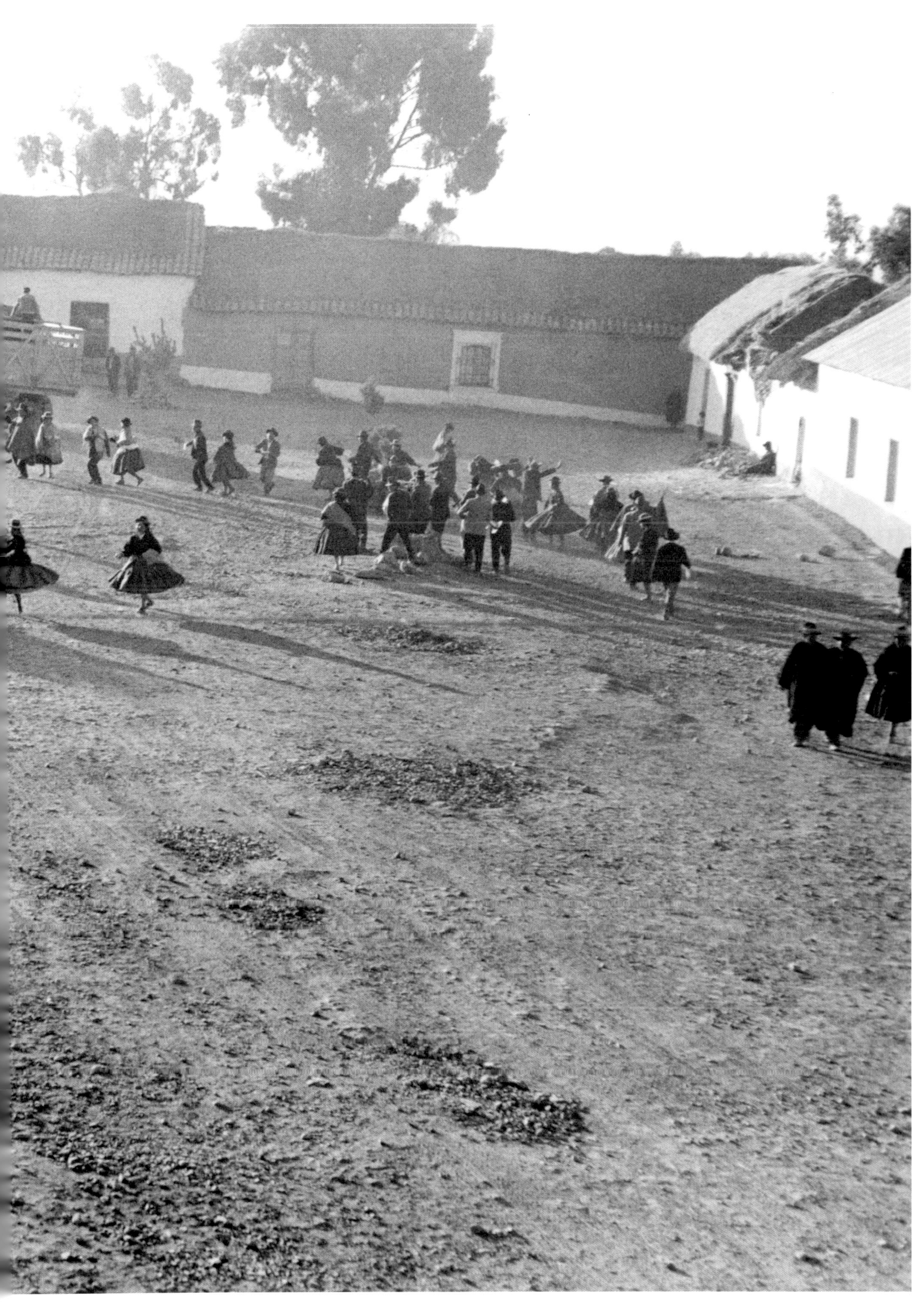

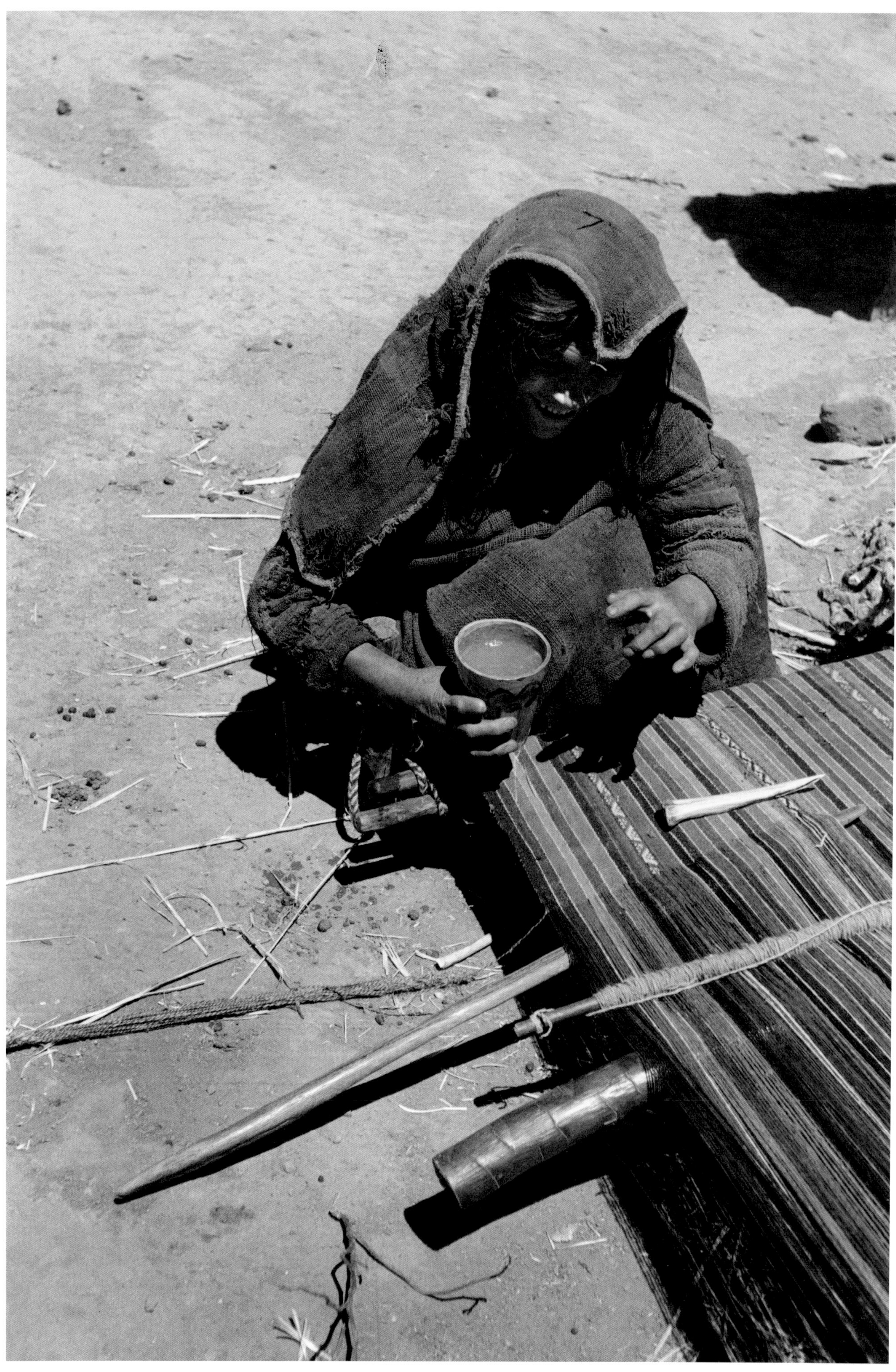

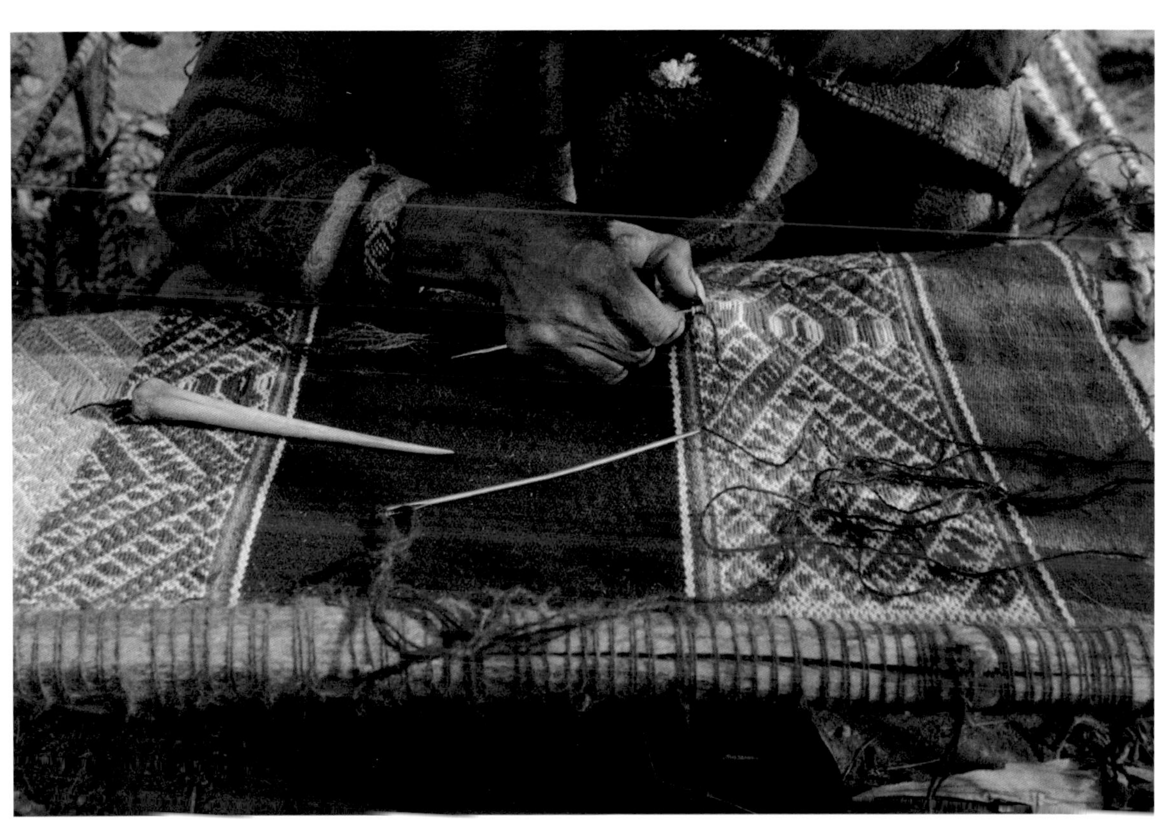

⇇ Chucuito, Peru, 1964

← Blessing the warp, Tinta, Peru, 1956

↑ Final passes, Ccapana, Peru, 1957

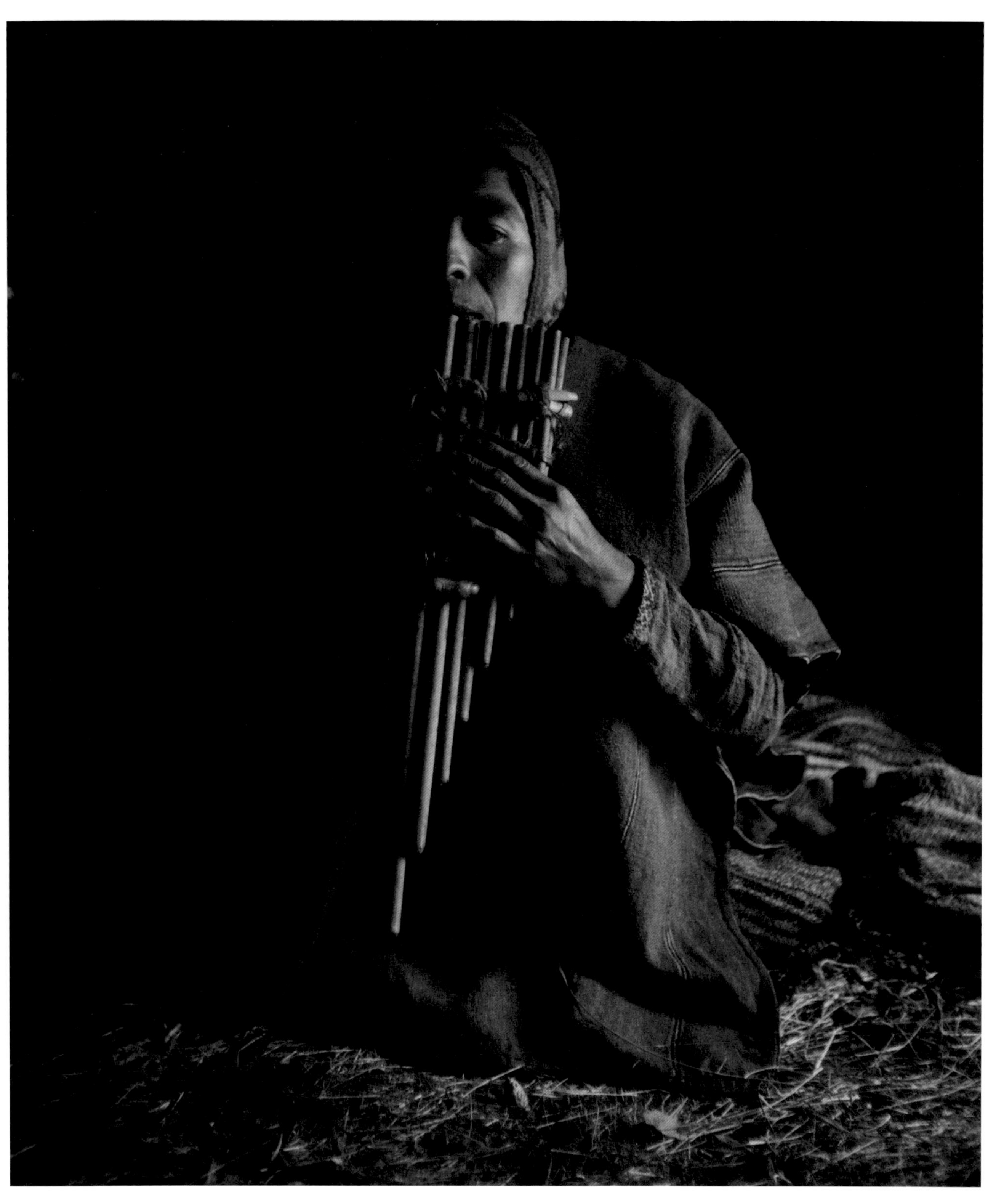

↑ Panpipes, Kiku, Q'eros, Peru, 1964

→ Near Pisac, Peru, 1956

⇉ Ocongate, Peru, 1964

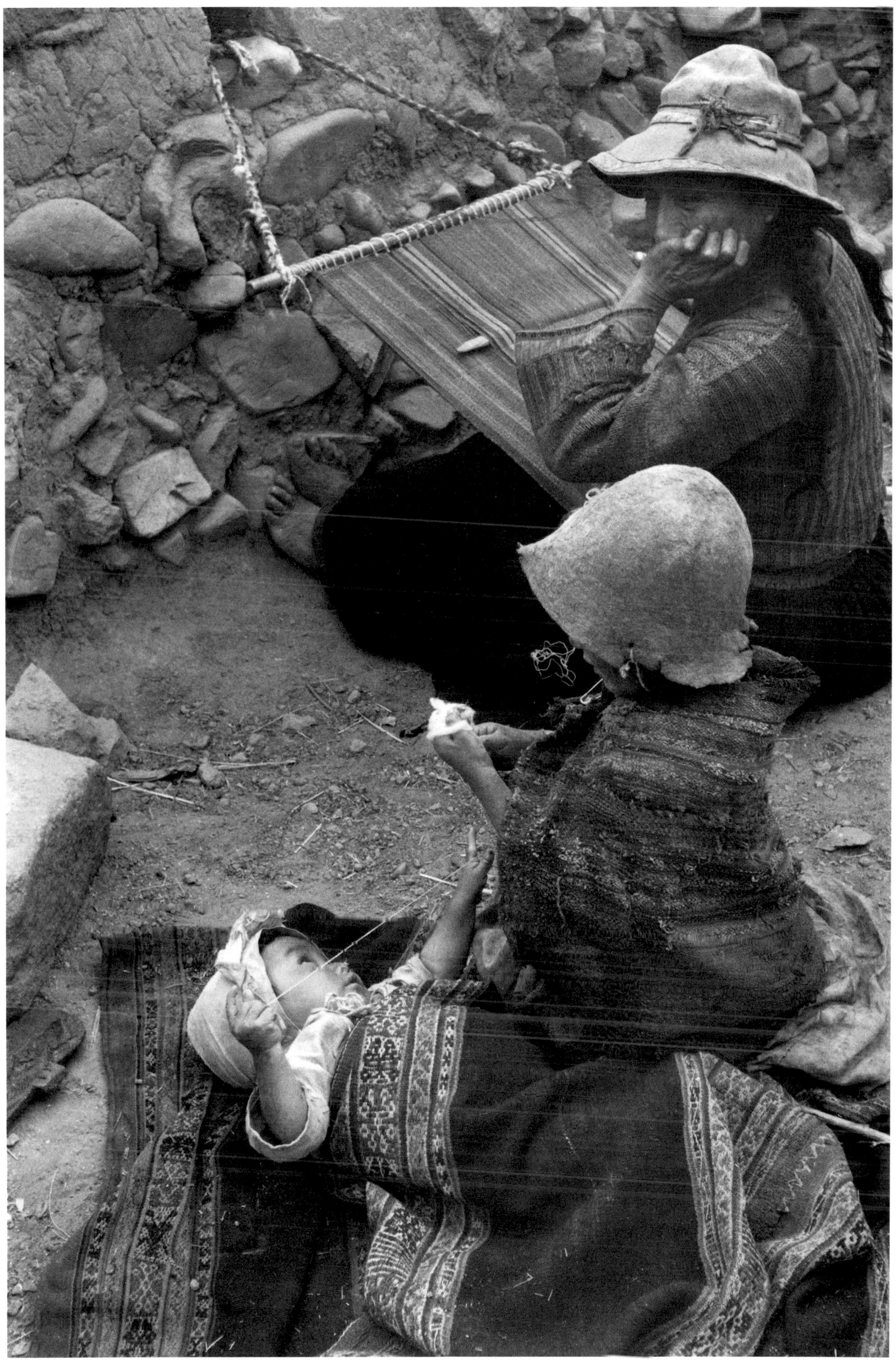

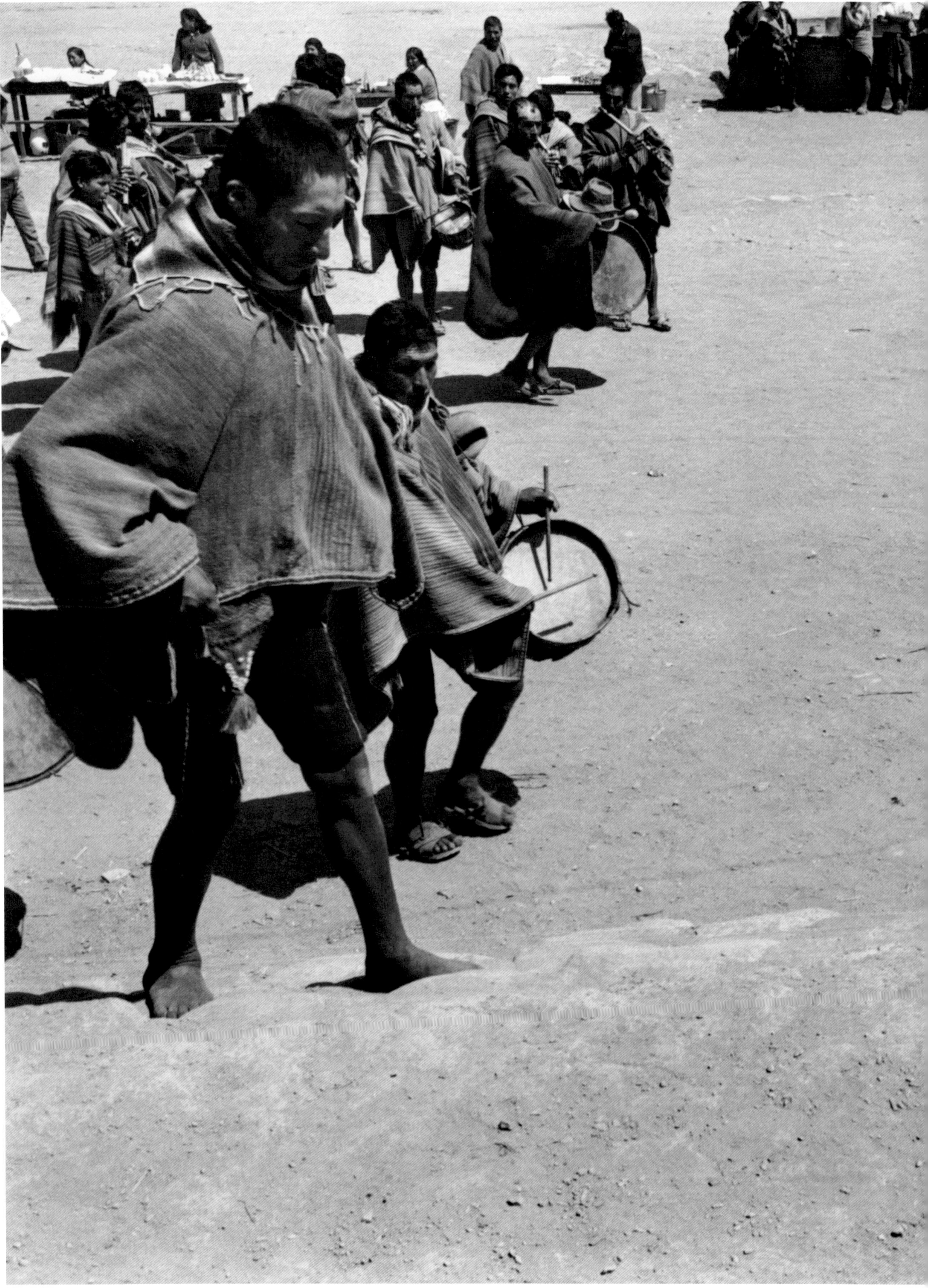

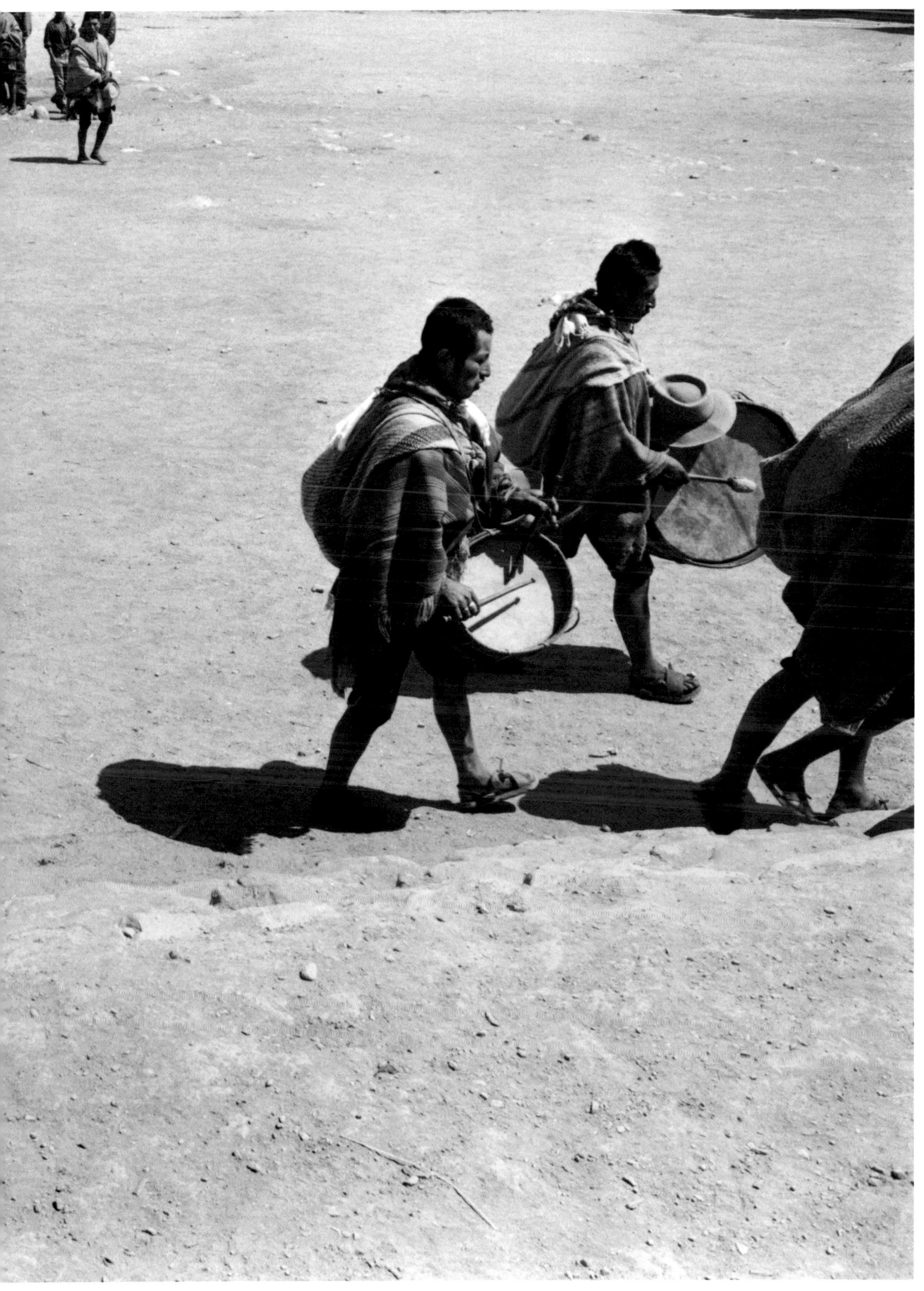

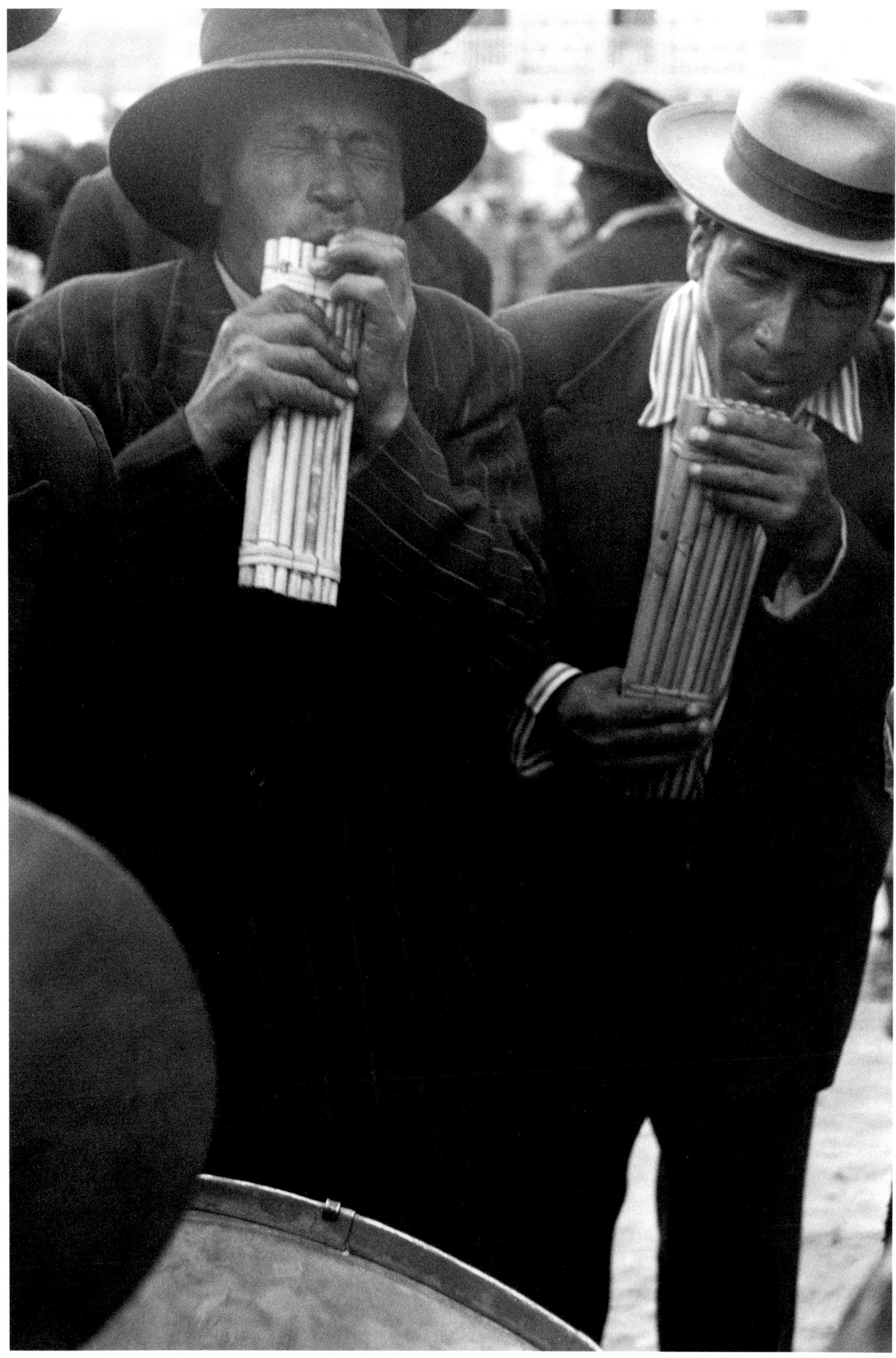

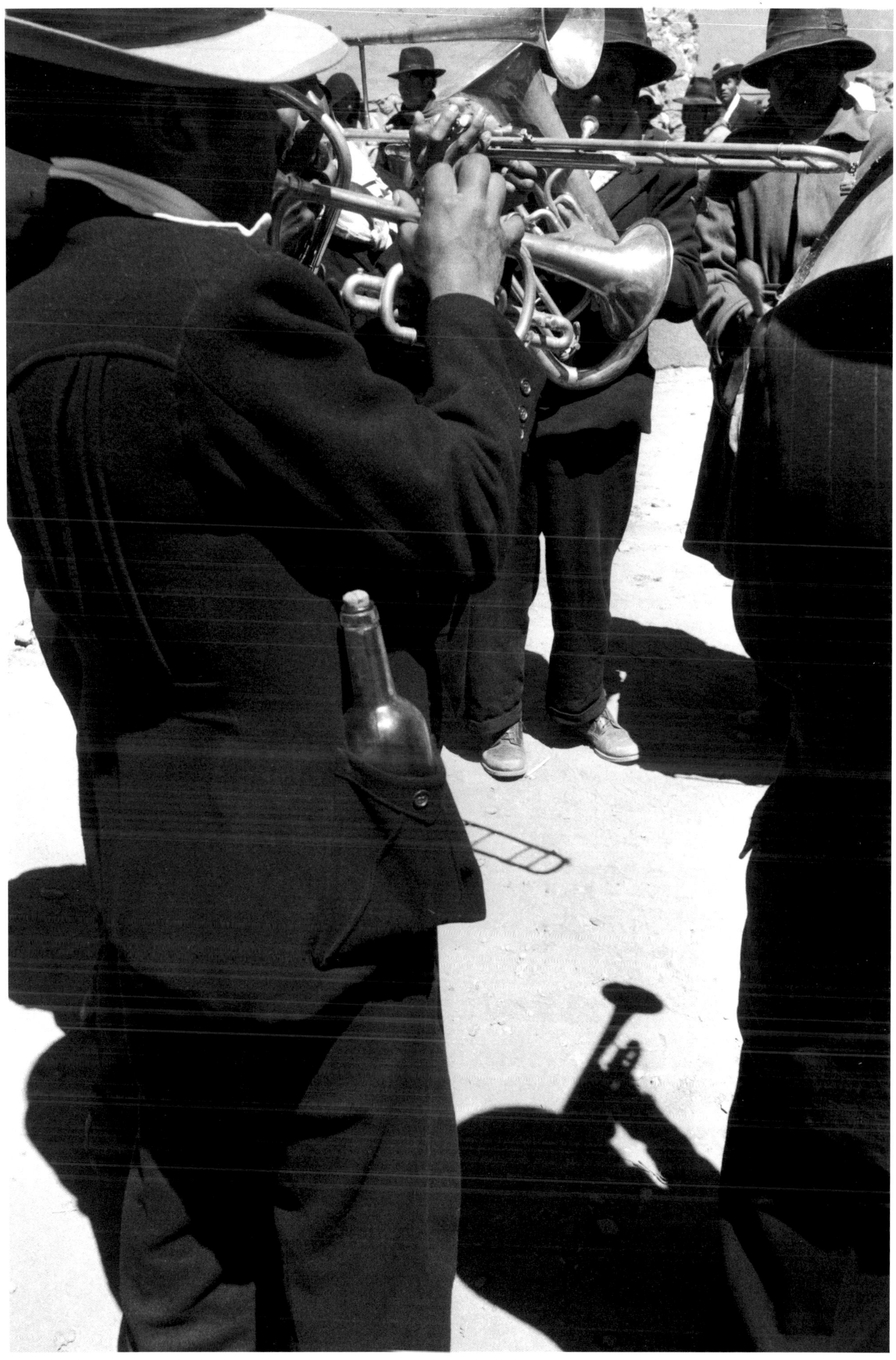

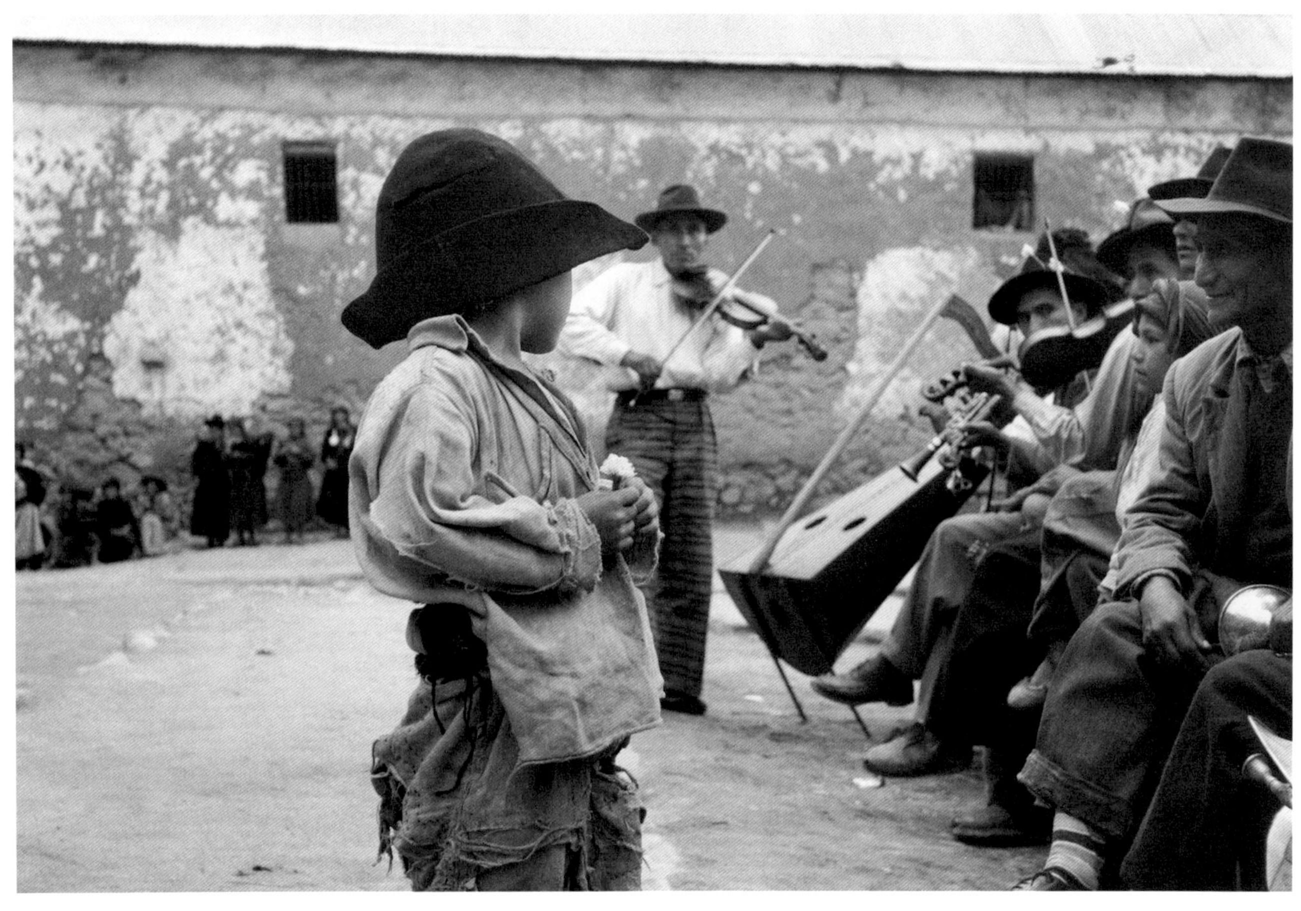

← Panpipes and Brass band Juli, Peru, 1956

↑ Fiddle and harp, Tupe, Peru, 1957

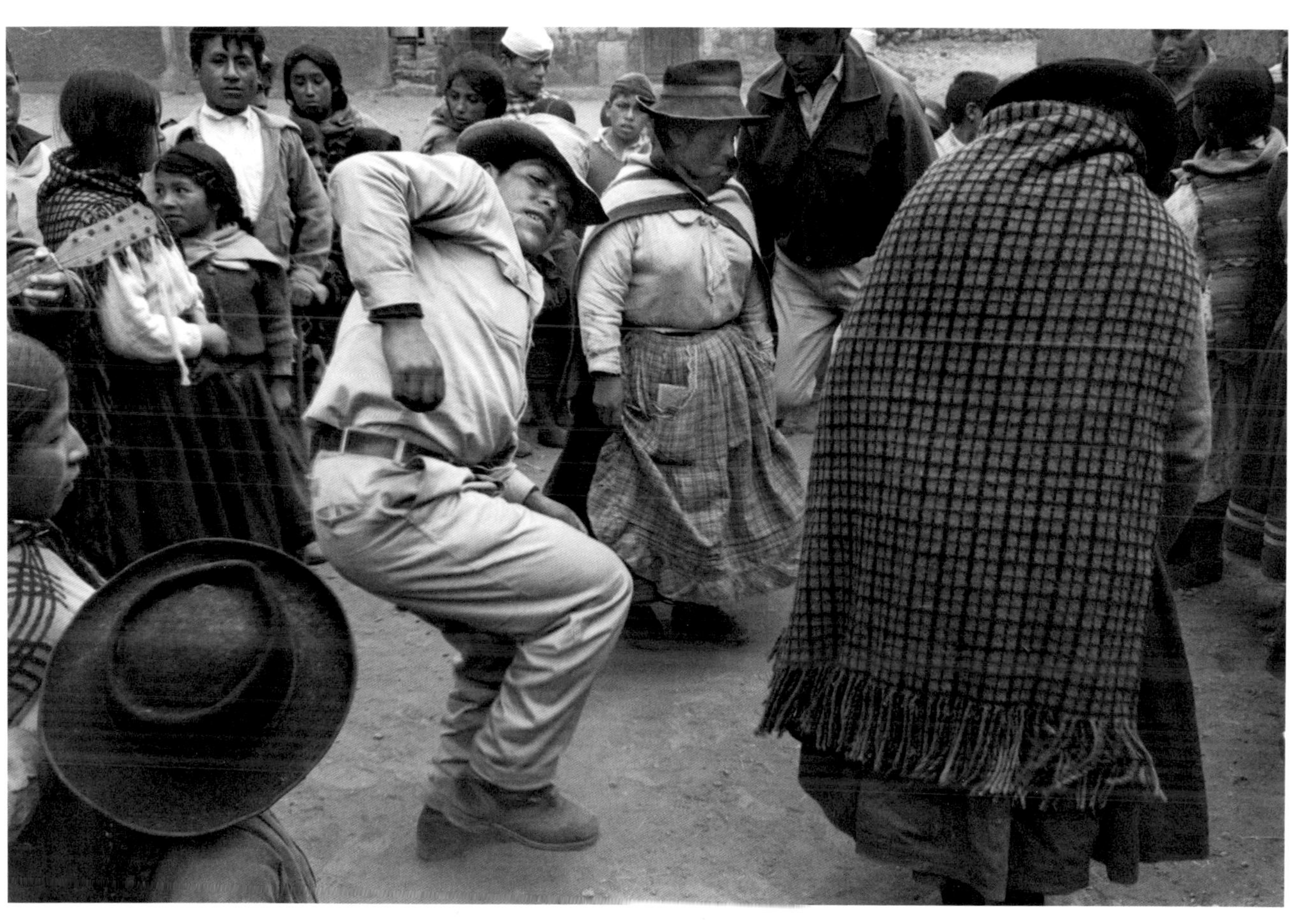

↑ Huayno dancers, Huancavalica, Peru, 1964

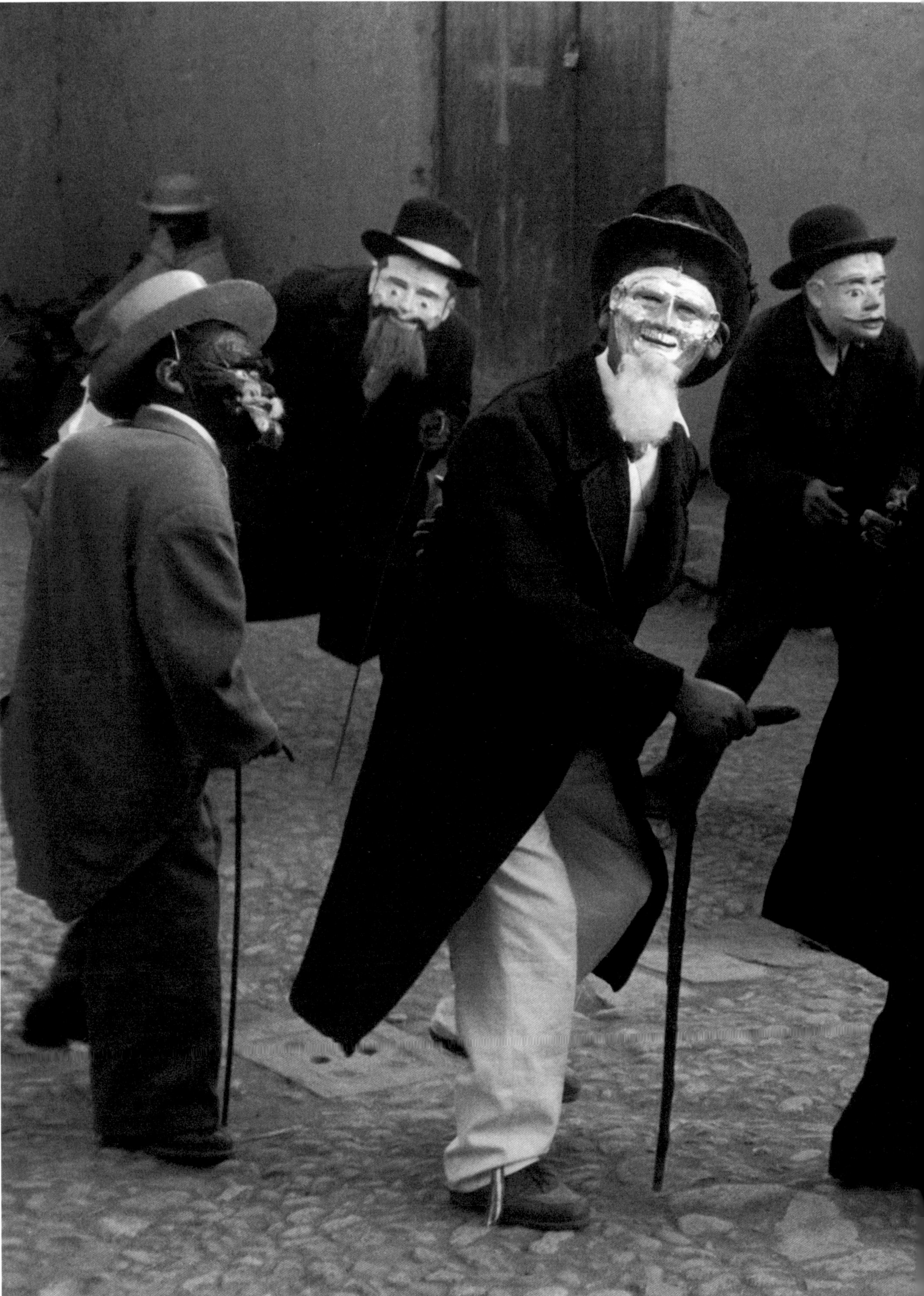

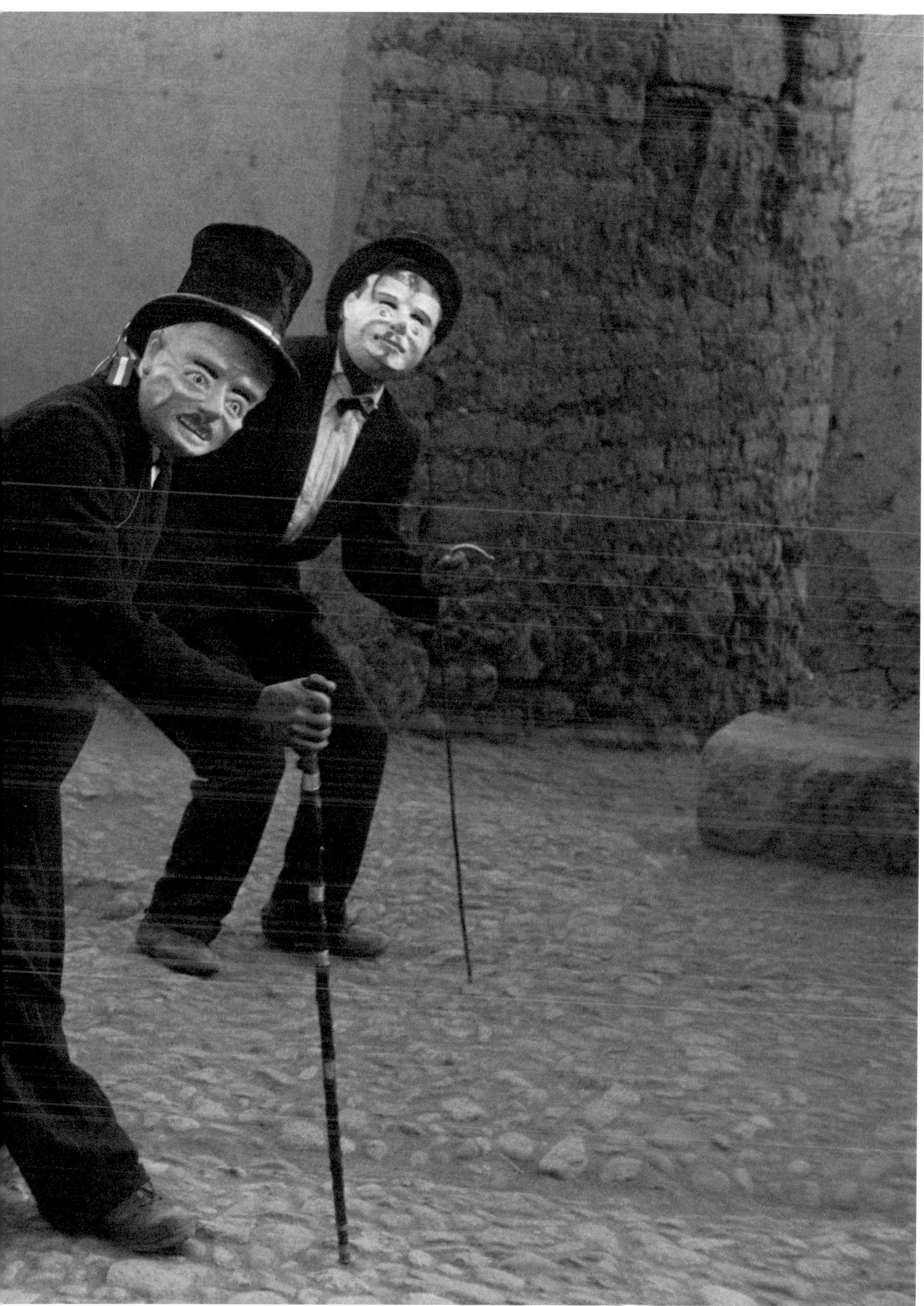

PULL MY DAISY, TIP MY CUP ALL THE DOORS ARE OPEN

On returning from Peru in 1957 I found a small loft in New York City and moved in among a community of artists and cooperative galleries. This was my home for the next seven years. It was during the time of Abstract Expressionism, the start of Pop Art, and the Happenings. There was a climate of creative ferment in the studios and galleries although an endgame atmosphere was hanging over that part of the city.

Abstract Expressionism was being carried forward by "second wave" artists, and they mingled with the originators at the Cedar Bar. It was always easy to speak with Franz Kline. Philip Guston was often still discussing art with younger painters into the night. Willem de Kooning's loft on Tenth Street had been the magnet that attracted the painters. There was loft space, light, and rentals that were cheap. The cooperative galleries formed here. It was a meeting ground for a smaller art world, where artists had shows with few prospects of sales or reviews.

⇇ Macchu Tussec dancers, Juli, Peru, 1957

→ Tenth street, New York City, 1959

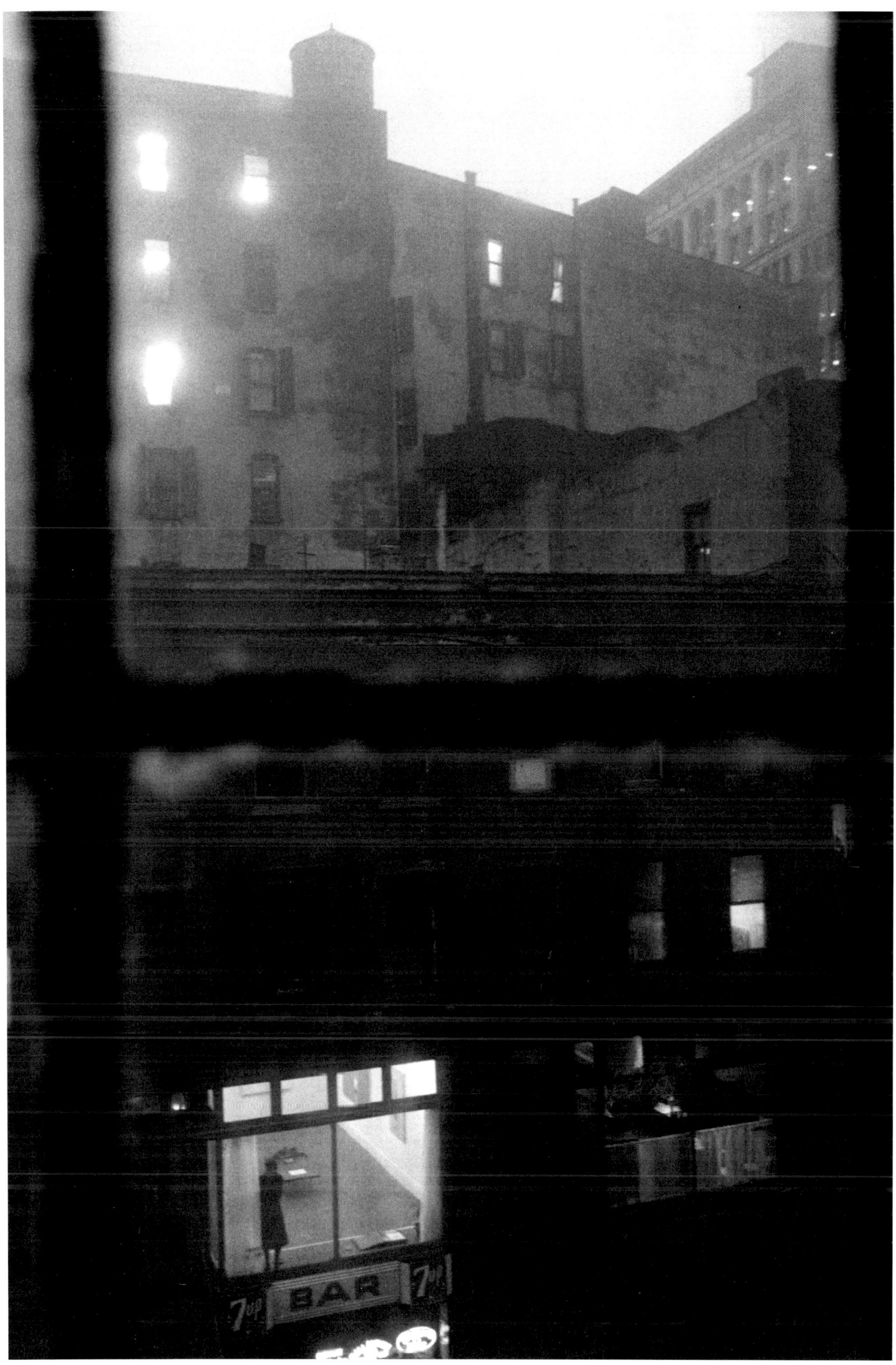
7up
BAR
7up

In the grimy no-man's land between Greenwich Village and the Lower East Side, the block I lived on had small industrial spaces and street level stores. It wasn't legal to live in the lofts, but we did. There were usually Bowery alcoholics sprawled out on the sidewalk. The photographer Robert Frank lived next door with his family. Also on the block was Merce Cunningham's lead dancer Carolyn Brown, and her husband Earle Brown, an experimental composer.

I attempted paintings and printed my photographs there. The little loft was also my desk, bedroom, and kitchen. My first serious love affairs took place here. A large glass window looked onto Third Avenue. Even in my sleep I could identify the sounds of mice in the cracker box heard over the trucks passing outside. The New Lost City Ramblers practiced music here, and Pablo and Andrea (Robert and Mary Frank's children) would come visit me, climbing the fire escape in the backyard.

In 1957 there was only one photography gallery in New York. Helen Gee's Limelight over on Seventh Avenue was where I had my first solo show. It was a frustrating time for independent photographers since the magazines and advertising agencies were the only places one could get work. In response, some of us attempted to start an informal organization of independents. The first meetings were held at my loft. The members were Lee Friedlander, Garry Winogrand, Simpson Kalisher, David Vestal, Saul Leiter, Walter Silver, Harold Feinstein, and myself. I think they chose my place for the gatherings because of the respect they had for Robert Frank, who lived next door.

In 1957, before his book *The Americans* was published, Robert showed me stacks of photographs he was looking at from his travels in America. I remember he had the floor covered with prints and he would just look at them. From thousands of images, he sought reactions—from friends, from himself. He was deliberating how to put them together. It was a much more troublesome statement than his early work. The message of personal chronicle and human compassion was less obvious. Instead, the photographs pointed to an emptiness in America. Robert had looked directly at difficult things while others had diverted their eyes. It wasn't about poverty and social patterns—it was the feeling of a hollowness and corrosion that was coming over American life.

From my Third Avenue base I went out on concert tours with the NLCR and on photography expeditions to the rural South. I shot my first test roll of movie film at the loft, a silent three-minute view of young Bob Dylan on my roof. In the loft I also photographed Dylan, Alan Lomax, and the Kentucky singer Roscoe Holcomb. The Stanley Brothers and Woody Guthrie visited, along with a stream of other musicians and artists. Over the distance of time, those years on Third Avenue seem very exciting, but in reality it felt mostly desolate and run down. Still, I liked the sober seriousness of my daily life.

Young artists appeared who questioned and defied what was going on in abstract painting. None seemed more different than the Pop artists. I was at a music party on the Lower East Side while on the floor below, Red Grooms, Claes Oldenberg, Jim Dine, Jay Milder, and others were engaged in a mock battle, decked out in lampshades, tablecloths, and wooden swords. Later they performed these skits in the galleries—absurd dramas and events which combined Dada with the outlook of Walker Evans. It wasn't certain whether they were inspired by popular culture, folk art, or just a desire to bring content back into art. The audience for these Happenings consisted largely of painters and the art world. The Beat poets also showed up. This mix of artists and ideas exploded into many separate establishments a few years later as recognition came from Uptown, and Soho emerged downtown.

→ Third Avenue backyard, New York City, 1960

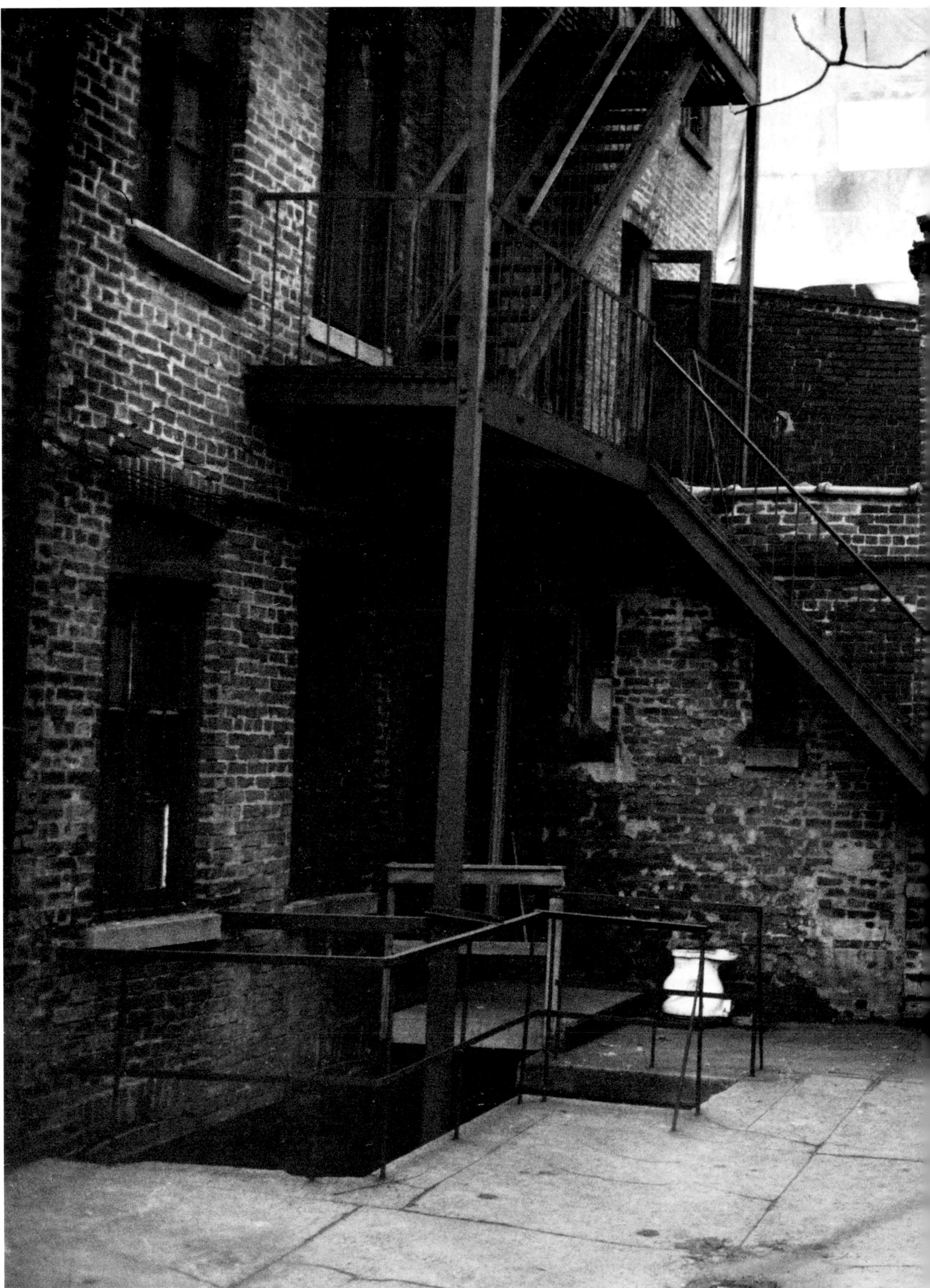

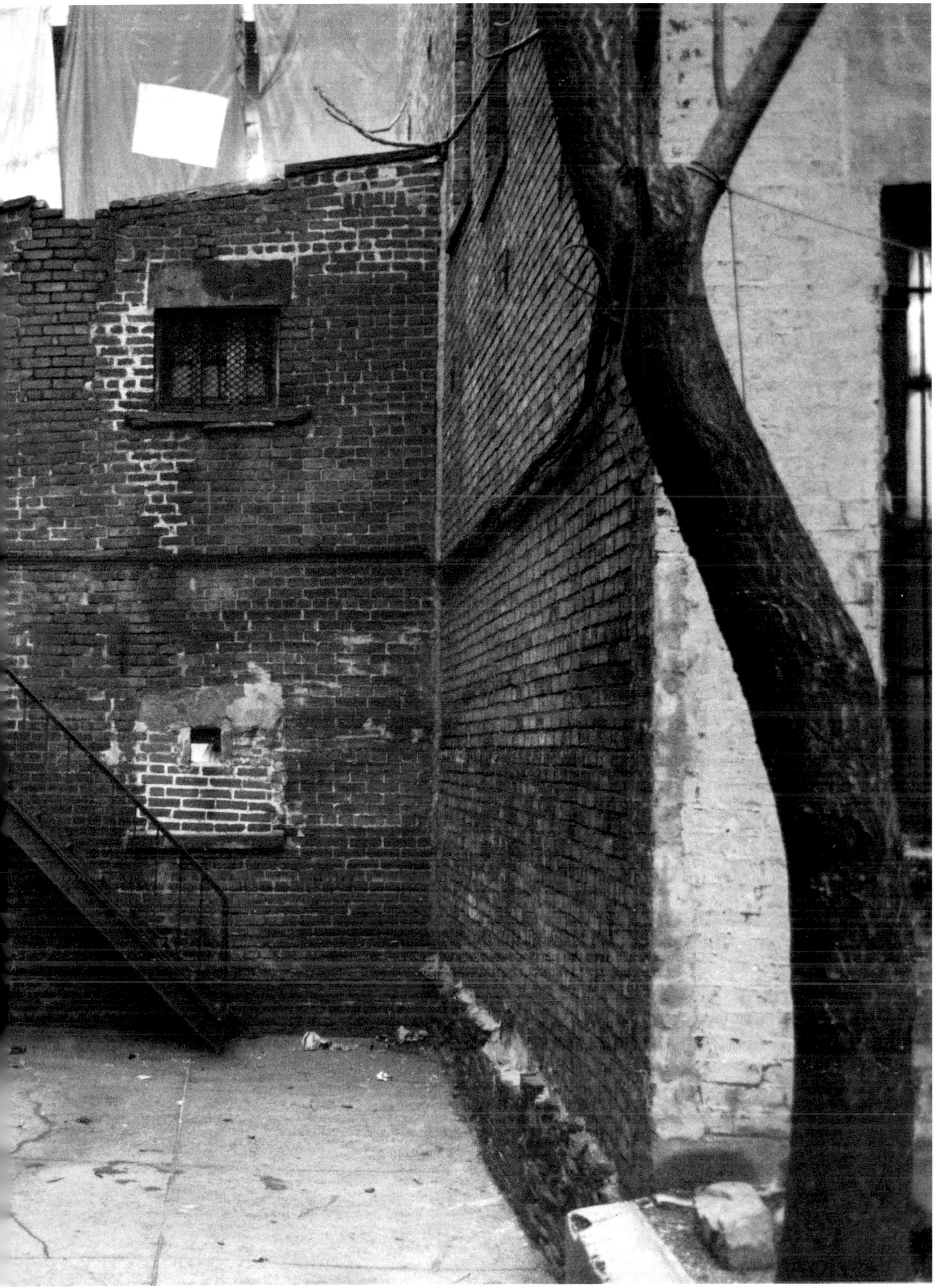

→ Cedar Bar, New York City, 1959

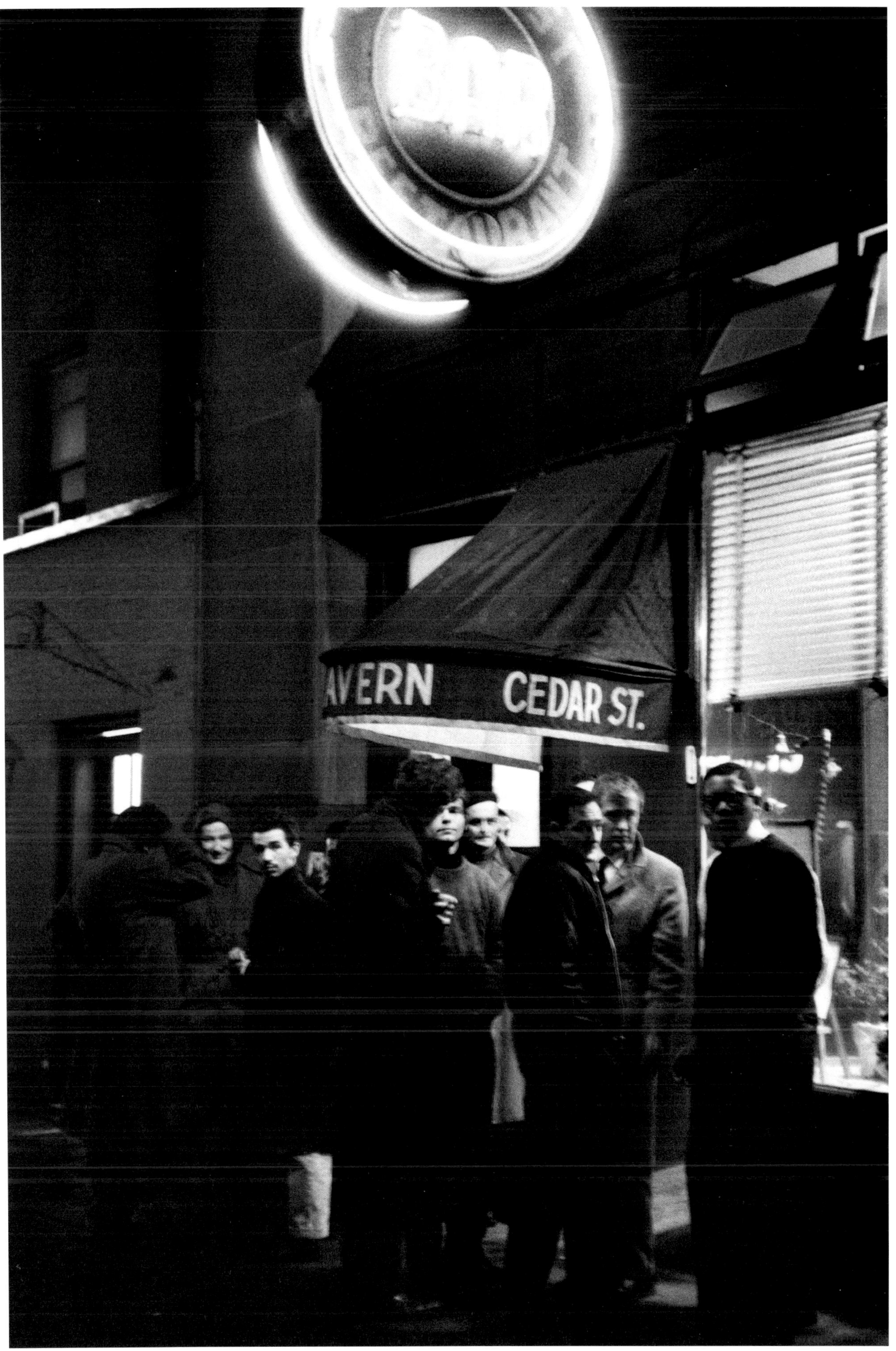
AVERN
CEDAR ST.

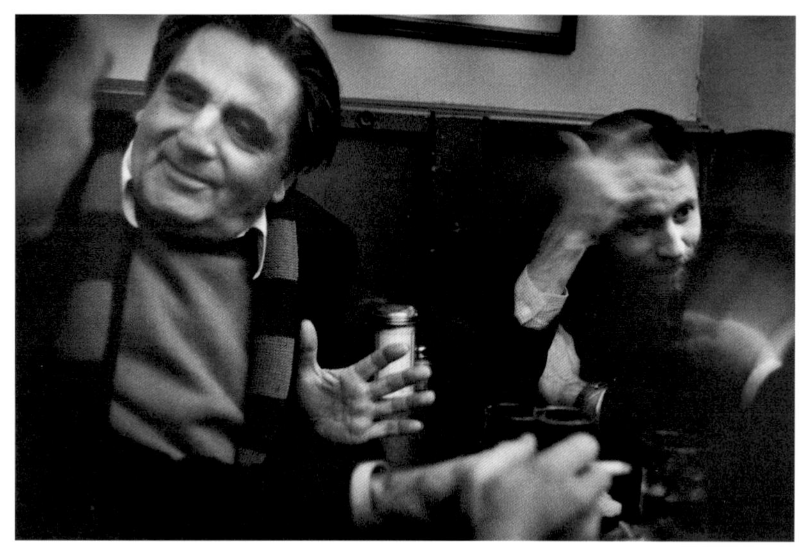

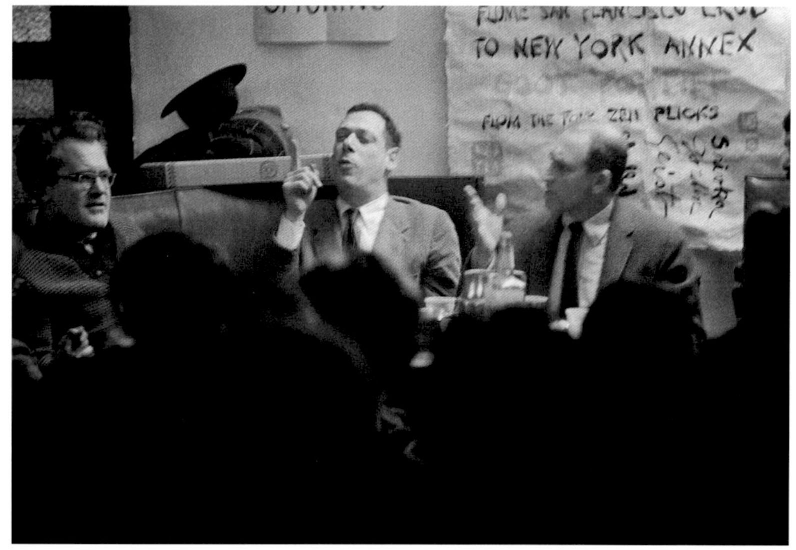

↑ (top) Kaldis, Allan Kaprow, Cedar Bar, 1959

↑ Hubert Crehan, Thomas B. Hess, Harry Holtzman, Artist's Club, 1959

→ Grace Hartigan, Cedar Bar, 1959

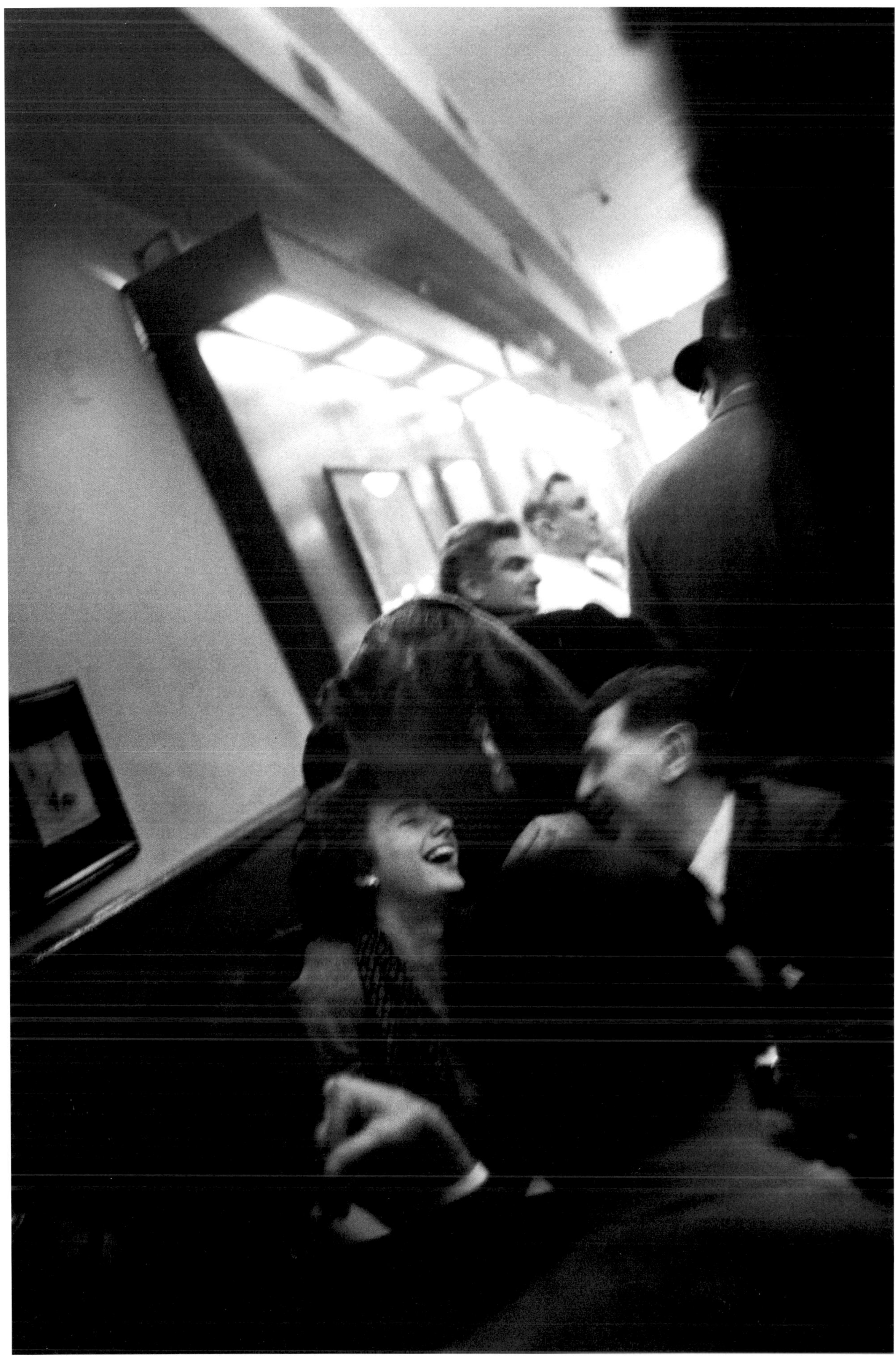

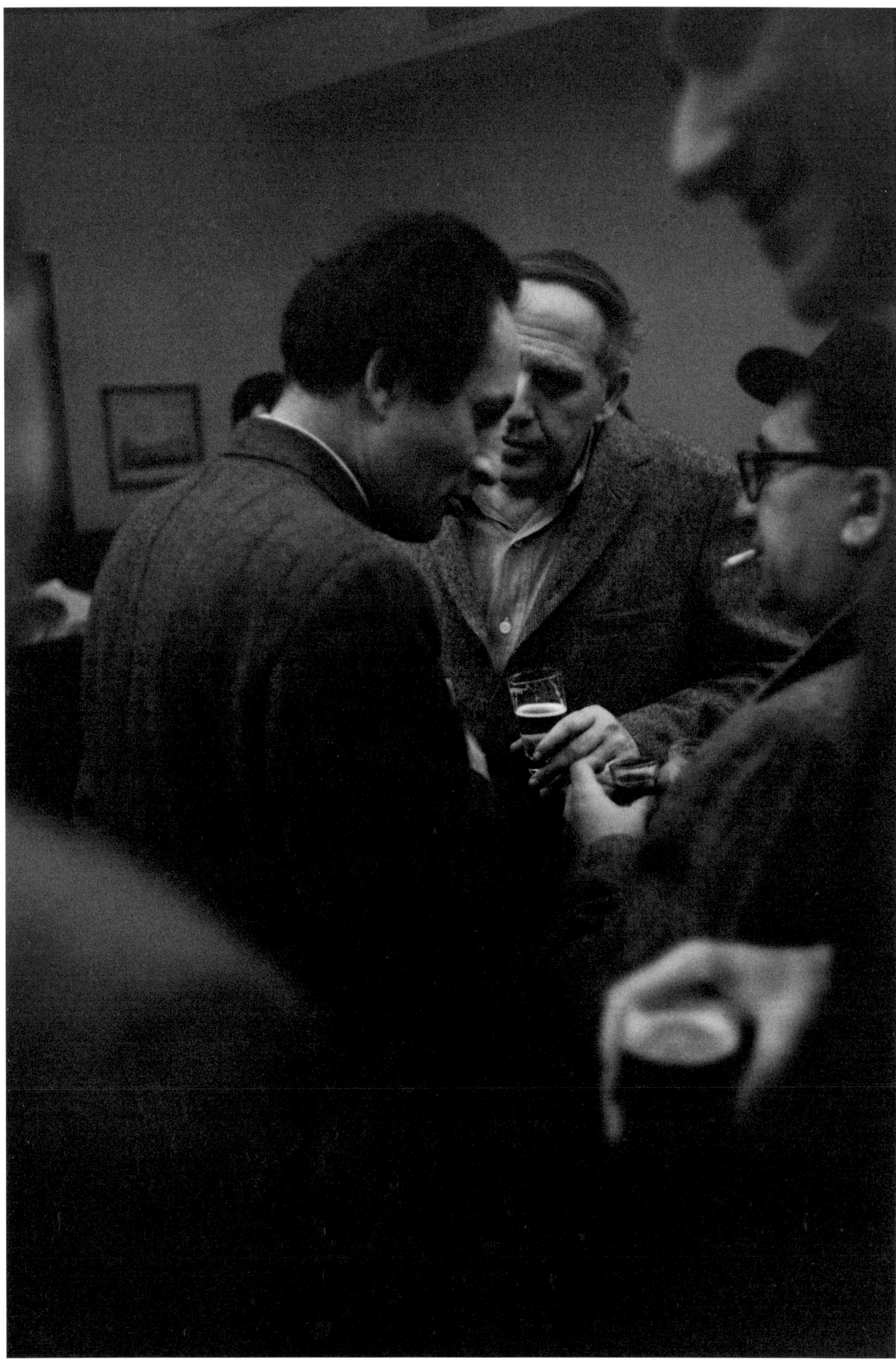

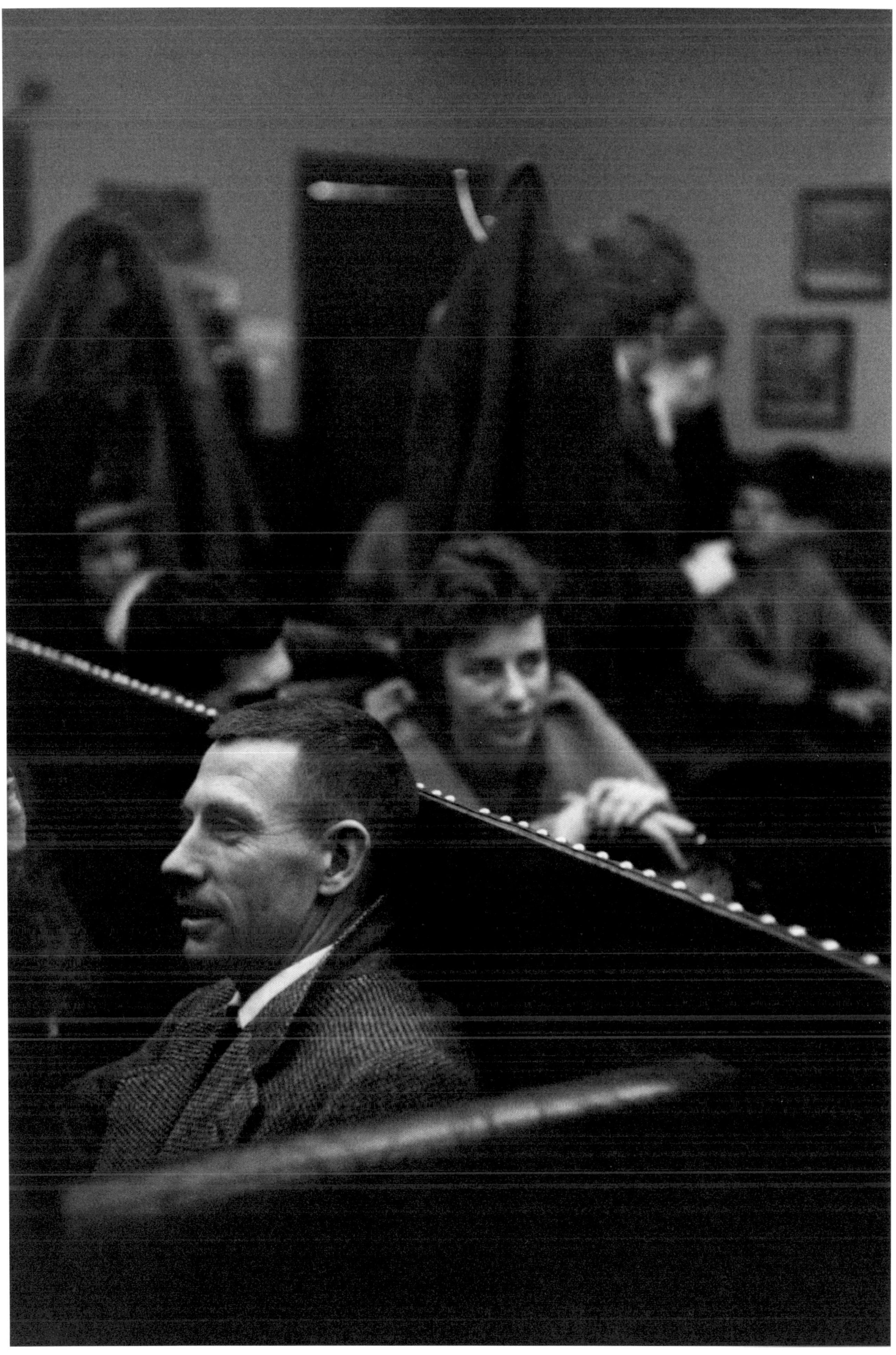

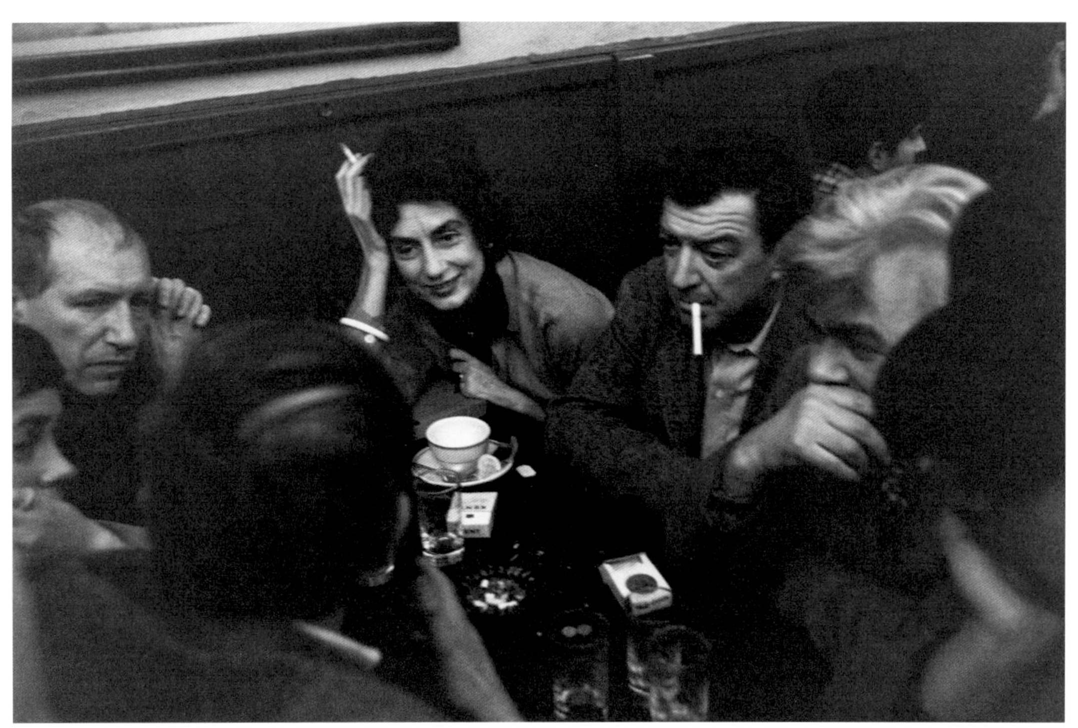

↖ Norman Bluhm, Philip Guston, Aaron Siskind, Cedar Bar, 1959

↖ Lester Johnson, Cedar Bar, 1959

↑ Jack Tworkov, Mercedes Matter, James Brooks, Gregorio Cavellon, Cedar Bar, 1959

→ Tanager Gallery opening, Tenth Street, 1959

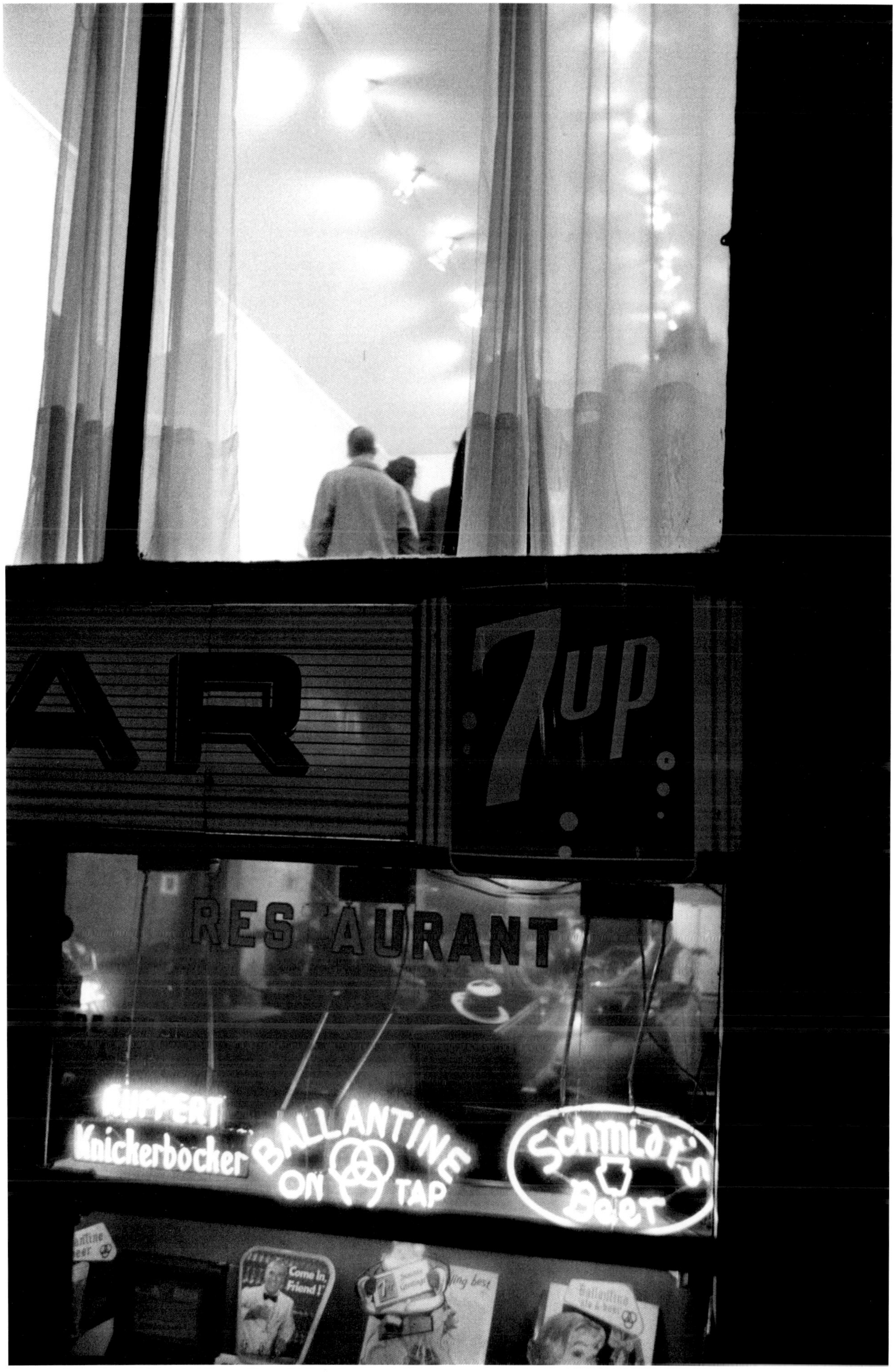
AR
7up
RES AURANT
Knickerbocker
BALLANTINE
ON TAP
Schmidt's
Beer
Come in, Friend!

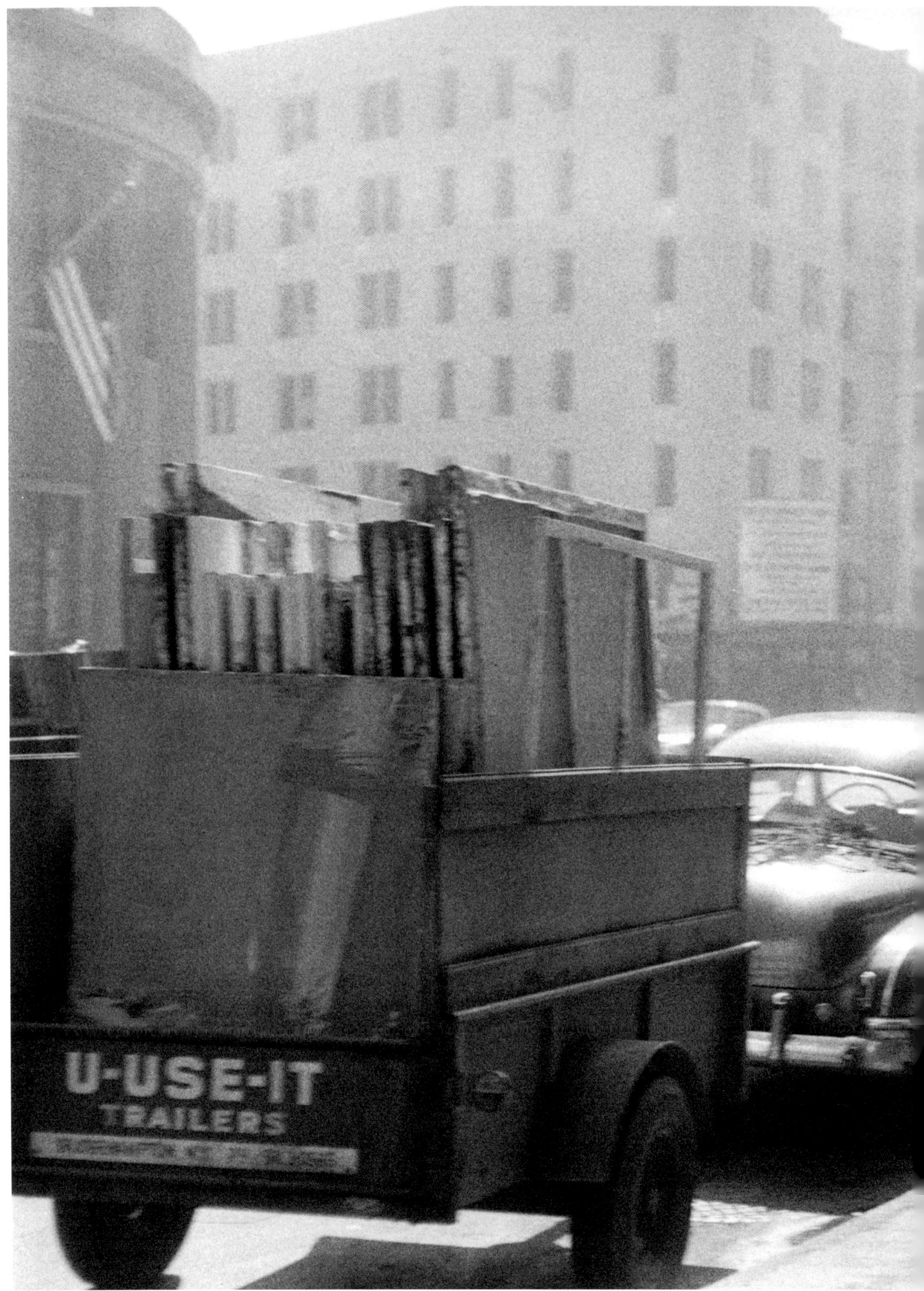
U-USE-IT
TRAILERS

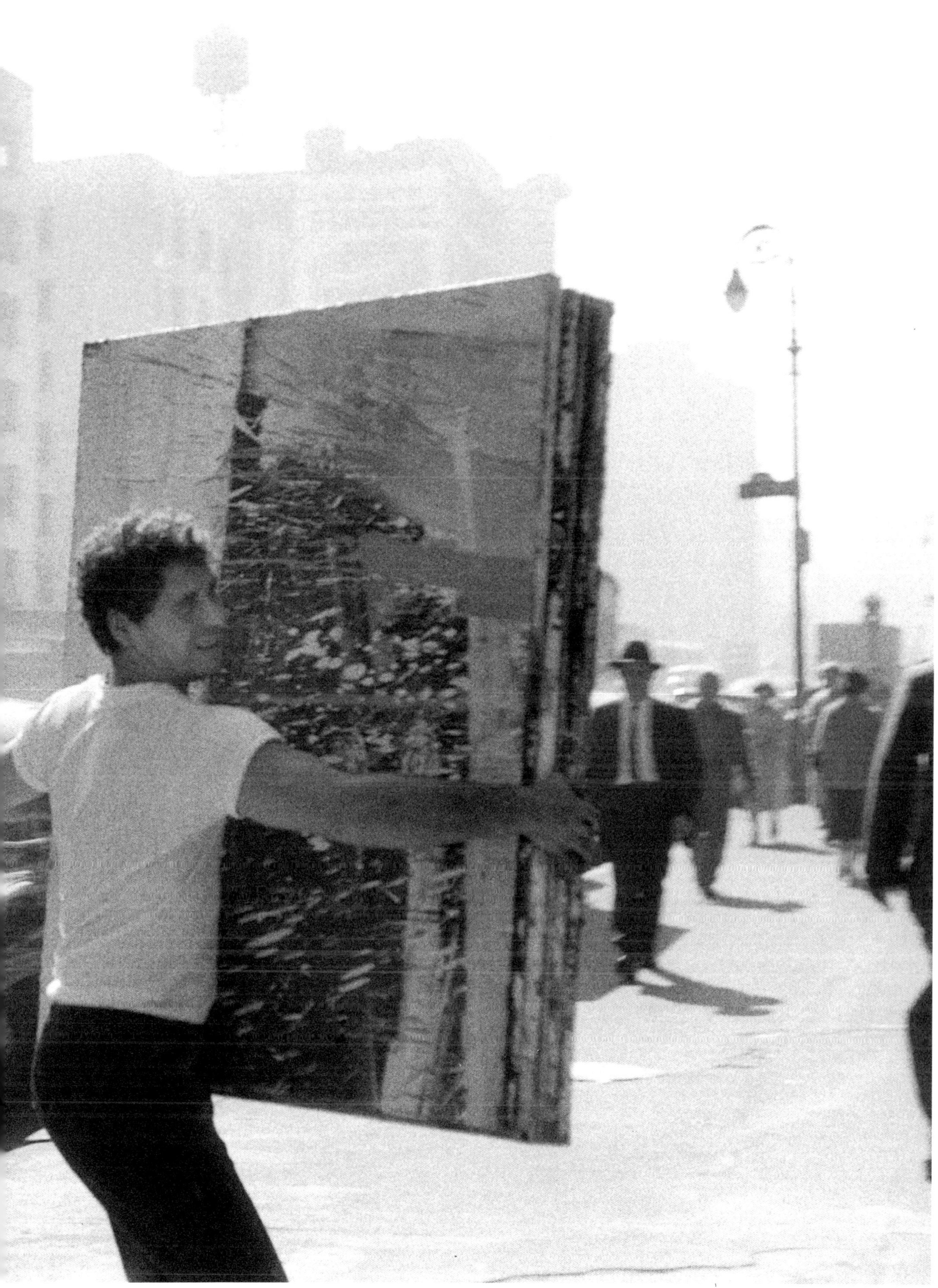

← Alfred Leslie, New York City, 1959

→ Franz Kline, New York City, 1960

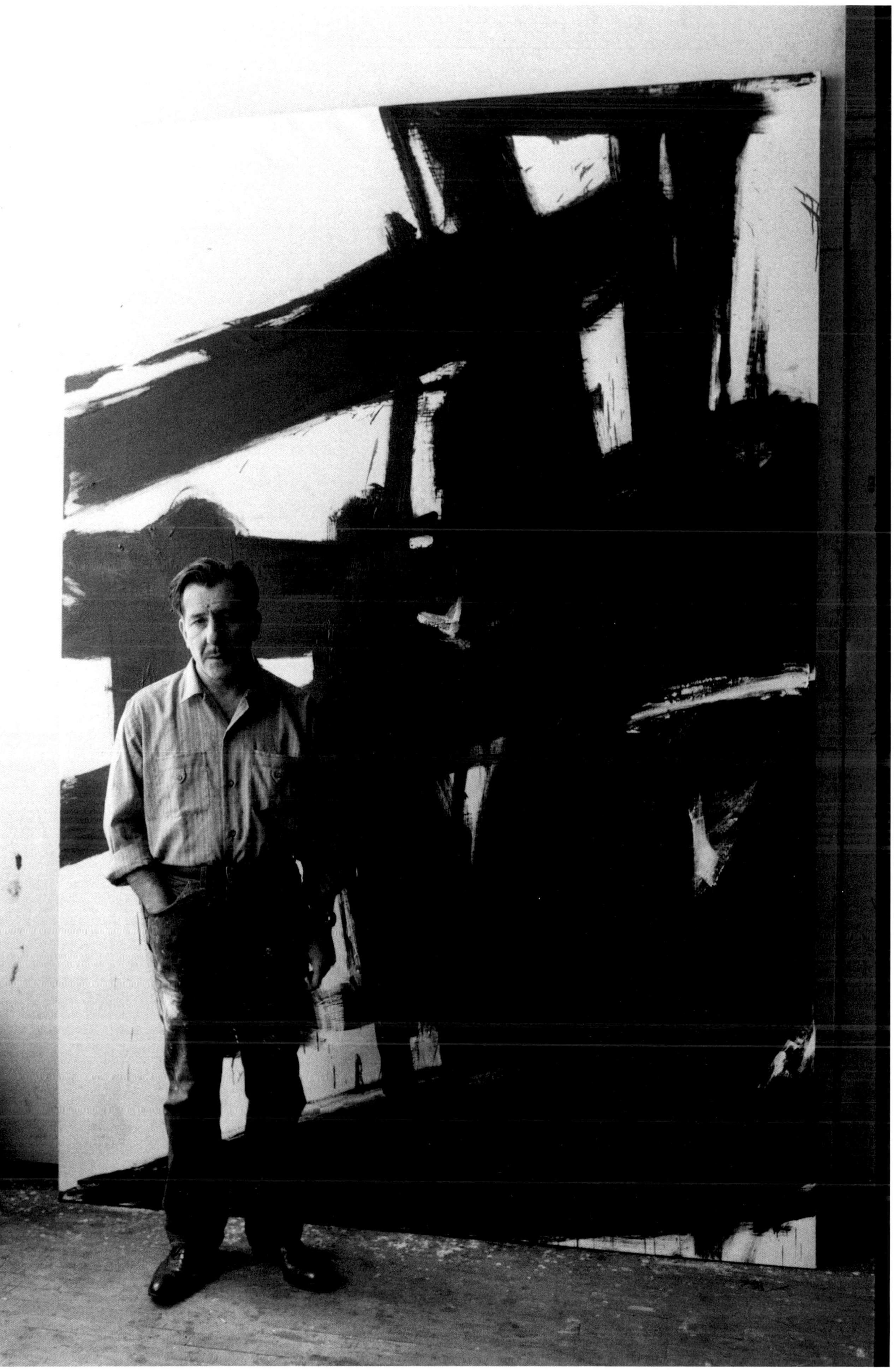

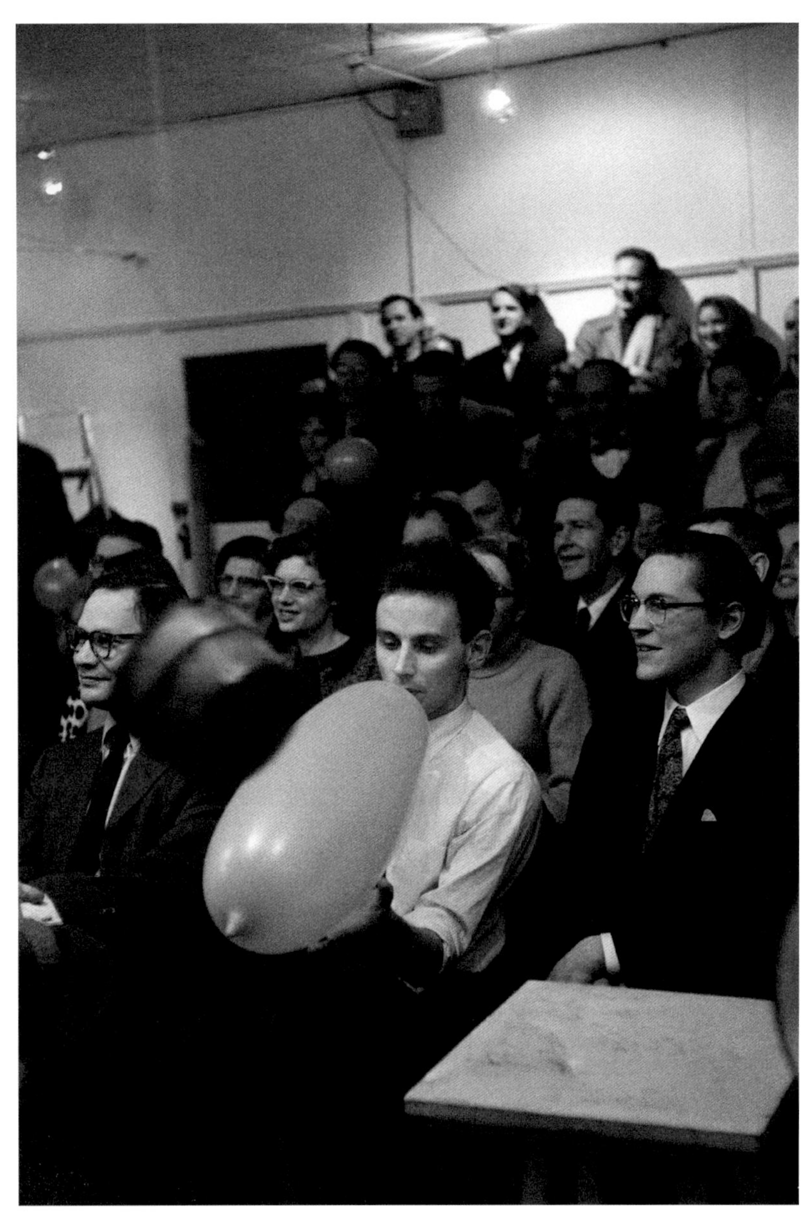

↑ Lucas Samaras, John Cage, et al, at "Happening," Reuben Gallery, 1959

→ Red Grooms crossing Third Avenue, 1960

⇉ Bob Thompson at Delancey Street Museum, 1959

⇉ Red Grooms "The Burning Building," 1959

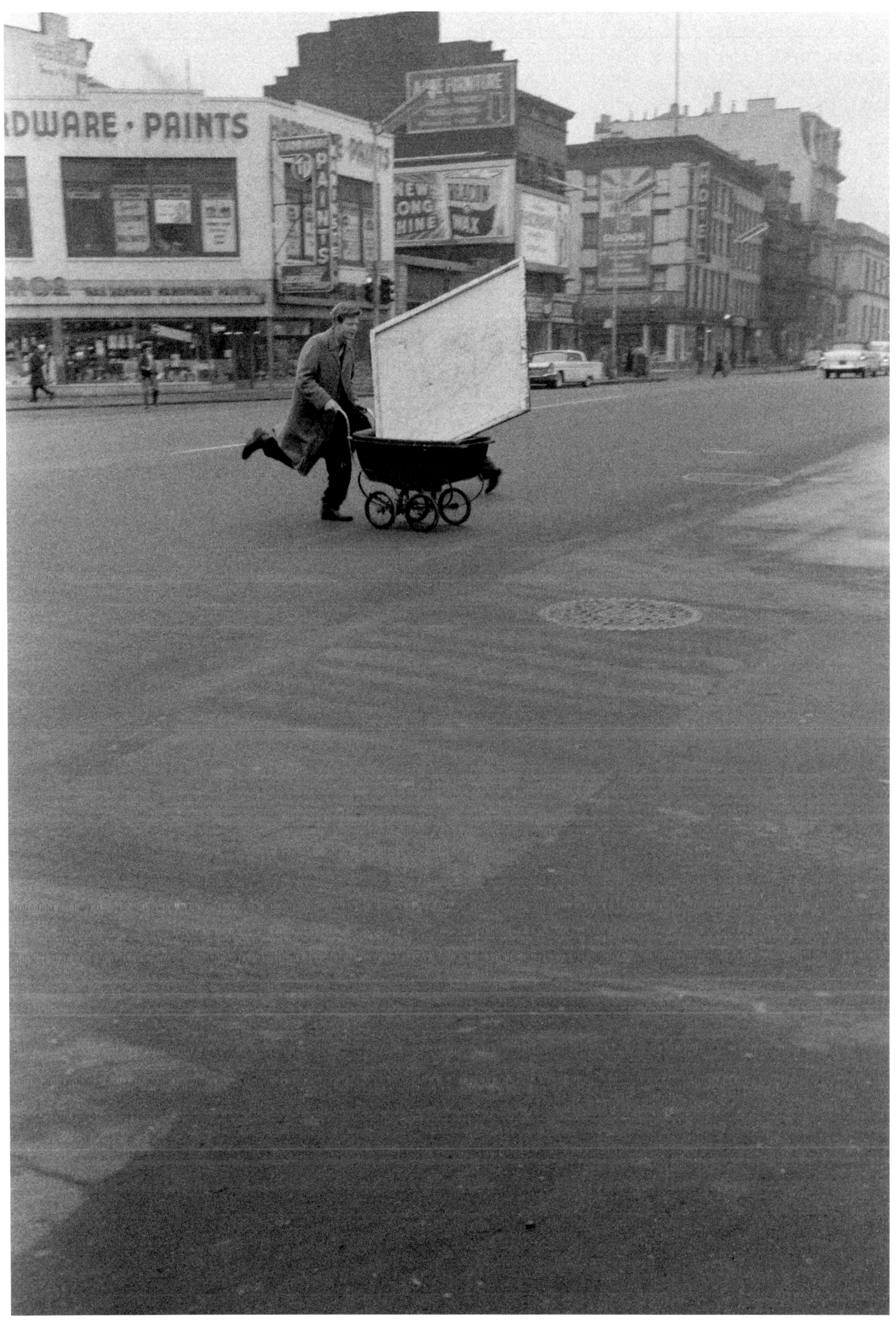
RDWARE • PAINTS
PAINTS
NEW
LONG
SHINE
WAX

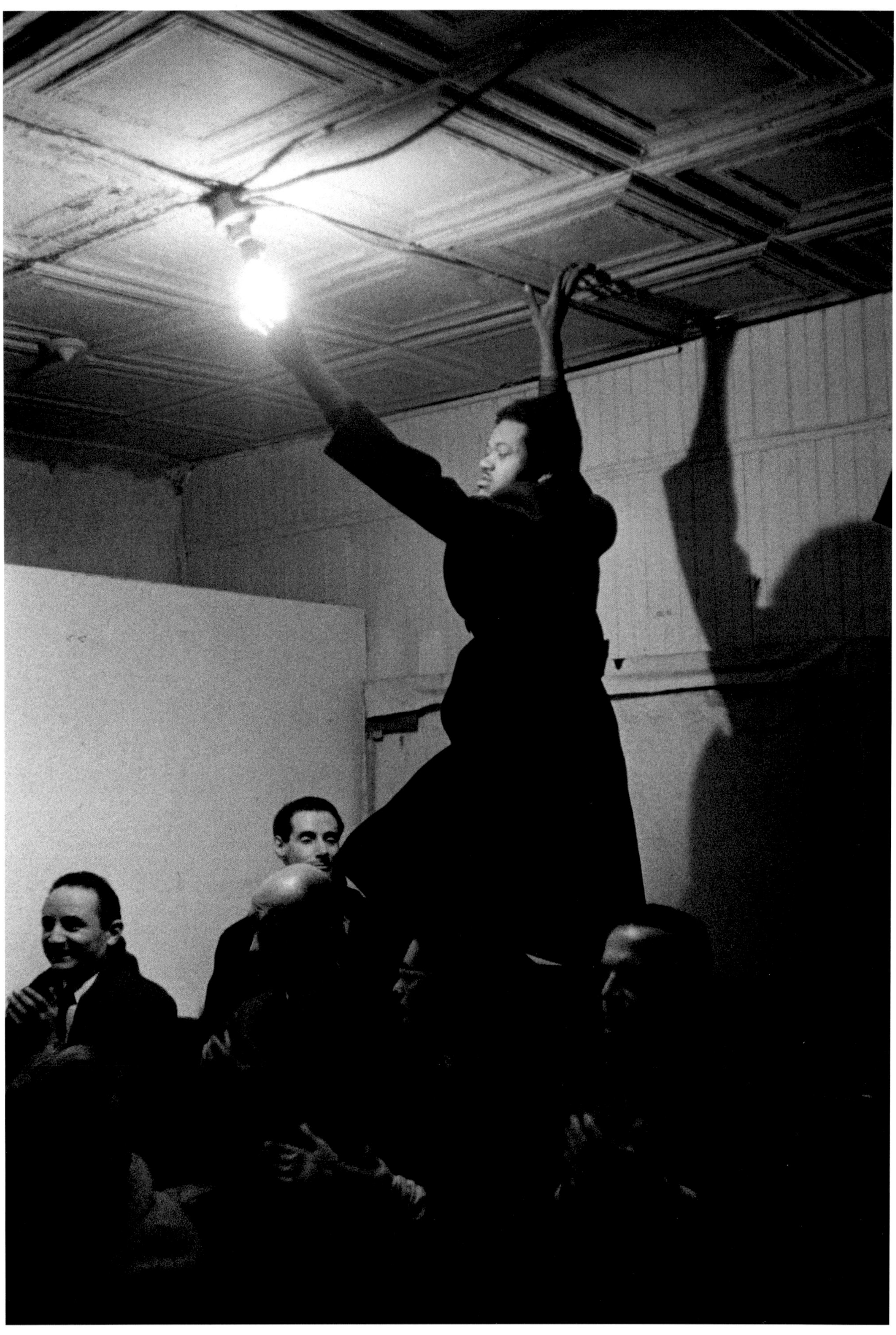

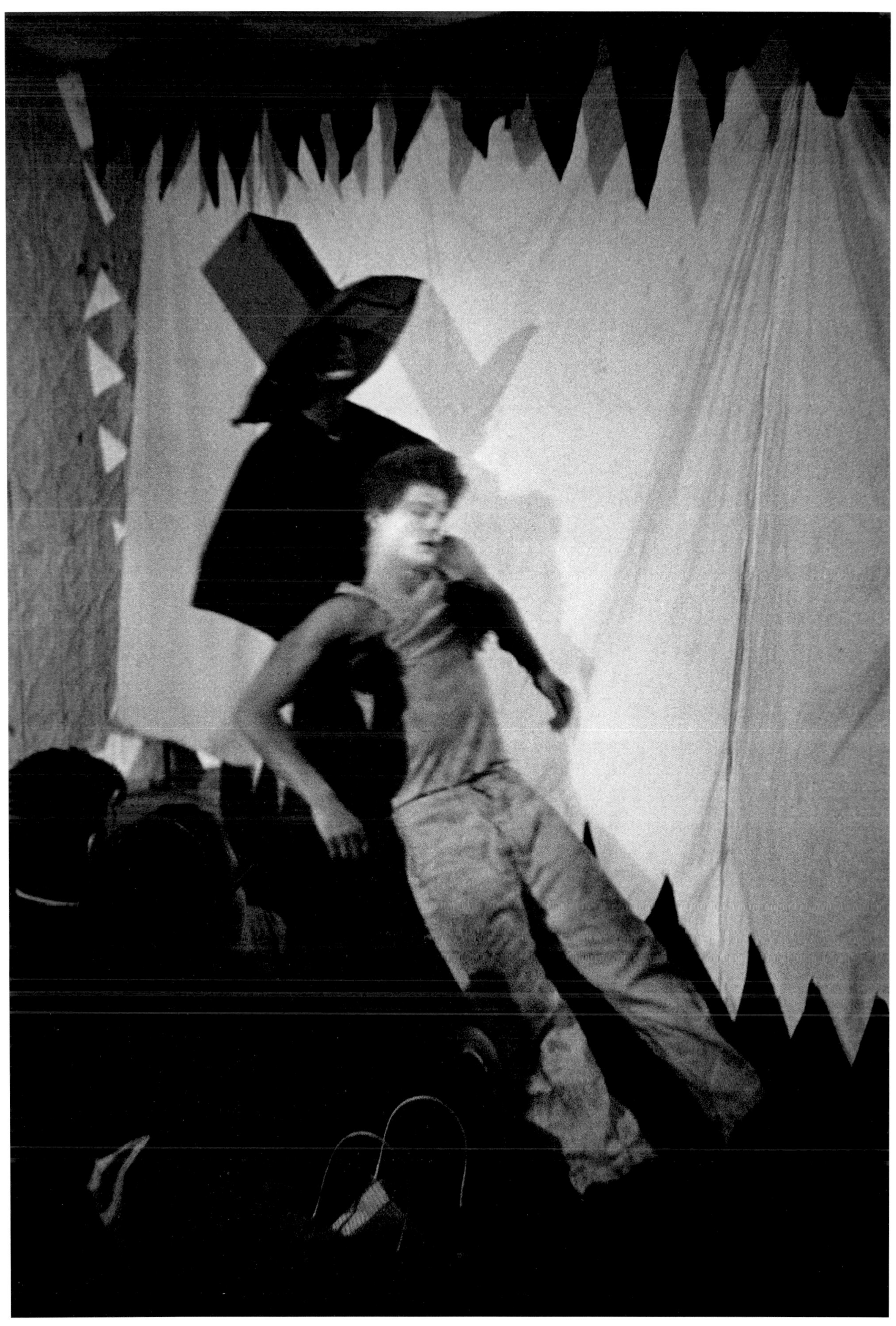

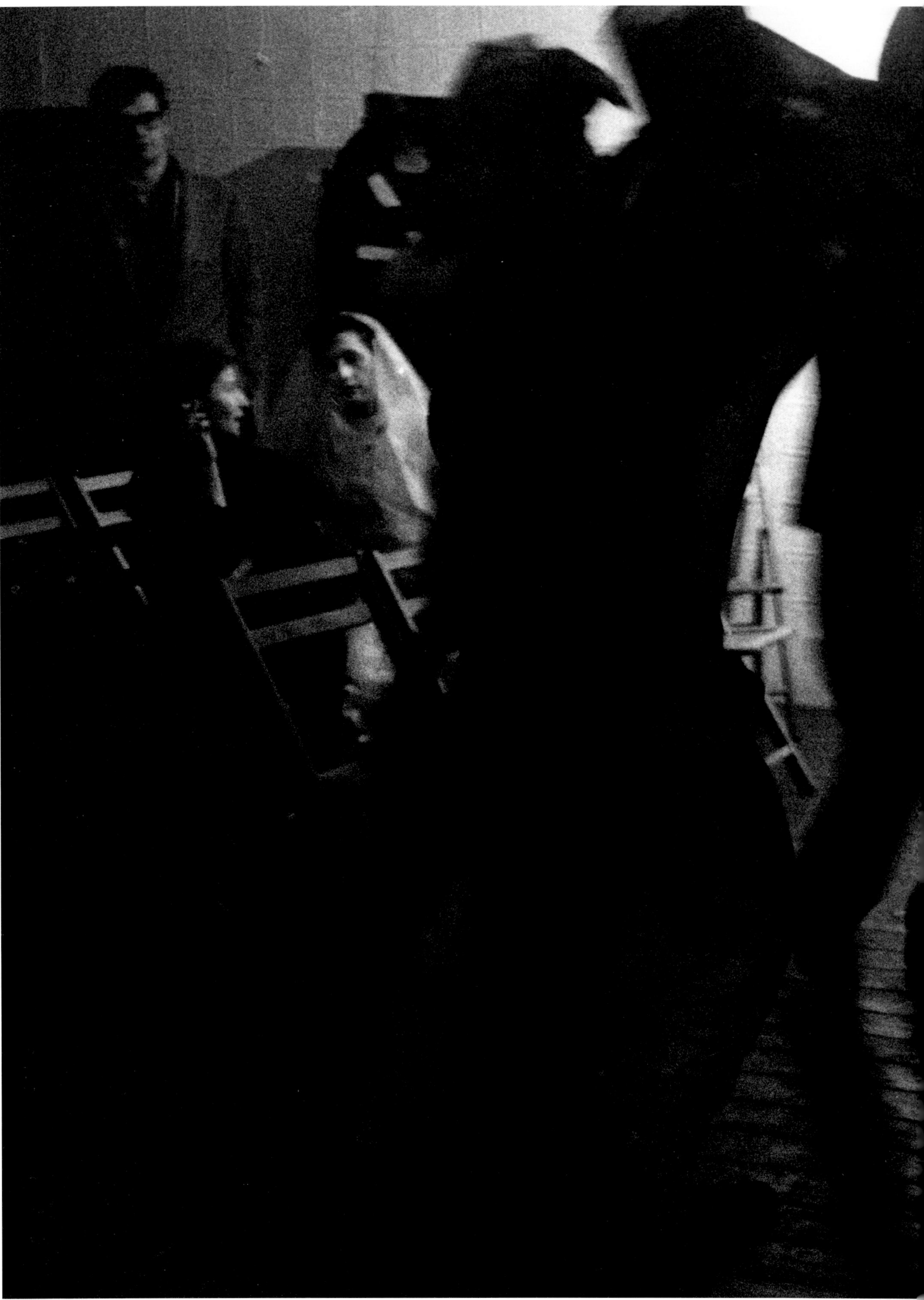

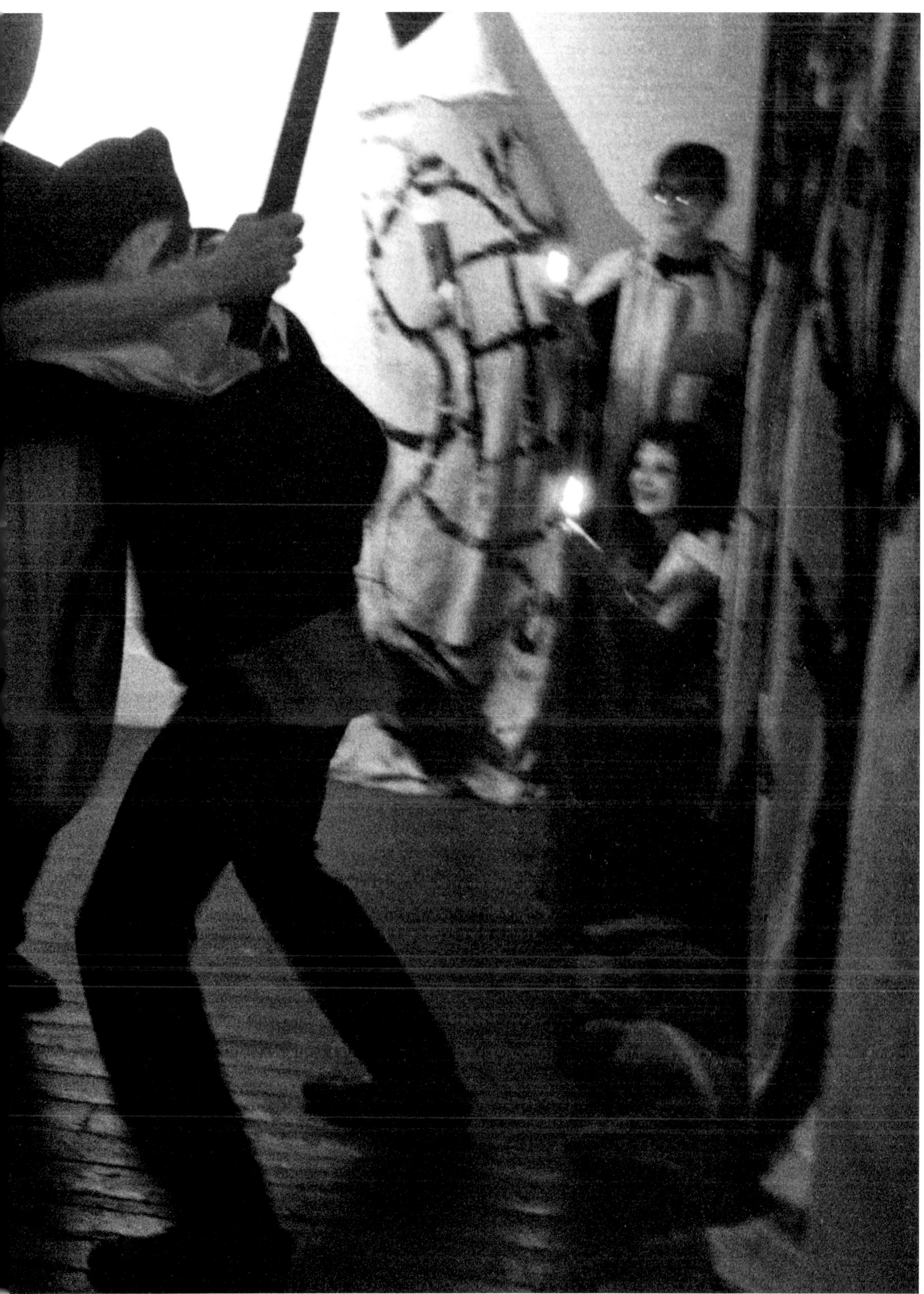

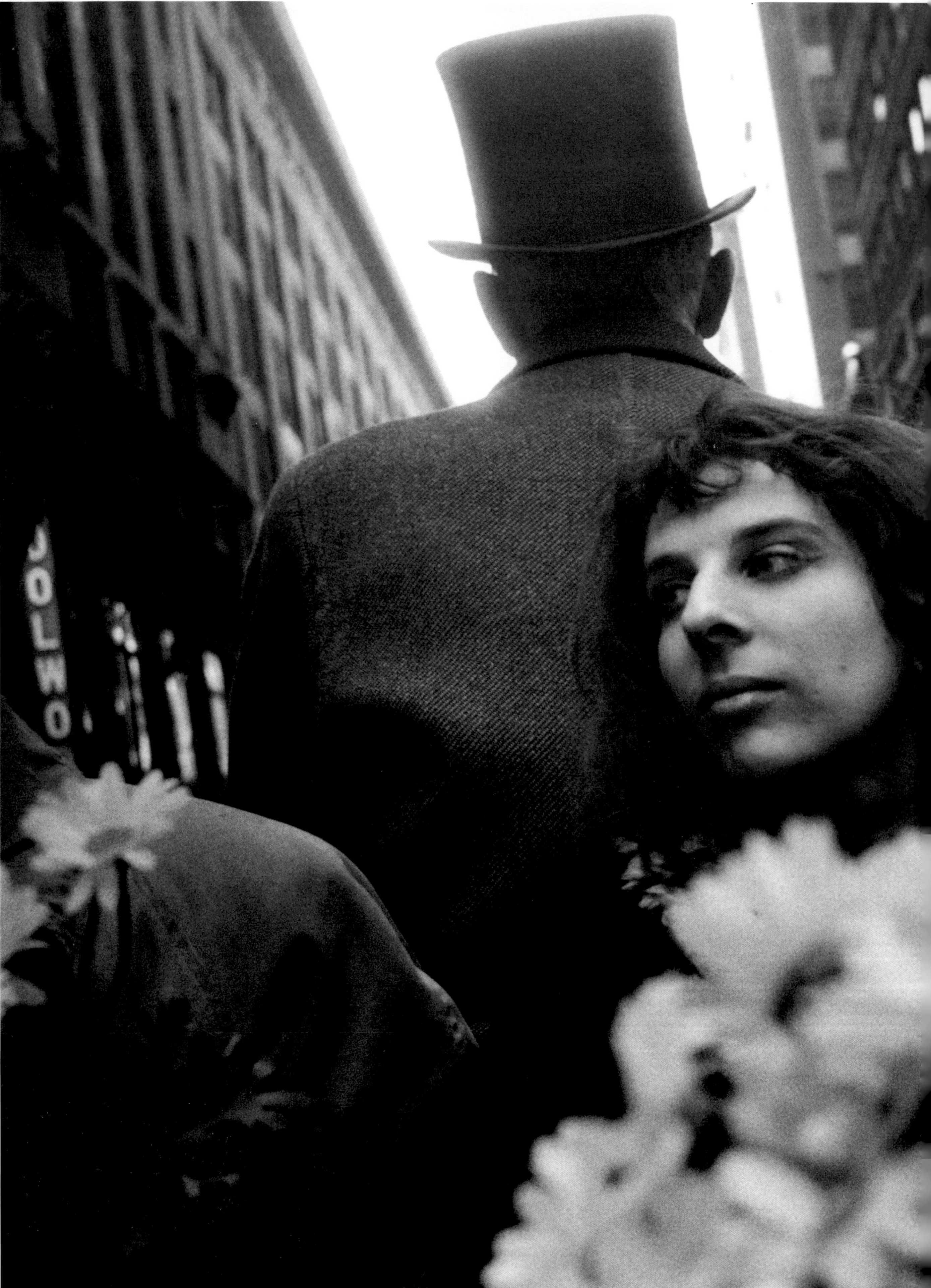
OLWO

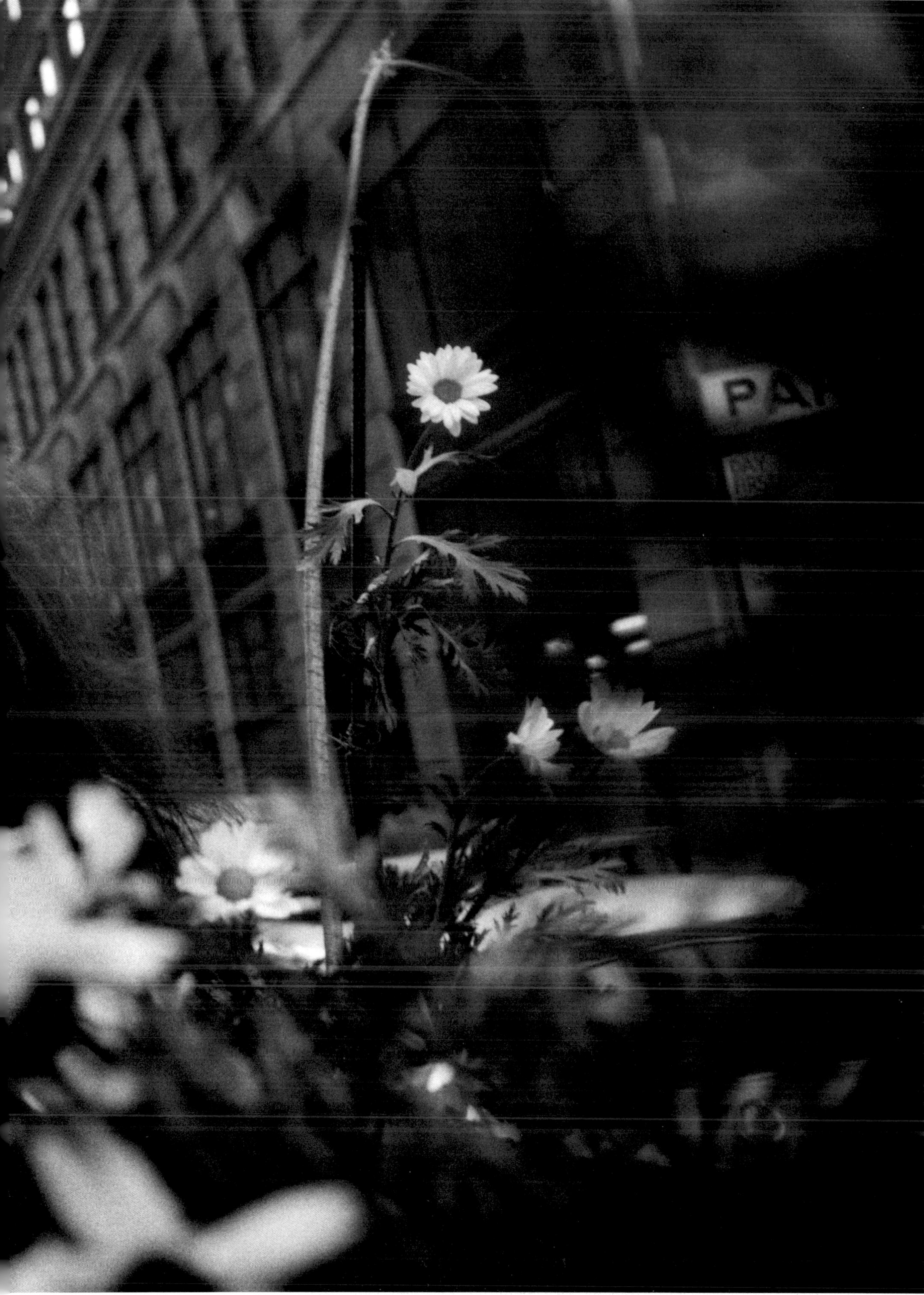

BEAT GENERATION In 1959 Robert Frank asked me to take production stills of the filming of *Pull My Daisy*, an experimental film about the Beat sensibility. The screenplay was based on a script by Jack Kerouac. The cast assembled by Robert Frank and Alfred Leslie consisted of painters, poets and musicians, plus one actress who was the wife of an artist (Delphine Seyrig played the harassed housewife in *Pull My Daisy* while she was an international film star in Europe). Although Frank and Leslie had a structure in mind, improvisation seemed to dominate the production. Frank focused more on composing images in the camera than in directing the "actors." Poets Allen Ginsberg, Gregory Corso, and Peter Orlovsky clowned their way through, with child-like involvement. Larry Rivers and David Amram played jazz. Frank's images caught the feel of loft living and the crazy openness of the Beat poets. In this setting the kitchen sink, the refrigerator, and even the cockroaches took on grimy meaning.

After the filming and editing were complete, Jack Kerouac came and improvised a text that brought the whole thing together.

"...dishes, toothbrushes, cockroaches, coffee cockroaches, stove cockroaches, city cockroaches, spot cockroaches, melted cheese cockroaches, flour cockroaches, Chaplin cockroaches, peanut butter cockroaches, cockroaches cockroaches, cockroaches of the eyes, cockroaches mirror, boom bang-Jung. Freud, Jung, Reich."

I met Jack on the sidewalk outside my loft and told him how I liked his book, *On the Road*, and added that it reminded me of Woody Guthrie's writing. There was a resemblance between their rambling sentences, free grammar, and the long lists of places and titles that evoked images of America.

Woody wrote lines like:
"Okema was one of the singingest, square dancingest, drinkingest, yellingest, preachingest, walkingest, talkingest, laughingest, cryingest, shootingest, fist fightingest, bleedingest, gamblingest, gun, club, and razor carryingest of our ranch and farm towns."

Jack was indignant. "Woody Guthrie's just a folksinger. I'm a poet, like Rimbaud and Verlaine."

continued on page 118

"Happening," Reuben Gallery, 1960

Mary Frank, 1960

→ Jack Kerouac and Allen Ginsberg, 1959

Robert Frank, Alfred Leslie, Gregory Corso, 1959

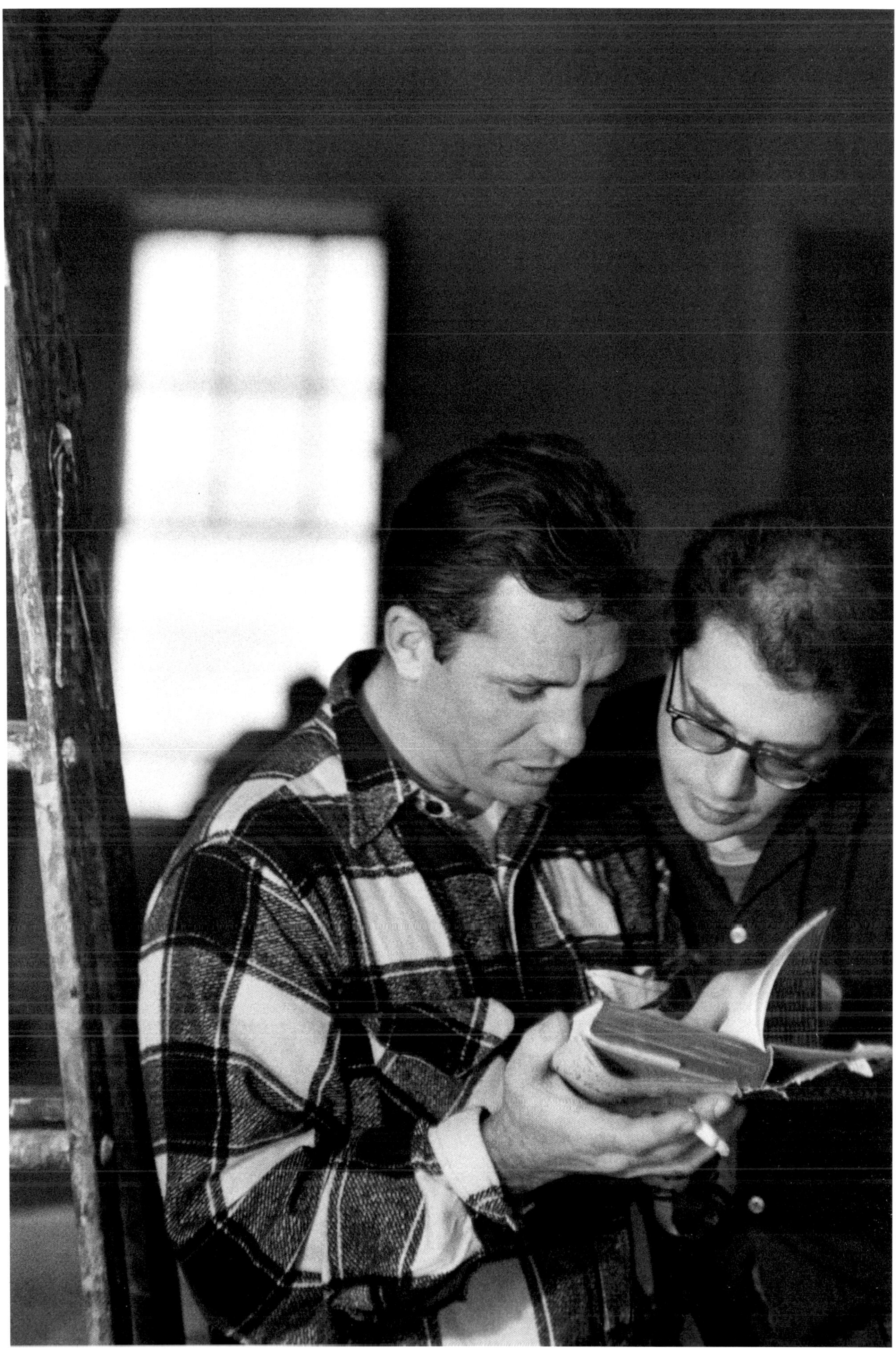

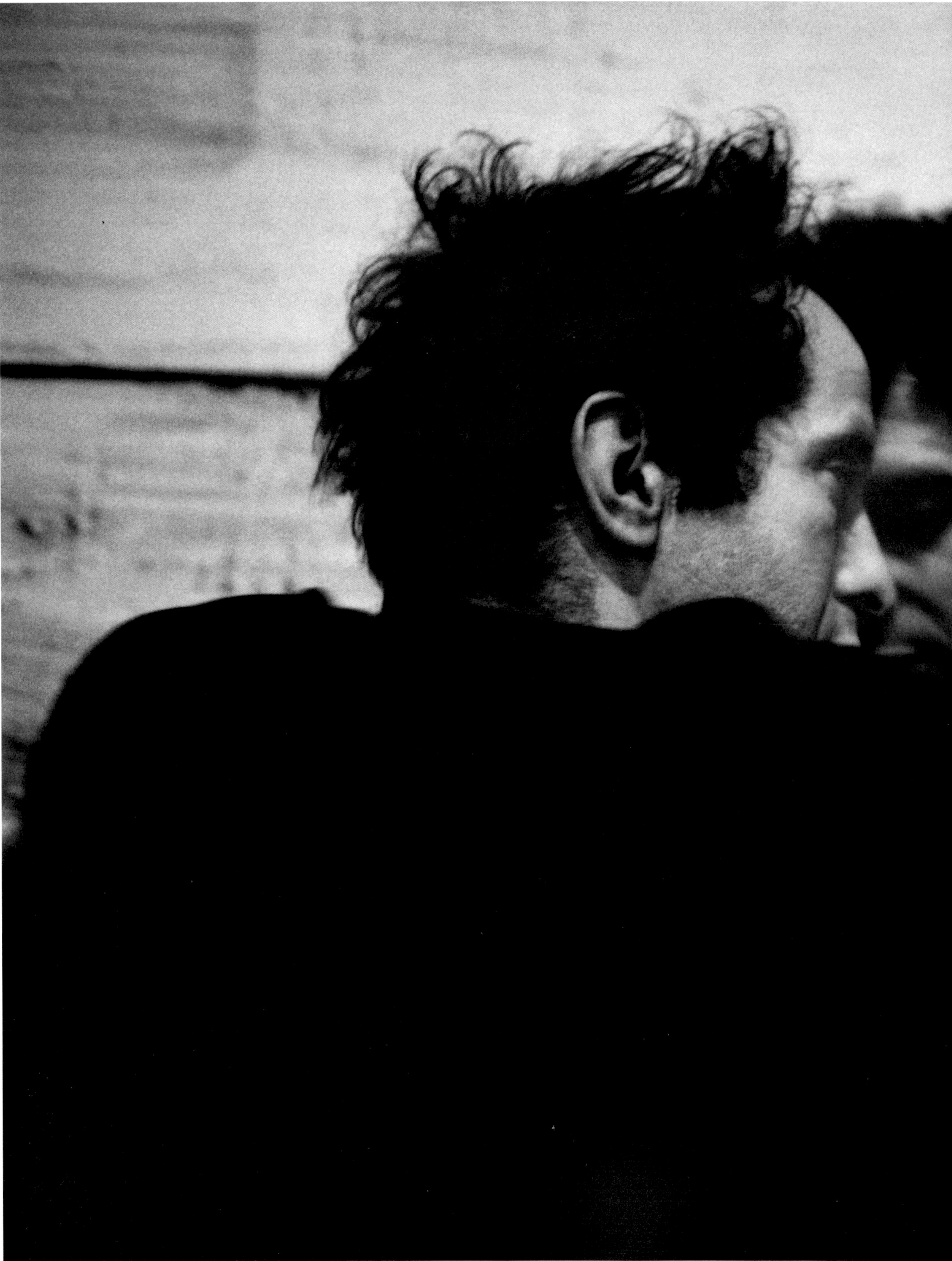

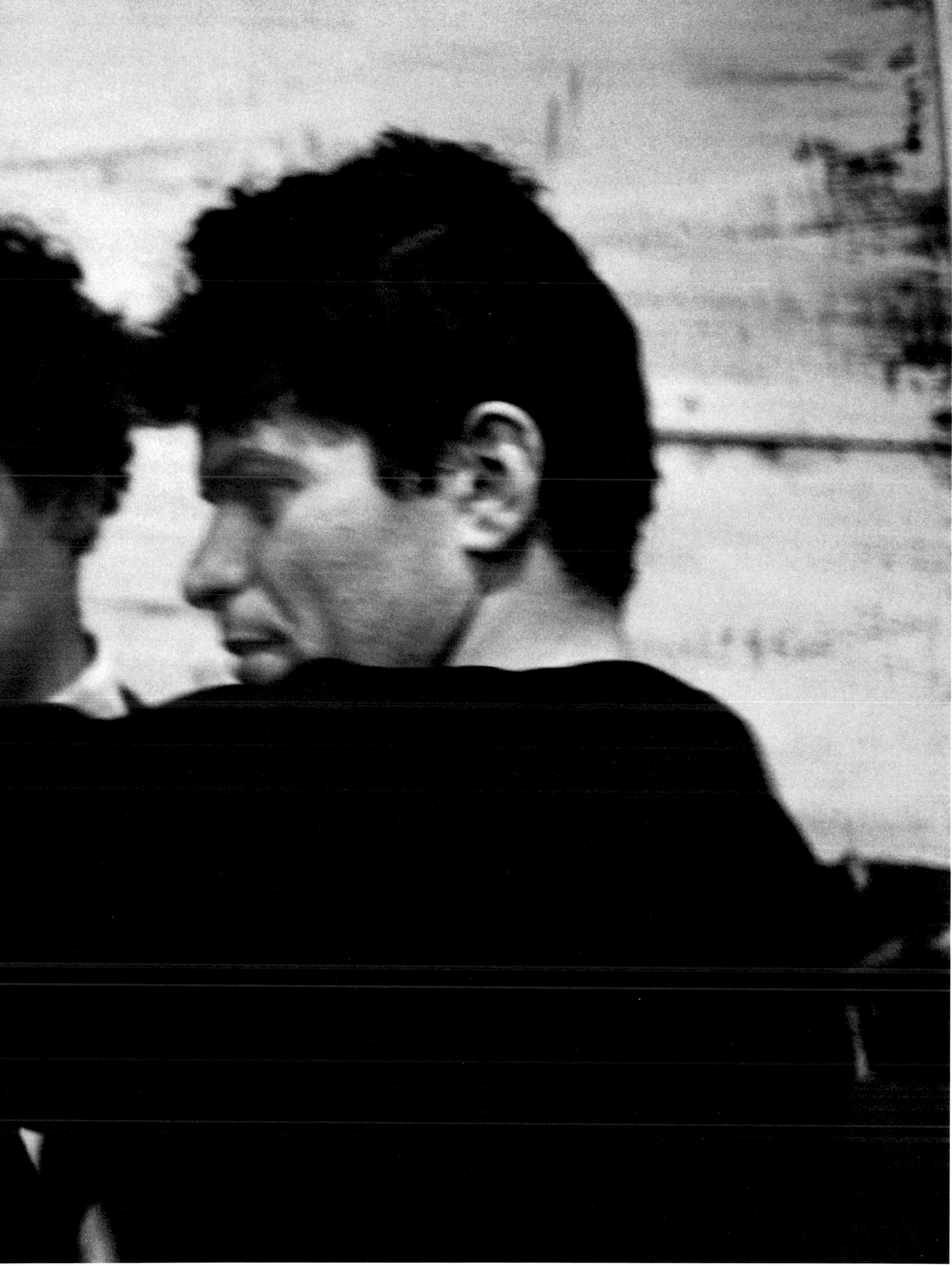

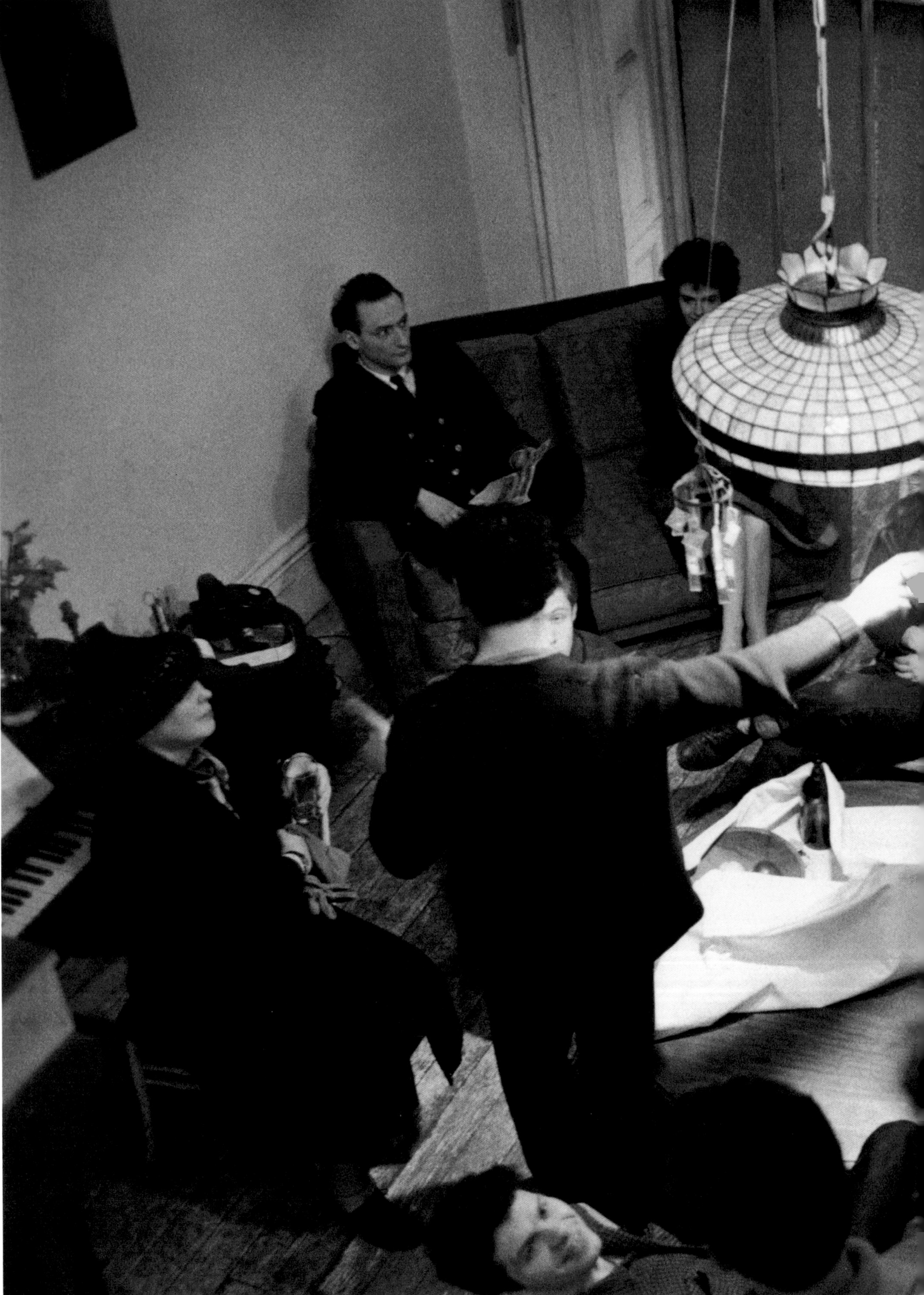

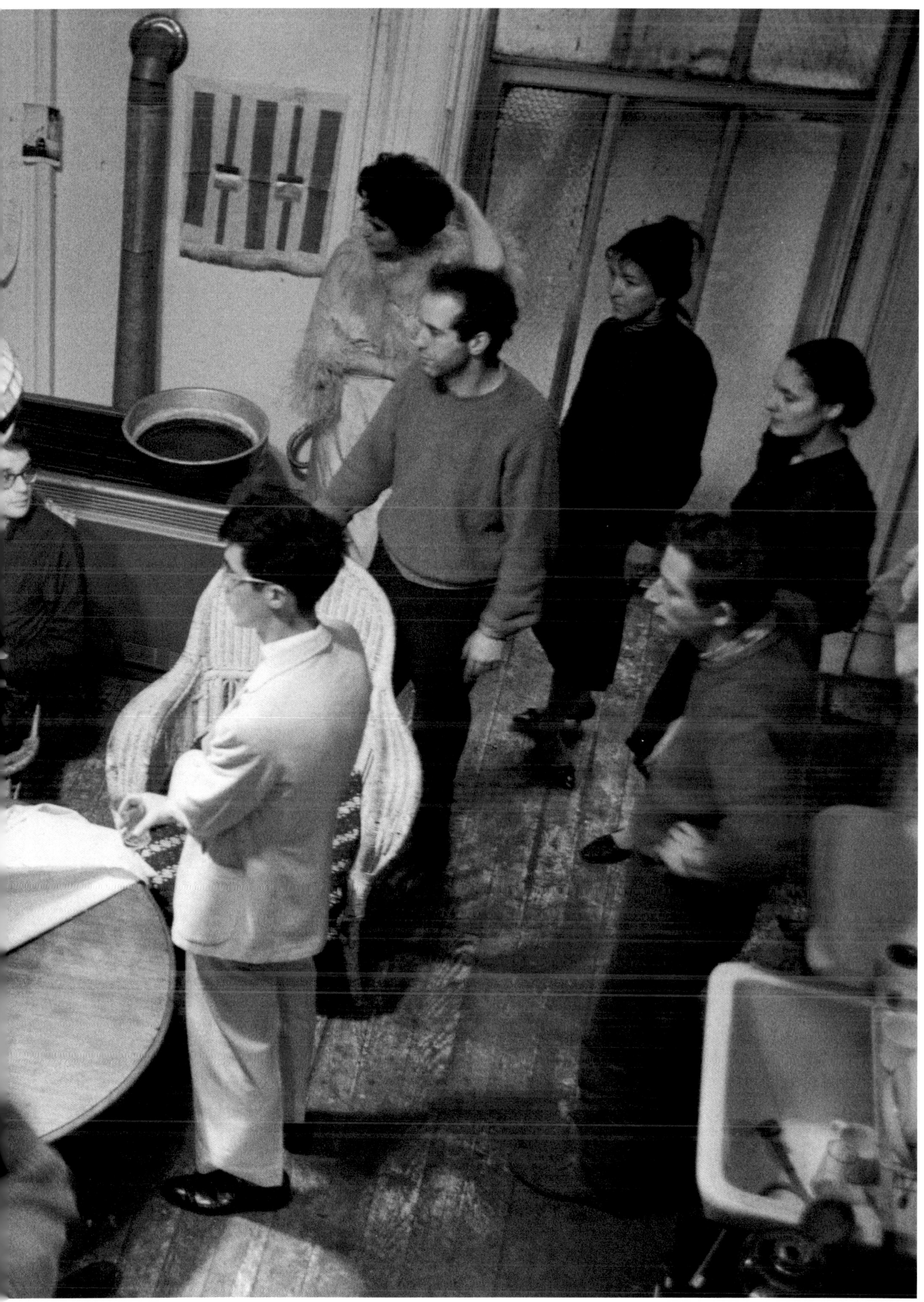

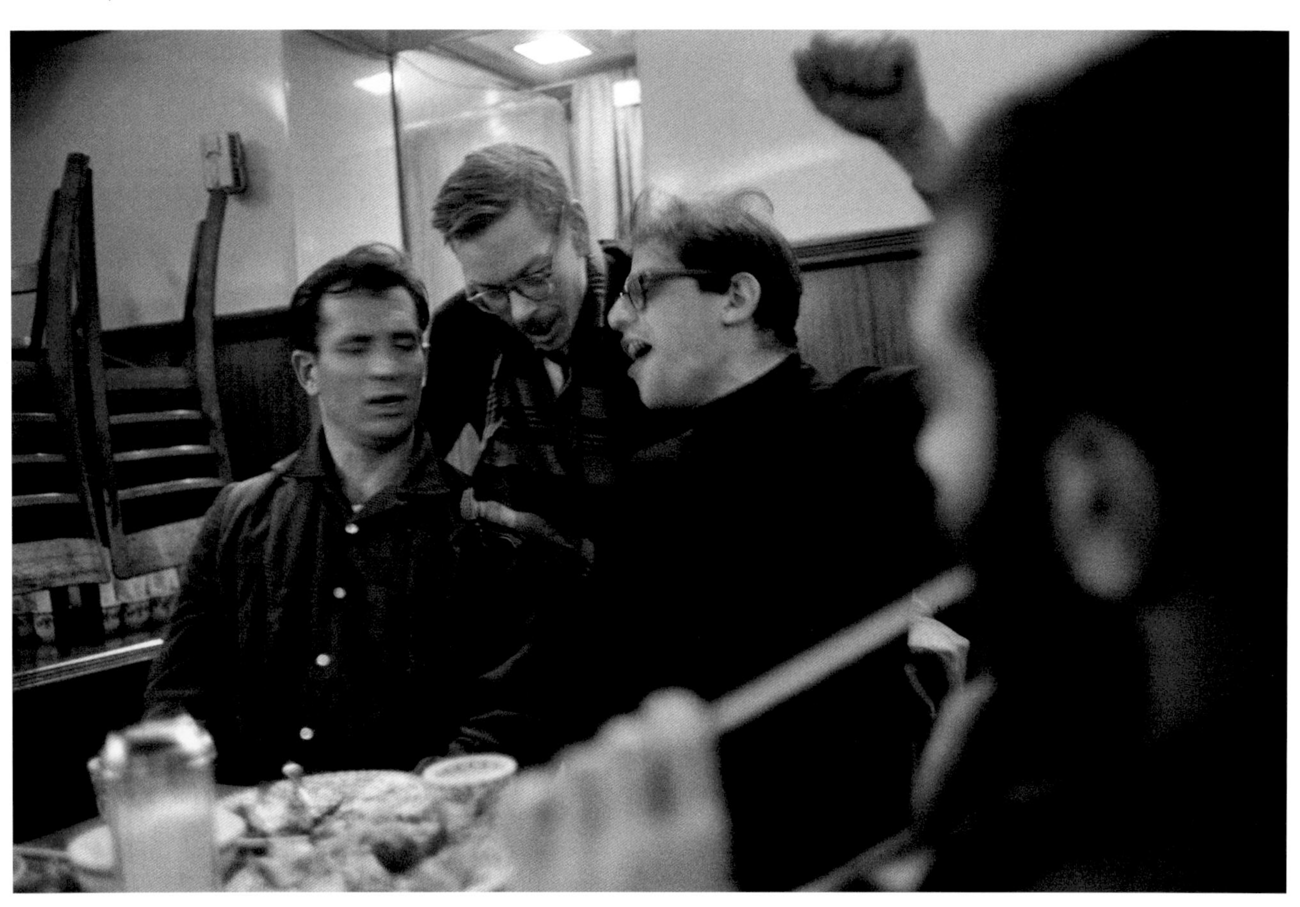

⇇ Cast *Pull My Daisy*: l-r, Alice Neel, Larry Rivers, Delphine Seyrig, Allen Ginsberg, Delphine Yungerman, Robert Frank, Sally Gross, Gert Berliner, Dick Bellamy, David Amram, Gregory Corso, Alfred Leslie, Peter Orlovsky (hidden).

↑ Jack Kerouac, Lucien Carr, Allen Ginsberg, 1959

→ Allen Ginsberg, 1959

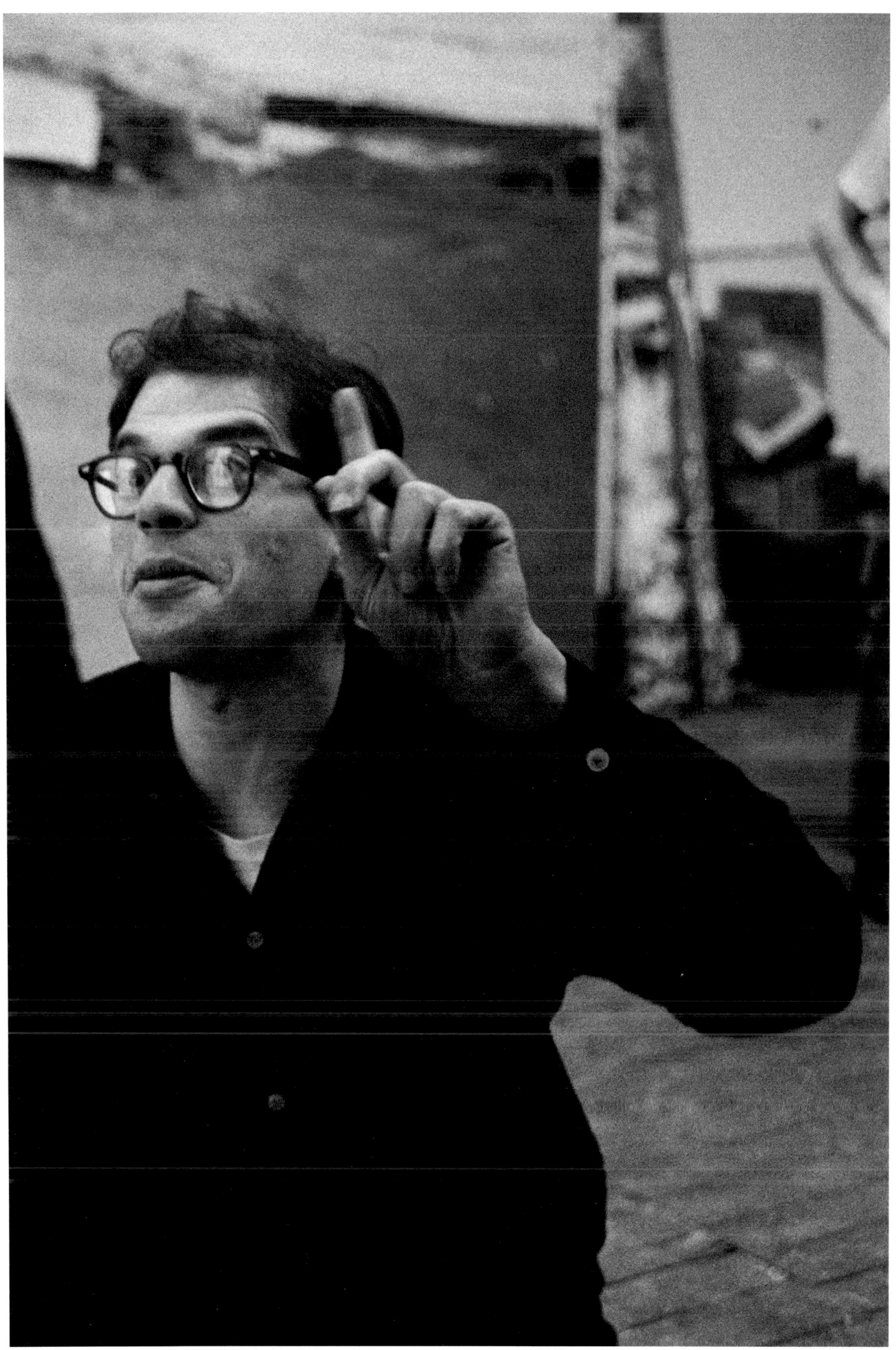

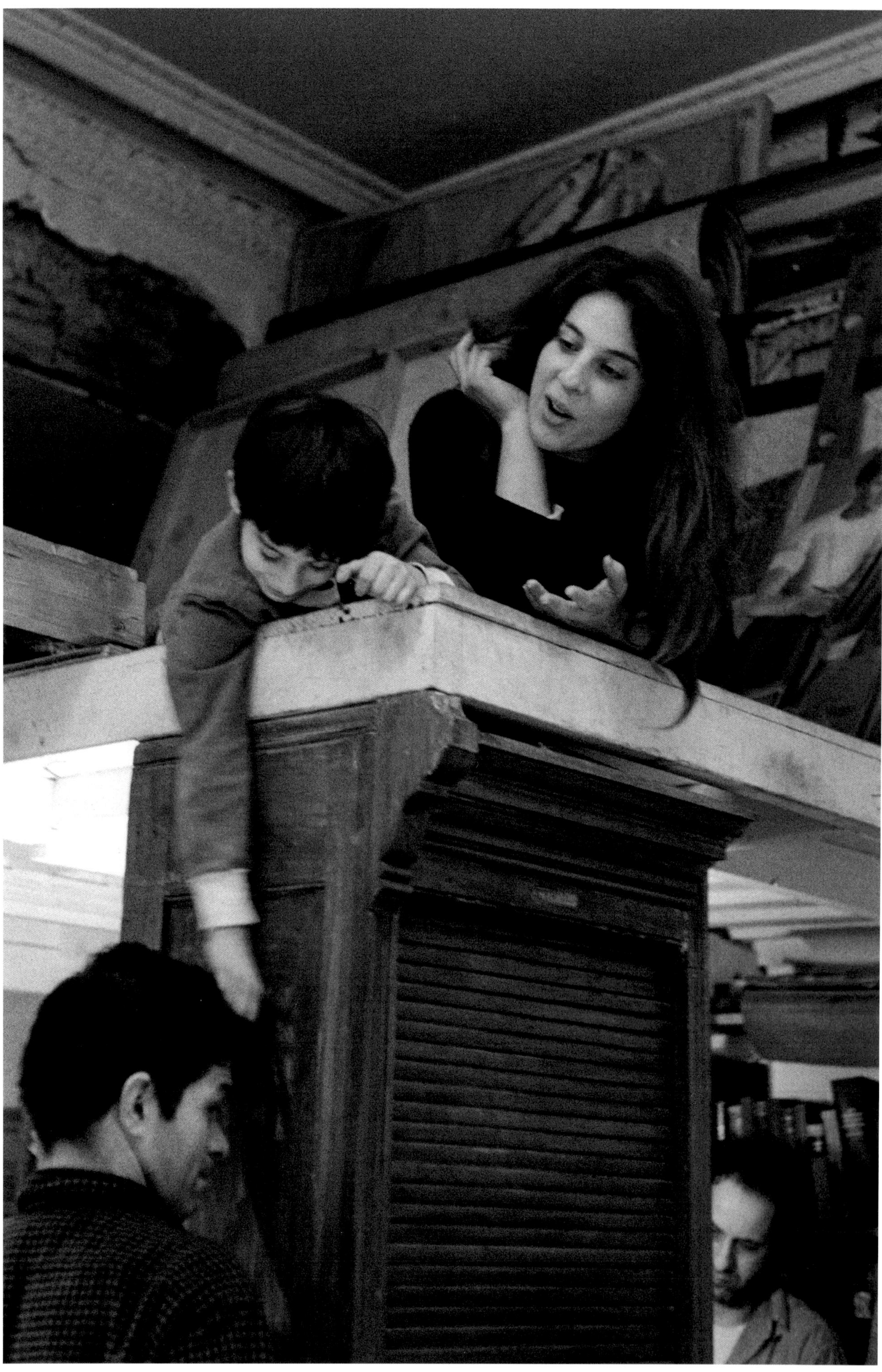

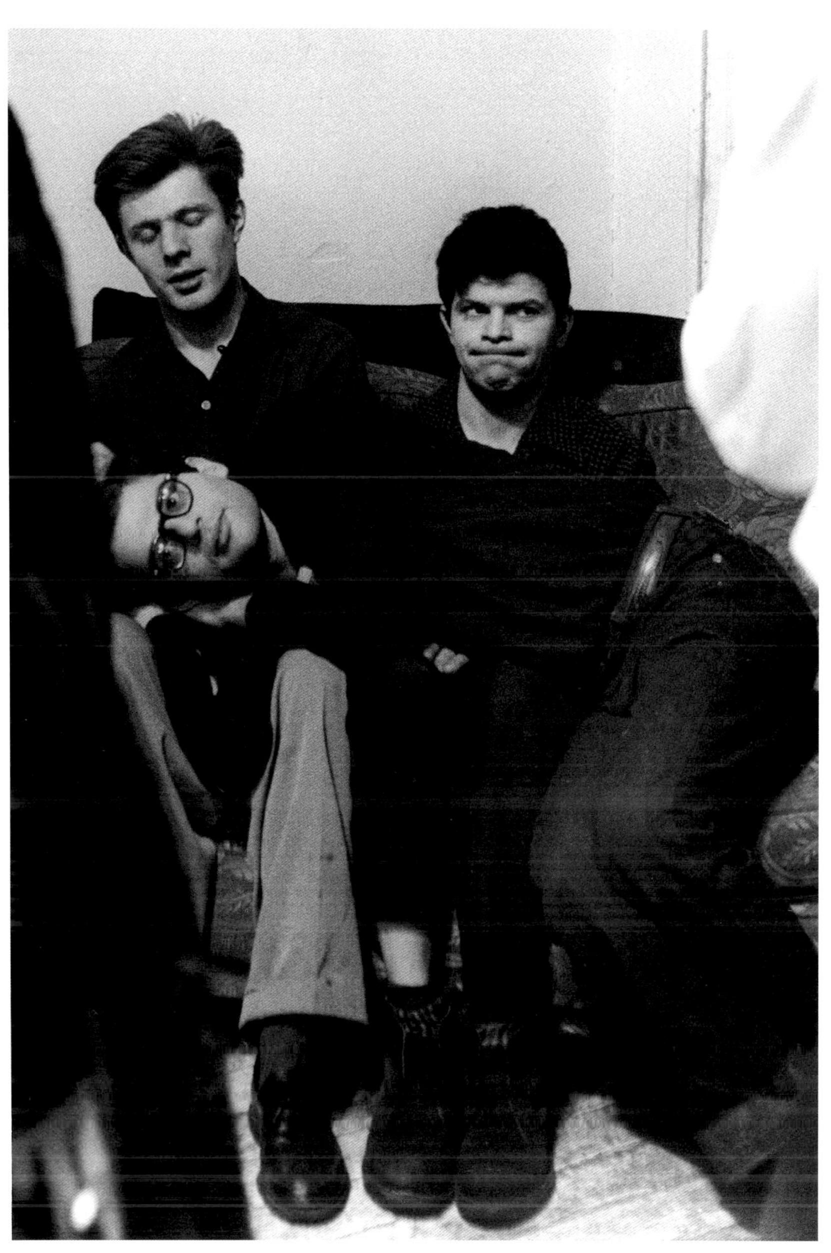

← Gregory Corso, Pablo Frank, Mary Frank, Robert Frank, 1959

↑ Allen Ginsberg, Peter Orlovsky, Gregory Corso, 1959

⇉ Jack Kerouac listening to himself on radio, 1959

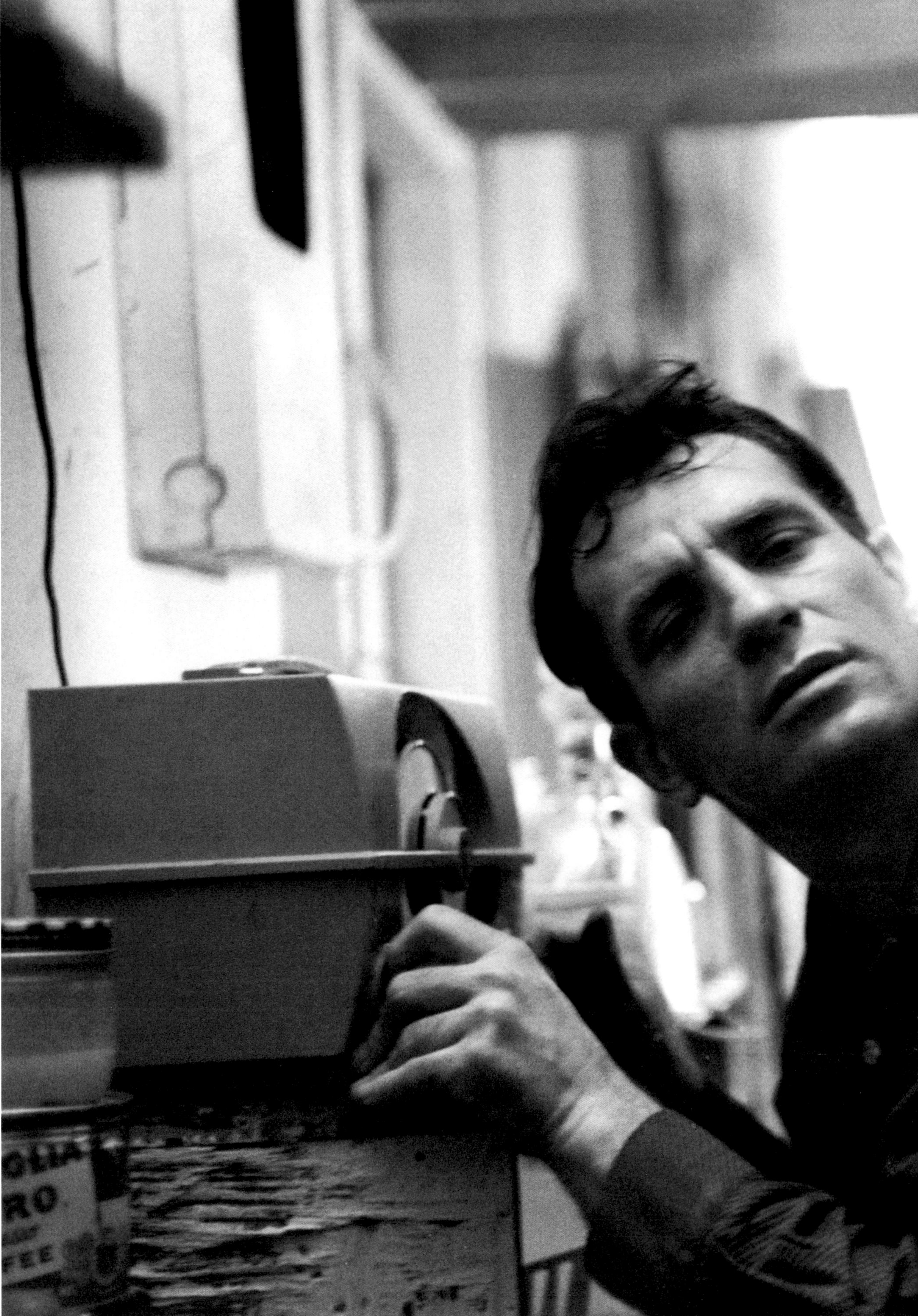

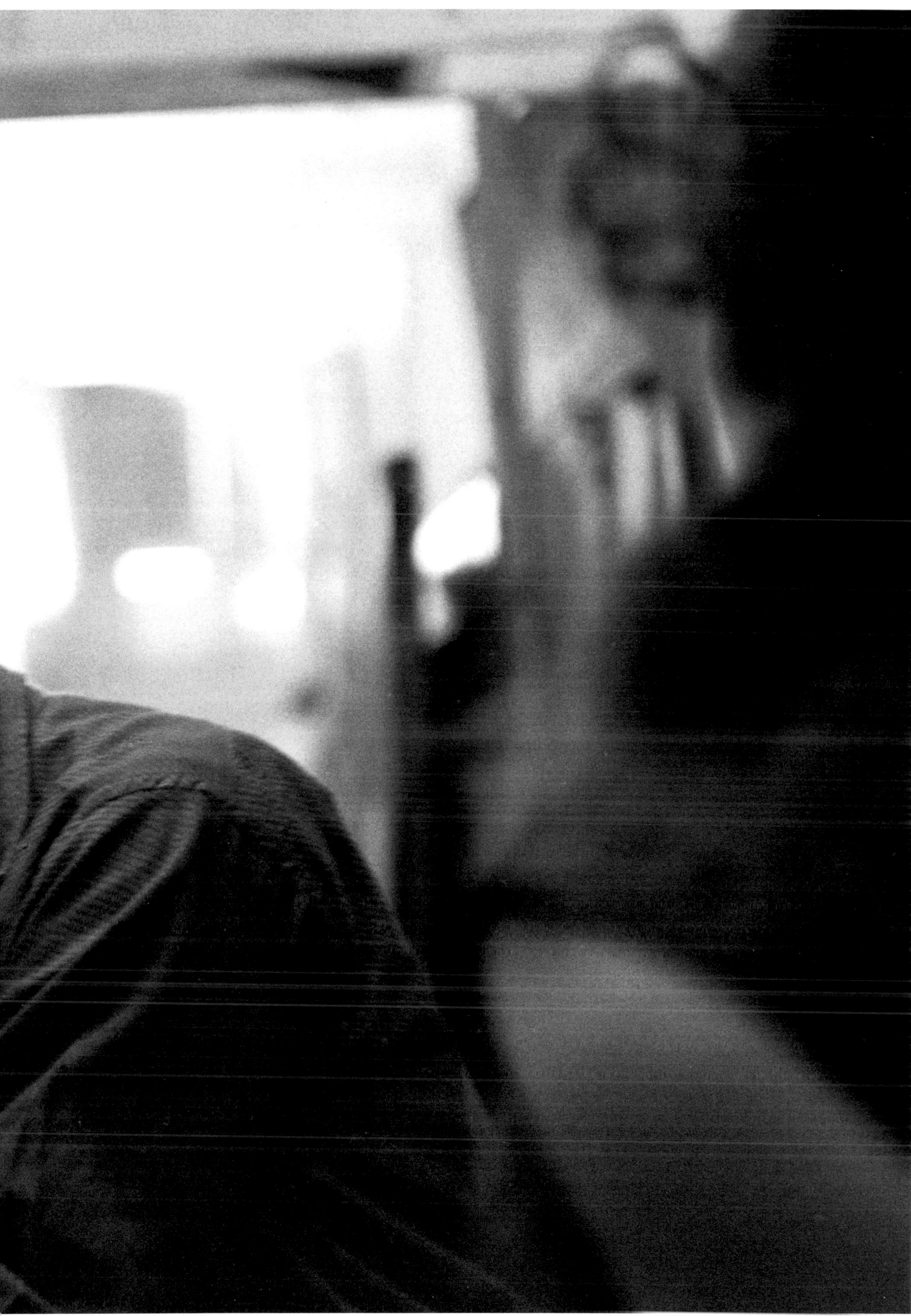

continued from page 106

Over the years, I have come to believe that Kerouac was right and wrong. His put-down of Guthrie, compared to his own high-art aspiration, was revealing. Woody was born into a middle-class Oklahoma family. He became a wanderer and dust bowl refugee when his father's business collapsed in the Depression. After that, solidarity with working class Okies became his identity. Jack, who was from a poor, French Canadian working class family, found his artistic persona as a trouble-raiser and provocateur within intellectual literary circles. Kerouac's roots were closer to the blue collar underclass than even Woody Guthrie's were.

After the filming of *Pull My Daisy,* many artists and writers came to the cast party. A reporter who said he was from *LIFE Magazine* approached Zero Mostel. Zero gave him one of his incredulous looks. "You're from *LIFE Magazine*? Well, fuck you." *LIFE* paid me for a "first look" at my Beat Generation photographs. I used the money to finance a trip to Kentucky.

→ Robert Frank and Jack Kerouac on set of *Pull My Daisy*, 1959

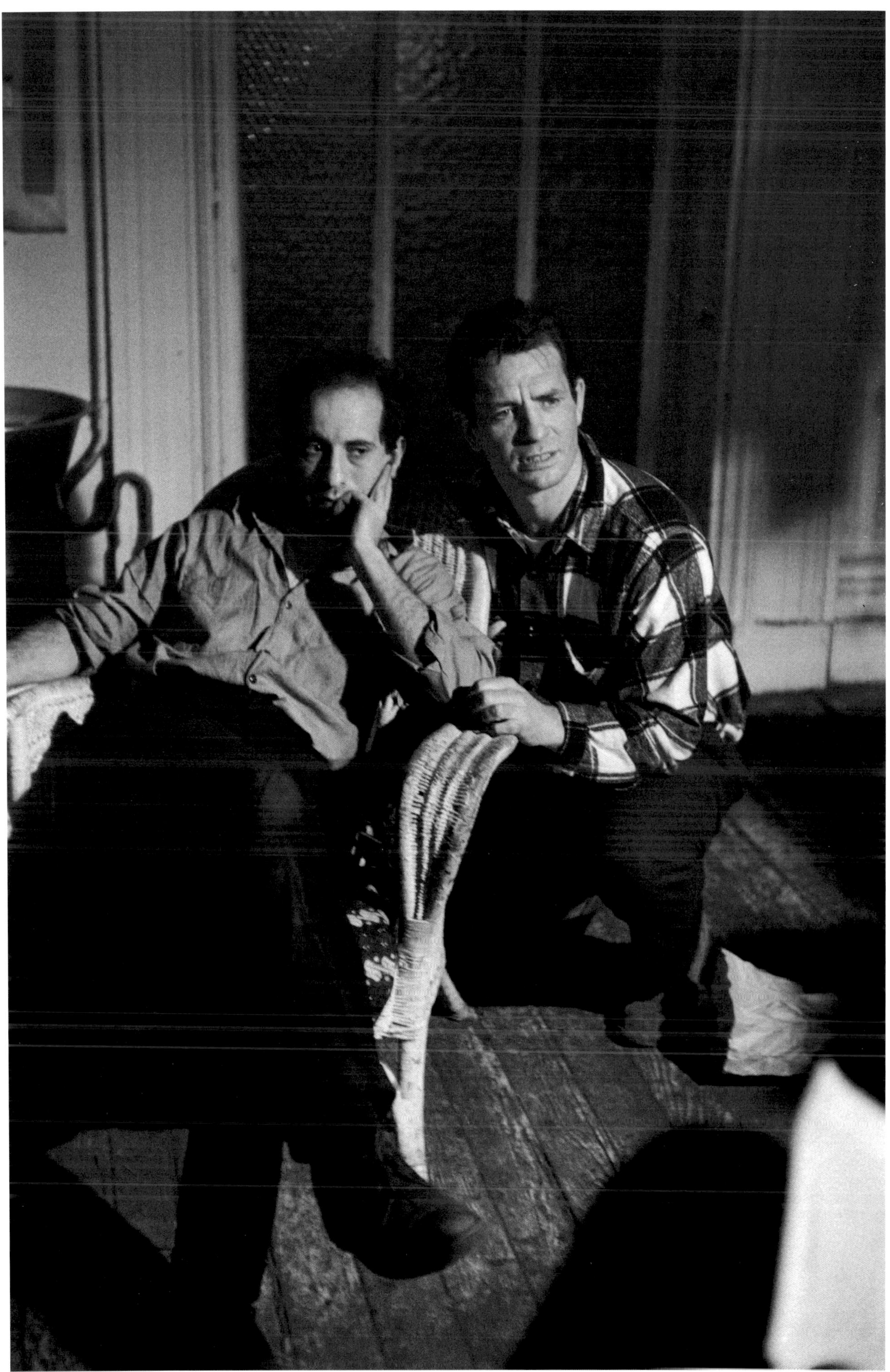

THE HIGH LONESOME SOUND In the spring of 1959 I traveled to eastern Kentucky to make recordings of the music and to photograph. While the rest of America was busy and prosperous, Kentucky was experiencing a depression caused by troubles in the coal mines. Since coal was the only industry here, everyone was affected. The prevailing sense was of poverty in a landscape of run-down coal mines, small farms, houses huddled away in remote hollows, and roadsides littered with junked cars too worthless to be hauled out of the mountains. There was a feeling of tension and potential violence between miners, unions, and operators. It seemed as if the rural people of Appalachia were stranded in an increasingly mechanized America. These were the descendants of the pioneers, still holding on to old American rural traditions, and suffering because of it. They were stuck in poverty while the rest of America was prospering. How different their lives were from what was on TV. Harry Caudill called it "Night Comes To The Cumberlands."

The Appalachian faces showed pride, stoicism, and a sort of playfulness. These were people known to be closed off and inaccessible. But when asked for their music, it opened direct paths to their hearts and memories. They sang with a passion that came from within themselves. It was not a styled performance; deep feelings were just beneath the surface. I still listen to the recordings of their voices. They sound more powerful now than when I recorded them. The Kentucky music had a clarity beyond anything America's mass culture offered. Fathers made banjos from coffee cans for their sons. Old Baptists wailed melodies sounding like Gregorian chants. Ballads were sung from a time before the record industry or radio. Blues, bluegrass, and old love songs were performed with an intense edge. I named it "The High Lonesome Sound."

→ Roscoe Holcomb, Daisy, Kentucky, 1959

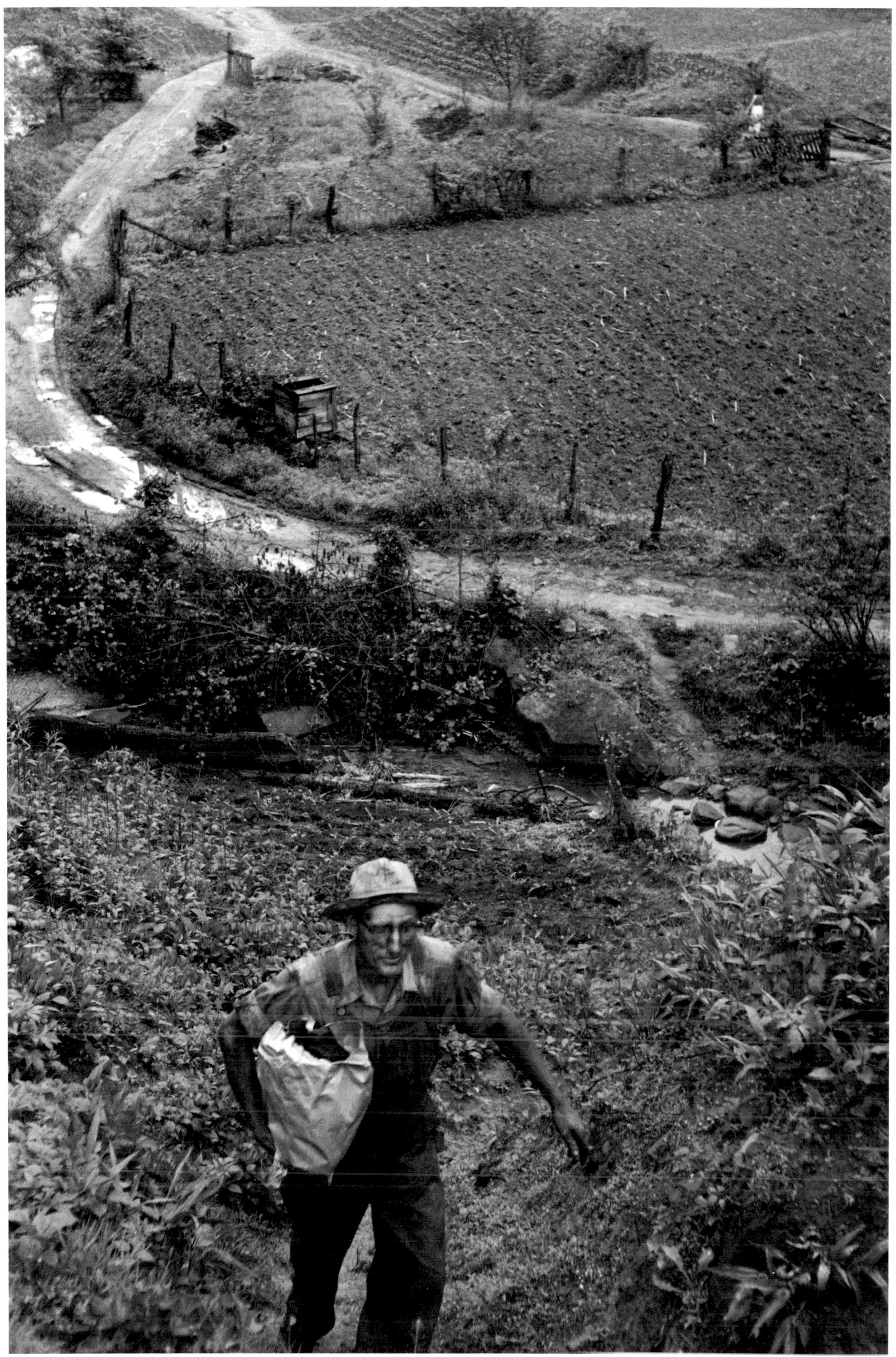

In 1959 I met Roscoe Holcomb. His intense singing, coupled with hard-driving banjo and bluesy guitar, was some of the strongest music I had ever heard. I got to know him, recorded him, filmed him, and we kept in contact for the remainder of his hard life. He told me, "Farming's about all there was in this country until the coal mines came in here. Man made his living on the farm."

"Course there was railroad work. That gave a lot of people work, 'n still they farmed, raised their own stuff to eat. It was one of the best livings a man ever lived when you raise all your vegetables and have three of four big hogs to kill. Plenty of milk and butter, 'n your own eggs. Raise your own chickens 'n you don't have to go to the store for it, you got it. It's all pure food, buddy, and that's the reason the old generation lived longer 'n stronger than they do today."

"I guess the coal mines have been here before my time, but there was only just a few.... The first mines started 'n they made their own pushcarts and pushed the coal out of the mines 'n hauled it in a wagon to the railroads. Then they got the trucks, 'n it kept building up. Then they got the coal machines to cut the coal and shoot it, and motors to haul it with.... But the big mines don't use no stock (mules, etc.) at all. It's all machine. It's getting too much machinery, taking the work away from the people."

"My living was hard labor: construction work, coal mines. It's all hard, hard living. But I love to work whenever I'm able."

I asked him, "Are you not working these days?"

"Ain't able. I don't know what's gonna happen. I thought I was getting better but it was just a thought. I wasn't. That's what got me worried. If I'se to get a job, I couldn't hold it. It would be more worries. A man just as soon have his brains shot out as to be in that condition, the way I feel."

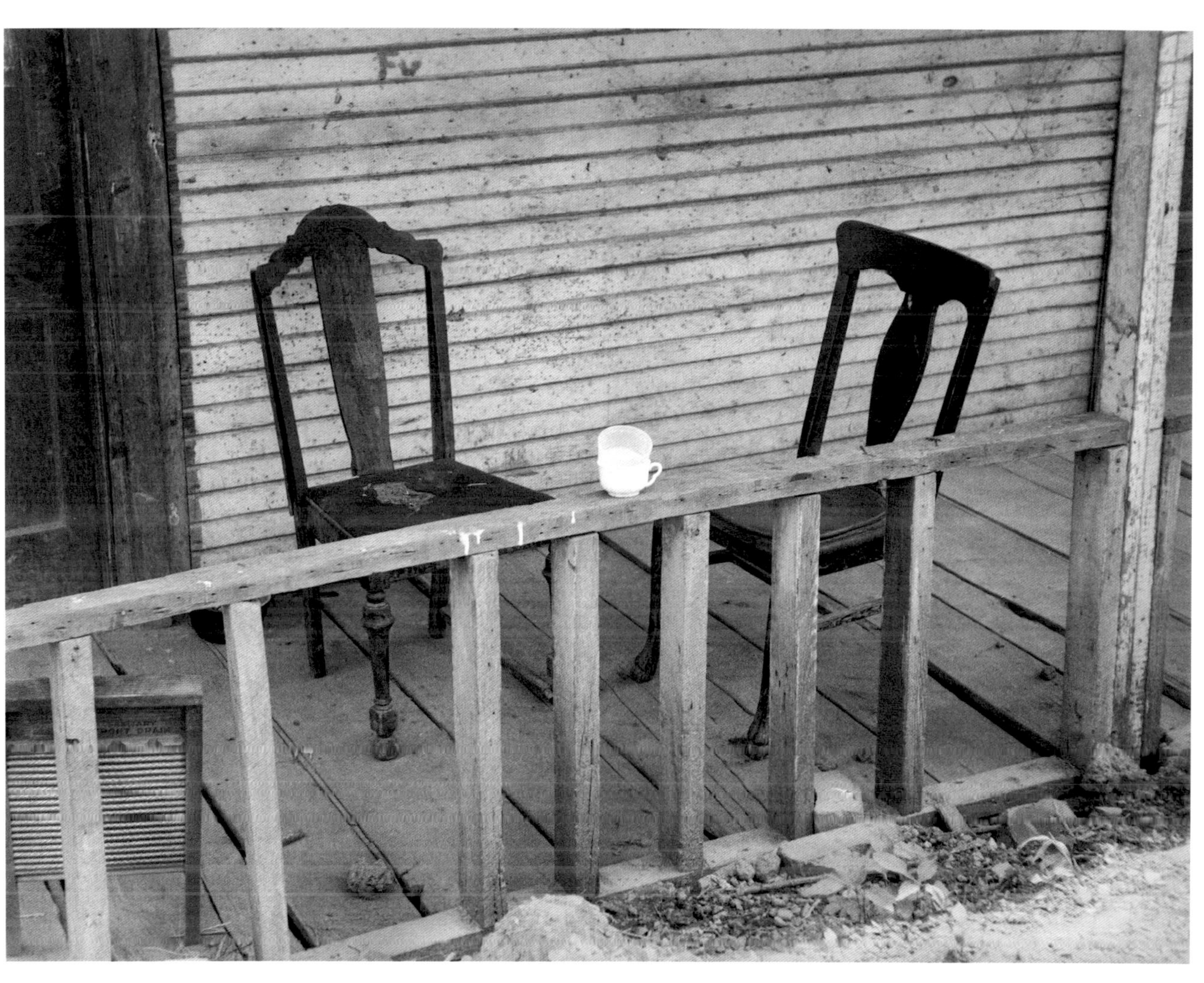

↑ Leatherwood, Kentucky, 1959

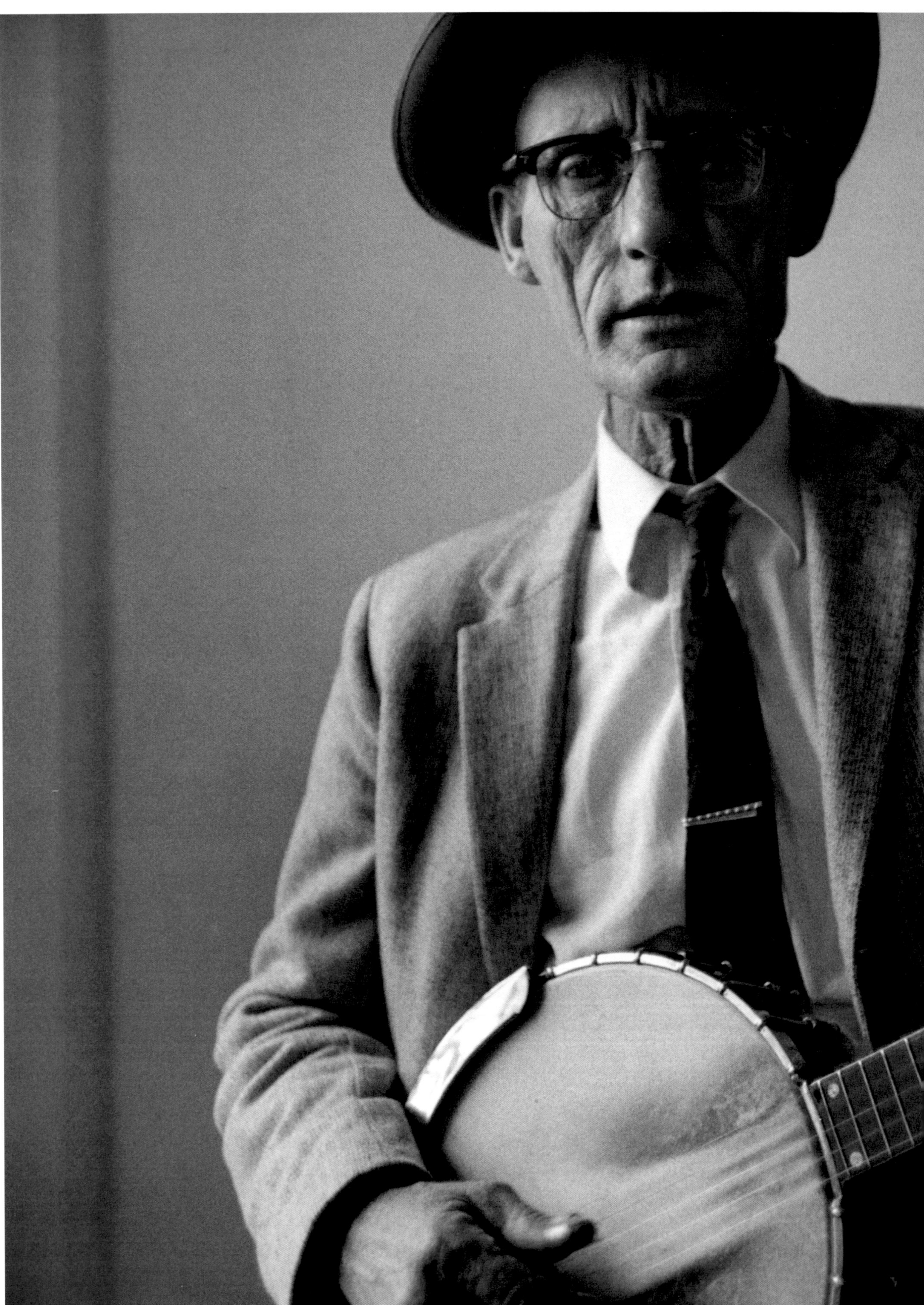

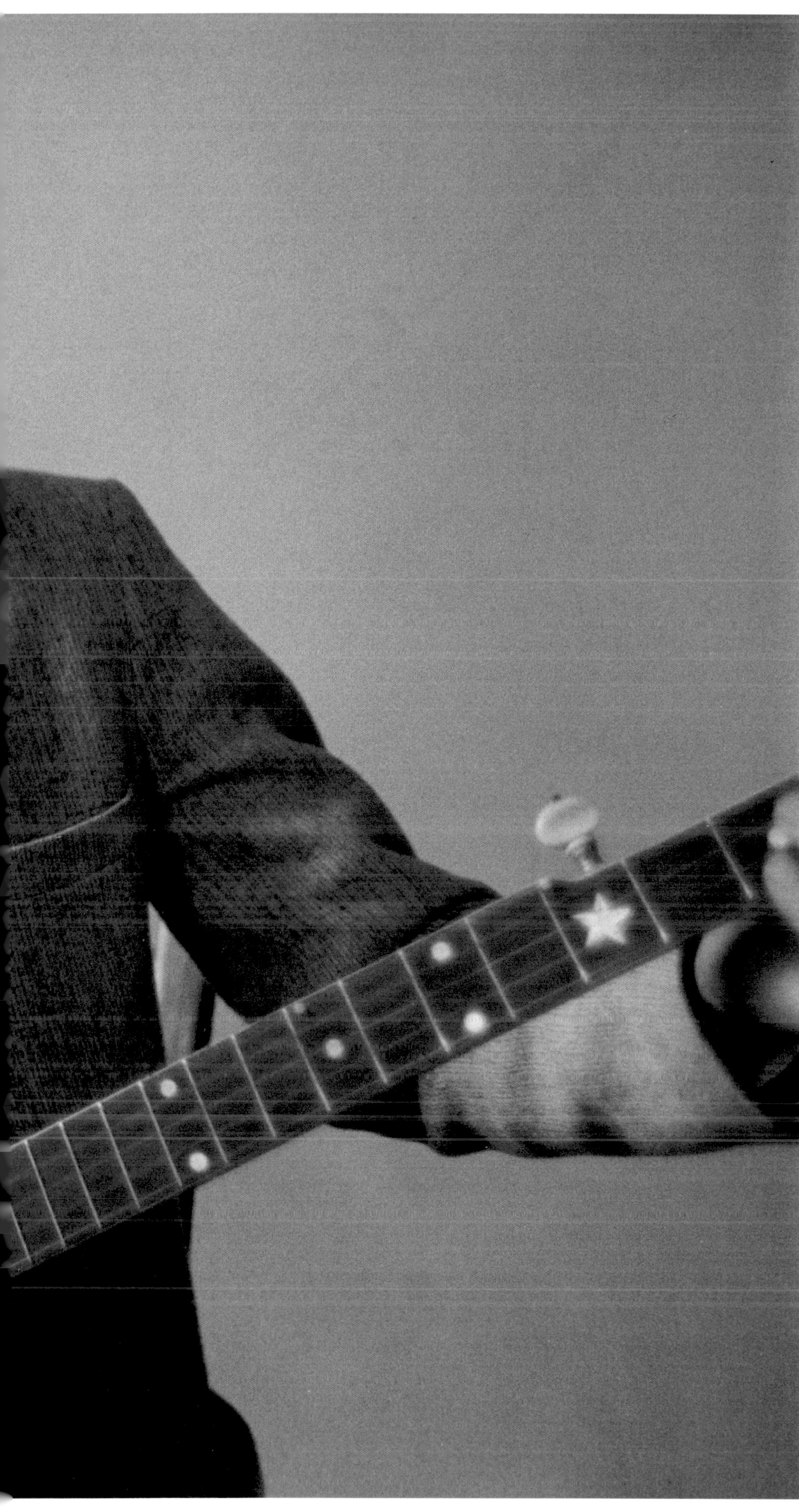

Roscoe Holcomb, 1964

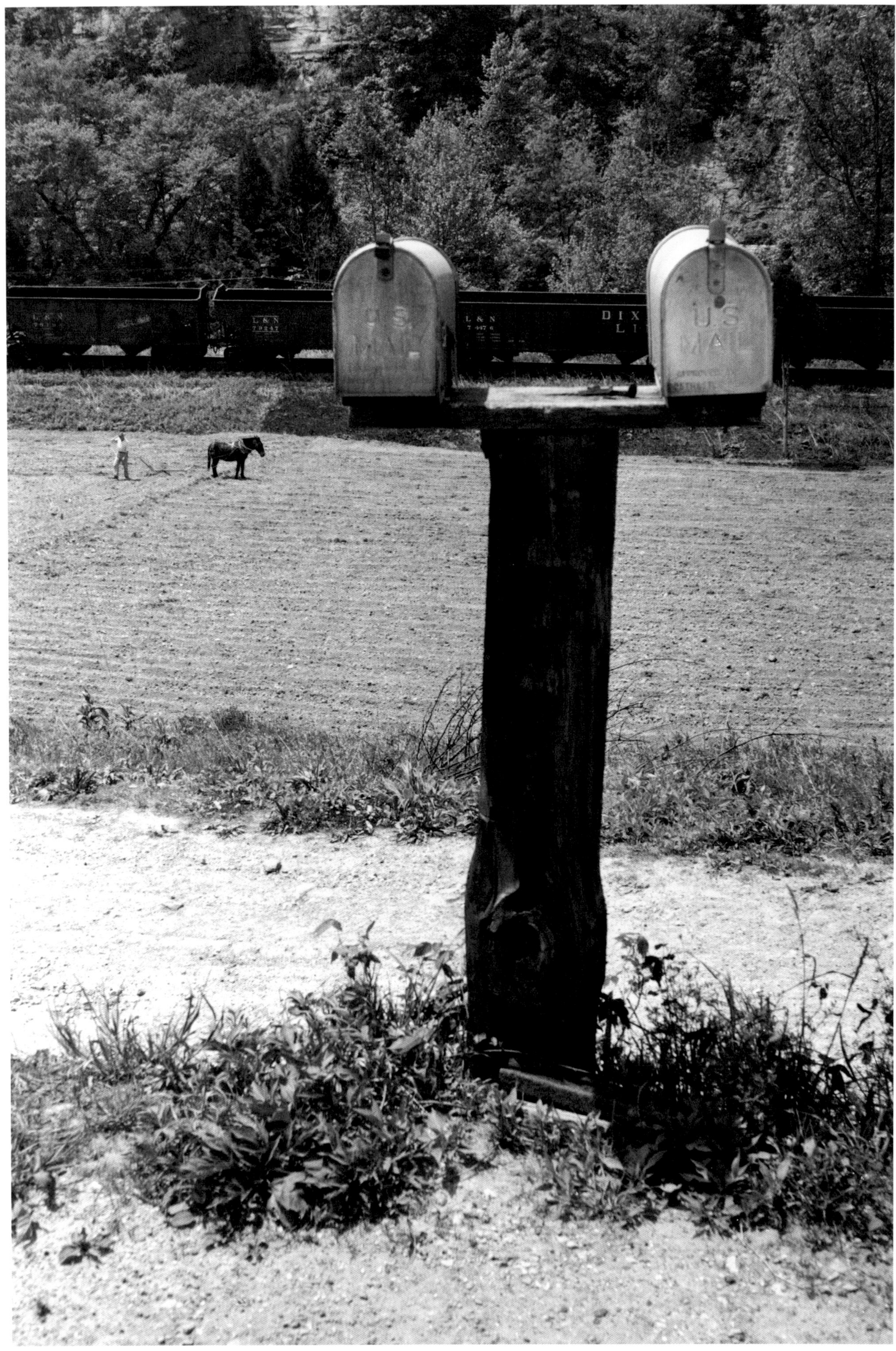
L&N
79247
L&N
74476
DIX
LI
U.S
MAIL

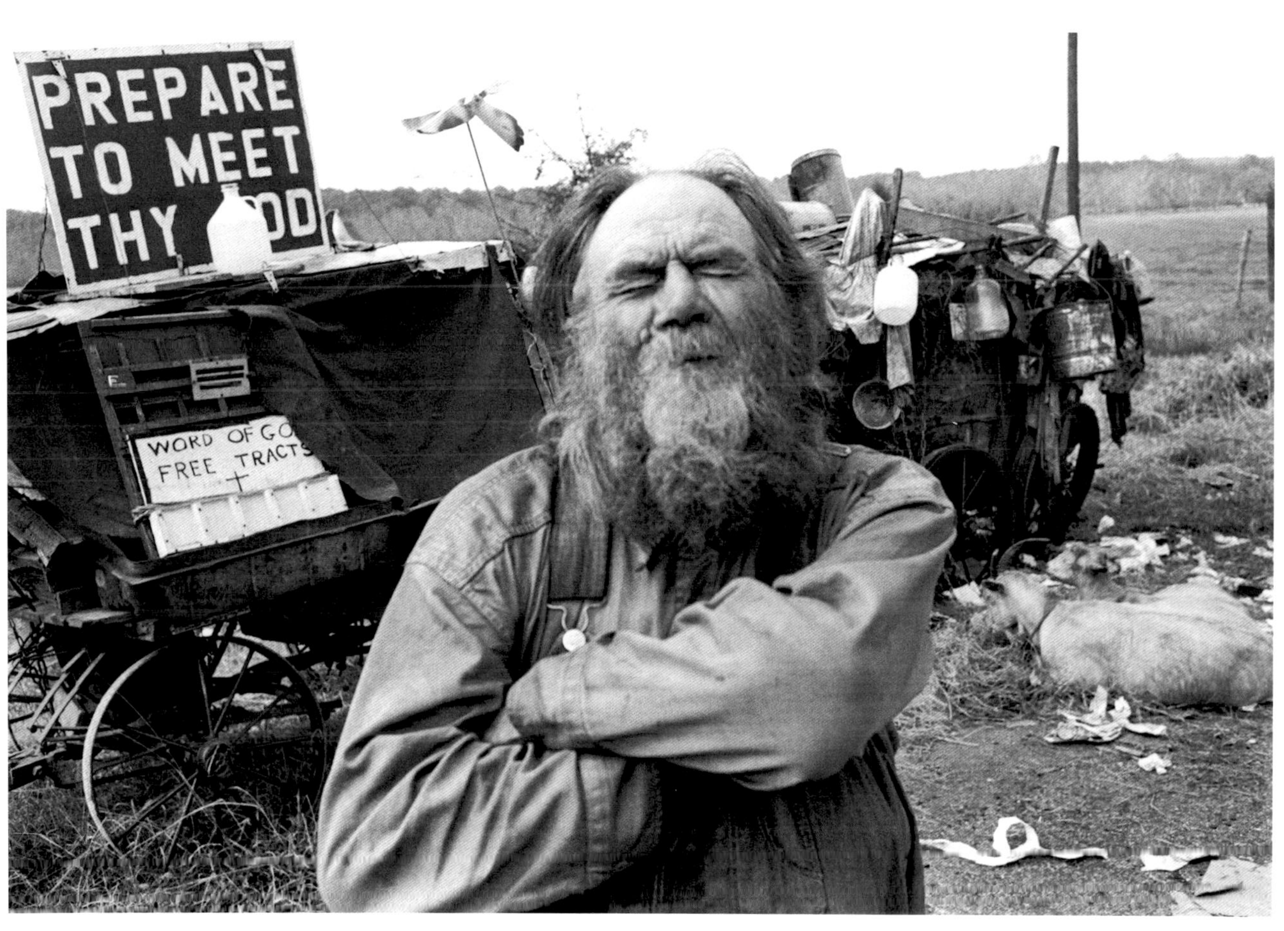

← Perry County, Kentucky, 1959

↑ The Goat Man, North Georgia, 1967

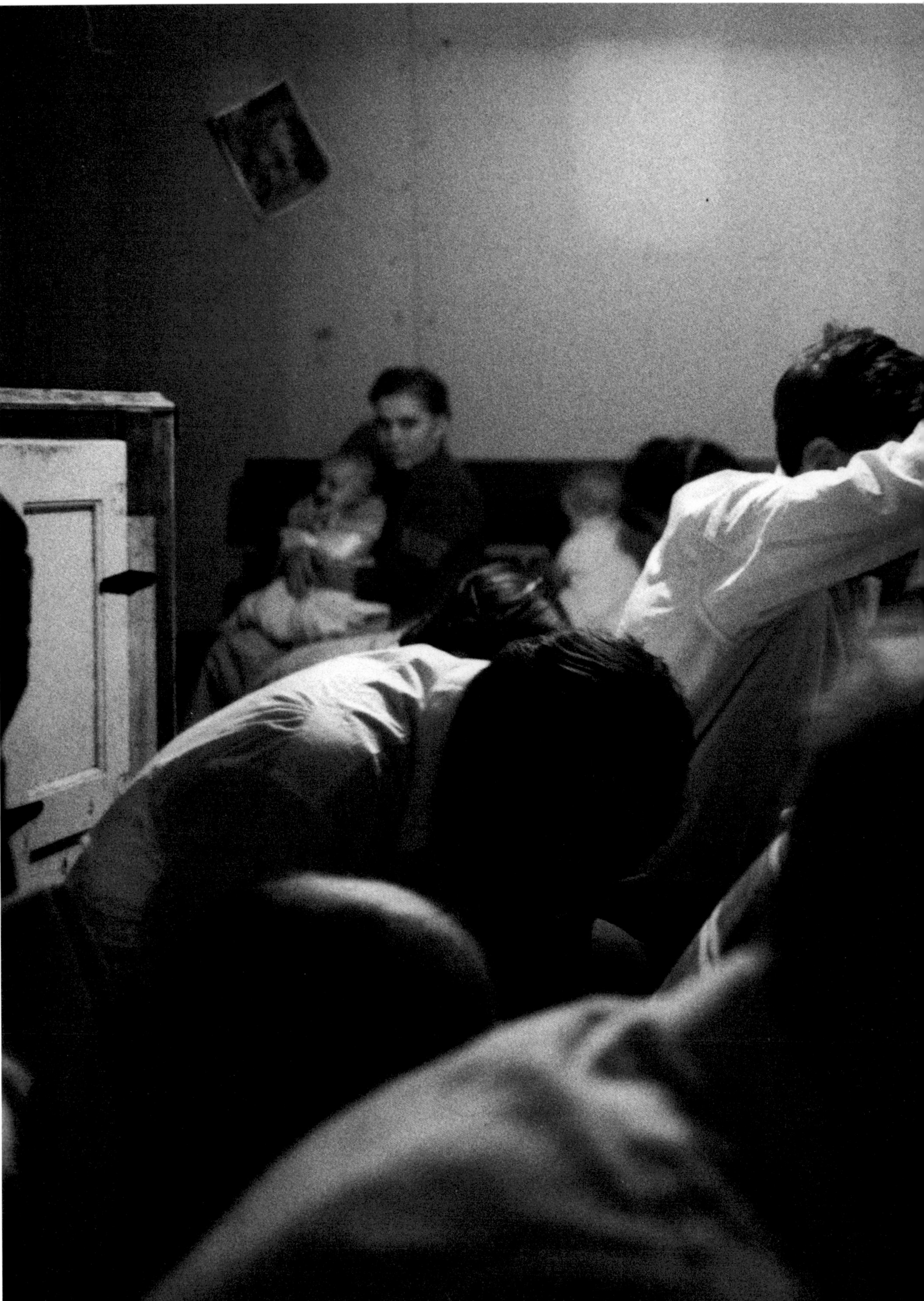

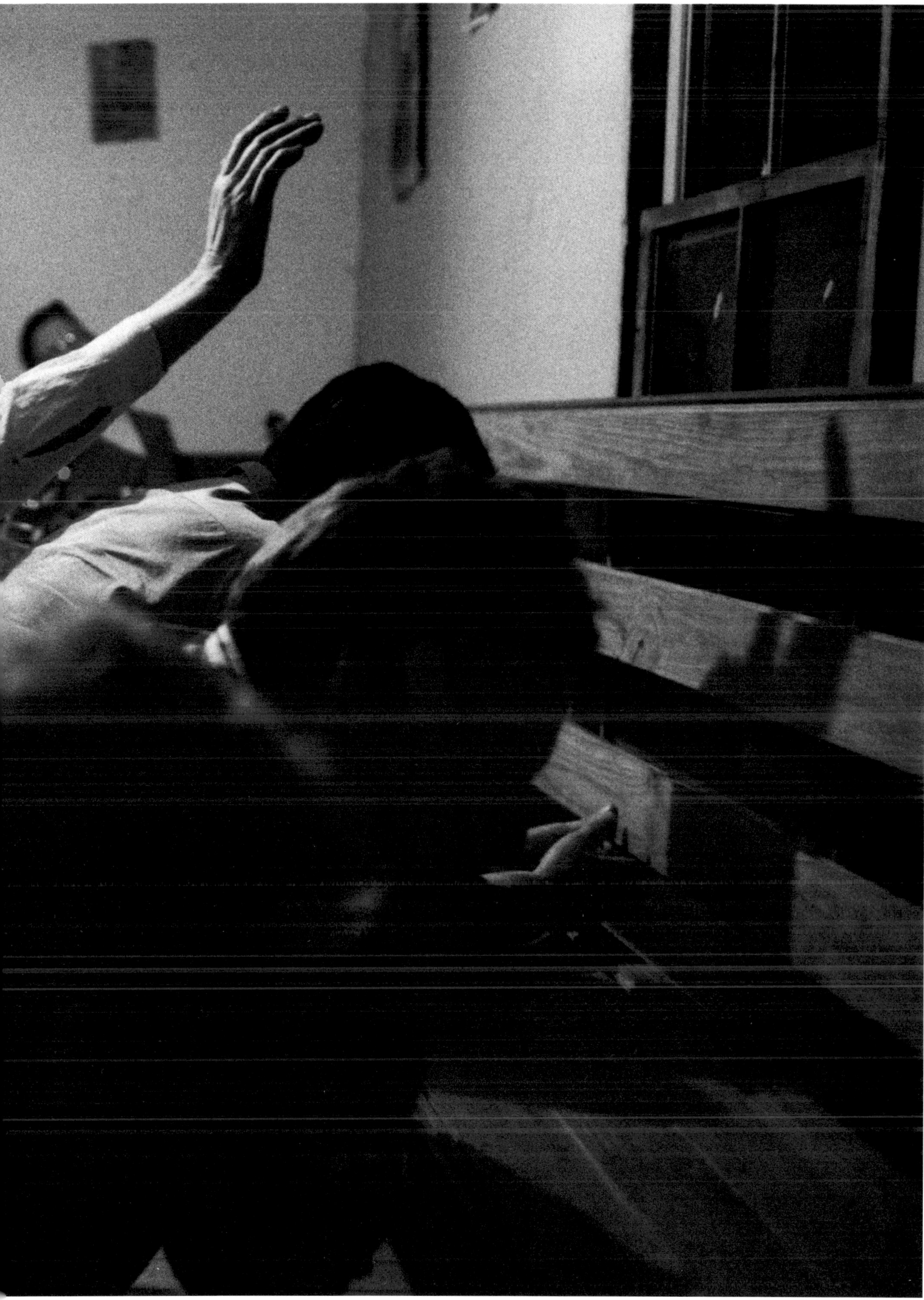

⇇ Holiness Church, Leatherwood, Kentucky, 1959

→ Roscoe Holcomb's hands, 1959

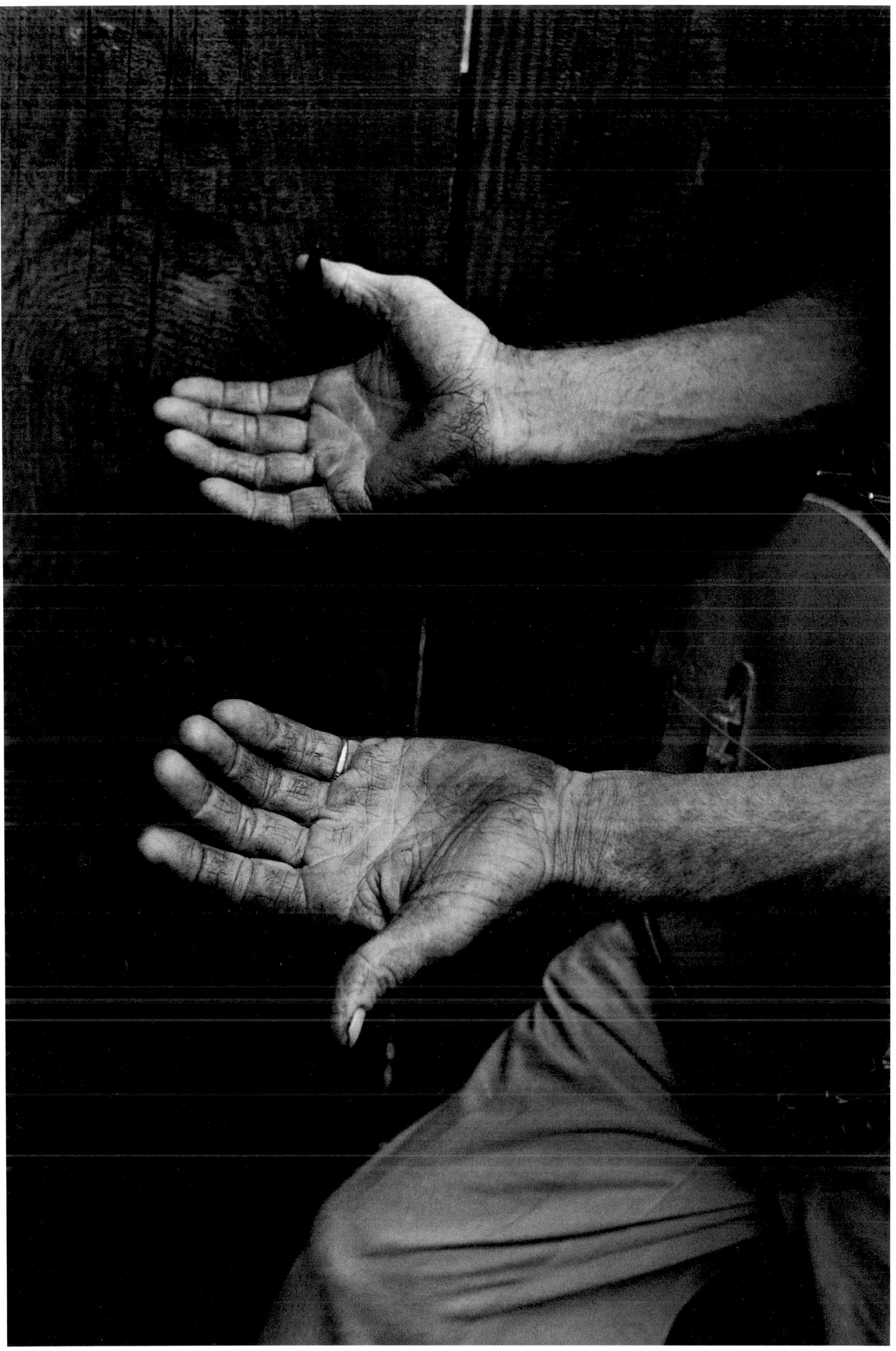

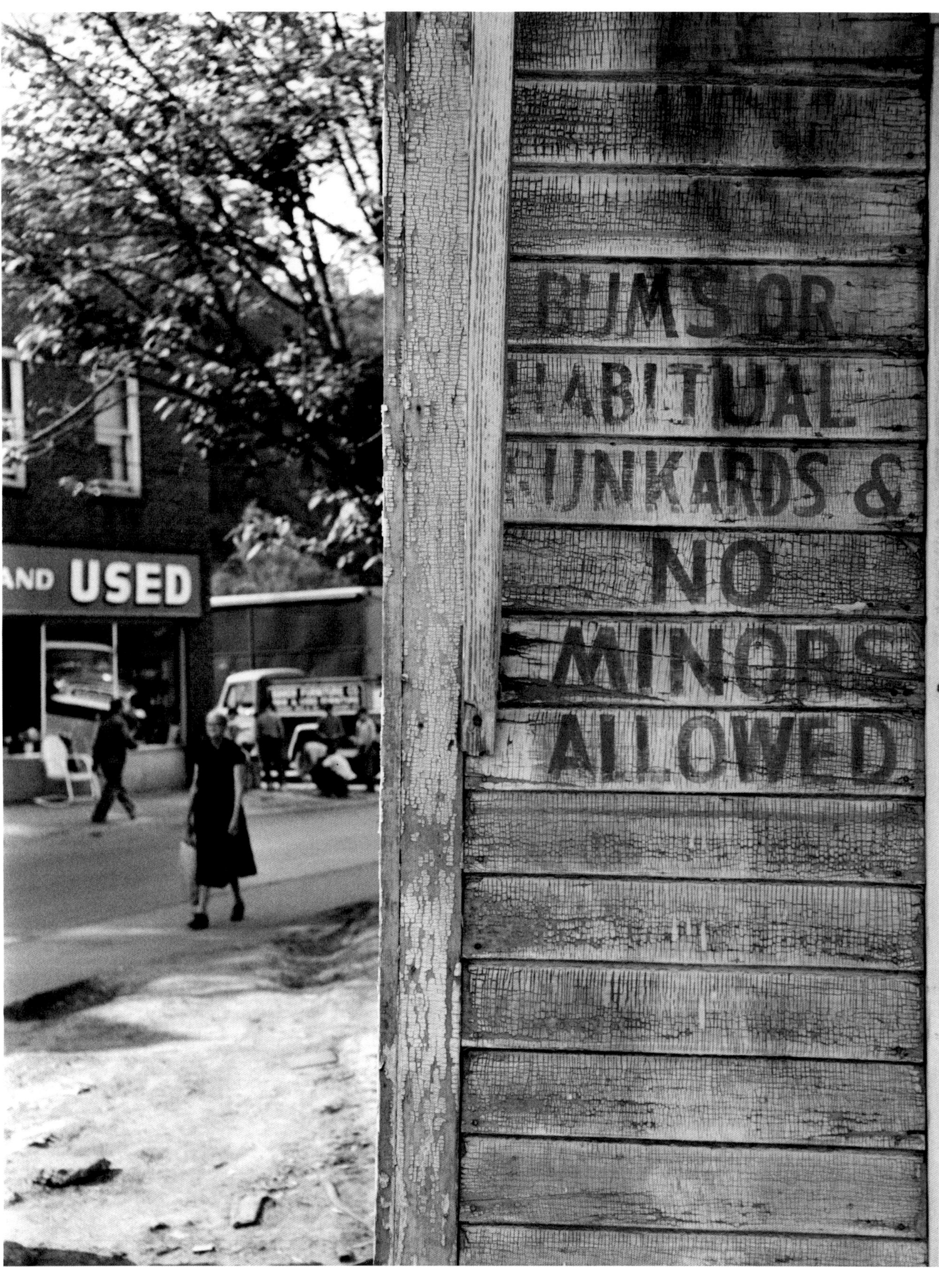
AND USED
BUMS OR
HABITUAL
DRUNKARDS &
NO
MINORS
ALLOWED

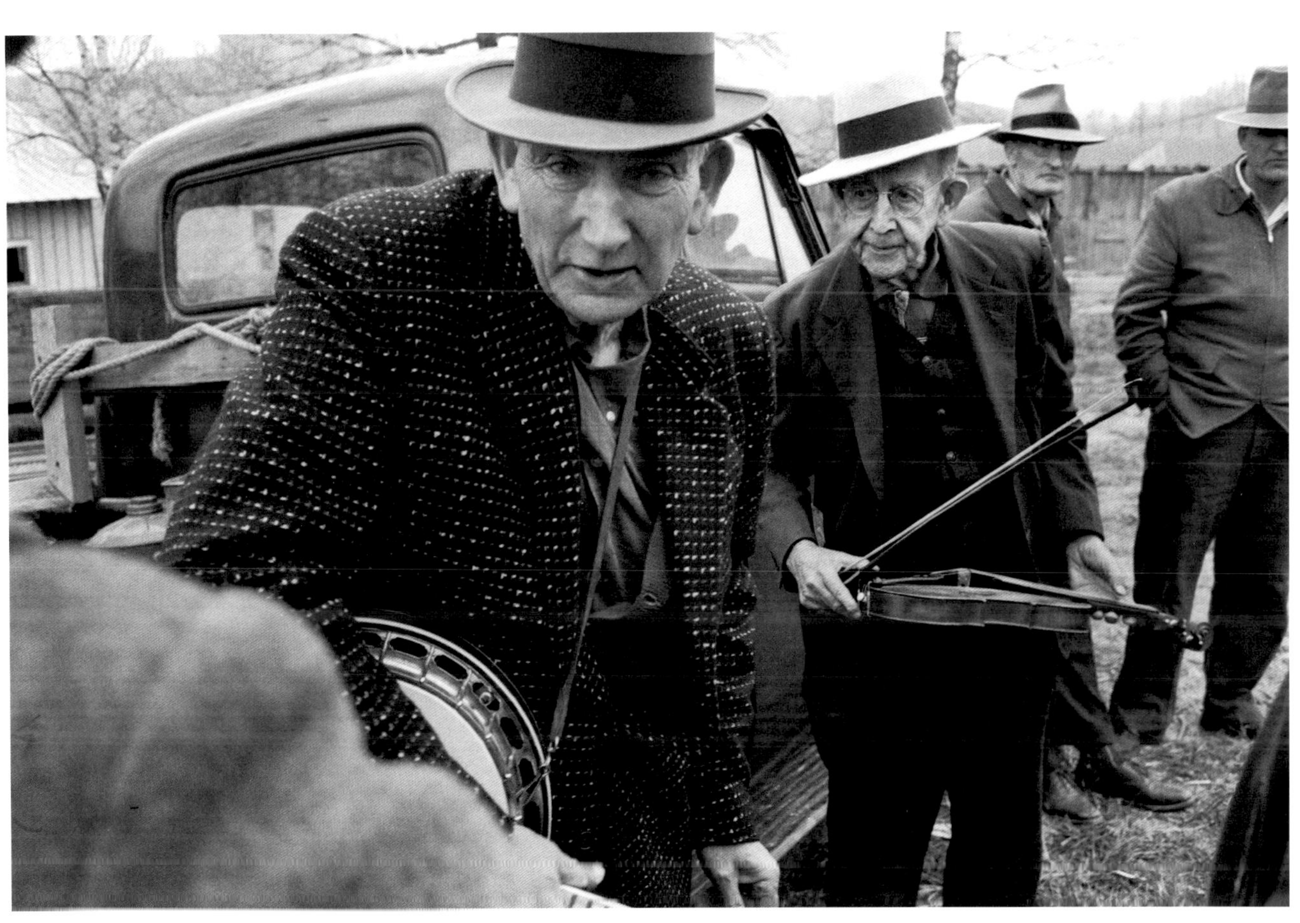

← Sign, Hazard, Kentucky, 1959

↑ Wade Ward and Charlie Higgins, Galax, Virginia, 1961

COLLECTING I'd heard a terrific fiddle recording done by Eck Robertson in the early 1920s and jumped at the report that he might still be alive. In 1963 I drove to Amarillo, Texas and found him there, making his living tuning pianos. We made recordings of his fiddling and listened to his fabulous stories. He told of his life in vivid detail and it struck me that the flow of his memories would overwhelm a tape recorder, burn out the tubes and stop the motors. Like John Henry, the man wins over the machine.

Eck had done heroic things: confident and proud of his fiddling, he travelled from Texas to New York to present himself at the Victor Record company, requesting that they record him. In 1922 this was unprecedented; up till that moment there had been no recordings by an American country artist. Victor accepted his music and he made the very first country music record.

Earlier in the century, he'd learned that the champion fiddler from the St. Louis Exposition was going to perform in Oklahoma. So Eck set out with horse and wagon to cross Texas to hear this musician. But after travelling hundreds of miles, a flooded river prevented him from crossing, and he missed the performance. I was amazed to realize the extremes he went to in pursuit of excellent music. He used to play his fiddle in theaters for early silent movies. Since there were so many cowboy pictures, he decided to dress as a cowboy himself, and claims to have been the first country musician to wear Western gear.

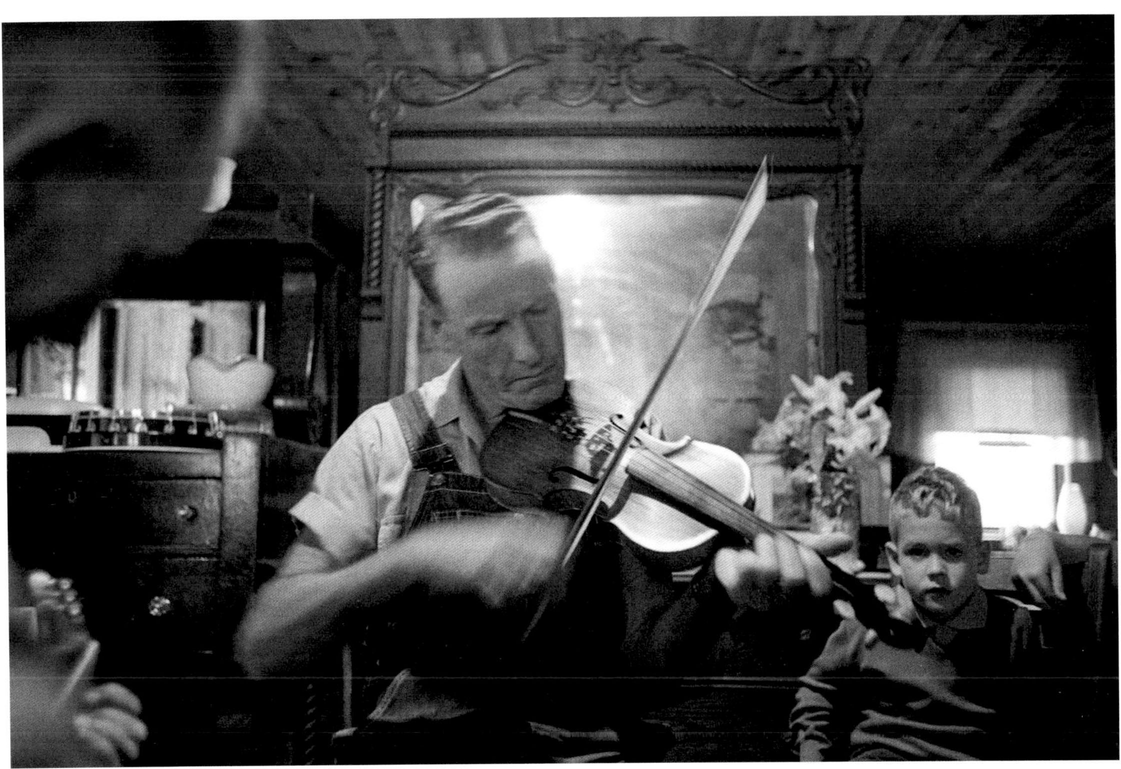

Old Time Fiddling was not much appreciated in the realm of the folk revival of the 1960s. But in a Georgia newspaper clipping from 1917 I read a description of a local fiddlers contest in which the contestants were allowed to play for awhile onstage in order to get "warmed up." They would be judged only on the performance which followed the warm-up. One old guy became so involved in his playing that they had to carry him off stage still fiddling away. He was so wound up in his "competition" tune that he couldn't stop.

Before there were bluegrass festivals, that kind of rural music was heard mostly at country parks, in bars, and in early morning (5 am) radio shows that farmers listened to before doing their chores. Bill Monroe, the creator of bluegrass, performed on the courthouse steps for coal miners in Hazard, Kentucky. I filmed and photographed him there.

This involvement with the music became my agenda, the focus of all my work. Photographing became another way to take part in the music. While we documented the sound of Old Time musicians, fiddlers, and bluegrass artists, the camera gave me a way to make a visual record. Some of my photographs of musicians were used on record covers. They became a moveable exhibition of my work.

↑ North Georgia, 1967

→ Old Fiddlers Contest, Galax, Virginia, 1962

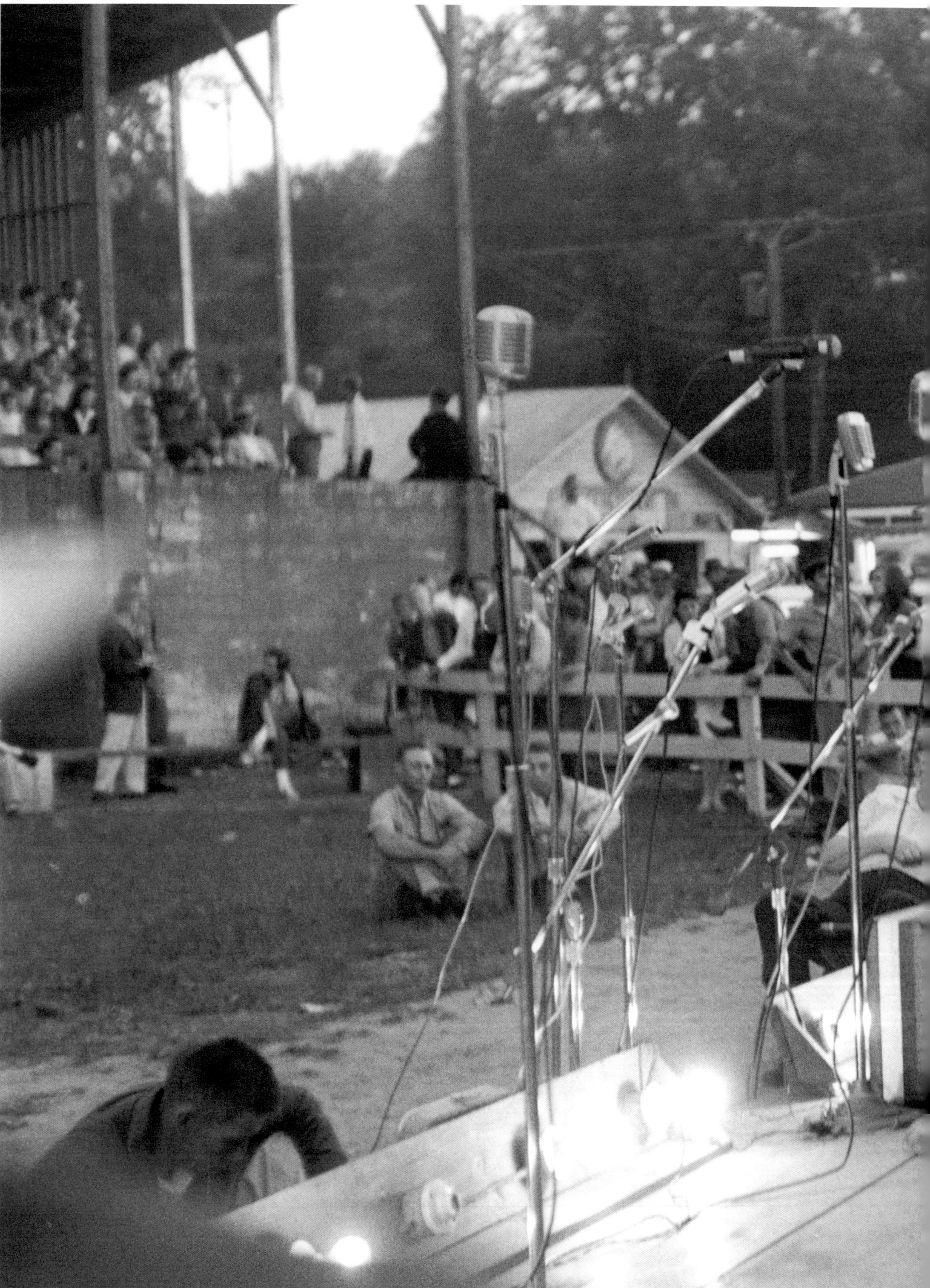

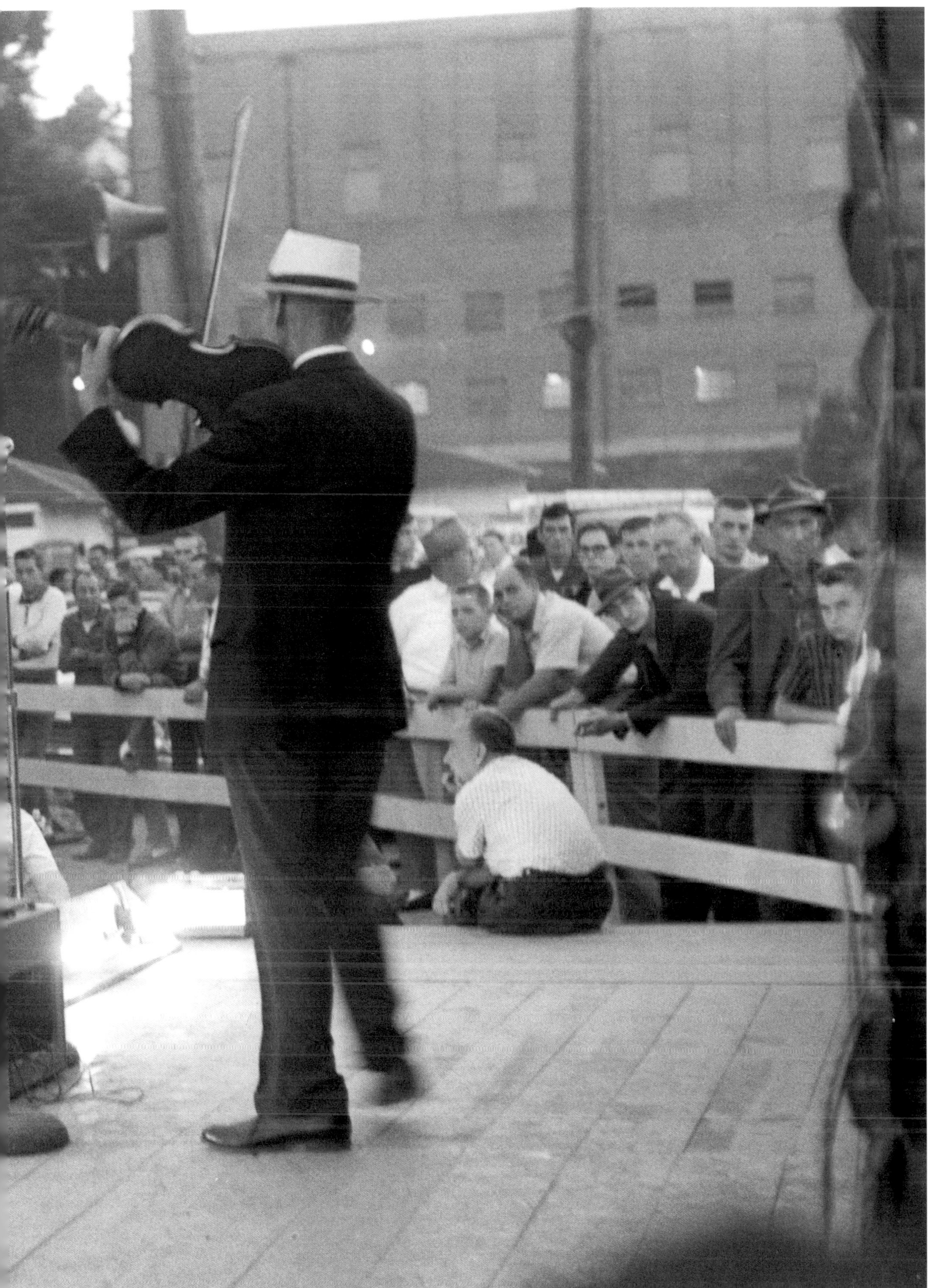

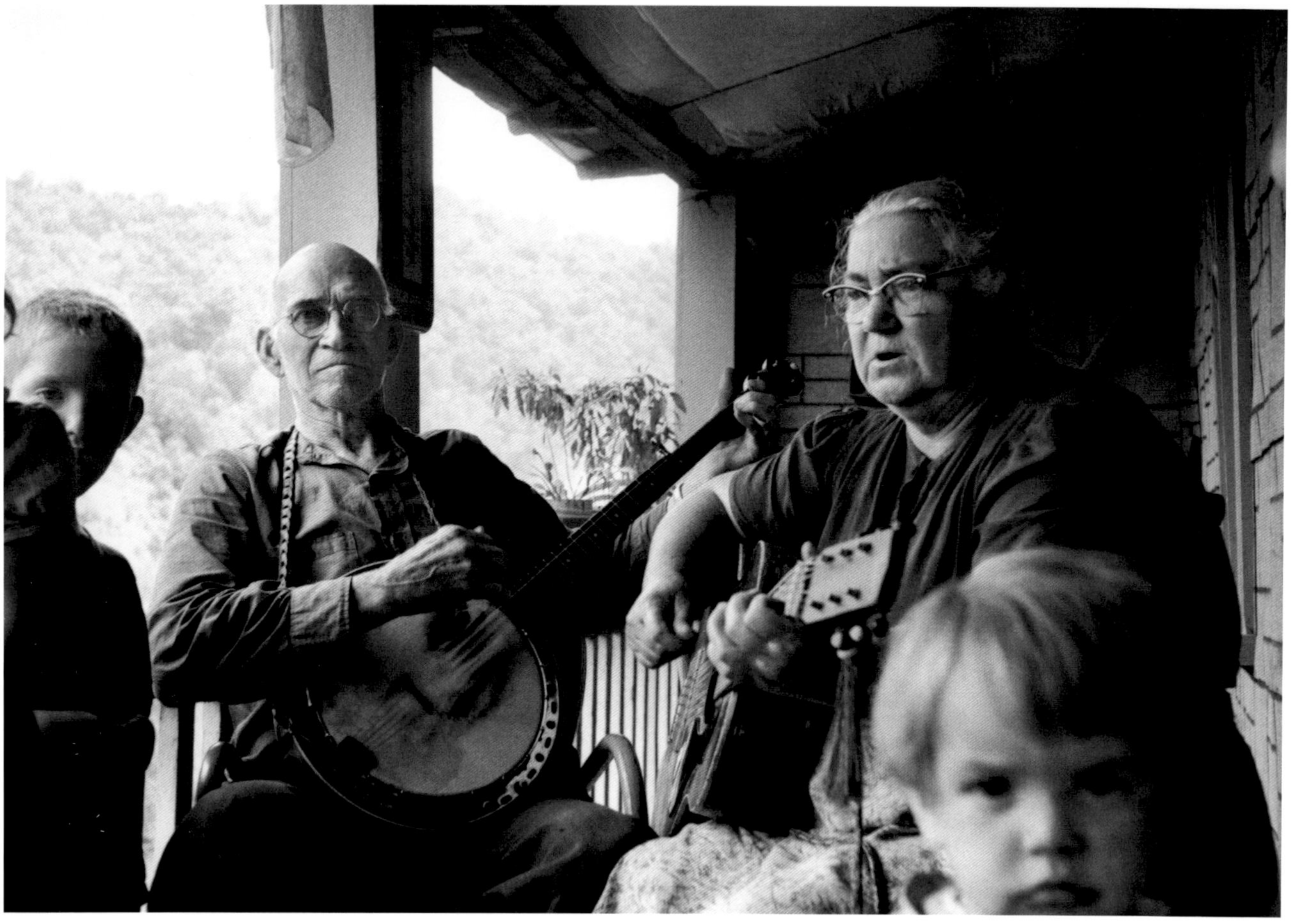

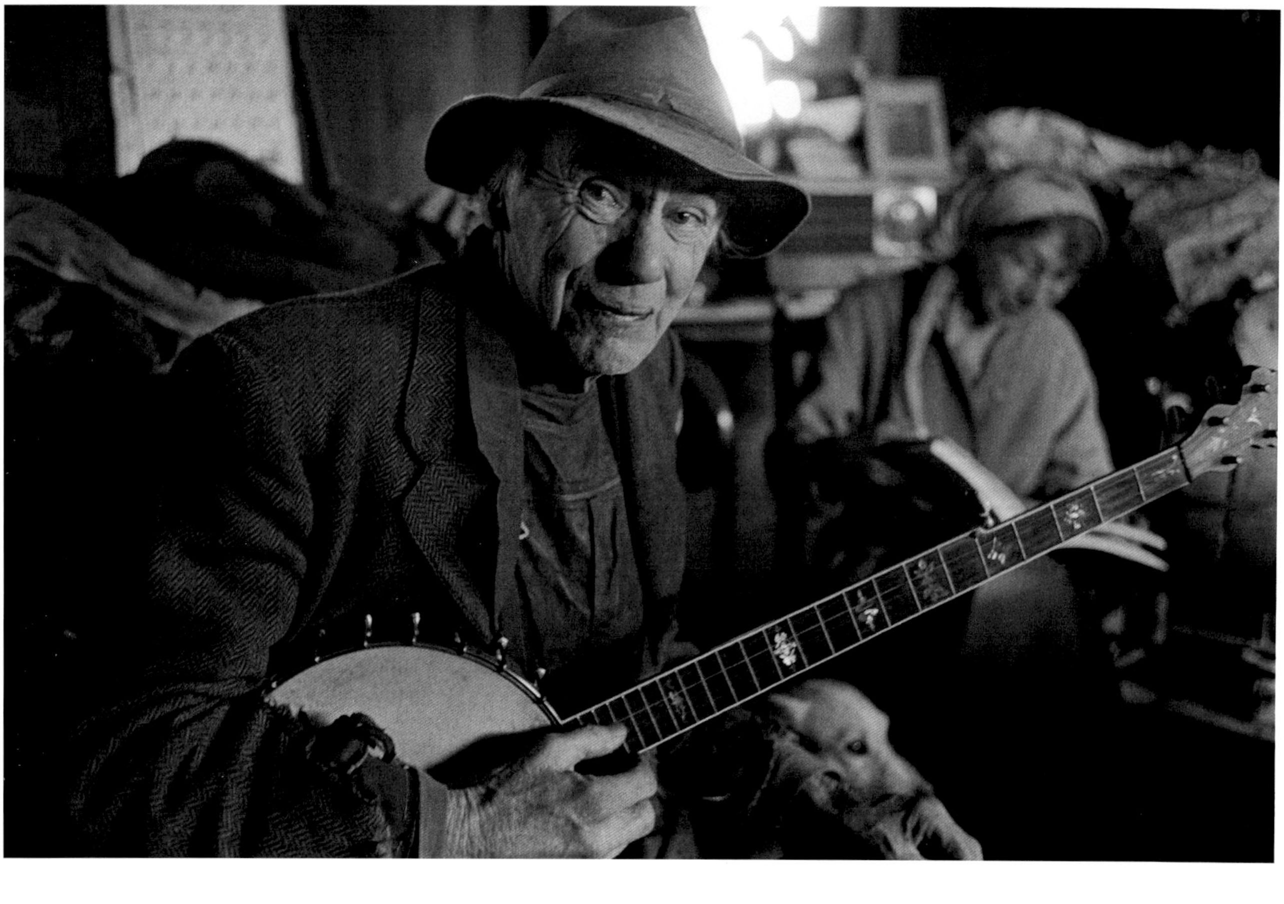

↑ (top) Mr. and Mrs. Sams, Combs, Kentucky, 1959; (bottom) Sidna Myers, Hillsville, Virginia, 1965

→ Eck Robertson, Amarillo, Texas, 1963

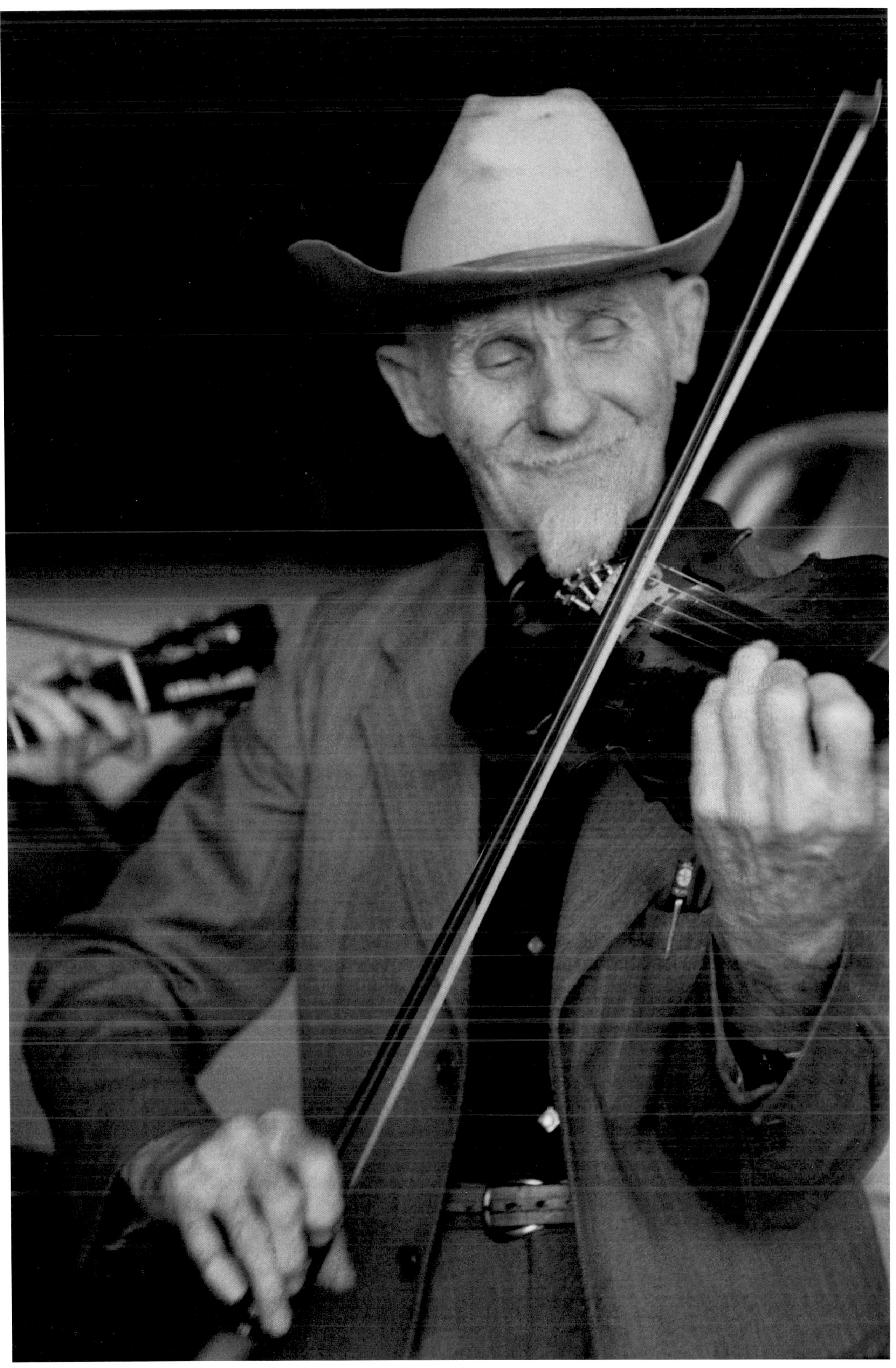

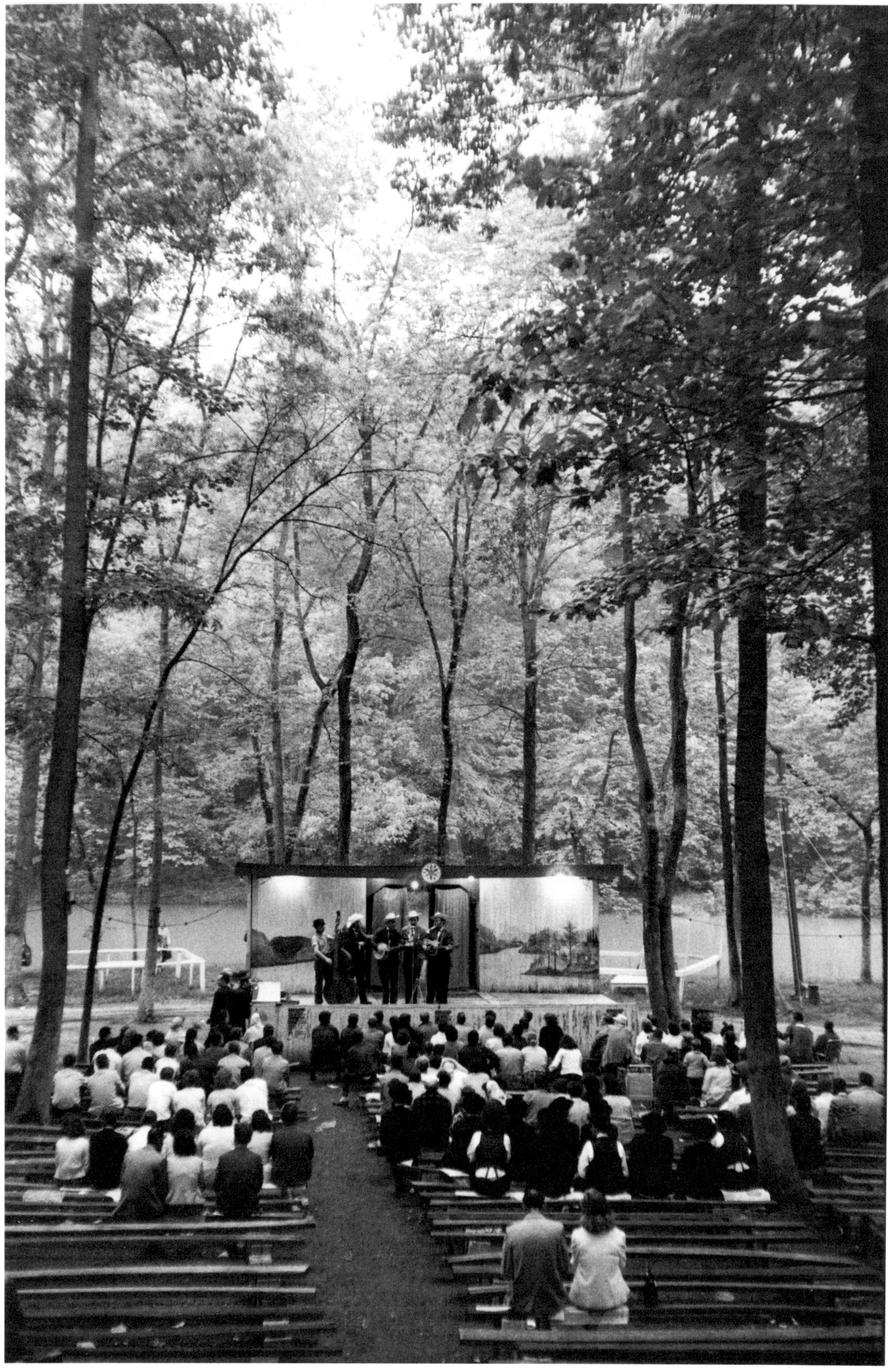

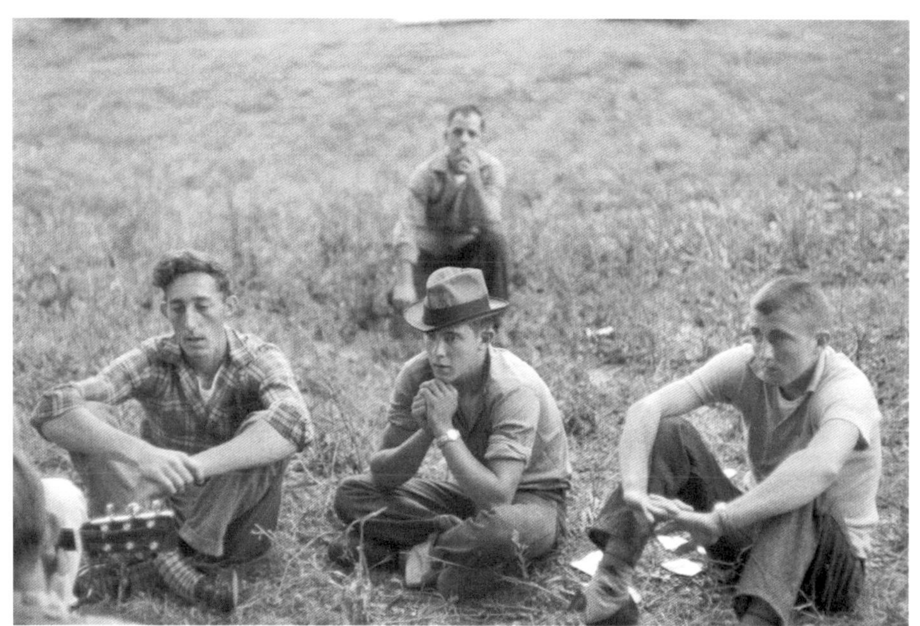

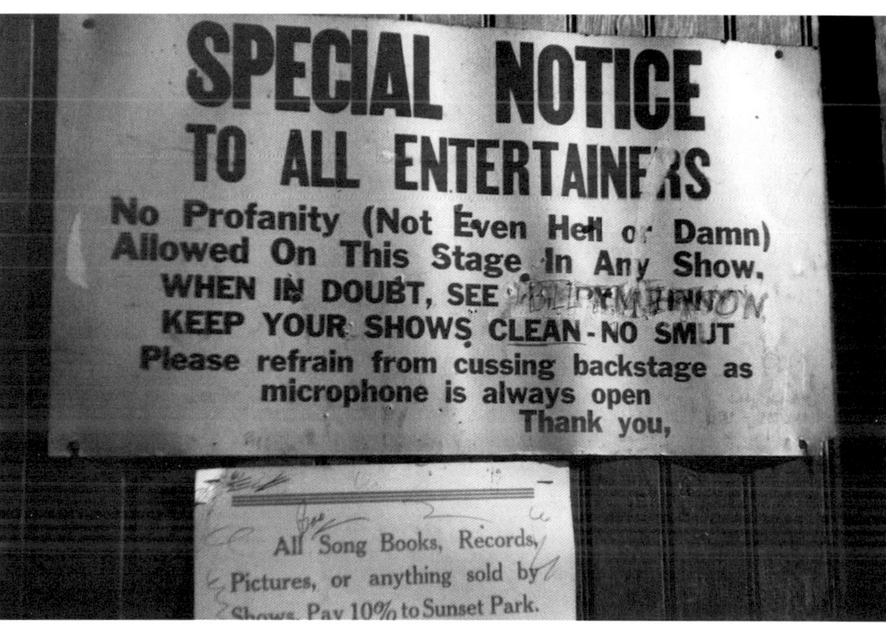

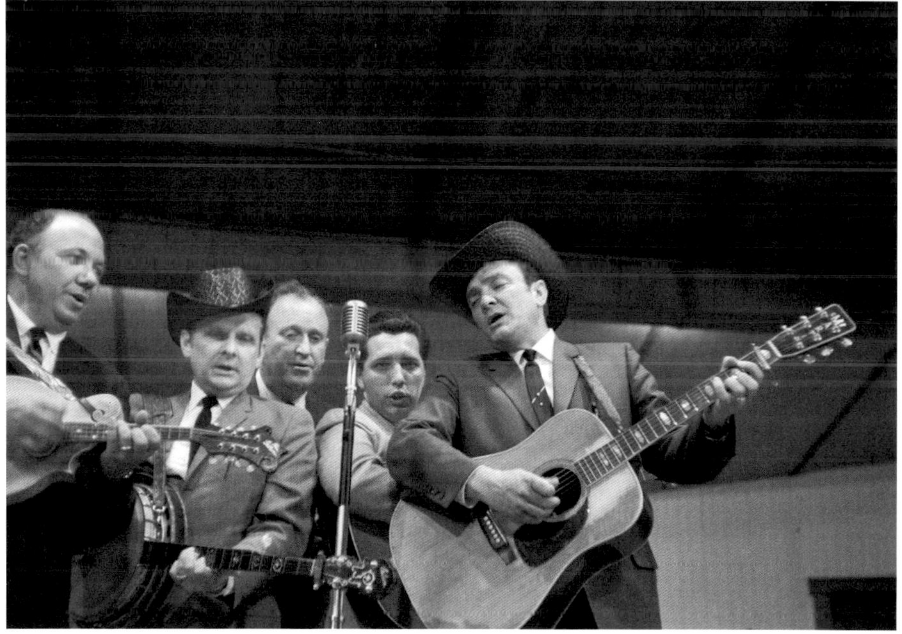

← Flatt and Scruggs, New River Ranch, Maryland, 1961

→ (top) Parking lot audience, Galax, Virginia, 1962

→ (middle) Backstage, Sunset Park, Maryland, 1961

→ (bottom) The Stanley Brothers, 1961

→ Bill Monroe and his Blue Grass Boys, Hazard, Kentucky, 1962

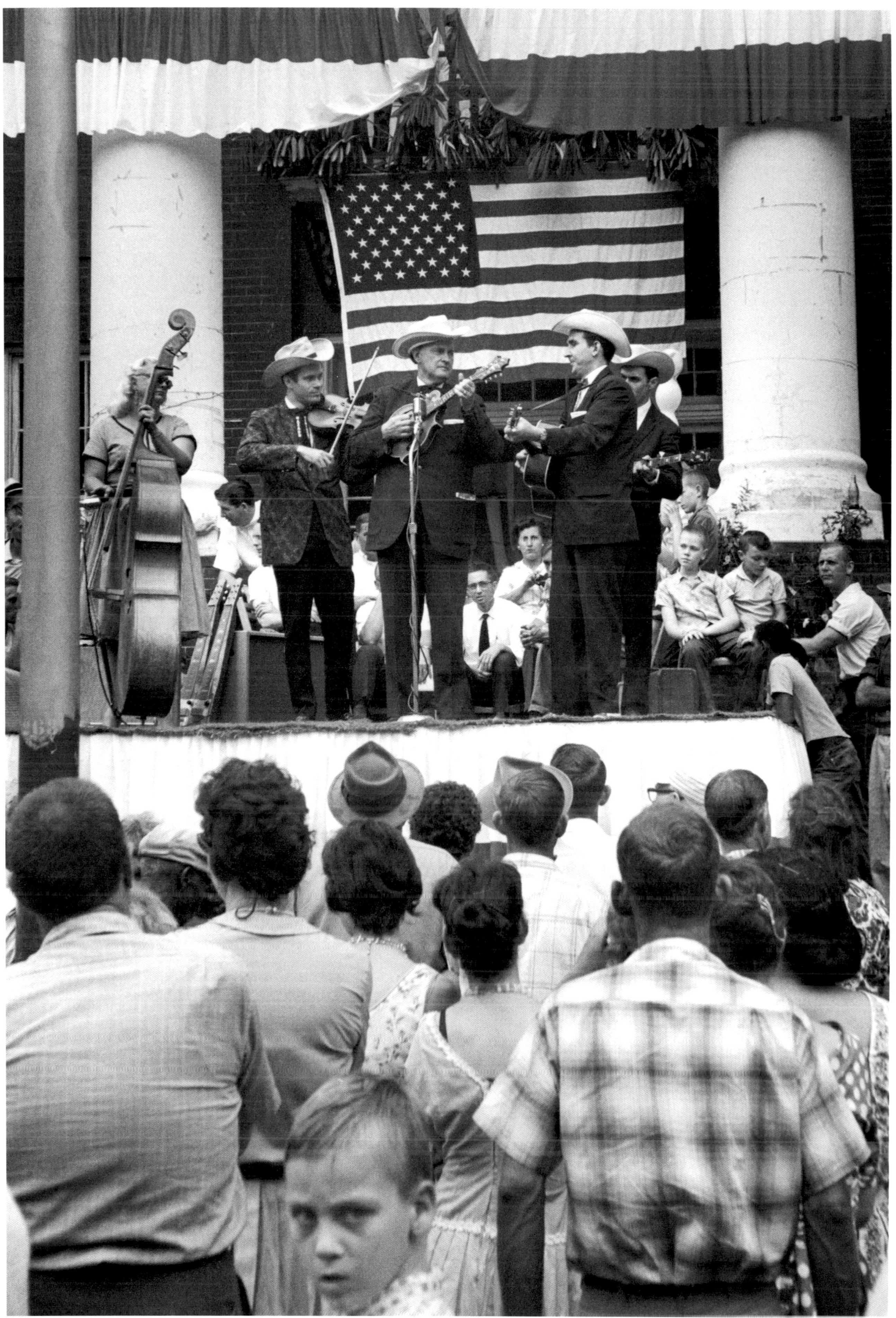

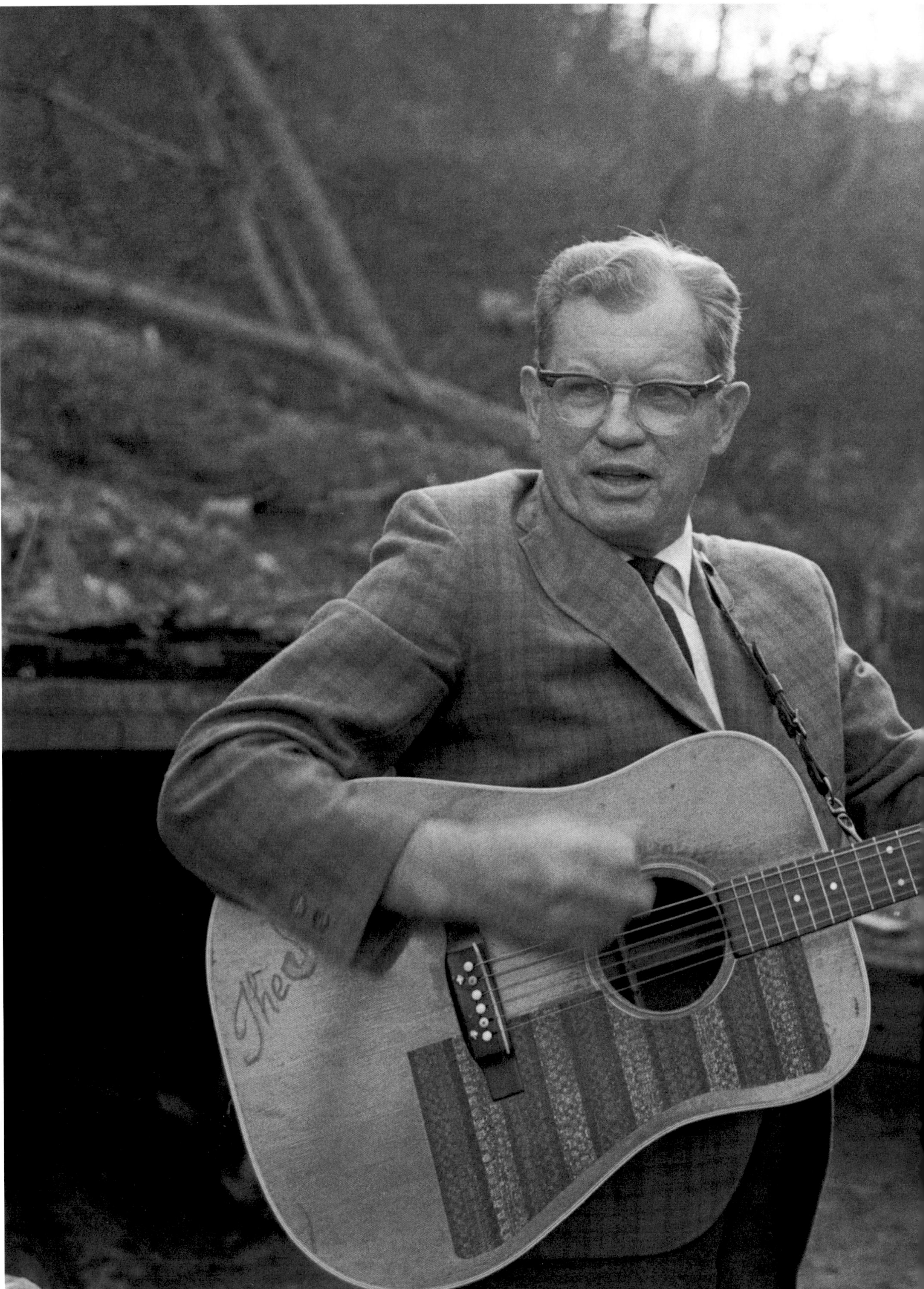
The

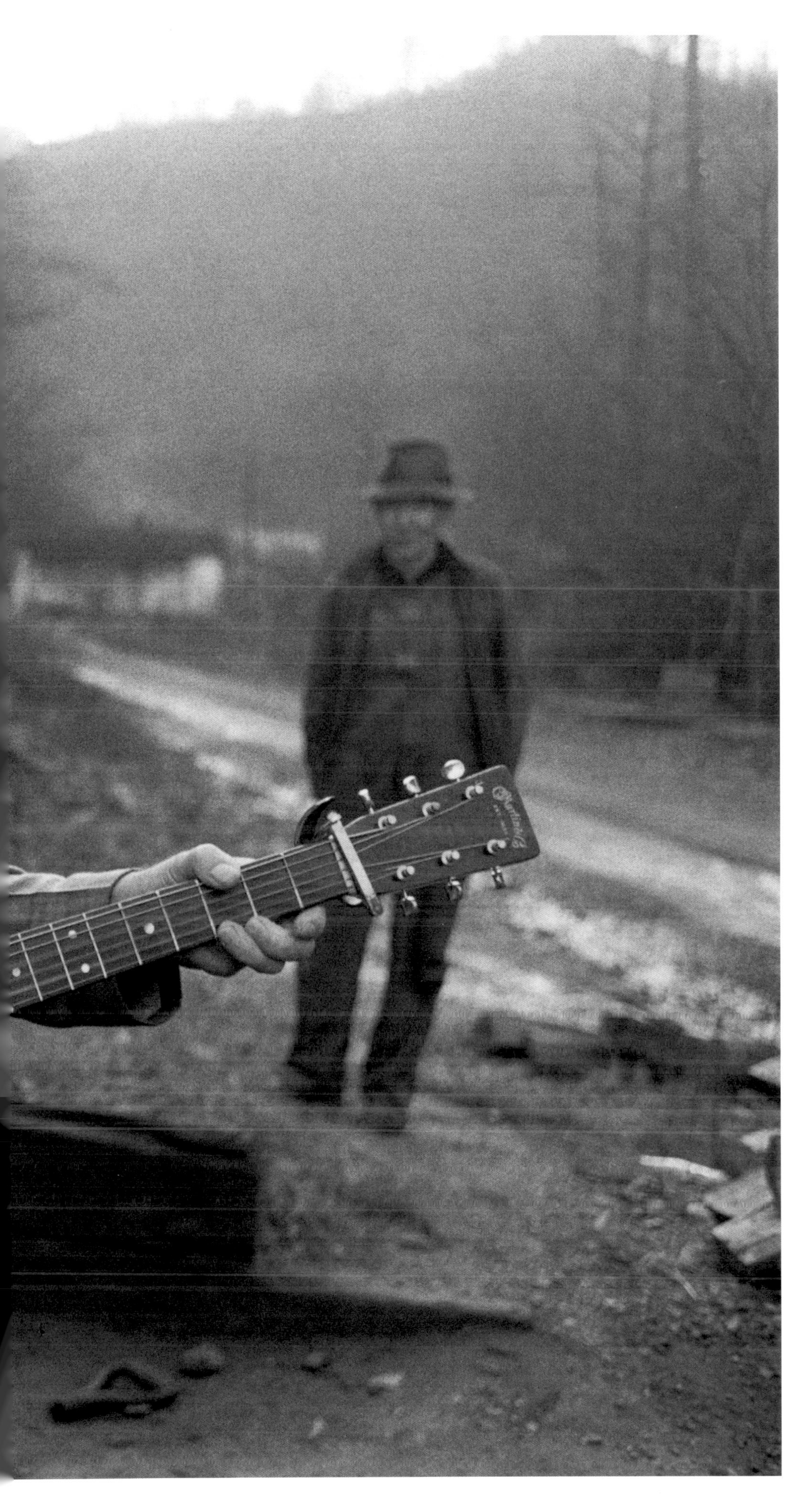

George Davis, "The Singing Miner,"
Lothair, Kentucky, 1968

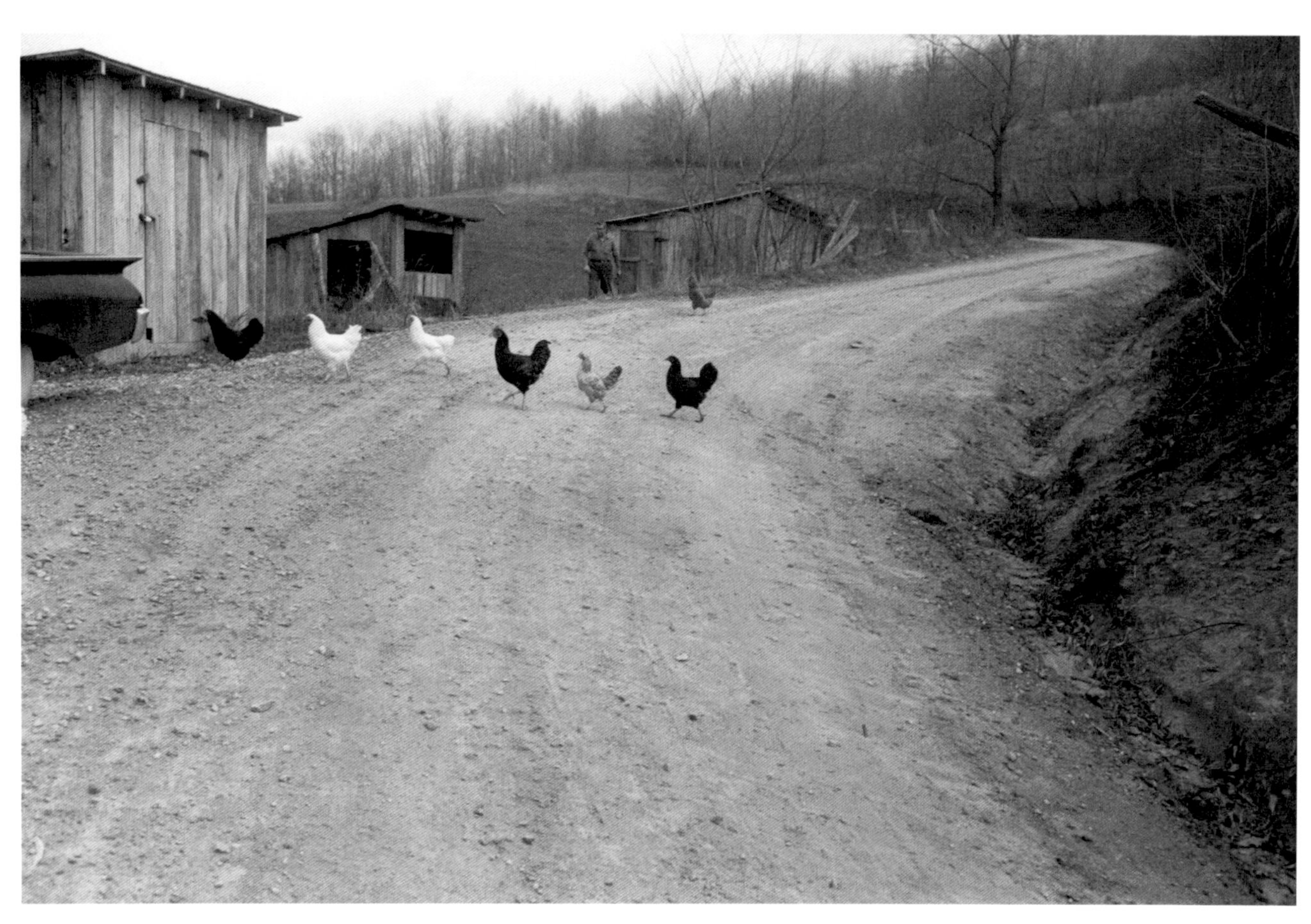

↑ At E.C. Ball's, Rugby, Virginia, 1965

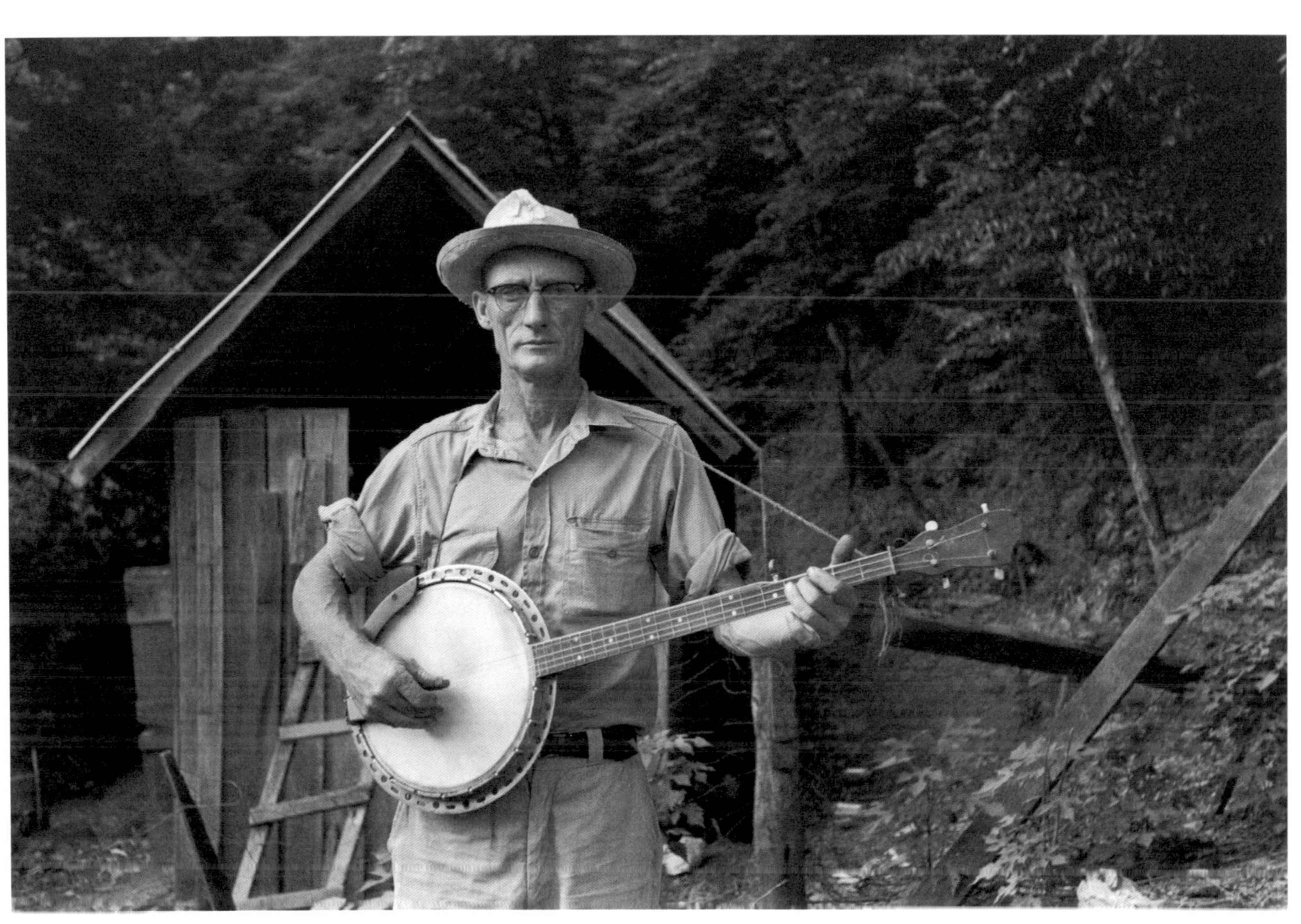

↑ Roscoe Holcomb, Daisy, Kentucky, 1959

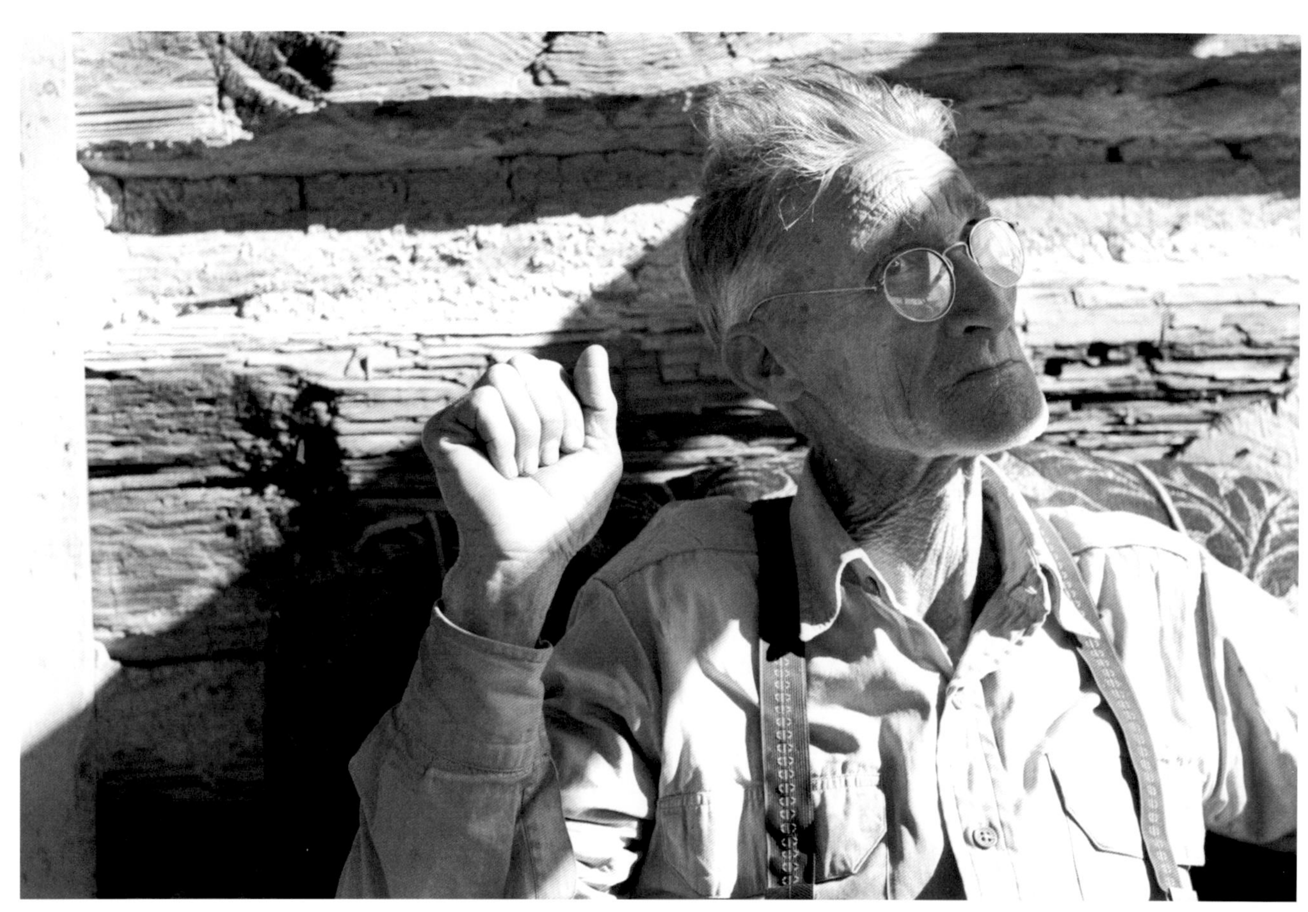

↑ Lloyd Chandler, Sodom, North Carolina, 1965

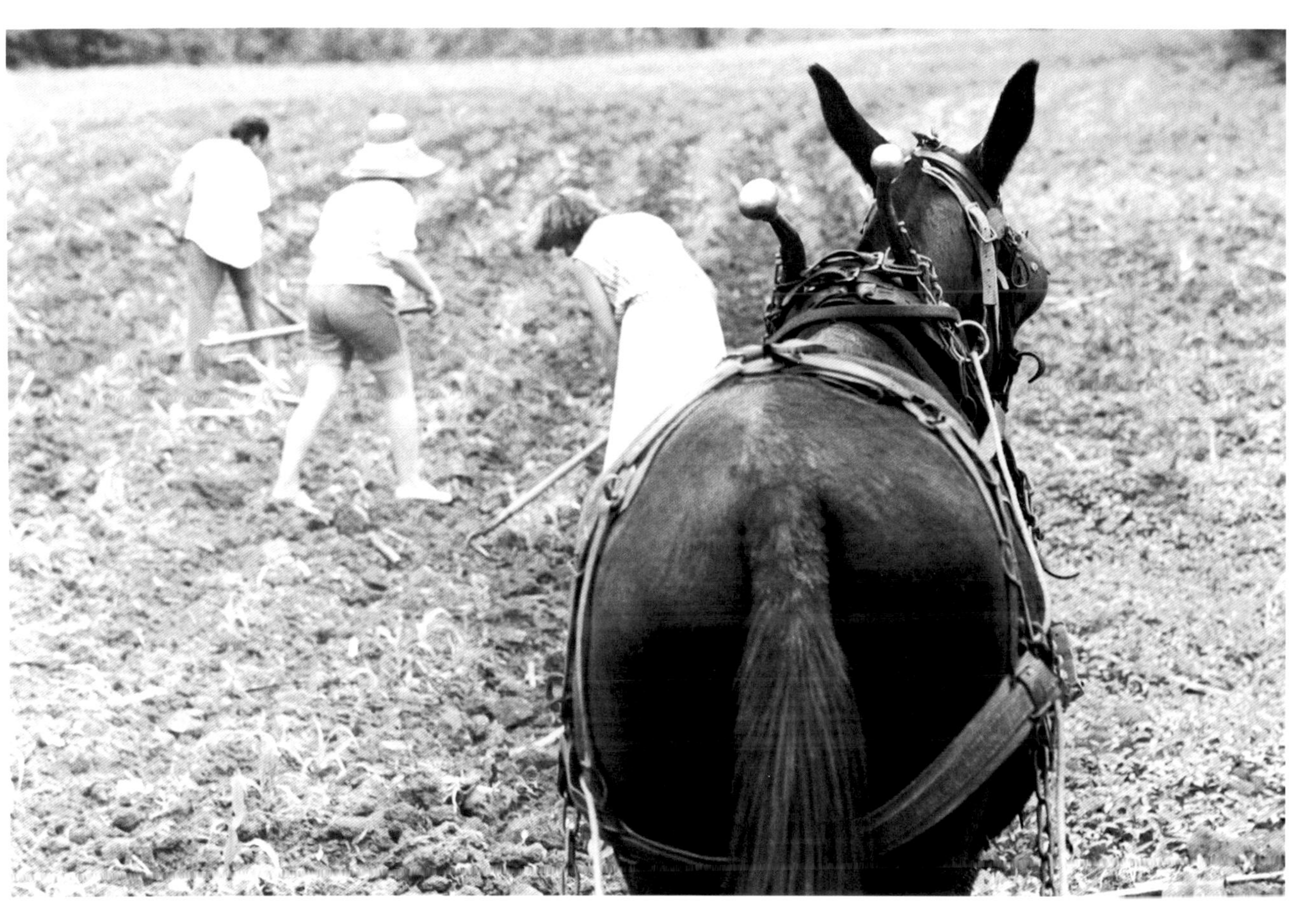

↑ Jeff, Kentucky, 1959

⇉ Holiness church service in a house, Daisy, Kentucky, 1962

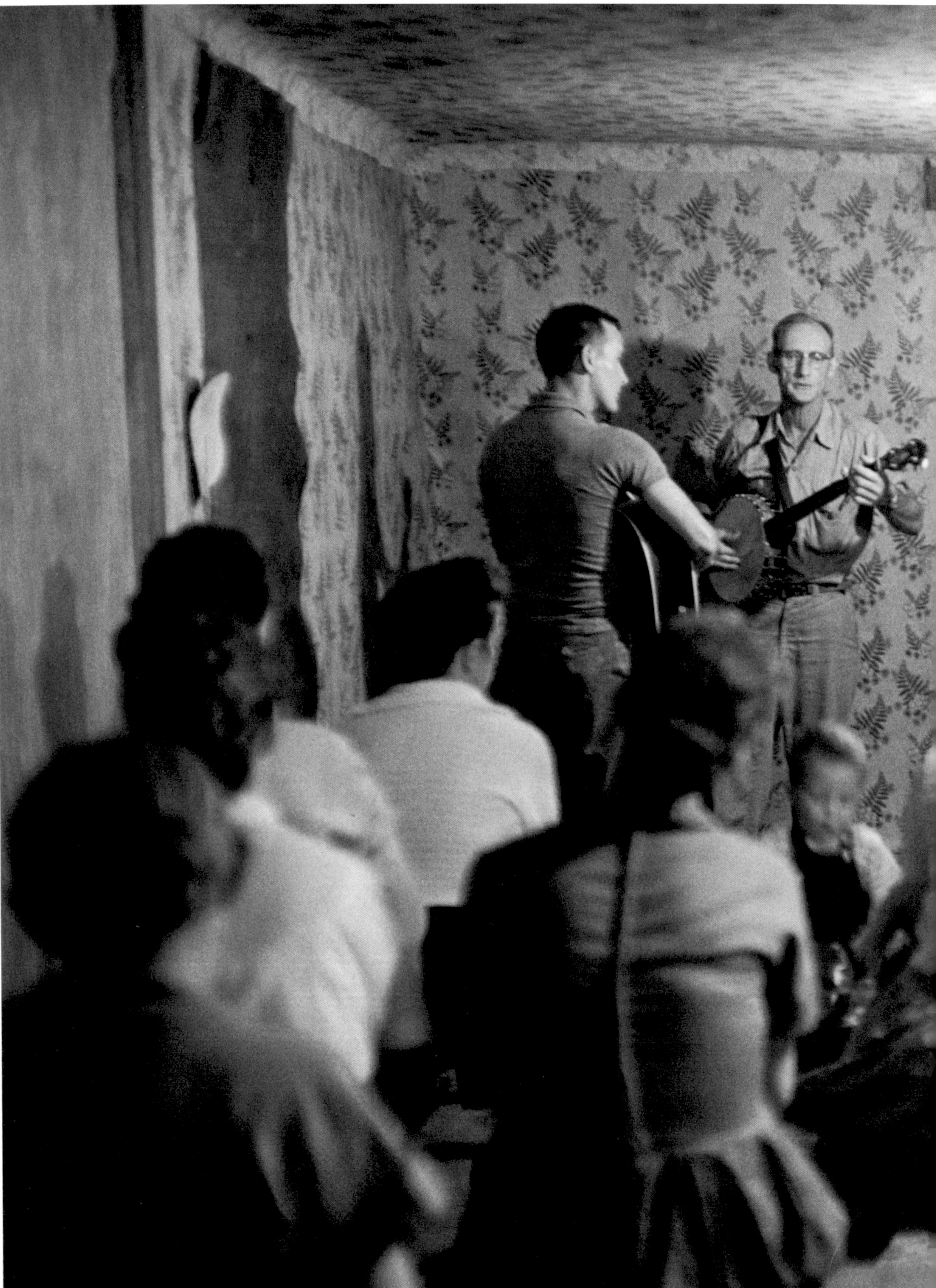

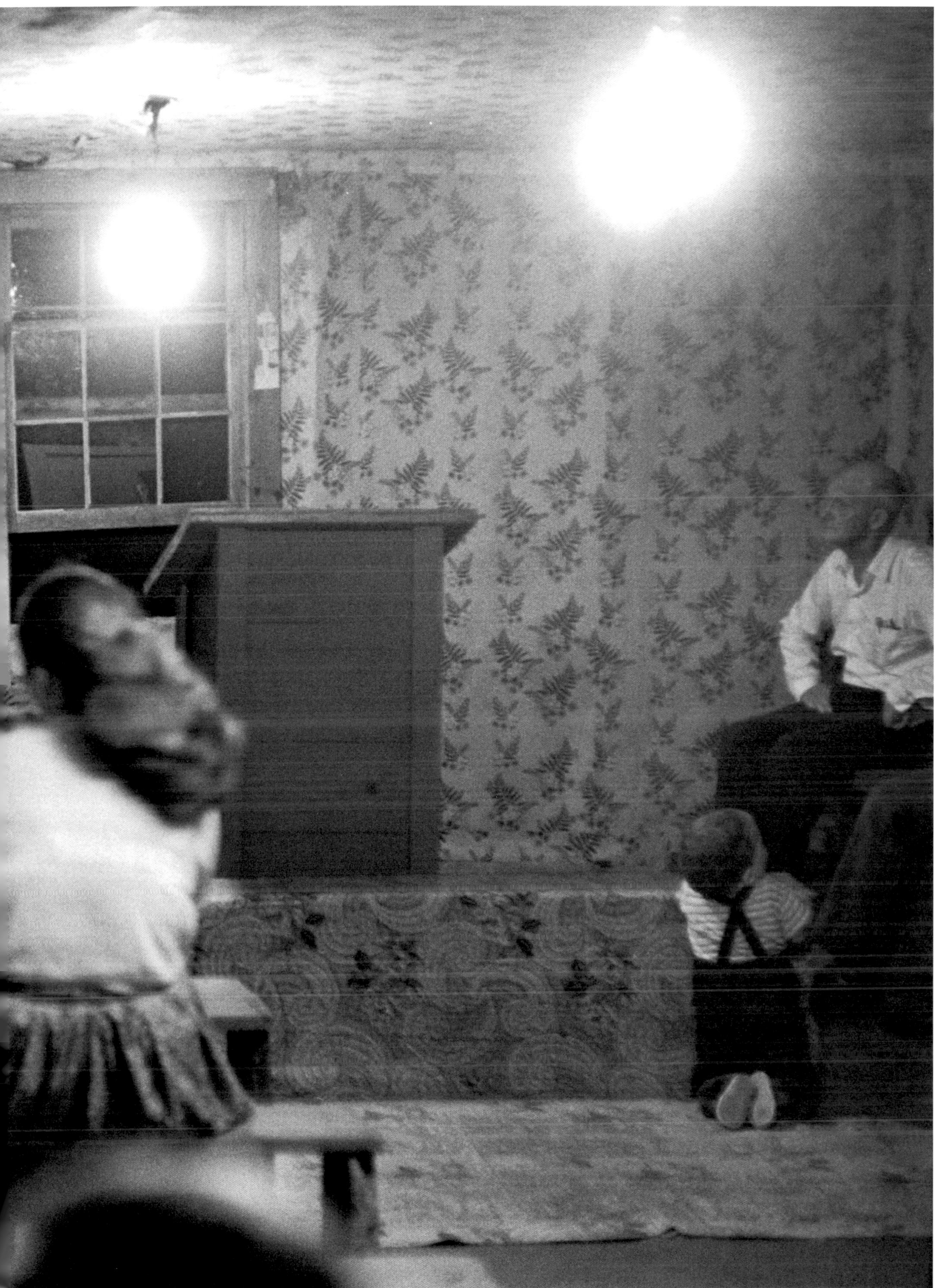

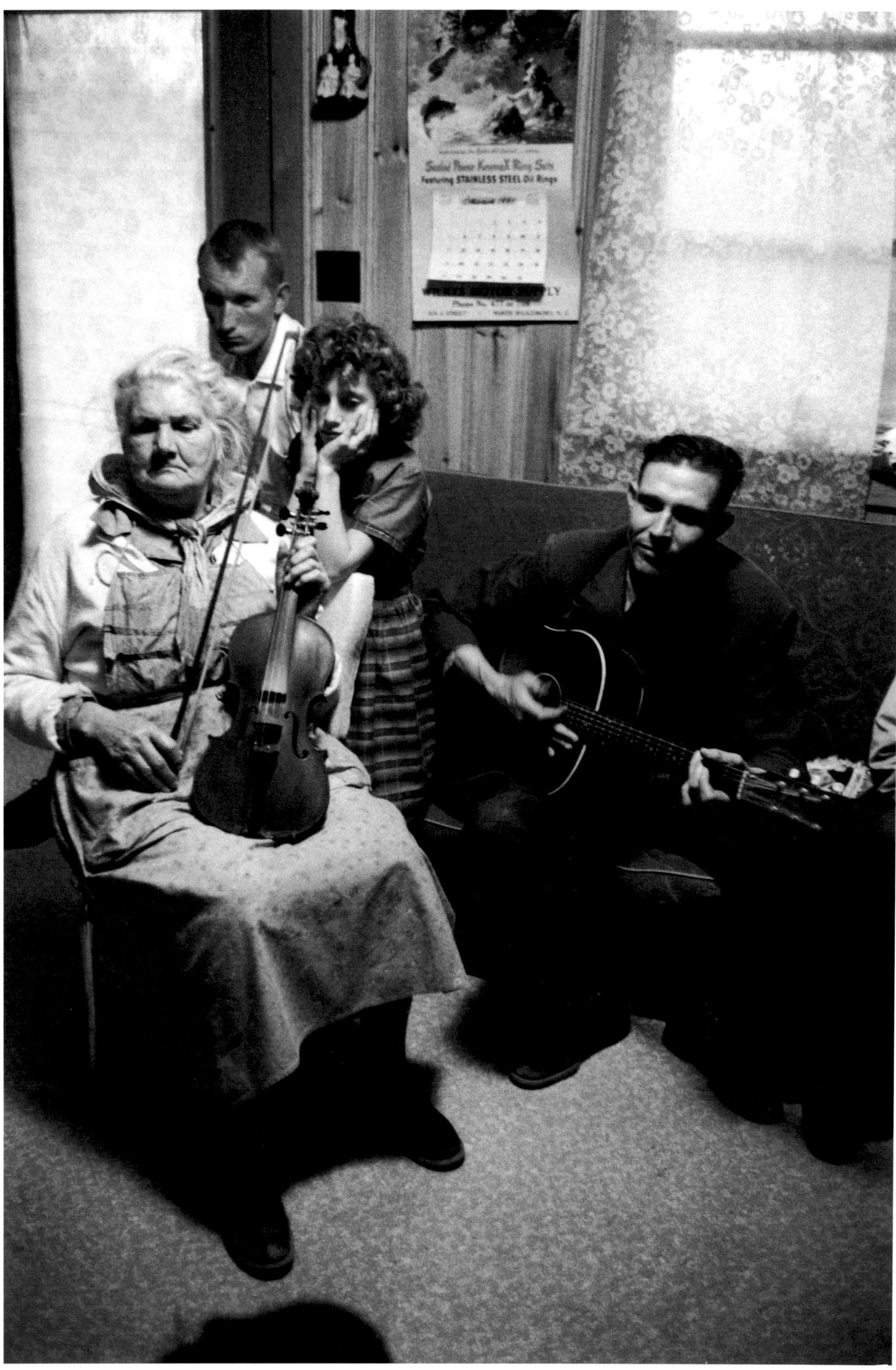
Featuring STAINLESS STEEL Oil Rings

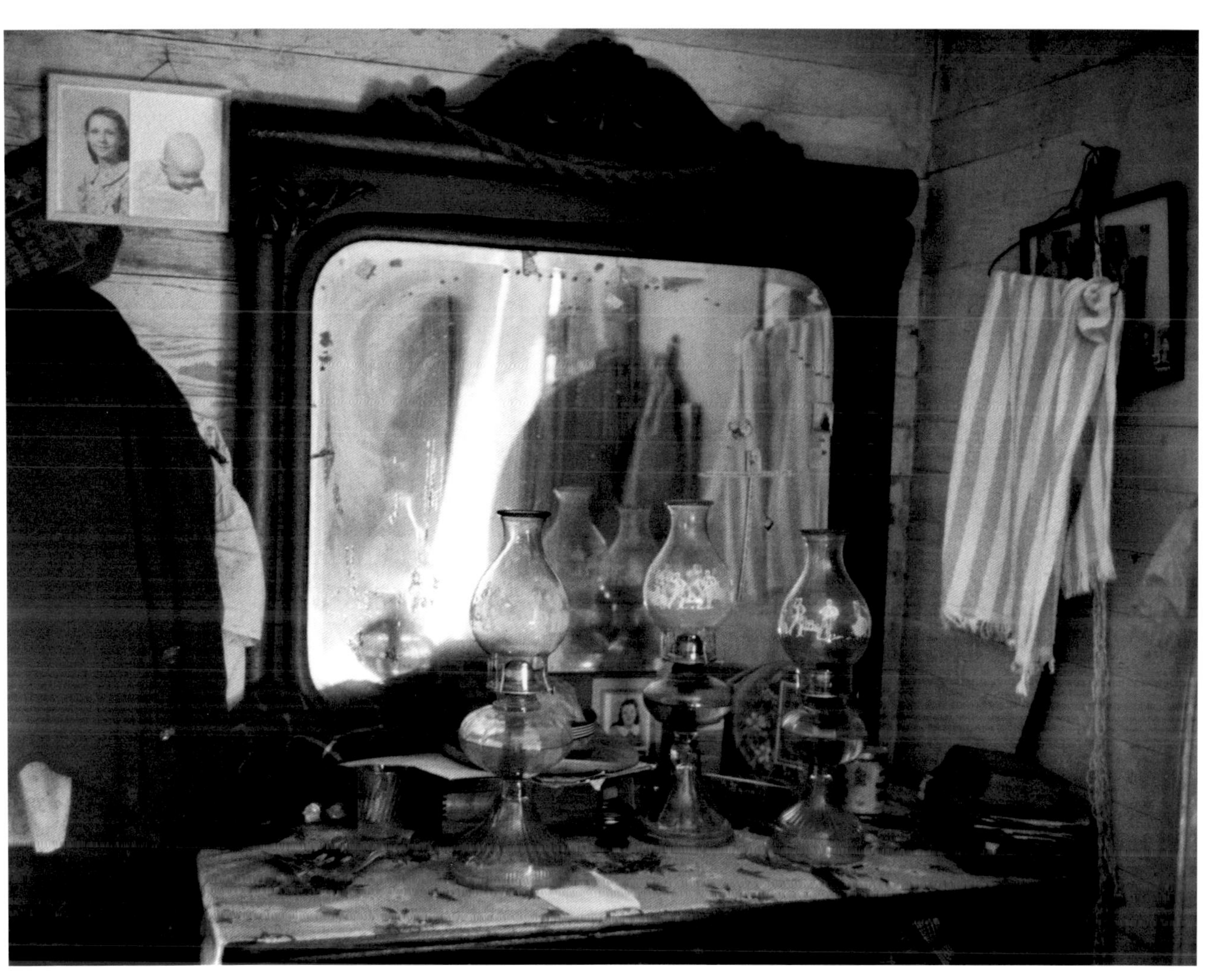

← Grandma Pearly Davis, Roaring River, North Carolina, 1961

↑ Pearly Davis' home, North Carolina, 1961

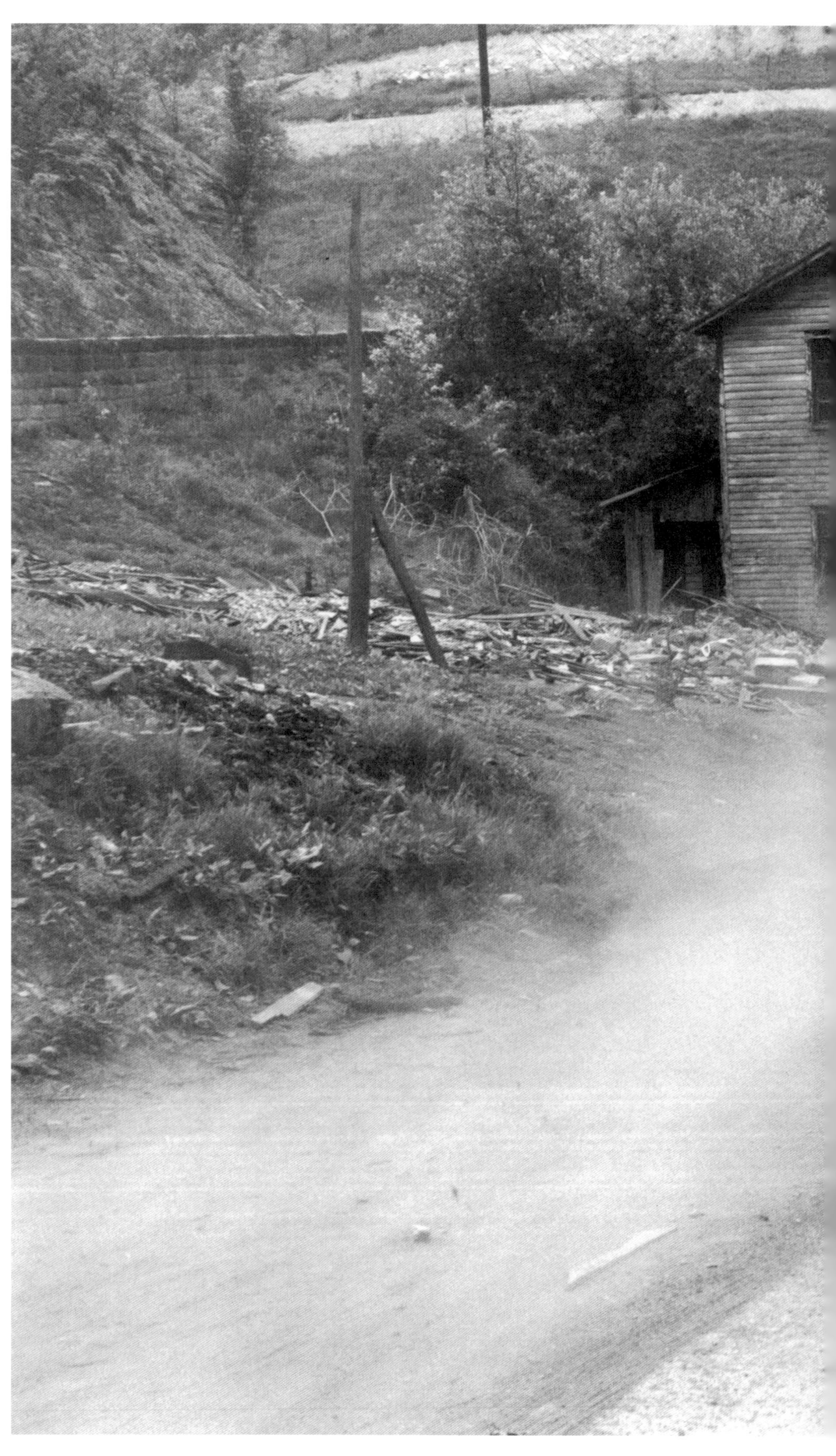

Vicco, Kentucky, 1959

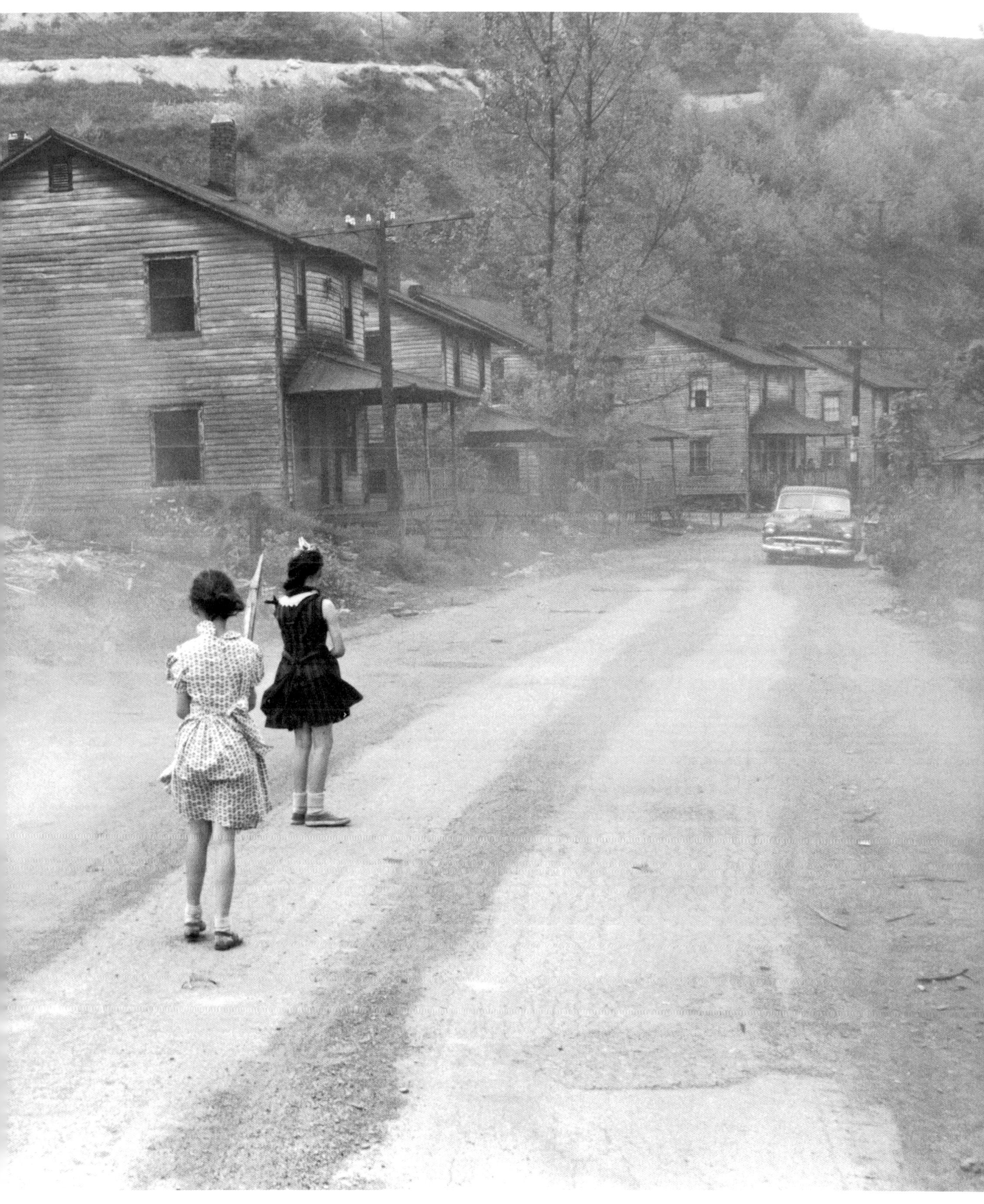

TO REVIVE US AGAIN We were engaged in a struggle for the image of American music. Ralph Rinzler, Israel Young, and myself founded the Friends of Old Time Music to put on concerts by traditional artists in New York City. This was our response to the commercial music industry which had sprung up around the folksong revival. We knew that if people could experience the real thing in all its complexity, they would see beyond the mass marketed entertainment which dominated the airwaves at that time. So we presented the first concerts of Roscoe Holcomb, Clarence Ashley, Doc Watson, Dock Boggs, Mississippi John Hurt, Gus Cannon, the Stanley Brothers, Bill Monroe, and many others. Next, Ralph Rinzler brought this message to the Newport Folk Festival and eventually to the Smithsonian Festival of American Folklife, which has been held annually on the mall in Washington, D.C. for almost thirty years.

Shortly after Bob Dylan's arrival in New York, making his own pilgrimage to Woody Guthrie, he asked me to do photographs of him. My loft and rooftop were the setting. There was no clear image of who Bob Dylan was, yet.

"...you are right john cohen—quazimoto was right—mozart was right...I cannot say the word eye anymore...when I speak this word eye, it is as if I am speaking of somebody's eye that I faintly remember...there is no eye—there is only a series of mouths—long live the mouths—your rooftop—if you don't already know—has been demolished." —Bob Dylan, "Highway 61 Revisited," 1965

In New York I'd often take an evening walk; my first stop was the Cedar Bar, final destination was The Folklore Center on MacDougal Street. Coffeehouses and "basket houses" were the venues for poetry readings and folk singers.

I felt a widening gap between the avant-garde artists in their studios and folksingers along MacDougal Street. The painters were into jazz which was performed at the Five Spot on the Bowery. The place was noisy and smoke-filled, and the customers talked over the music while the musicians played for each other. The Beat poets were also into jazz, but the coffeehouses where they recited were in the Village. They shared the spotlight with the guitar-picking folksingers.

→ Bob Dylan on my rooftop, Third Avenue, New York City, 1962

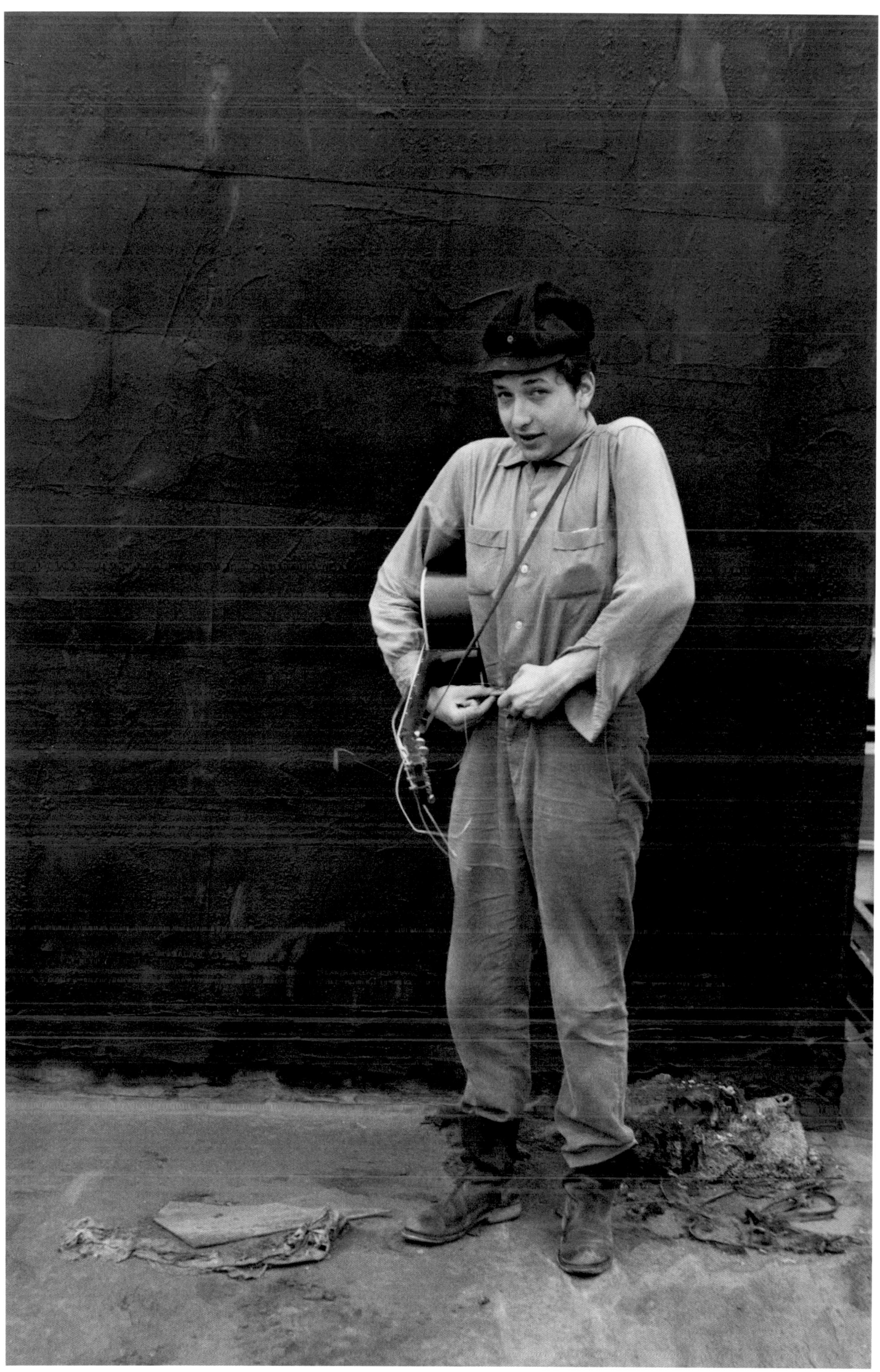

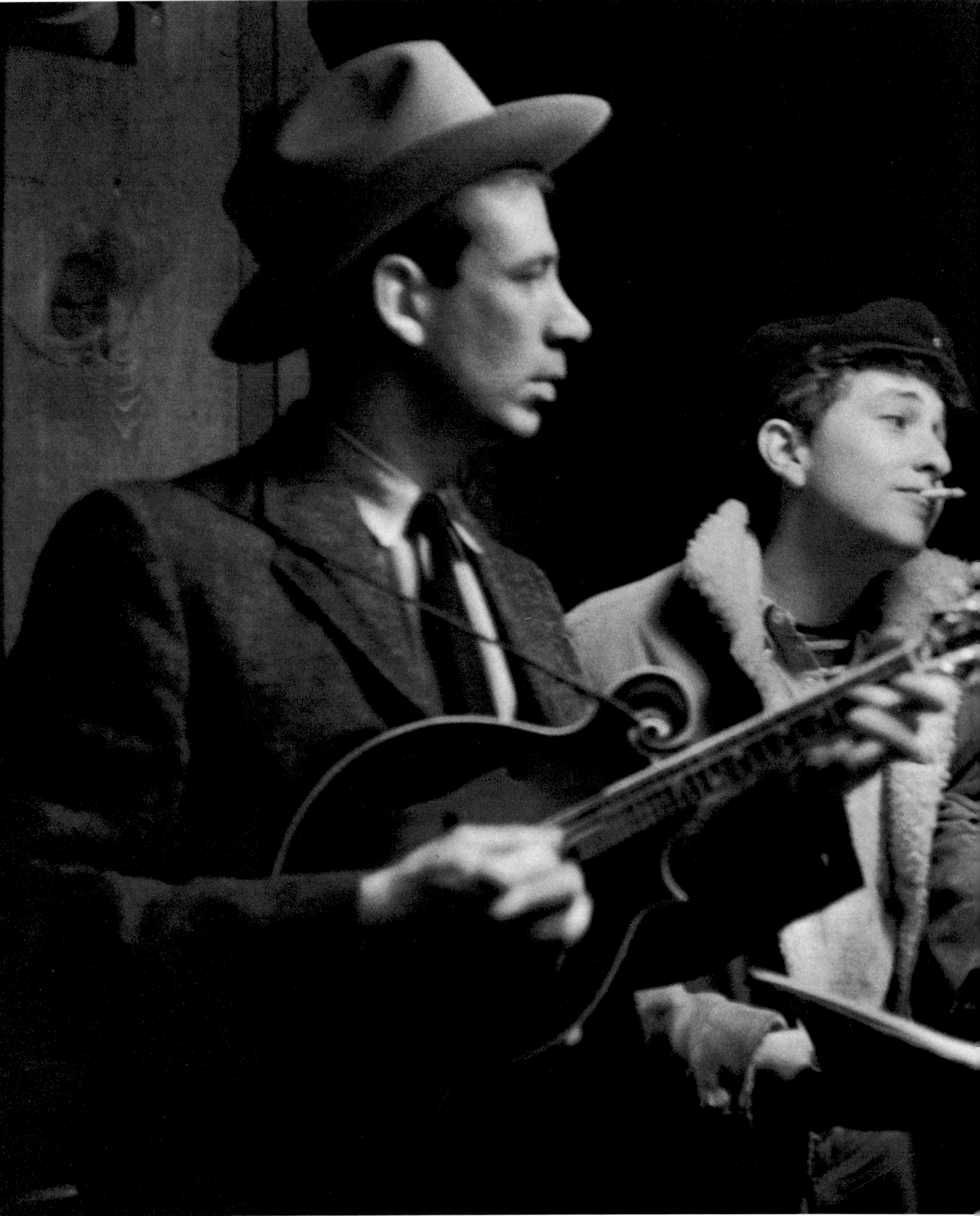

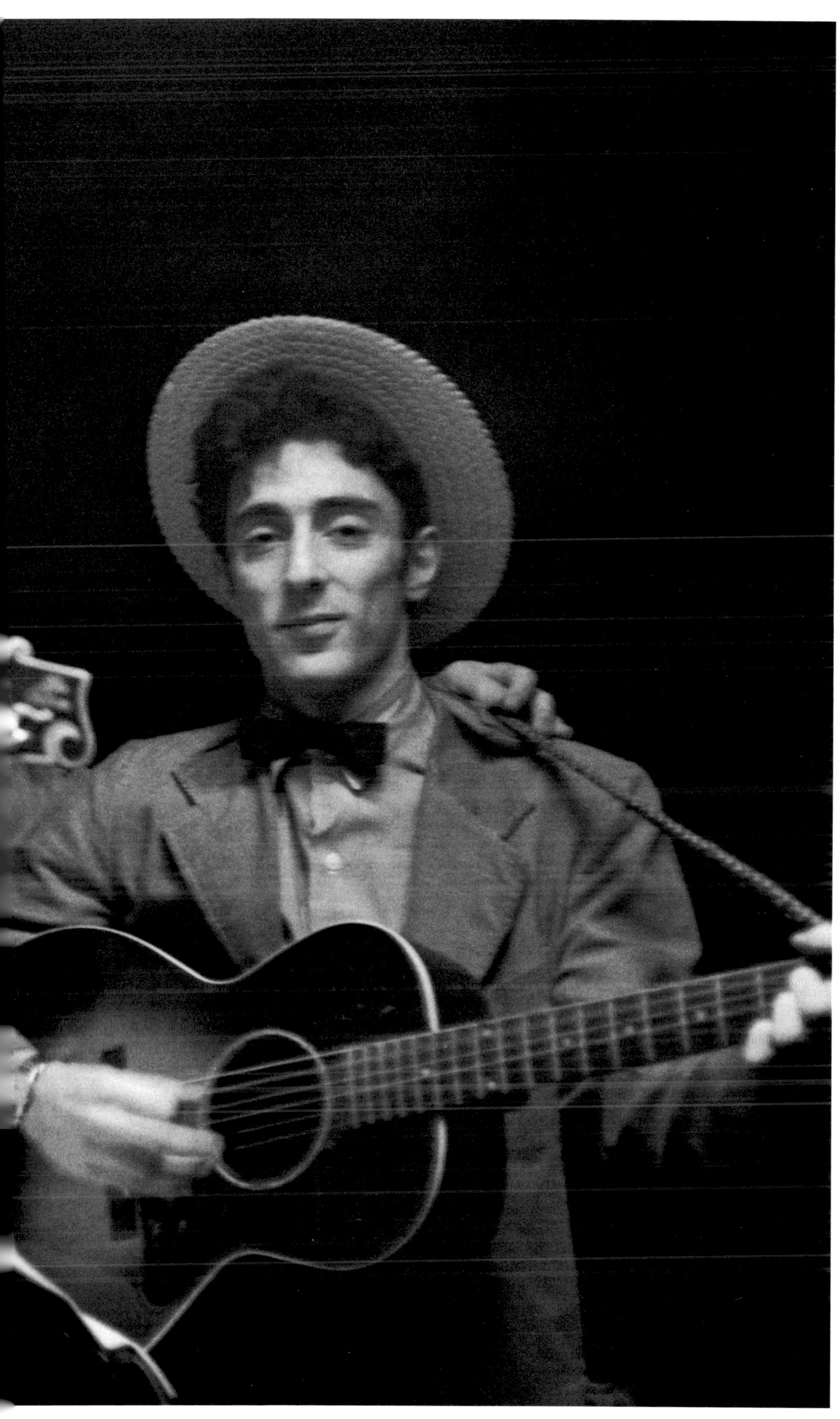

← Ralph Rinzler,
Bob Dylan, John Herald at the
Gaslight, New York City, 1962

→ Bob Dylan at my loft,
Third Avenue, 1962

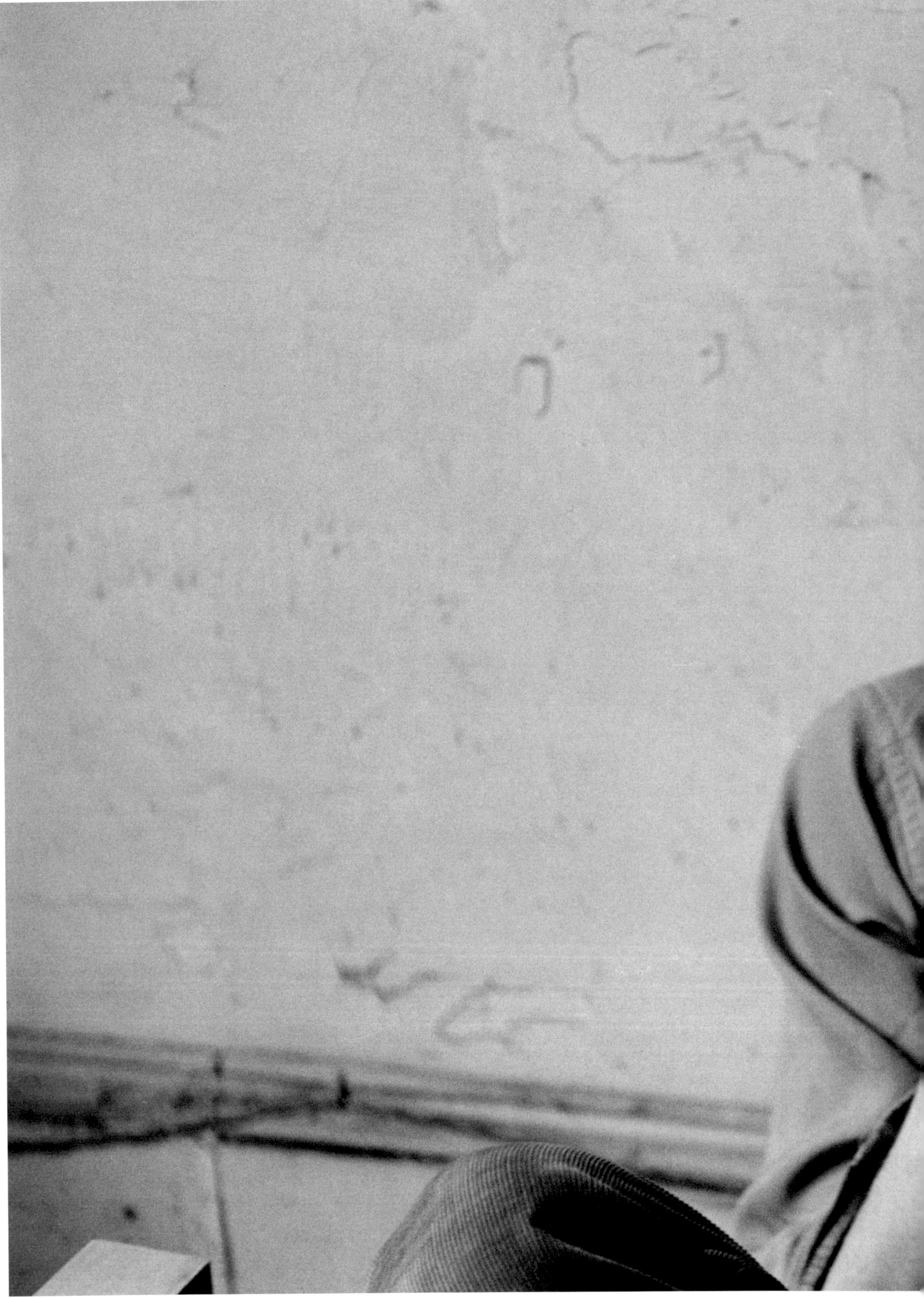

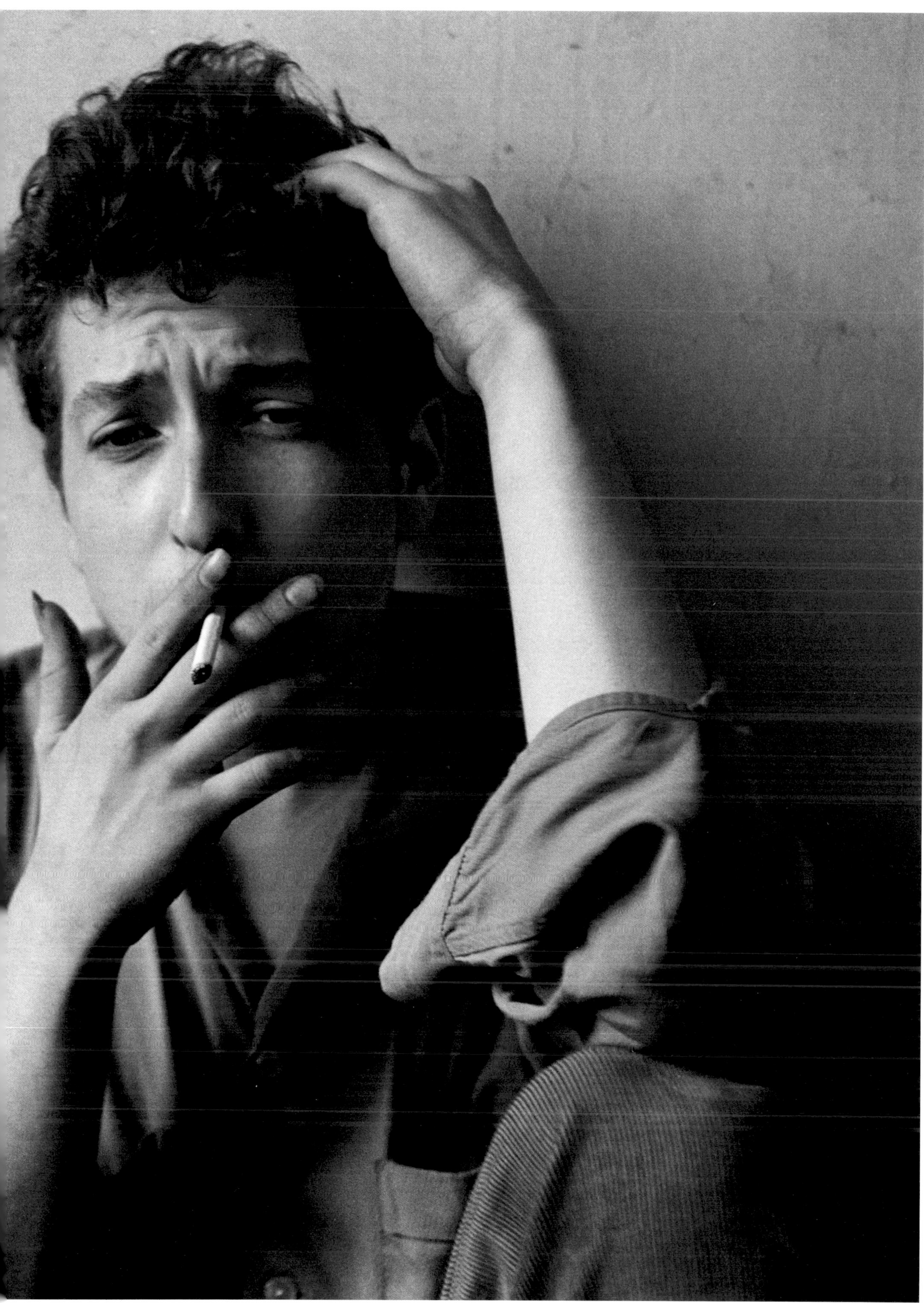

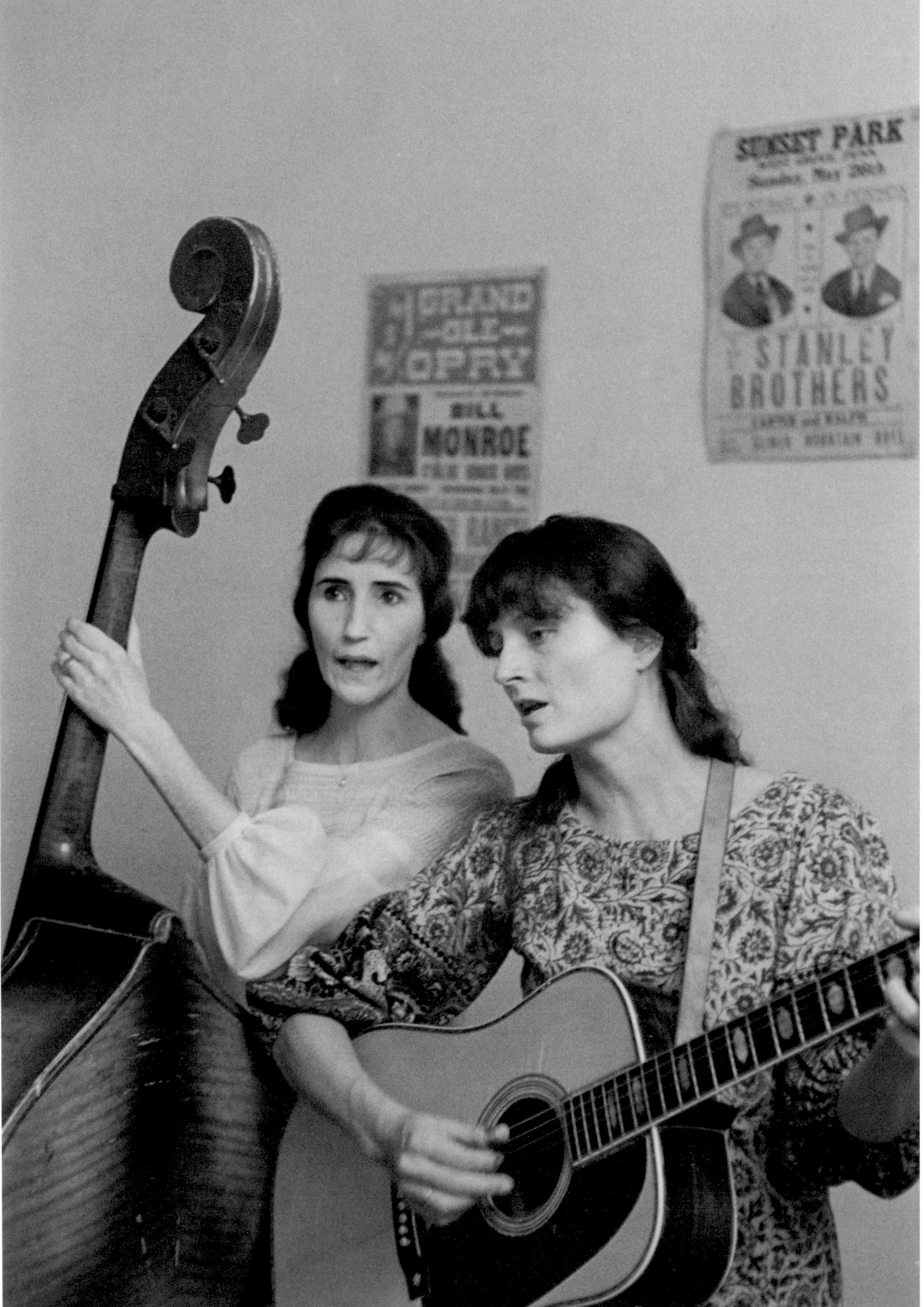
GRAND
OPRY
BILL
MONROE
SUNSET PARK
STANLEY
BROTHERS

← Hazel Dickens and Alice Gerrard, Washington D.C., 1965

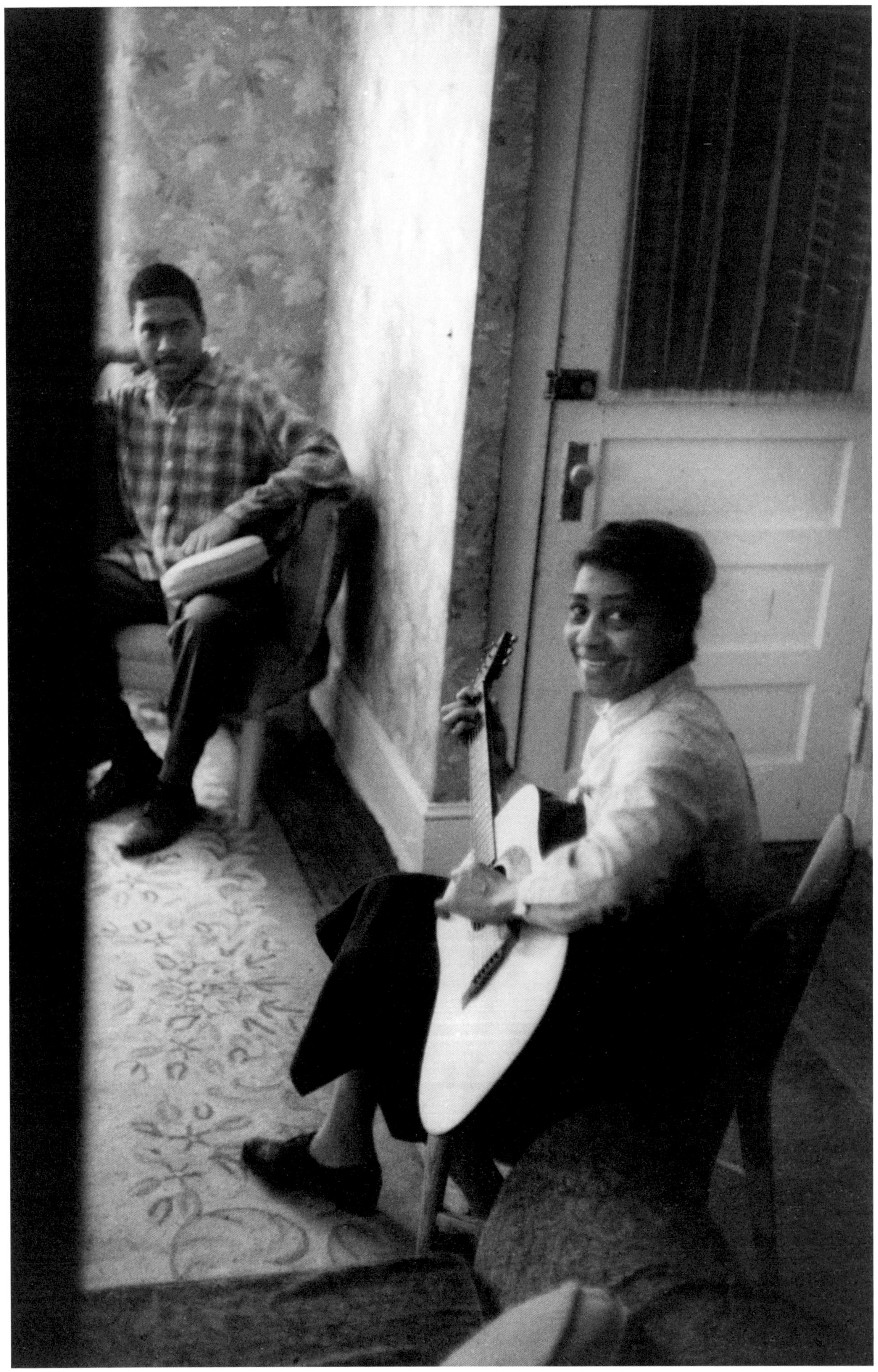

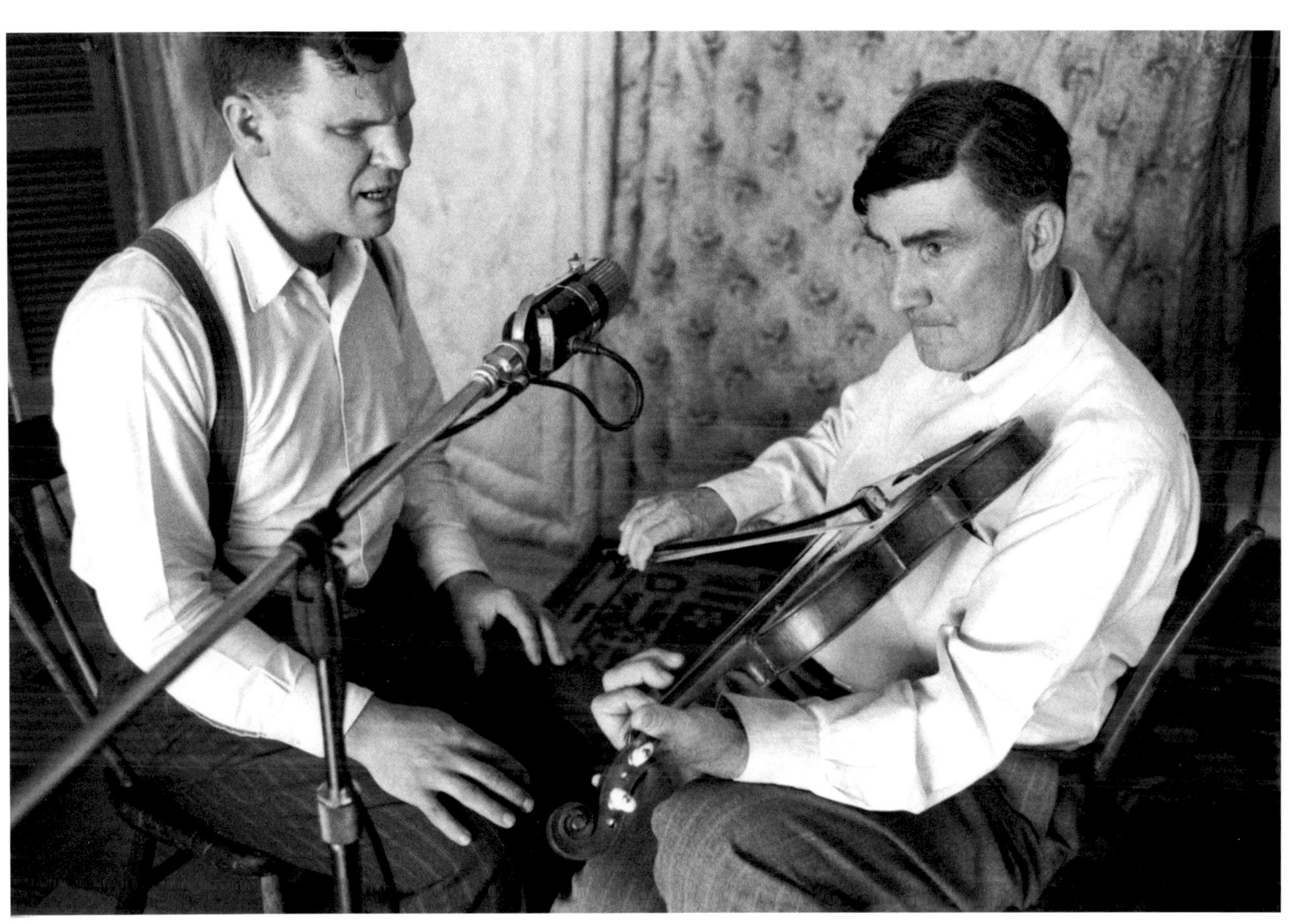

← Elizabeth Cotten, Washington D.C., 1960

↑ Doc Watson and Gaither Carlton, first New York trip, 1961

↴ Muddy Waters and Isaac Washington, New York City, 1959

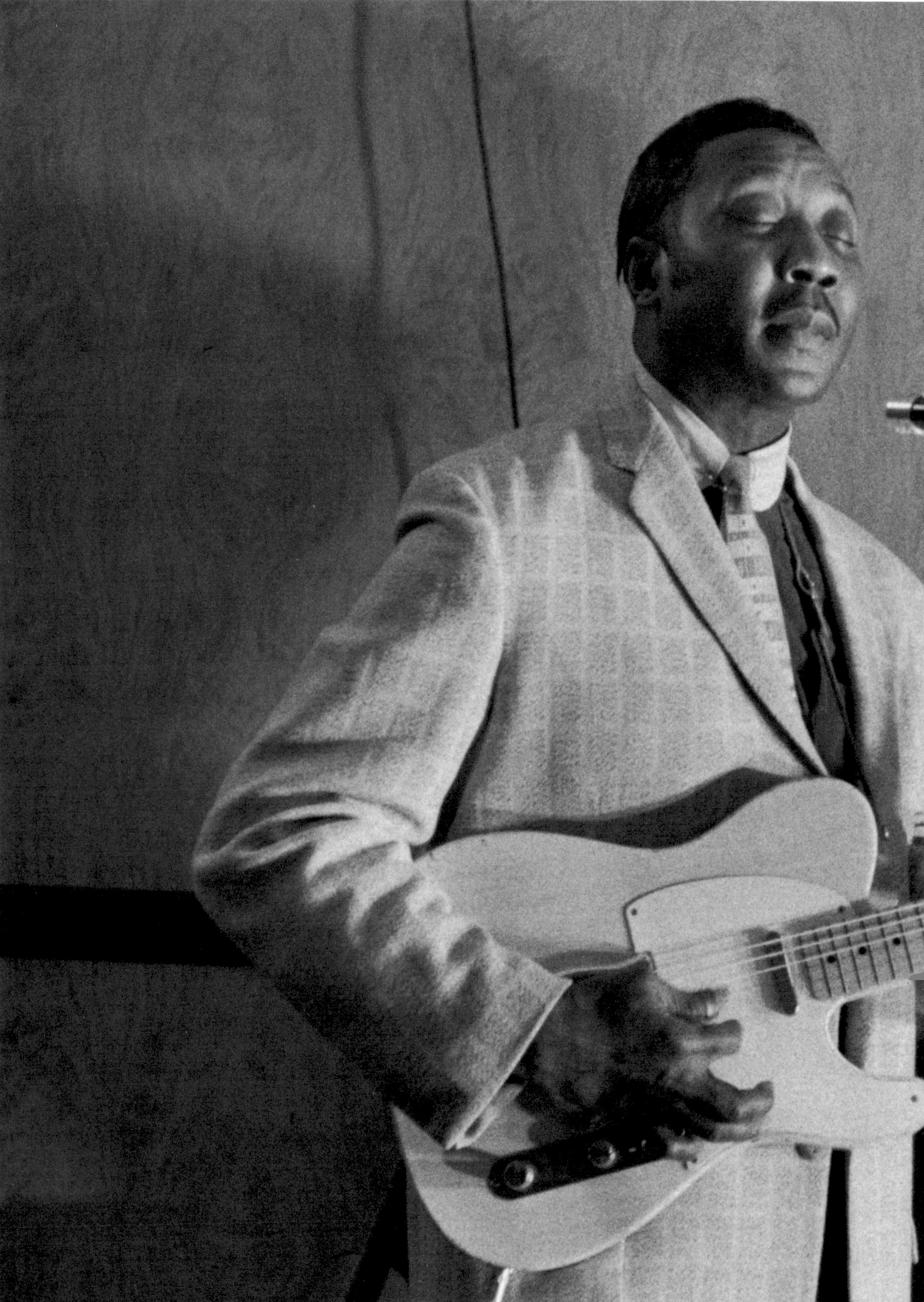

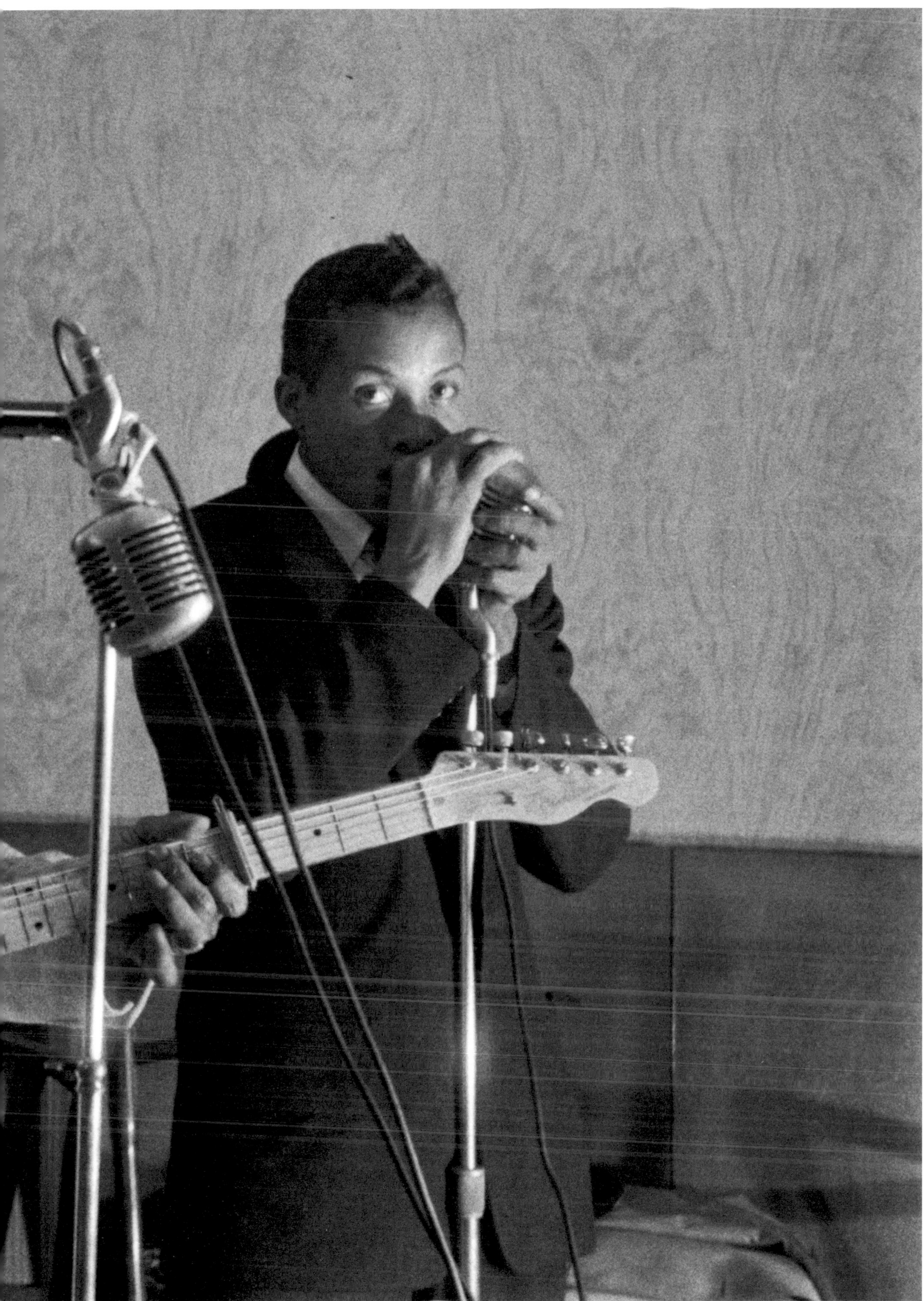

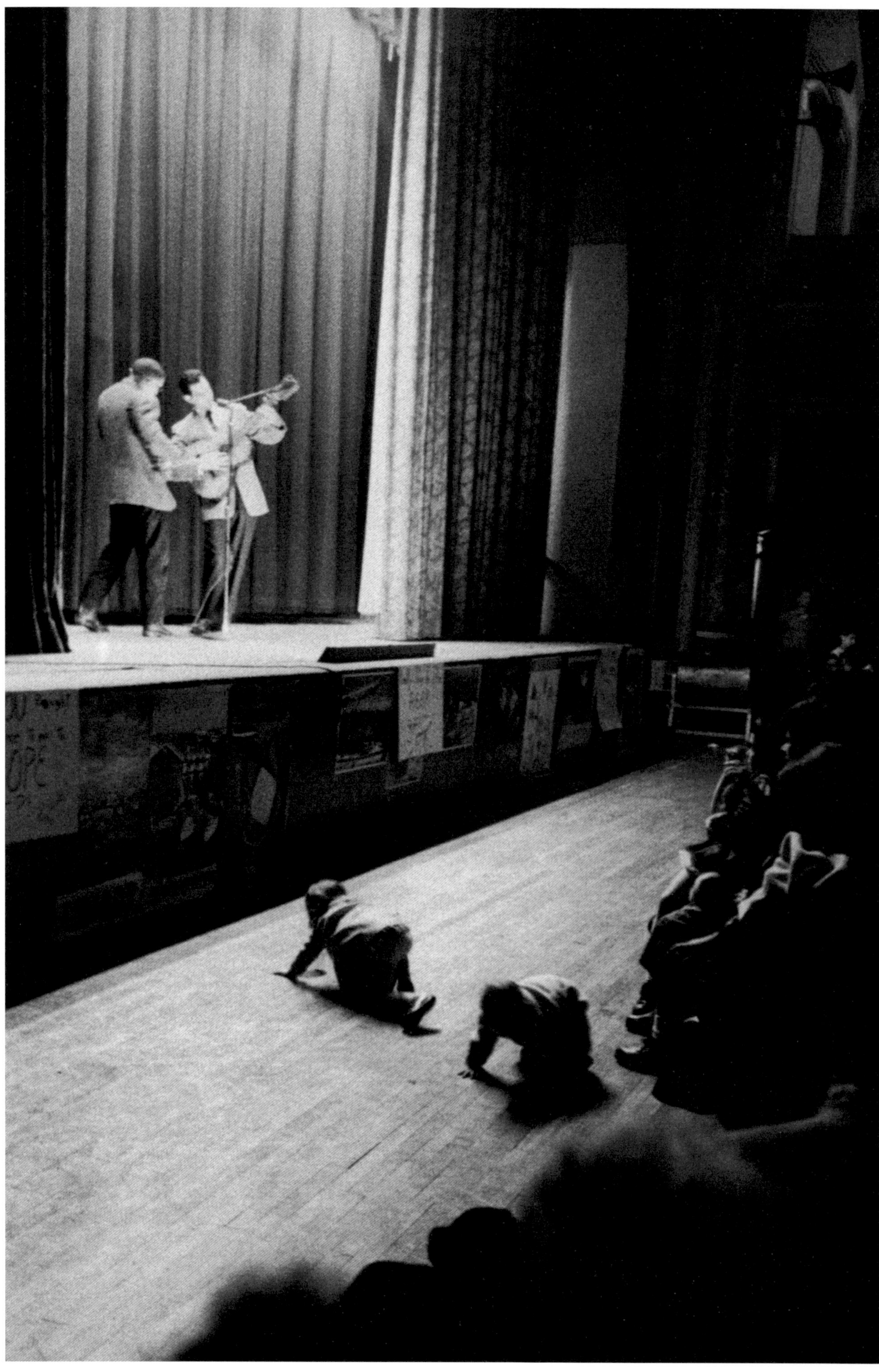

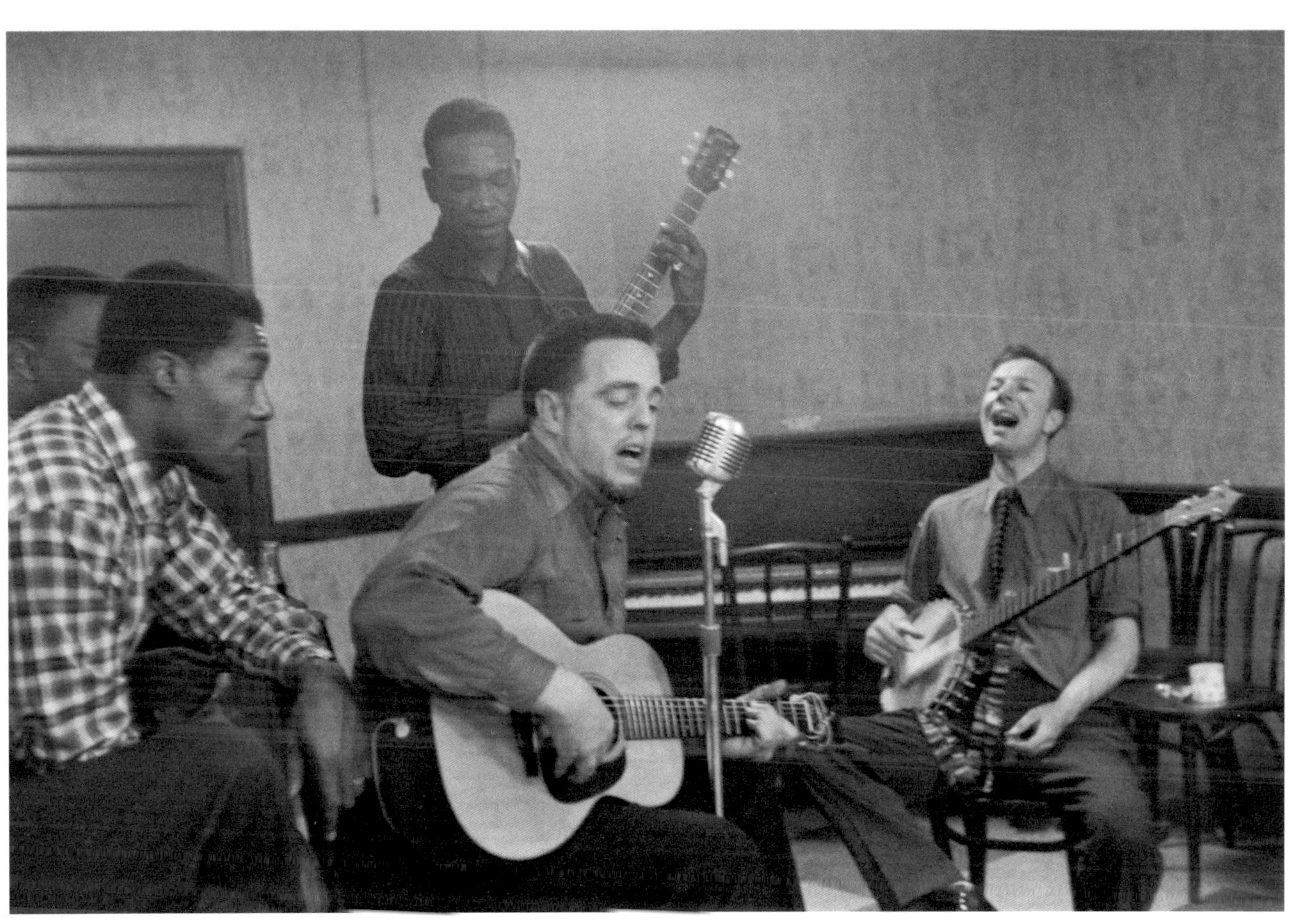

← YMCA concert, New York City, 1961

↑ Alan Lomax and Pete Seeger, "Folksong 59," New York City, 1959

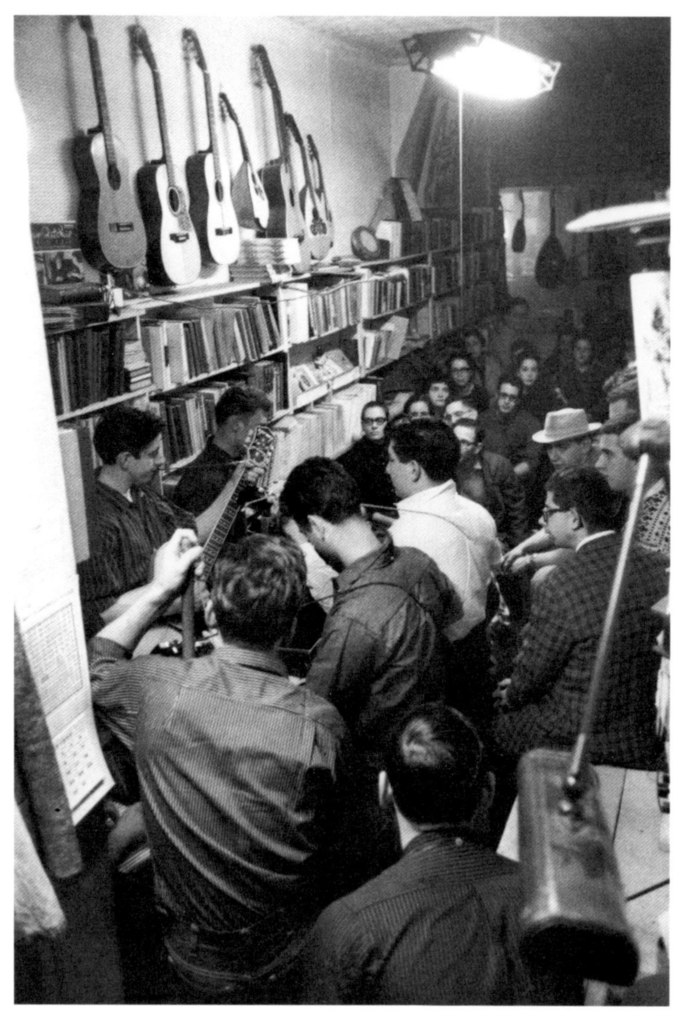

In 1957, before the Beatles, a Skiffle group from Britain did a brief concert at The Folklore Center on MacDougal Street in Greenwich Village. These guys looked more like Elvis than like Pete Seeger. They had just come off a ship and we didn't realize how much they announced the Rock 'n Roll approach and style that came to dominate popular music from then on.

↑ Early Skiffle Band, at The Folklore Center, New York City, 1957

→ (top) Geno Foreman and Eric von Schmidt, Indian Neck Festival, 1960

→ (bottom) Skiffle singer, 1957

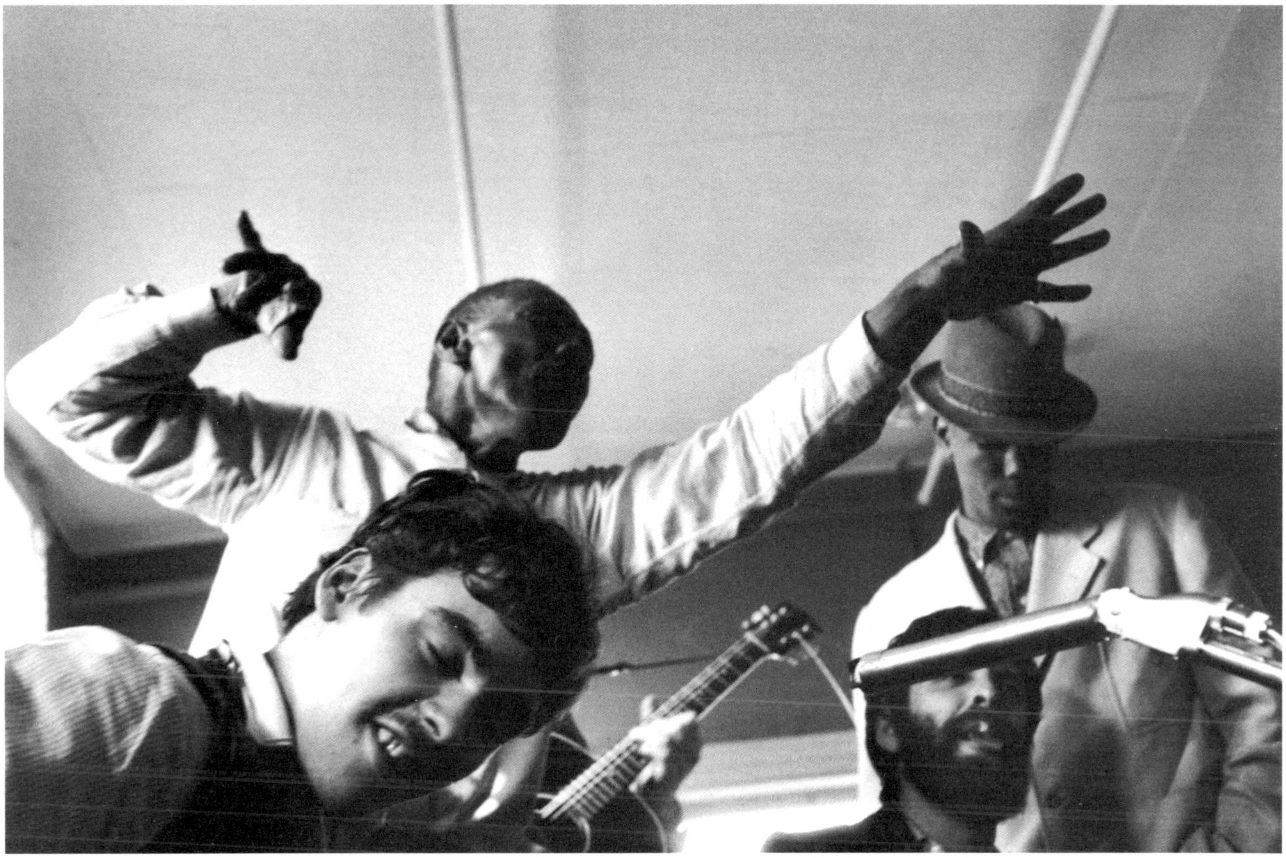

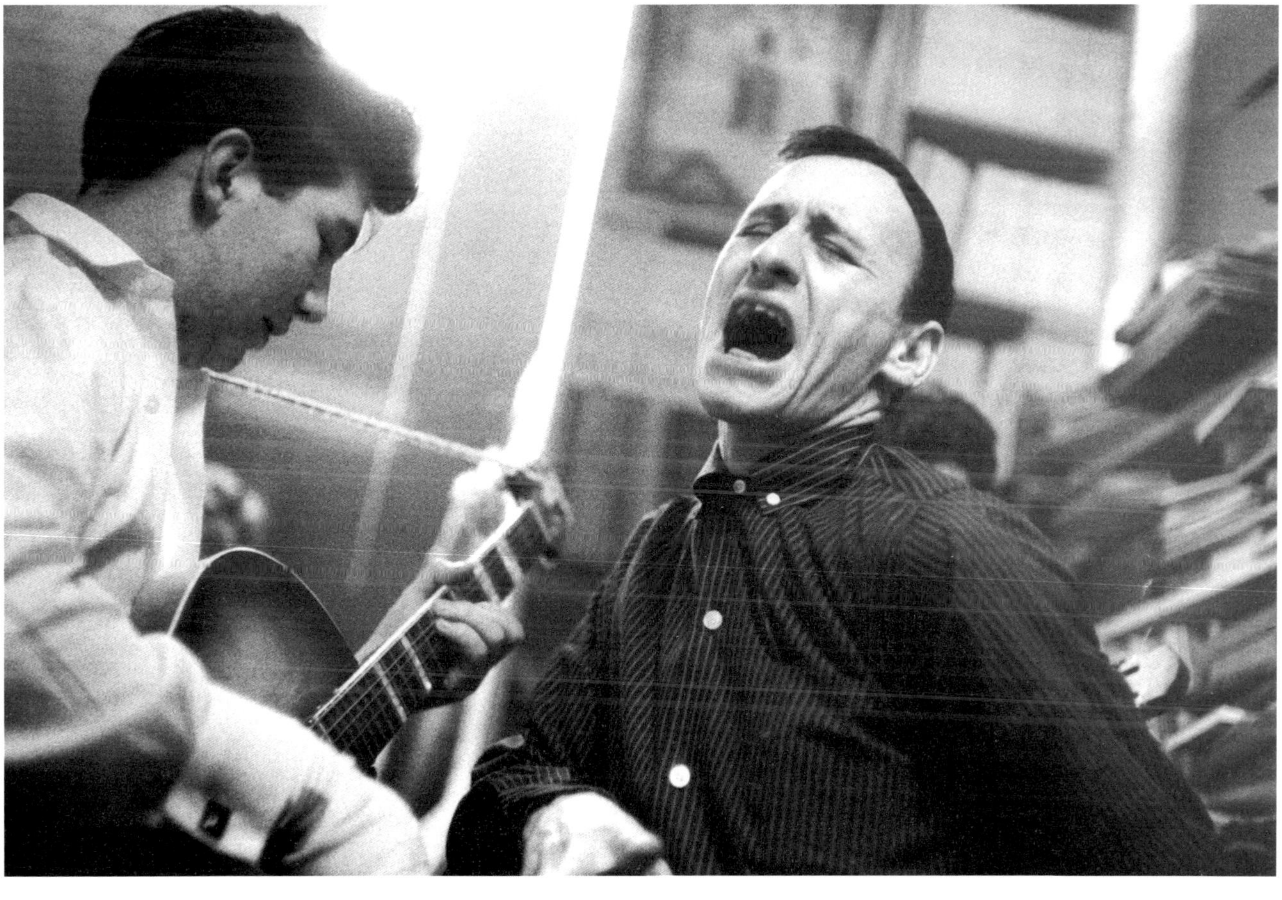

The split between high art, folk, and popular culture didn't seem to bother Bob Dylan who absorbed it all into his music. In early autumn, 1962, Dylan showed me the words to his new song "A Hard Rain's Gonna Fall." At first it resembled the old ballad "Lord Randal" or "Where have you been Billy Boy." Then it seemed like an early French symbolist poem to me, and I invited Bob to look at some of that poetry at my loft. I thought his verses were very strong although I couldn't imagine how he would fit them to music. One night during the Cuban Missile Crisis, when it felt like the world was on the brink of atomic collision, Dylan and I sang together at the Gaslight cafe. We did an old Carter Family song, "You're Gonna Miss Me When I'm Gone," not certain if there'd be anyone left to miss us.

Then there was Harry Smith, the off-beat elusive genius who had compiled the *Anthology of American Folk Music* for Folkways Records from old commercial discs. It became a bible for us and affected the way we heard traditional music. His insight into American music coupled with his mysticism, anthropological investigations, experimental films, collections of string figures, paper airplanes, Seminole patchwork, and Ukrainian Easter Eggs. Guided by intuition and obscure connections, emancipated by mind-altering substances, he explored the patterns of sight and sound, created a crazy atmosphere, visualized the invisible, and influenced everyone from the singers to the avant-garde and the Beat poets.

→ Harry Smith at the Chelsea Hotel, New York City, 1969

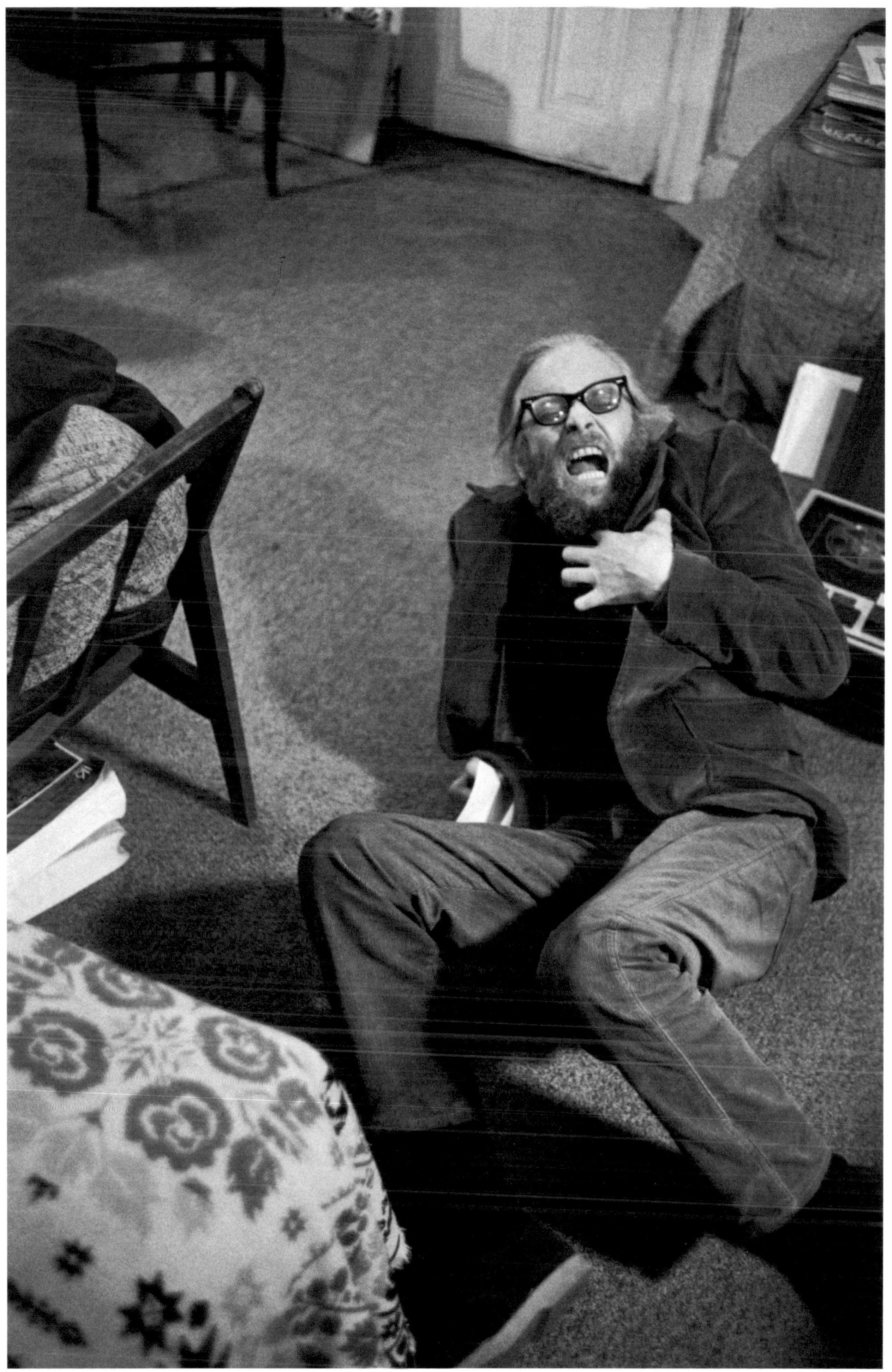

Woody Guthrie's disease was destroying him. He was shedding his image as the Dust Bowl Balladeer. Instead, his humanity and incredible inner strength emerged and became an inspiration to us. Woody's creative spirit was being transformed in a new generation.

→ Woody Guthrie, Cooper Union, 1959

⇉ Jack Elliot and Woody Guthrie, New Jersey, 1961

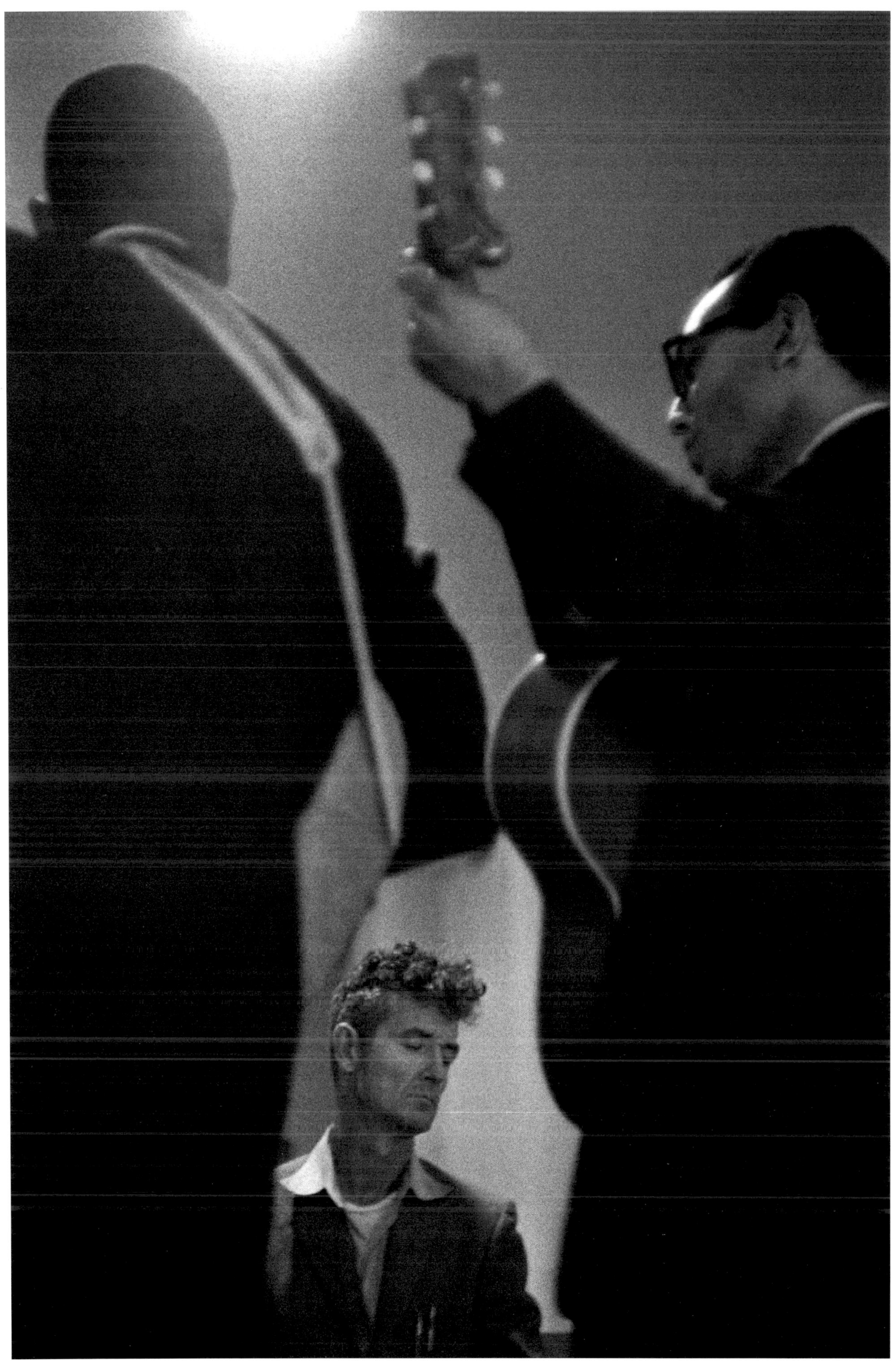

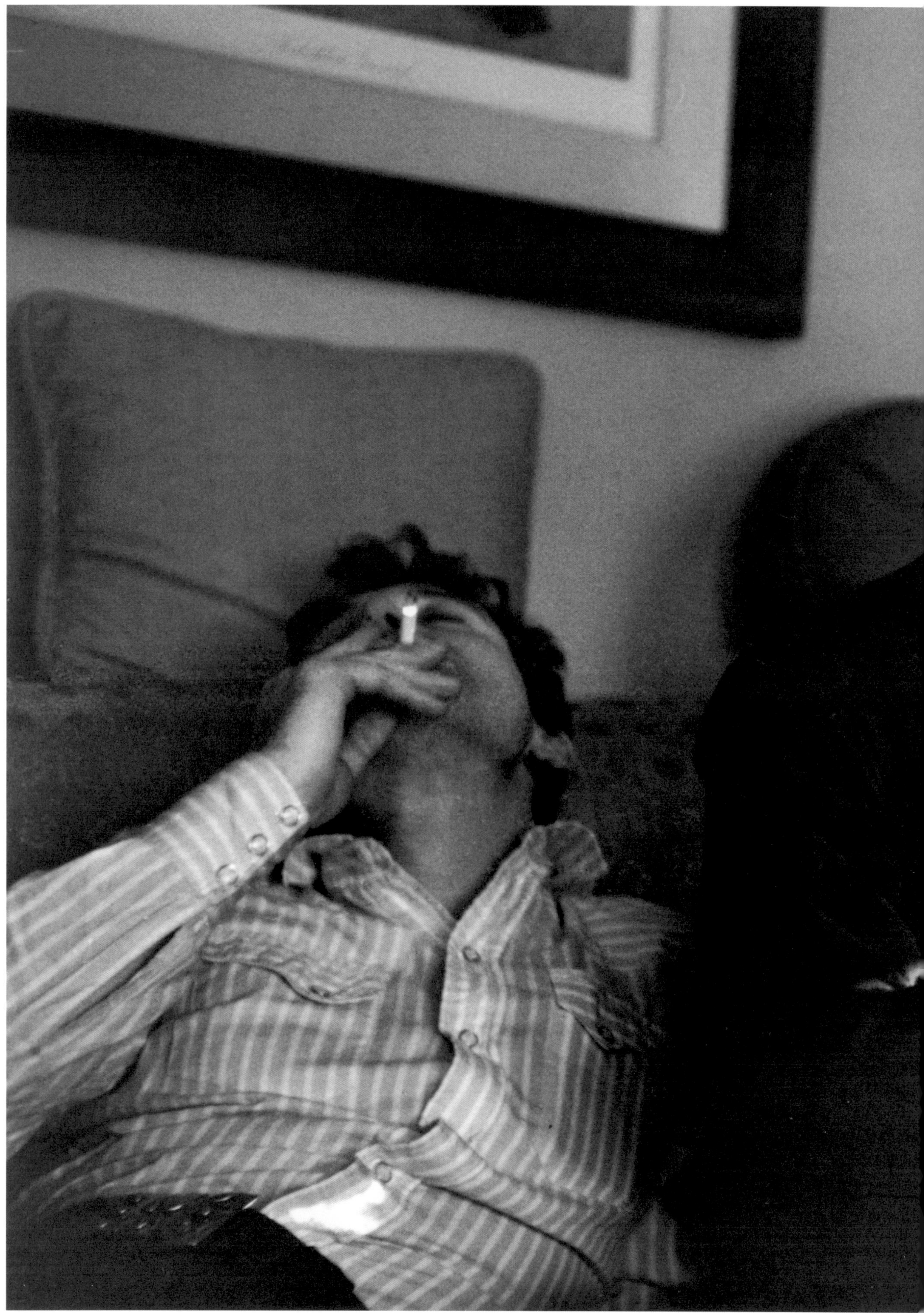

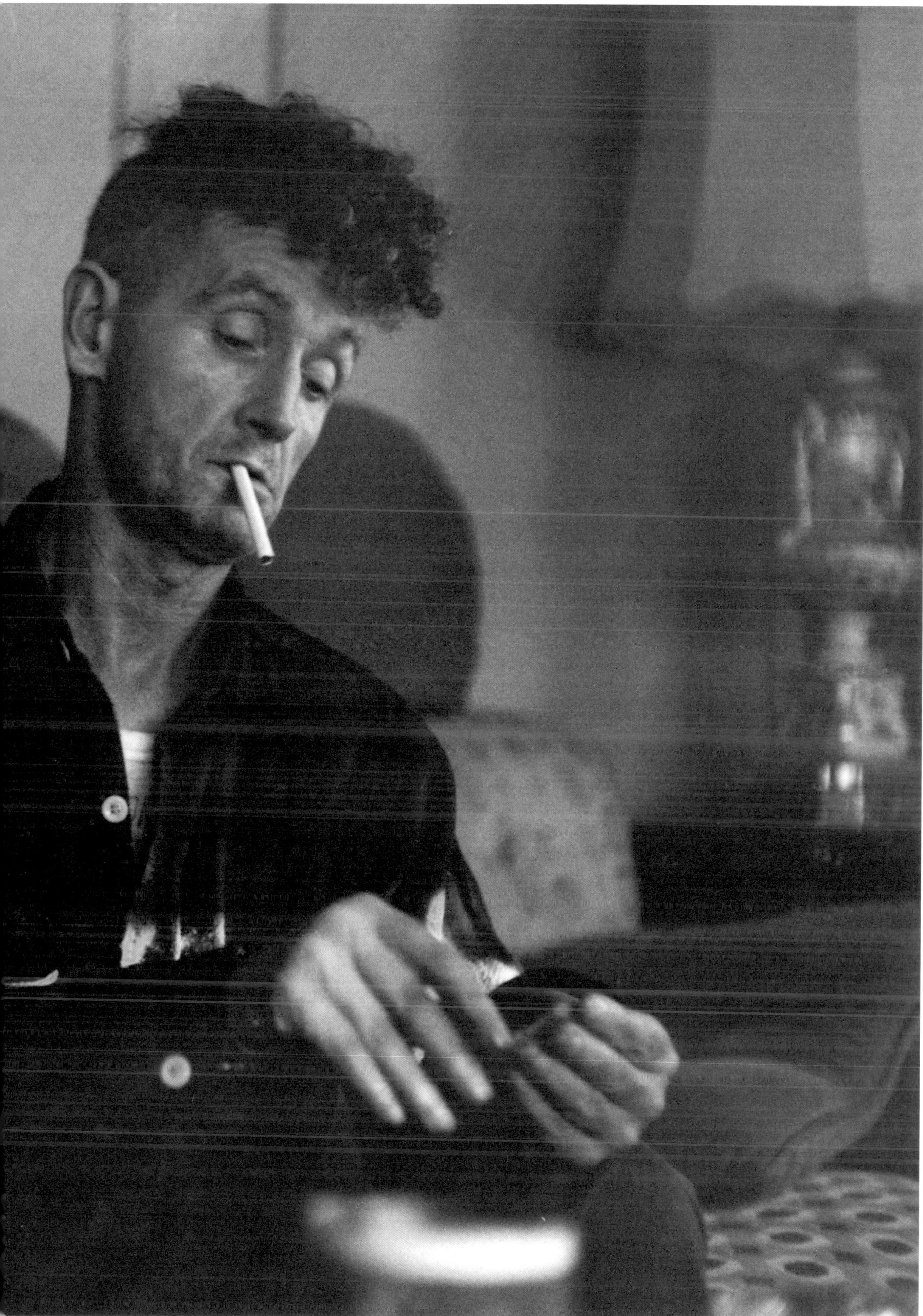

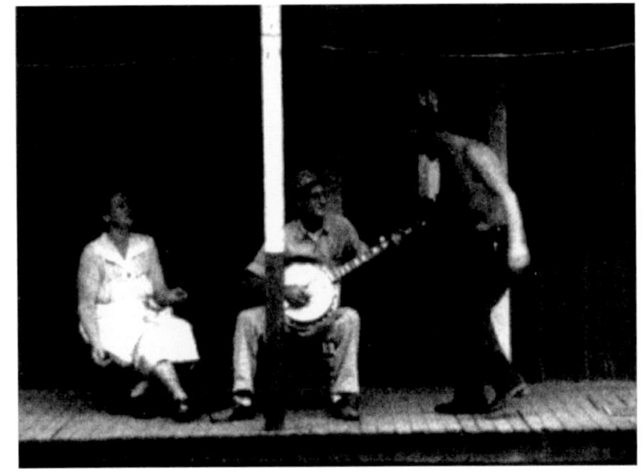

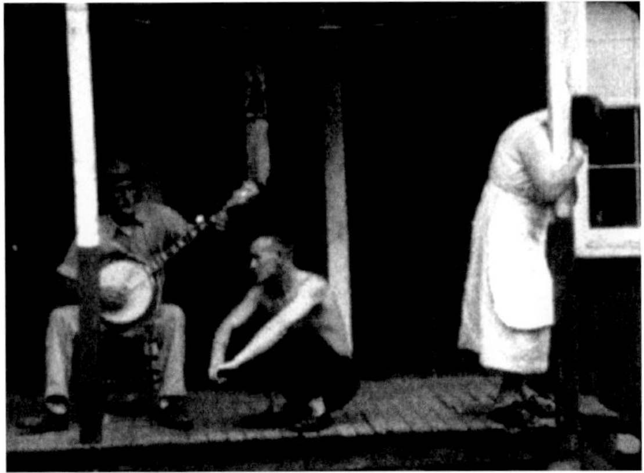

I MADE FILMS TO BRING THE IMAGES AND SOUND TOGETHER I needed a way to recapture the impact of music heard in its own native setting. There was another vision I had to get at, and sound recordings and still photographs were not enough to convey this feeling. My first film presented eastern Kentucky music in its intense home setting, a collision of images that would be experienced together with the sounds of mountain music. The film was an improvisation on the reality around us.

But I hadn't thought about how to edit a film, and had to approach that complicated process. It took hours, weeks, months and resembled the studio life of a painter. Compared to the actual filmmaking which was about action, physical energy, and human interchange, the editing was a quiet, contemplative and solitary process.

Over the years I have made fifteen films about traditional music. Each new film came from the previous one. I called them musical documents, and they conveyed the setting of the music, showing how it was part of daily life, ritual, and festival.

When the music led to political issues and social injustice, the films became controversial and were forbidden in some places. Anthropologists and ethnomusicologists distanced themselves. Since I couldn't compromise my purpose or abandon my path, I ceased making documentary films in 1992.

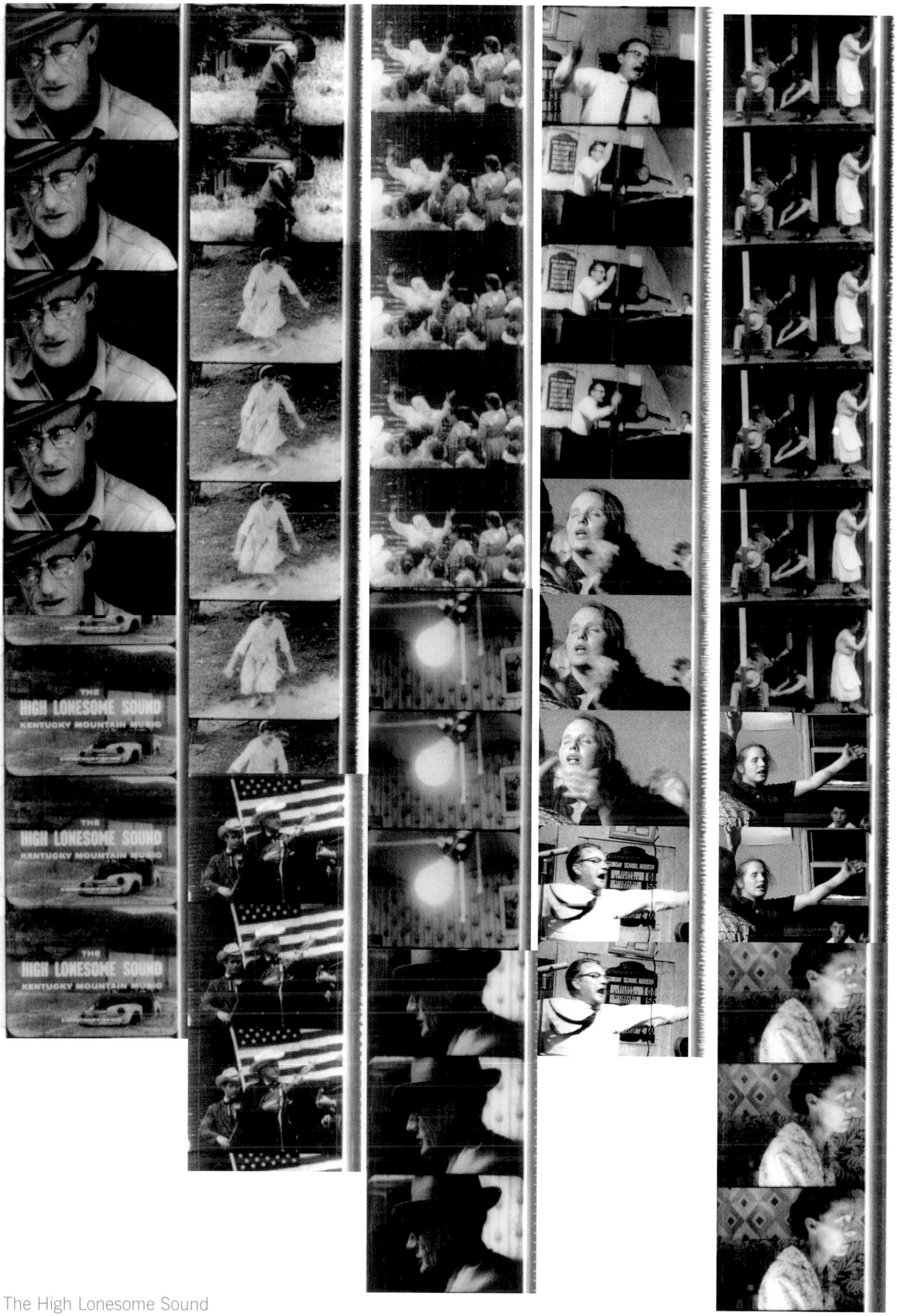

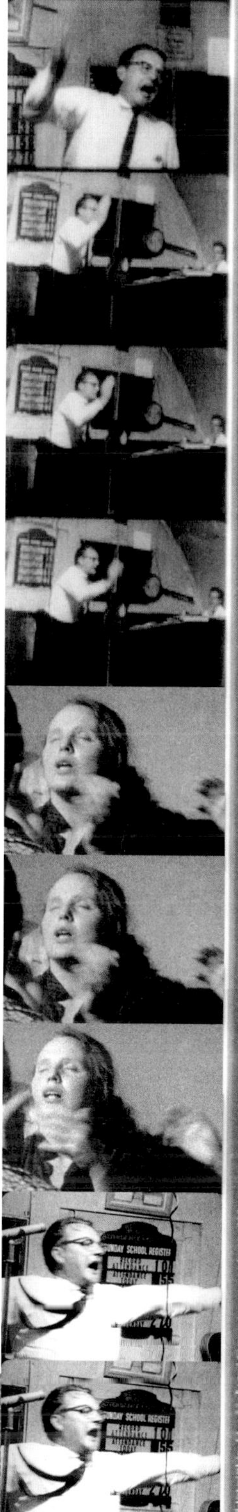

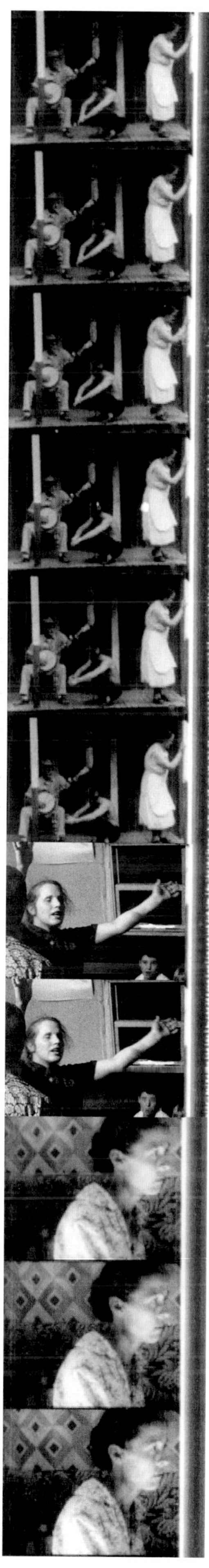

The High Lonesome Sound

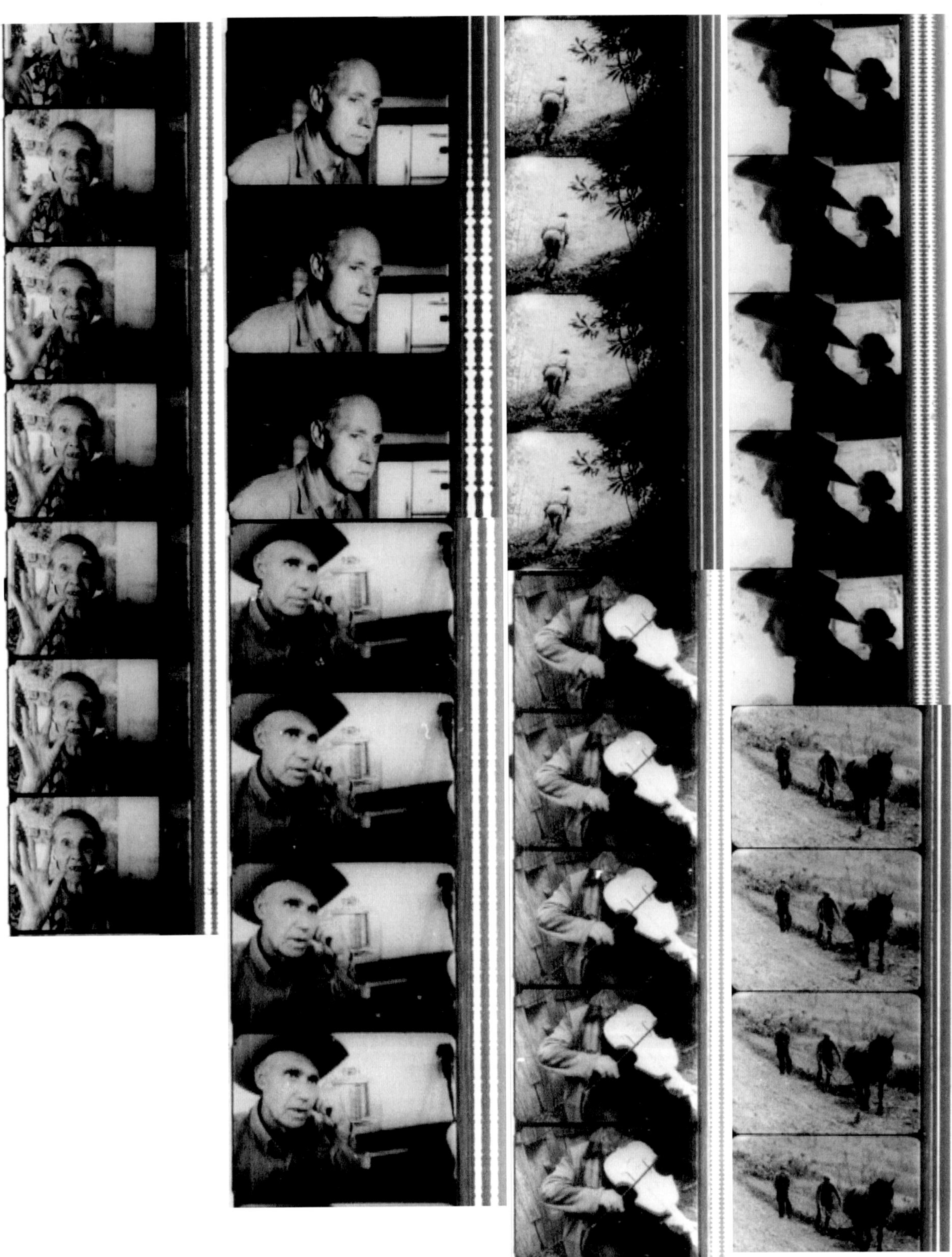

The End of an Old Song

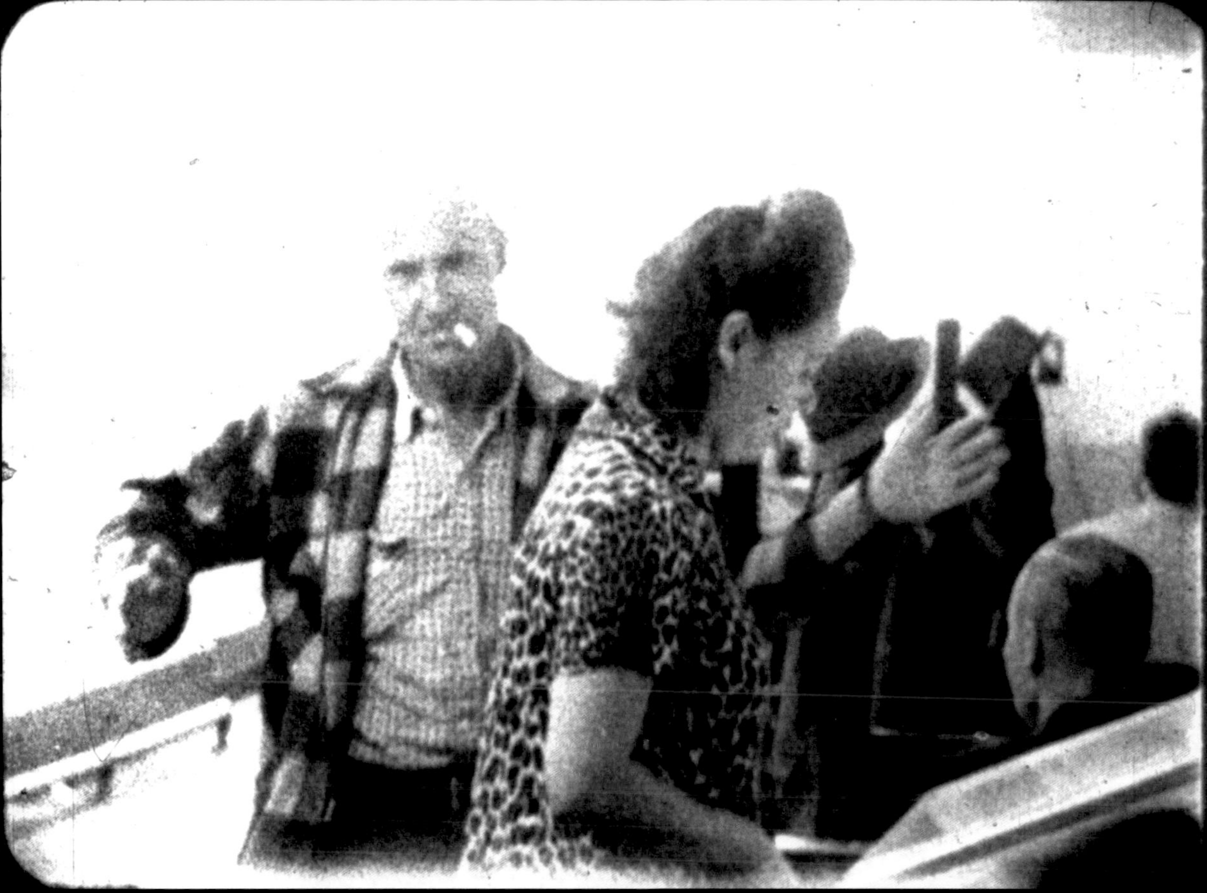

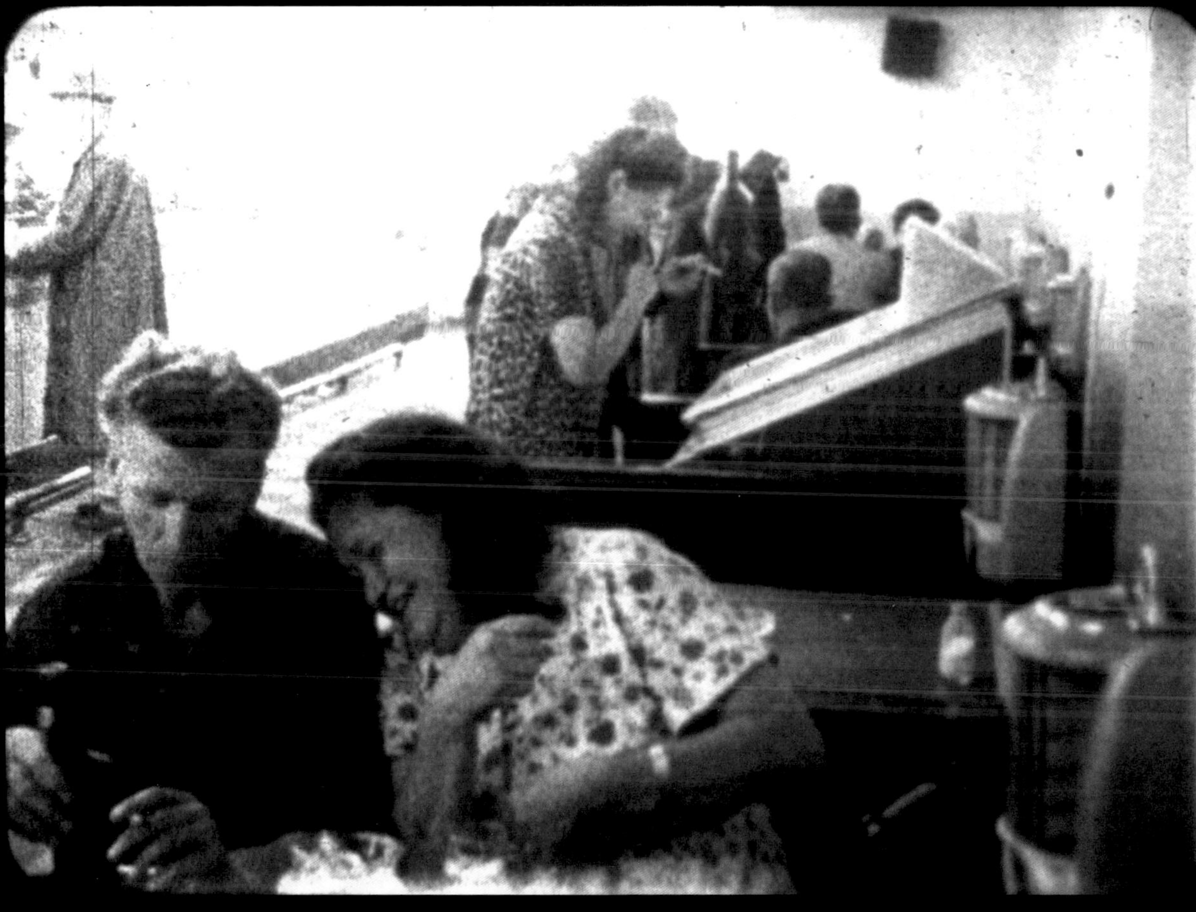

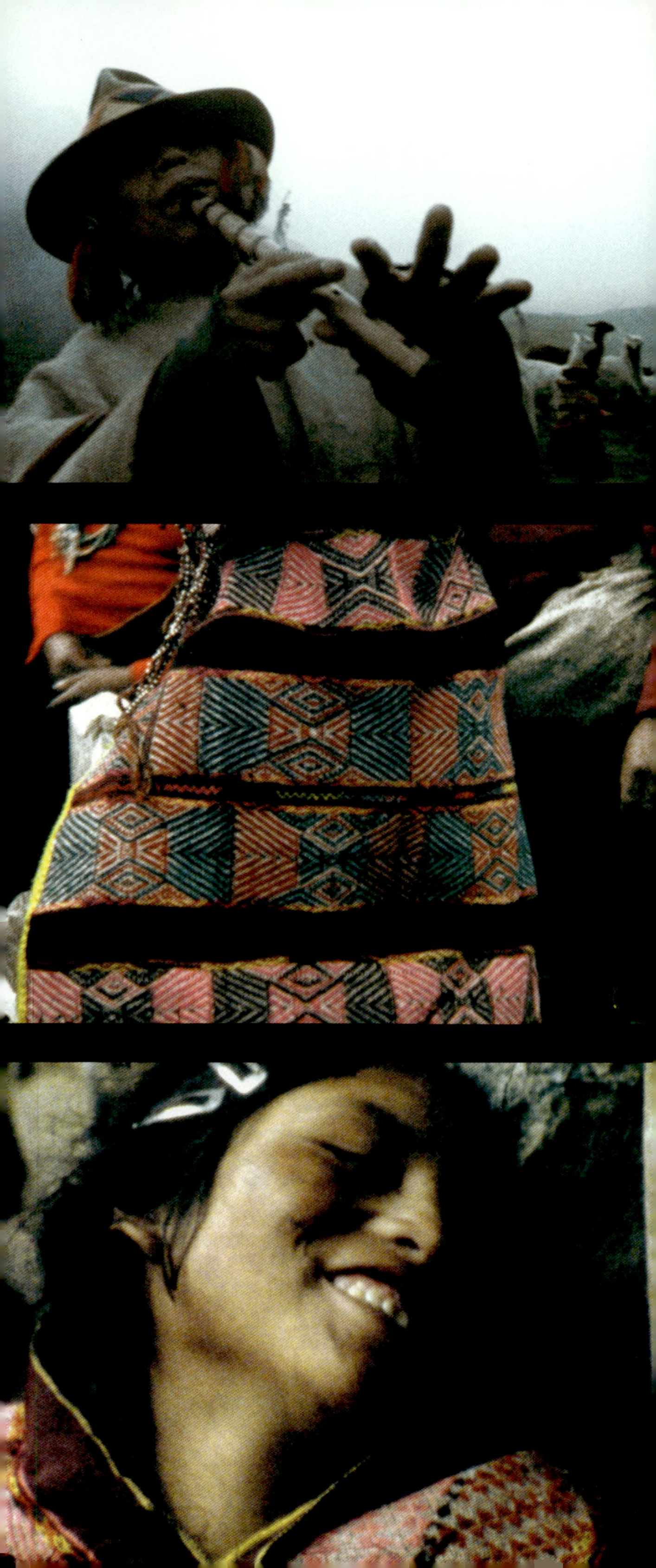

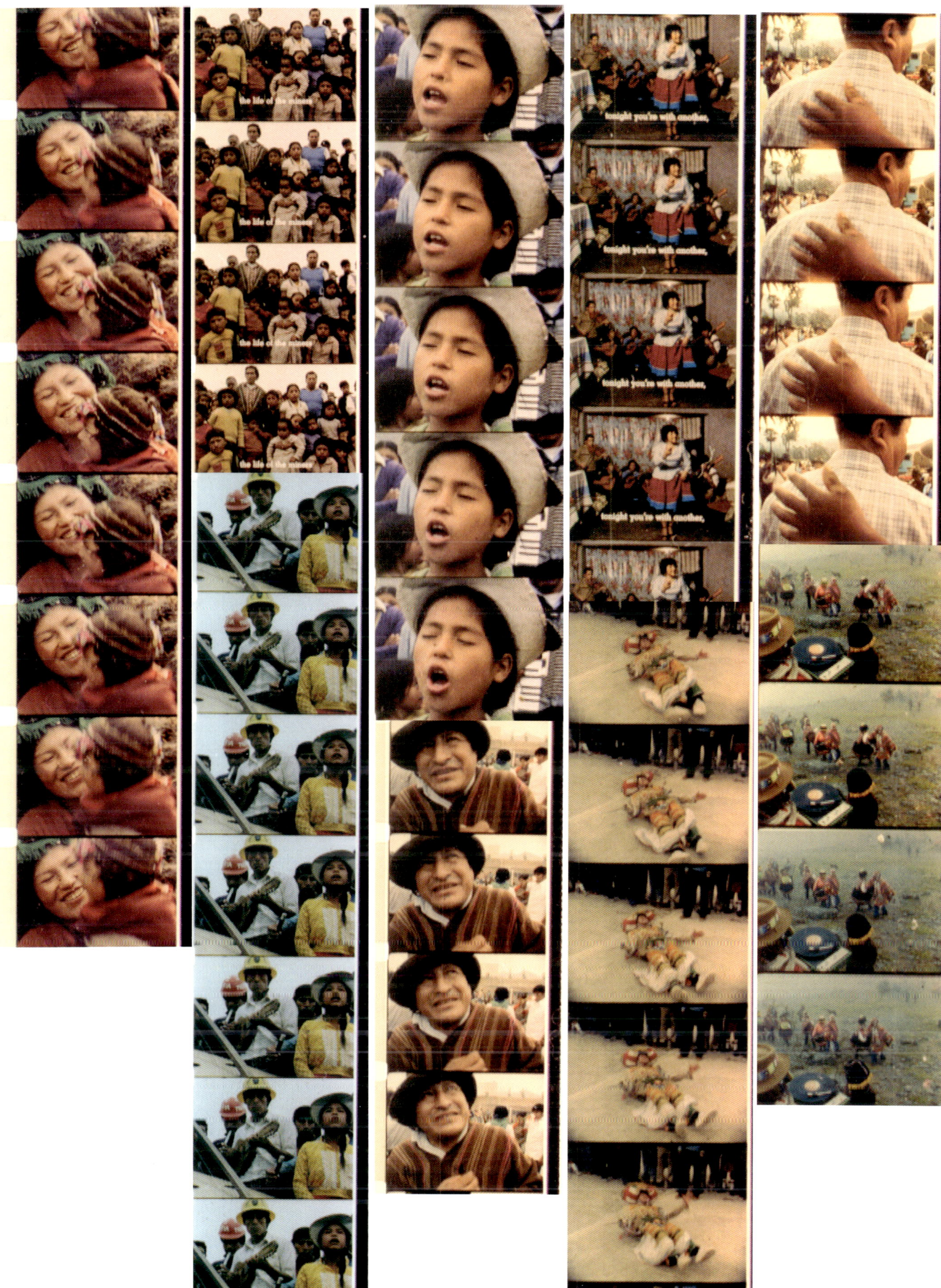

Mountain Music of Peru

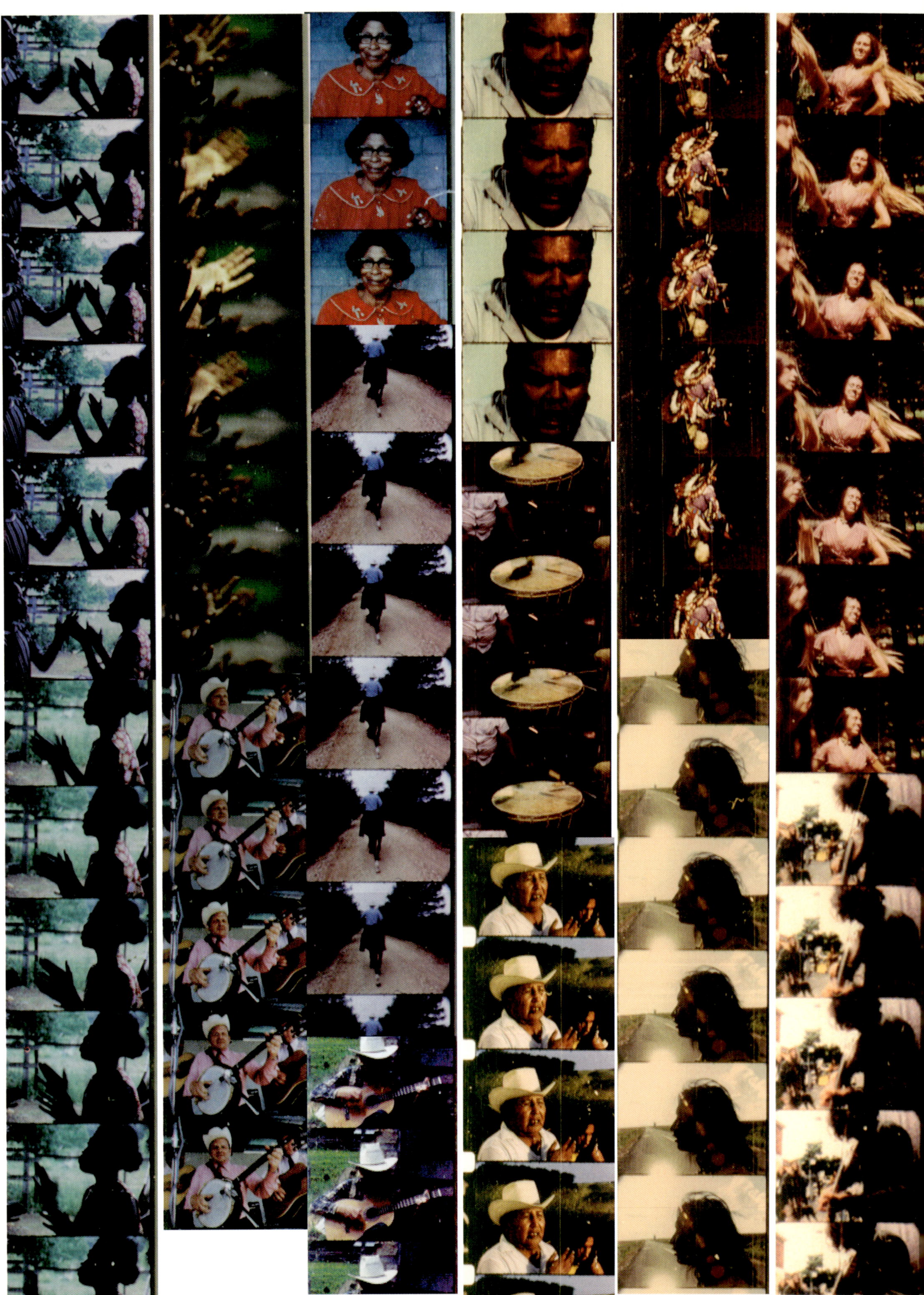

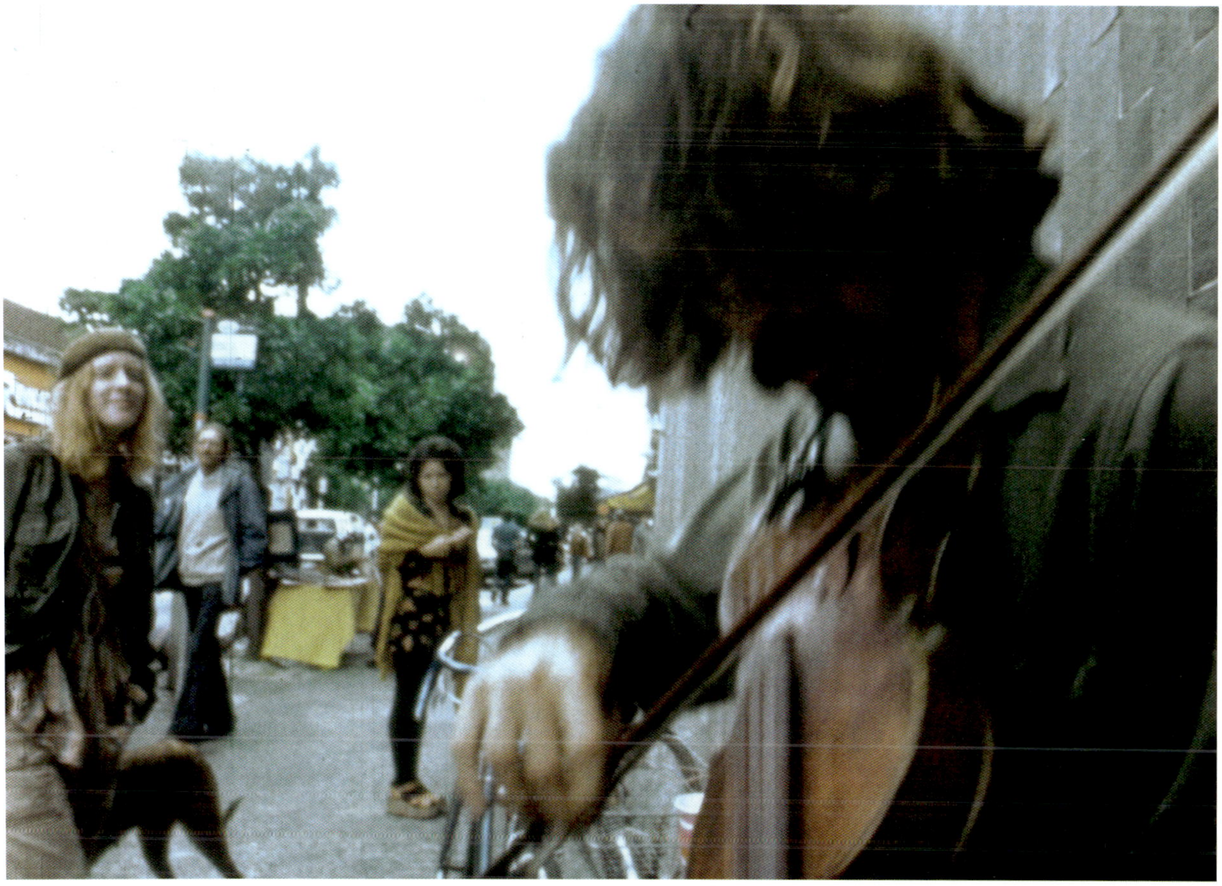

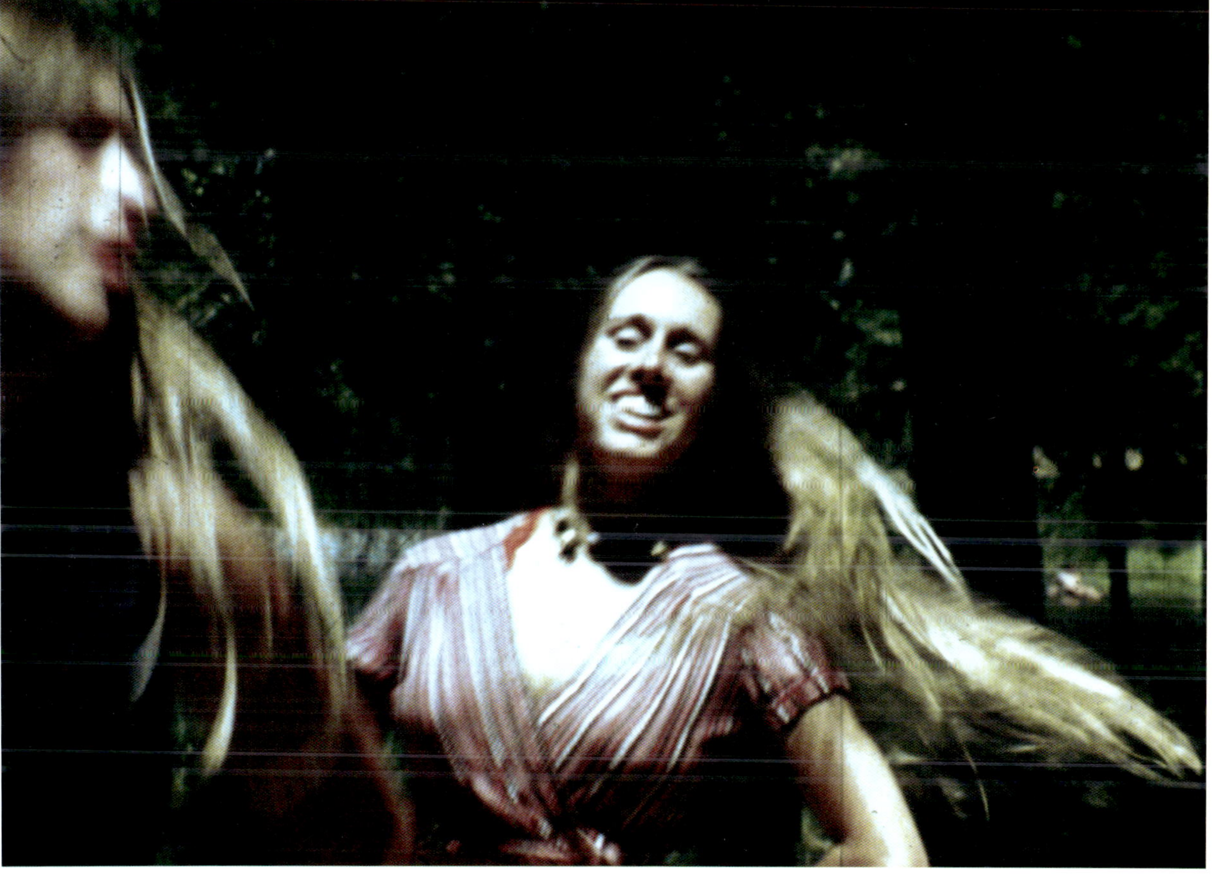

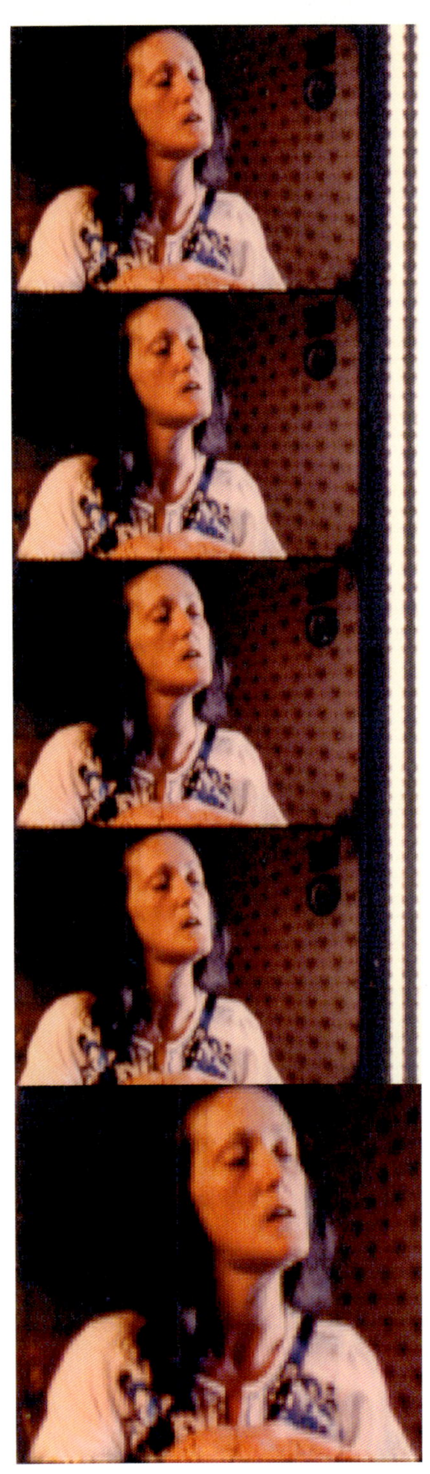

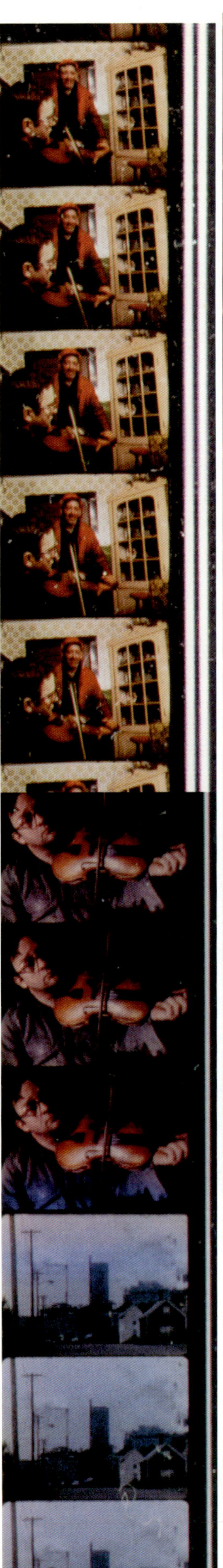

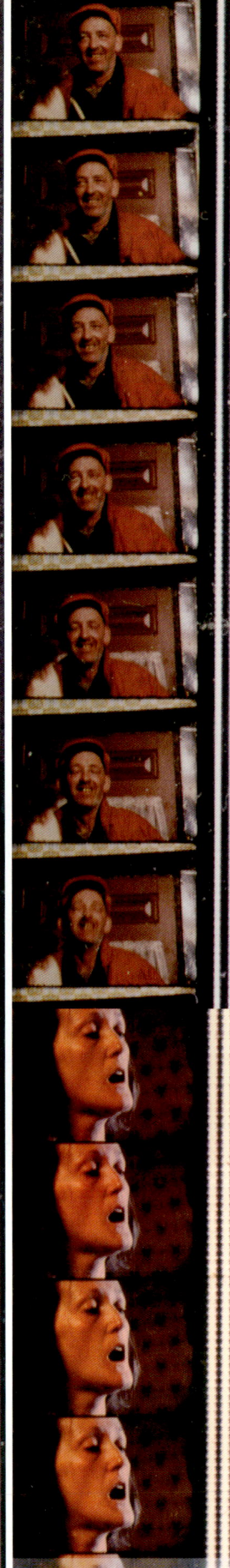

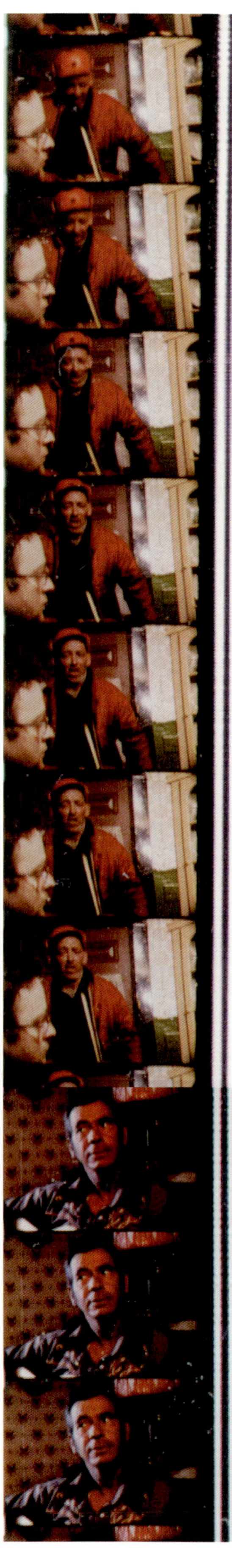

Post Industrial Fiddle

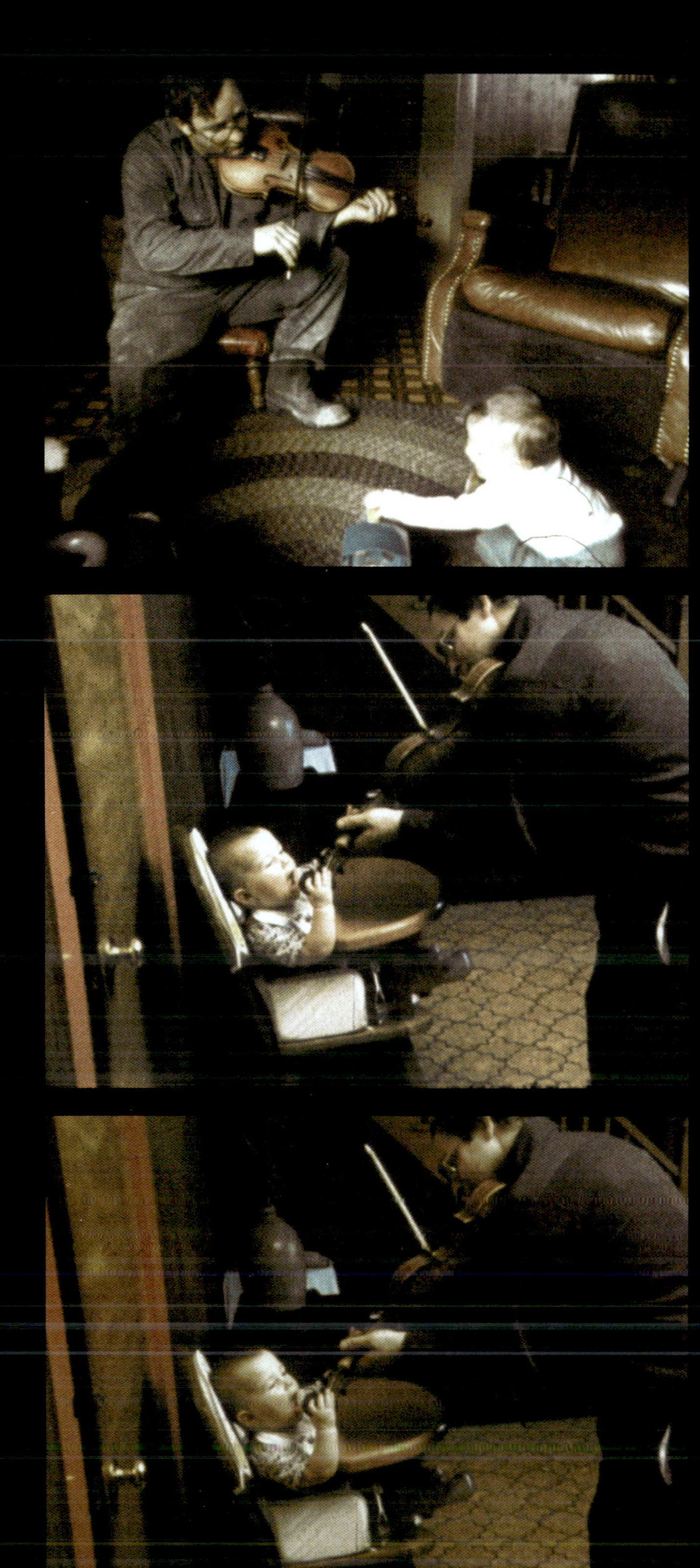

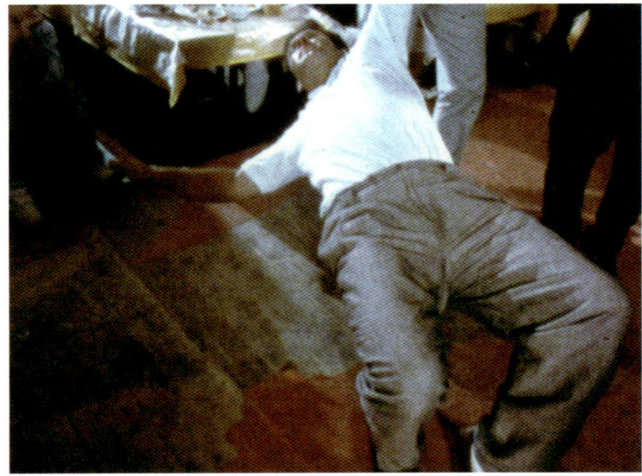

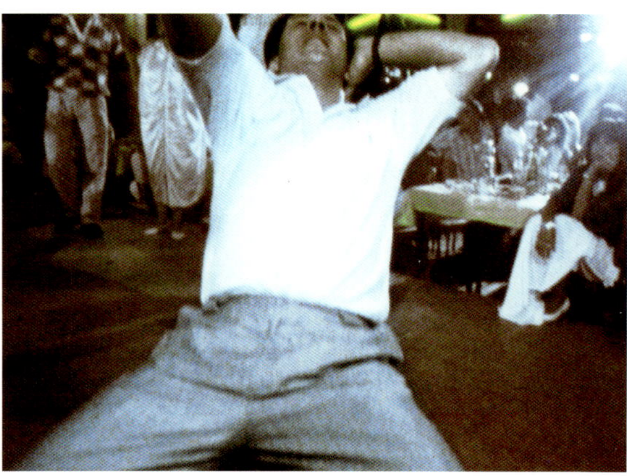

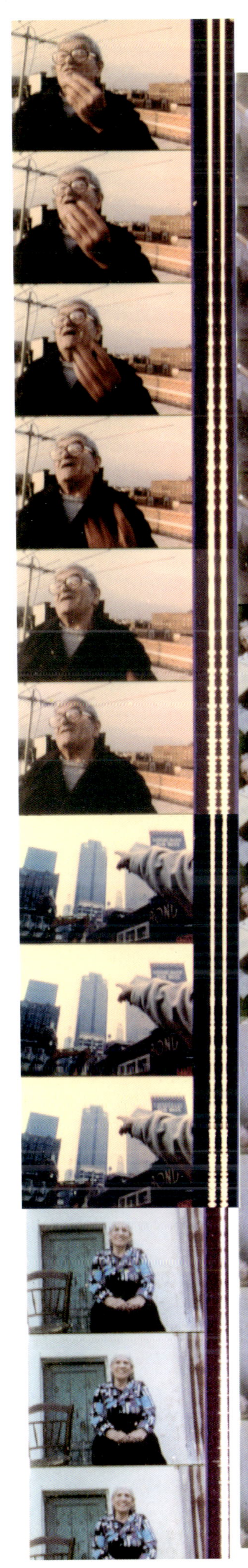
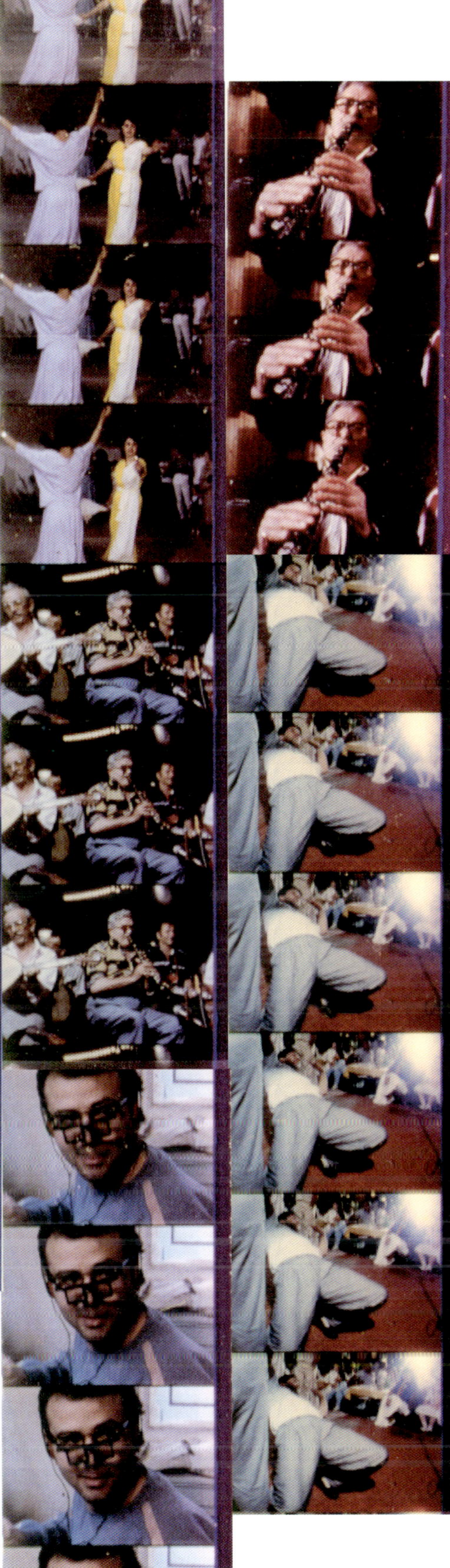
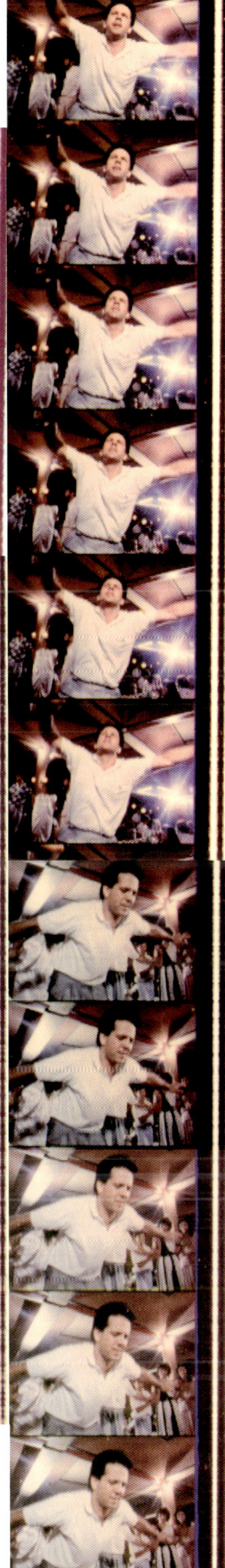
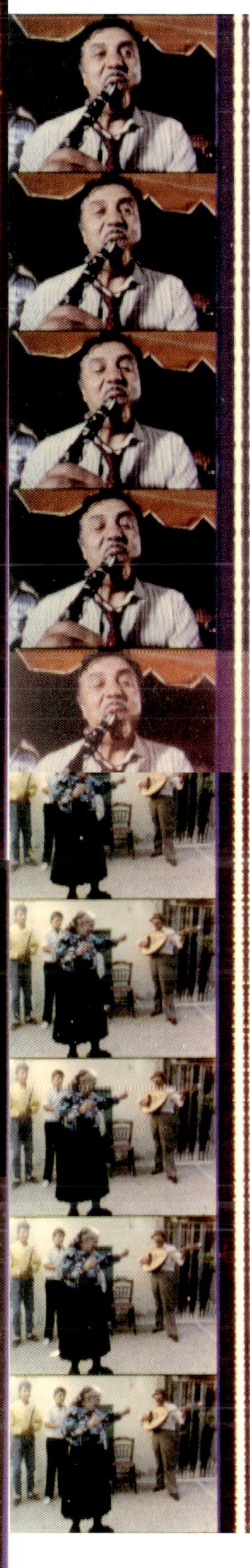

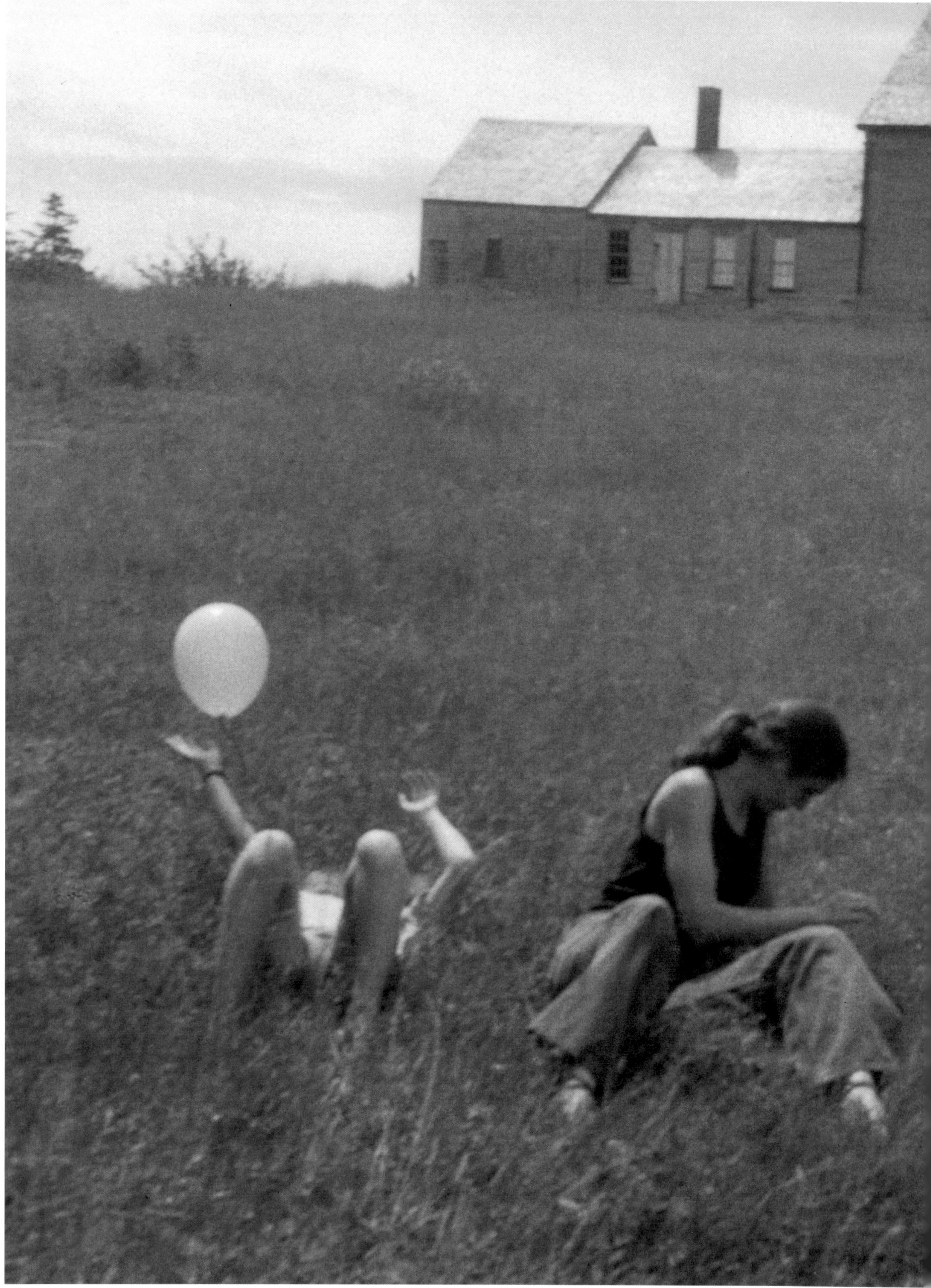

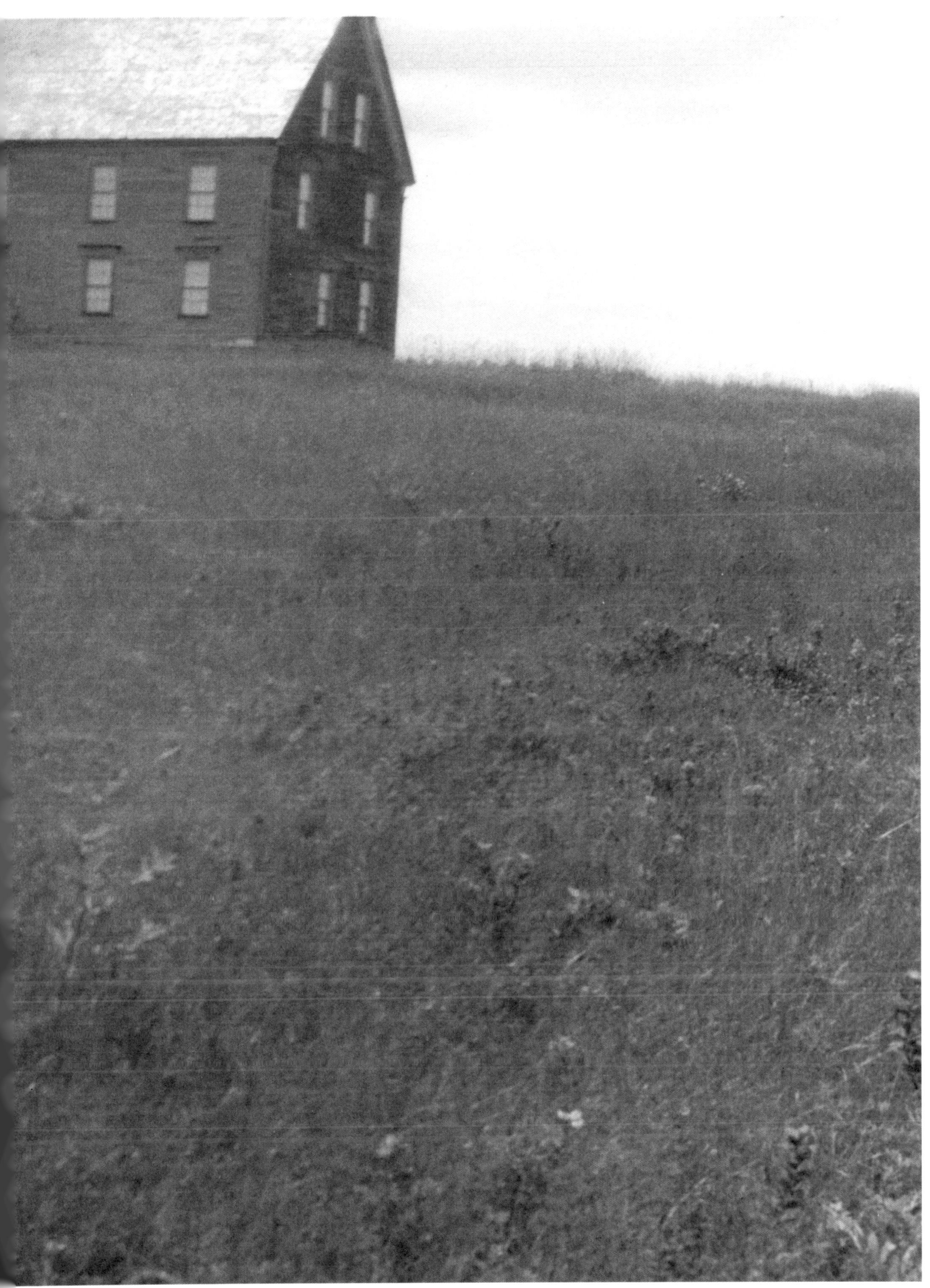

UP AND OUT My grandfather was an Orthodox Jew who observed ritual practices on Saturday in the synagogue. Once, when I was a small boy, I went with him there on High Holy Days and sat among his congregation, surrounded by old men who were doing mysterious, unfathomable things that I'd never seen before. Nobody explained why they took the Torah scrolls out of a cabinet and carried them between the aisles. Nobody explained why all the men kissed these scrolls as they went by, or why the women were sitting separated upstairs in the balcony. I have never forgotten the singing. It had a sound which was weird and deep. The melodies had unfamiliar intervals and took strange turns in the way the men sang, with an unrythmical muttering; they were never in step with each other. I didn't hear anything like it again for many years, but I recognized the feeling it generated in me when I heard the Old Regular Baptists in Kentucky. It was slow paced and unrelated to modern or popular music. Some of the Q'eros songs in Peru also had this quality, and the impact on me was always the same: a sound coming from a deep spiritual place and from a different, past, unending time.

I had reached the place where the music alone didn't communicate what I felt, and the still photographs by themselves couldn't convey what I felt, and I was carrying around a growing frustration that I might never communicate what I had to say, so I made films about music, and that challenge was so great and transformative that it became my main effort for they next twenty years as I watched my family grow up, and out.

⇇ Sonya & Penny, Maine, 1974

→ Penny, Peru, 1964

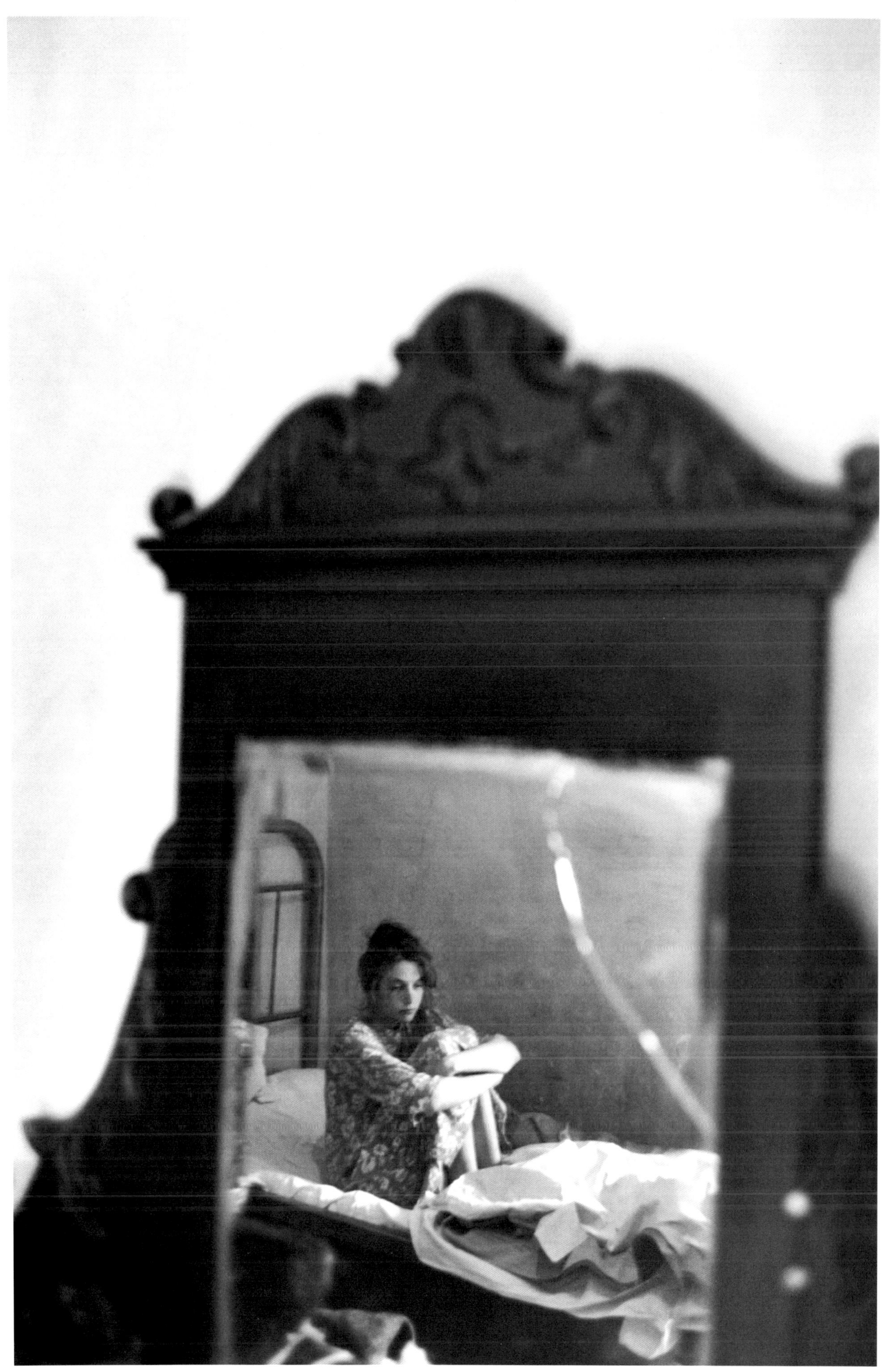

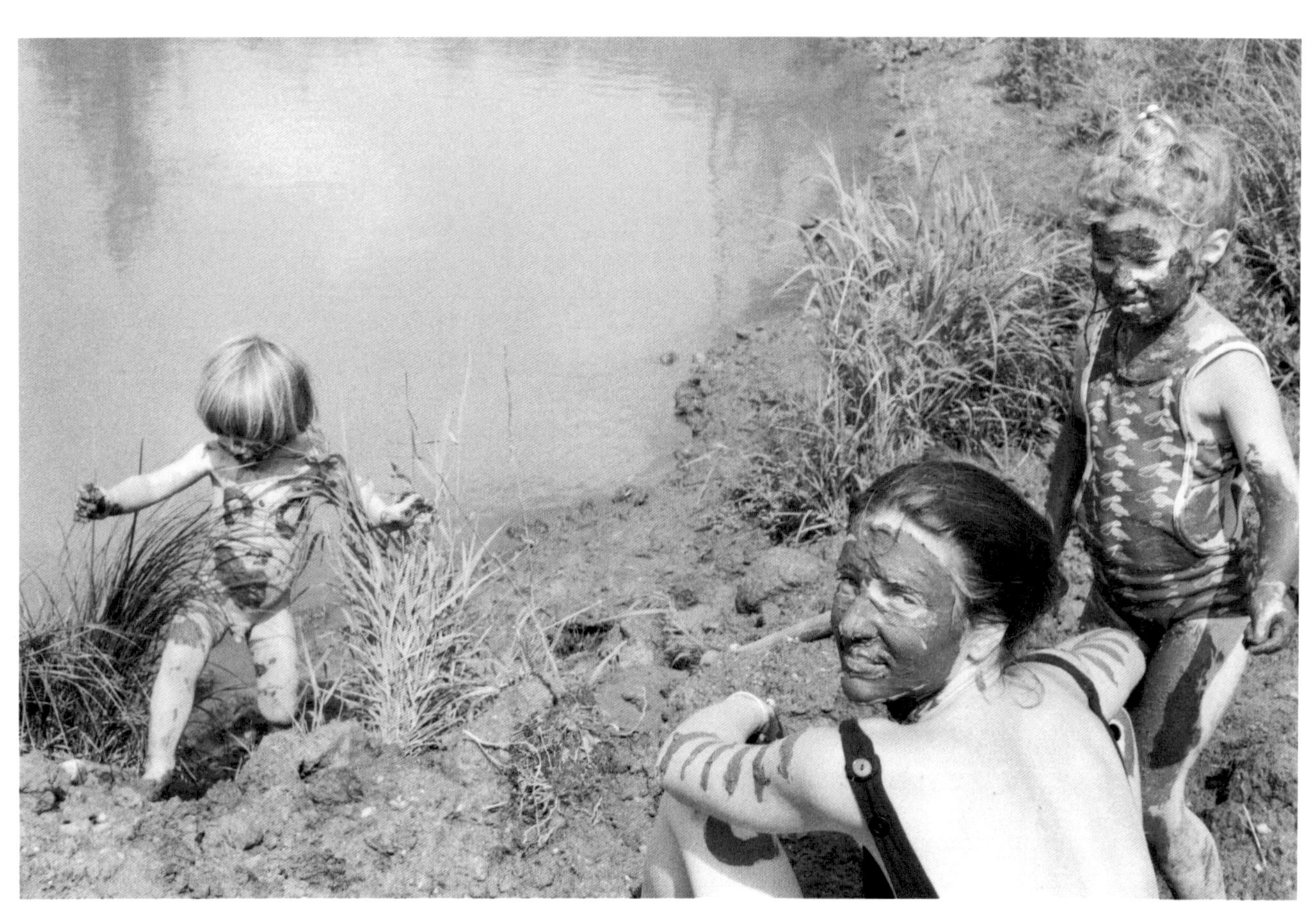

↑ Rufus, Penny, Sonya, Putnam Valley, 1971

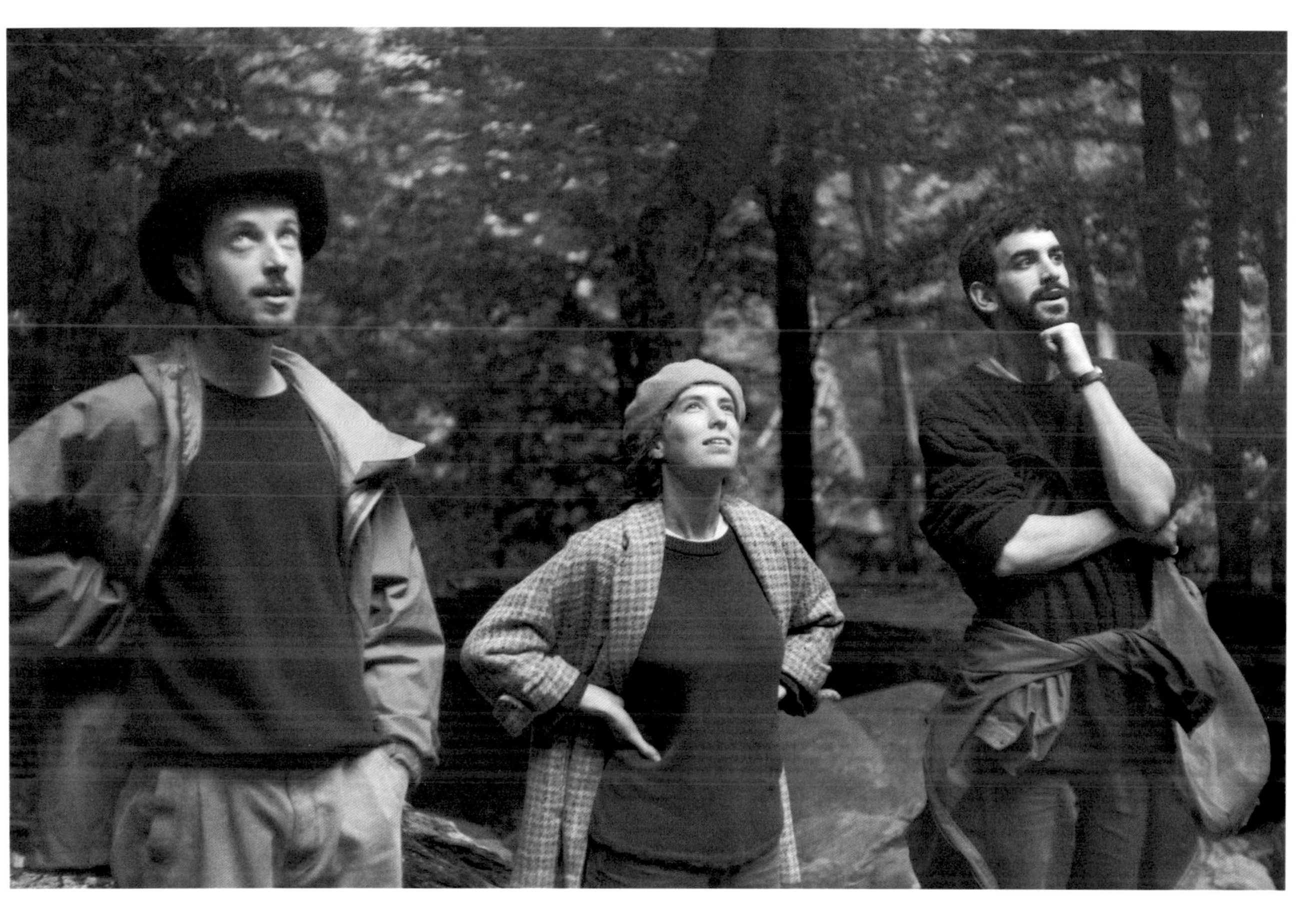

↑ Rufus, Sonya, Reid, New York State, 1996

→ Dio, Sonya, Texas, 1998

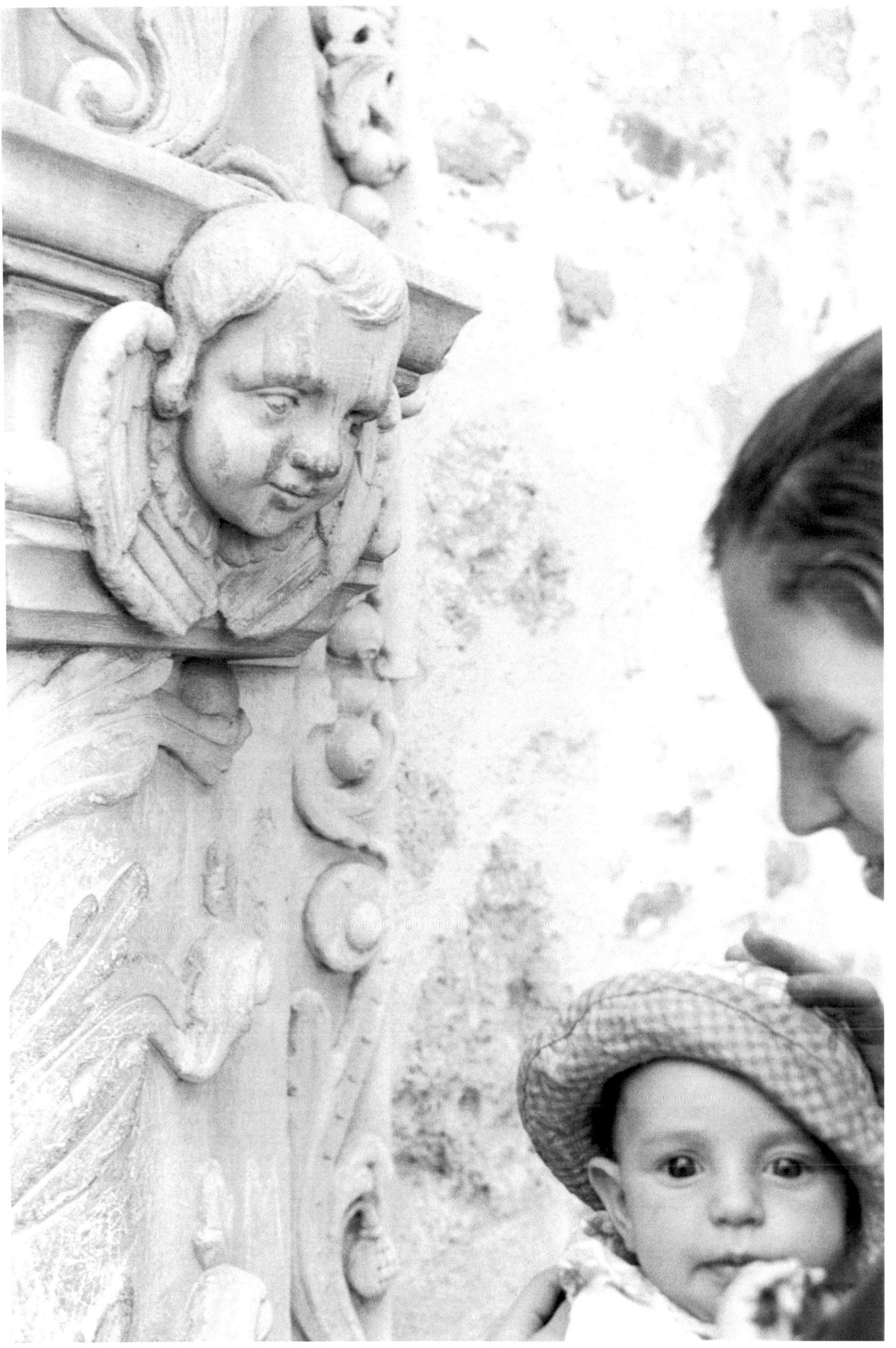

With thanks to those who helped make this book possible; their advice and friendship have been indispensible. Herbert Matter and Robert Frank started me down the trail. Stuart Alexander, Deborah Bell, Ed Grazda, and Paul Roth offered reassurance and encouragement. John Jacob suggested the sequencing of the pictures while David Gates provided early insights to the text. Philip Brookman offered deep artistic challenges and visions. His insights and direction were the first and final straws.

Special thanks go to my daughter Sonya Cohen, who generously guided me through the daily maze of the early layouts. Also thanks to Richard Benson and John Robinson who supervised the duotone separations, Yolanda Cuomo whose intuitions shaped the design, Sid Kaplan who breathed inspiration on the final prints, and to Daniel Power and Craig Cohen whose dedication to the artist's book made this publication possible.

FILMS BY JOHN COHEN

The High Lonesome Sound, 1962

The End of an Old Song, 1970

Fifty Miles From Times Square, 1972

Musical Holdouts, 1976

Q'eros: the Shape of Survival, 1979

Peruvian Weaving: a continuous warp, 1980

Sara and Maybelle, 1981

Post Industrial Fiddle, 1982

Gypsies Sing Long Ballads, 1982

The Ballad and the Source, 1983

Mountain Music of Peru, 1984

Choqela: Only Interpretation, 1985

Pericles in America, 1988

Dancing with the Incas, 1990

Carnival in Q'eros, 1992

FIELD RECORDINGS

Mountain Music of Kentucky

Mountain Music of Peru, vol 1 & 2

High Atmosphere

Huayno Music of Peru

The High Lonesome Sound: Roscoe Holcomb

Old Love Songs and Ballads

RECORDINGS WITH THE NEW LOST CITY RAMBLERS

NLCR Vol 1 the early years 1958–1962, NLCR Vol 2 1963–1973,
Songs from the Depression, Modern Times, Gone to the Country,
String Band Instrumentals, There Ain't No Way Out,
40 Years of Concert Performances, Stories The Crow Told Me

COMPANION RECORDING

There Is No Eye: Music for Photographs

www.johncohenworks.com

THERE IS NO EYE

Published in the United States by powerHouse Books,
a division of powerHouse Cultural Entertainment, Inc.
180 Varick Street, Suite 1302, New York, NY 10014-4606
telephone 212 604 9074, fax 212 366 5247
e-mail: eye@powerHouseBooks.com
web site: www.powerHouseBooks.com

First edition, 2001

Library of Congress Cataloging-in-Publication Data:

Cohen, John
There is no Eye: John Cohen photographs/essay by Greil Marcus.
p. cm.
ISBN 1-57687-107-X
1. Portrait photography. 2.Cohen, John. I. Marcus, Greil. II. Title.

TR680.C566 2001
779'.2'092–dc21

2001046177

Hardcover ISBN 1-57687-107-X
Limited Edition ISBN 1-57687-119-3

Duotone scans by GIST, New Haven
Printing and binding by EBS, Verona
Associate Designer, Kristi Norgaard

A complete catalog of powerHouse Books and
Limited Editions is available upon request;
please call, write, or eye our web site.

Also available:

A special powerHouse Collector's Edition with a signed and numbered
silver-gelatin print; call 1-877-266-5797 to order.

A compact disc collection *There is No Eye: Music for Photographs*,
Smithsonian Folkways Recordings (UPC # 0-9307-40091-2-3,
ISBN 0-9704942-3-8) call 1-800-410-9815 to order.

10 9 8 7 6 5 4 3 2 1

Printed and bound in Italy

BOOK DESIGN BY YOLANDA CUOMO, NYC